To Ride a Grey Ghost

To Ride a Grey Ghost

The Gator Navy in the Pacific, 1975

JOEY FOGARTY

ABOOKS

Alive Book Publishing

To Ride a Grey Ghost
The Gator Navy in the Pacific, 1975
Copyright © 2020 by Joey Fogarty

For information, contact ALIVE Book Publishing at: alivebookpublishing.com, or call (925) 837-7303.

Book Design by Alex Johnson

ISBN
978-1-63132-086-6

Library of Congress Control Number: 2020901064

Library of Congress Cataloging-in-Publication Data
is available upon request.

First Edition

Published in the United States of America by ALIVE Book Publishing
and ALIVE Publishing Group, imprints of Advanced Publishing LLC
3200 A Danville Blvd., Suite 204, Alamo, California 94507
alivebookpublishing.com

PRINTED IN THE UNITED STATES OF AMERICA

10 9 8 7 6 5 4 3 2 1

To
Violet and Mel

Foreword

In writing this sea story, my aim is not to bring to the reader yet one more high-stakes thriller the likes of which seem to flood the magazine aisle at the local supermarket, but rather that side of the fleet seen only by the men who man the grey ghosts of the U. S. Navy. The story of the long, hot, sometimes dangerous, and always critical watches in a ship's engine room. The hole snipes in particular and the lifer corps in general, regardless of their rating. This is a story of that lifer corps that makes the navy work. The culture that it breeds and the rare breed that rules that culture. Not all, or even a majority of career navy men resemble some of the characters in this story, but there is not one fleet sailor, career or not, that does not remember one. This story is for them.

Introduction

I will never forget the day my old man told me that it was time to leave home. He was finishing the last six-pack of Genesee cream ale and called me in from the driveway where I was clearing last night's snow. He asked me how old I was first.

"Eighteen, sir," I replied.

"Then you're old enough to know what side you're gonna part your package on, right?" he asked.

"Yes sir," I replied, somewhat taken back by the bluntness of his question.

"OK," he said, "that's man enough for me, and I'm not supporting two men. Out," he said with his thumb cocked over his shoulder.

"What, you mean right now?" I asked him.

"I'll give you thirty days to find work or join the military, they're always hiring," he said. "You've been boosting six-packs here and there too," he said as he held up an empty can of Genny, shaking it to reinforce his point.

"Now that's where I draw the line," he said. "Eating like a horse is tough enough, but boosting the old man's beer is asking for trouble. You need to make plans about what you're going to do in this asshole town or hit the road somewhere that'll do you some good," he advised.

The next morning I headed down to the federal building, and after a while settled on the navy due to the crackerjack uniform and the 'Join the Navy, see the world' logo on the large poster out front. I let the family know that evening at dinner, and the old man nodded in approval.

"It'll be good for you, square your ass away," he said. "Good for you, kid, make sure you measure up."

"I won't let you down, Pop," I promised.

"Oh, you won't be letting me down, you'll be letting yourself down. Your future's yours to win or lose," he said. "When you get older you will find that it was the best decision you ever made," he added.

"It'll give you a trade to apply someday that will come quicker than you think, and you won't be looking like a girl any more either, sweetheart," he added as he made the scissors hand gesture towards my shoulder-length hair.

"What's your next move?" he asked.

"Well, I already passed the entrance battery, and they said I should strike for a hull tech position. I take my physical Friday. The recruiter said I'll fly out of Albany April third," I replied.

"Where to?" he asked.

"San Diego," I replied.

"Lucky you, kid, wish I were going with you on this one. The climate in this neck of the woods sucks, just like this town sucks." He looked out the dining room window at the snowy, windy streets of Plattsburgh, New York. The old man was having a hard time adjusting to civilian life, having been discharged after thirty years due to alcohol problems. He did not like it one bit.

The recruiter called two days later and told me to meet him at the federal building at noon, where he then gave me a ride to the trail ways bus station on upper Cornelia street. After that, with my reporting orders in hand, I settled in for the 150-mile ride to Albany airport where I was soon on my way to sunny San Diego.

Chapter 1
Boot Camp, San Diego, CA.

The plane touched down at seven p.m. and after checking in at the military information desk and presenting my reporting orders, I was told to wait outside where about twenty other guys were standing around smoking nervous puffs of cigarettes. After about fifteen minutes, a grey bus with Navy markings pulled up in front of us. Two-third class petty officers with shore patrol arm bands and billy clubs stepped off and told us to climb aboard.

"No smoking, no talking, no gum!"

Everyone took seats and was silent as the grey bus pulled away from the airport and headed for Worm Island. The bus arrived about ten minutes later and crossed over the Humpty-Dumpty Bridge that separated the recruit training center from the rest of the naval base. A tidal estuary from San Diego Bay wedged Worm Island on the south and the Marine Corps recruit depot on the east. The bus dropped us off at the receiving and outfitting center where three guys wearing white chasers' helmets were waiting to direct us to the second floor of the building, where there was about sixty racks side by side. On each rack were placed two sheets, a grey wool blanket, and a pillow.

"Anybody gotta use the head do it now because once you hit the rack you stay!" commanded the chaser. When all had settled down, the overhead lights were secured, and one of the chasers remained in the large room as a sound and security watch. While everyone made the motions of pretending to be asleep, you could sense the nervous tension in the darkness. The only sound was the rhythmic footfalls of the chaser as he slowly walked around the room. The other two had taken up station just outside the double swinging doors. They would relieve each other every two hours until it was time to give us our 'grand morning welcome' to navy basic training. I was surprised I had drifted off under the circumstances and sound asleep when they came barging through the swinging metal doors banging metal trash can lids and yelling for everyone to get up. Everyone began hopping out of their racks and getting dressed in the rush of fear, adrenalin, and excitement this moment of confusion was meant to be.

"Get your asses up, get your asses dressed, and get your asses below!"

Once everyone was rushed down stairs into the court yard, we formed up as best we could in the early morning darkness with a chill breeze coming in from San Diego Bay. There were more chasers this time around, I noticed; six in all, and they were different from the other three.

"It's chow time, worms," said the biggest of the six. After they had us lined up two abreast as best they could considering our present state of confusion, the biggest chaser then spoke again. "This dirt lot you will cross is called the field of no return," he began.

"When you reach the other side you will fall under the uniform code of military justice, so if anyone has any last minute contraband, this is your last legal chance to get rid of it, no questions asked," he added. As we crossed the dirt lot in the darkness, I noticed several guys dropping whatever it was they needed to drop. When we had crossed the field of no return, the head chaser ordered us to halt and then sent one of the other chasers to the rear of the column.

"This man has been detailed aft to ensure that you paid attention, from now on you fall under U.C.M.J. It's one rough code people; it'll fuck you hard without kissing you first."

With the big chaser at the front of the column, and the other chaser at the rear, the other four took up station, two on each side. They marched us about a quarter mile across a large concrete parking lot known as a grinder to the front of a large lit-up (mess decks), a large cafeteria really. Upon entering, I witnessed a scene that took us all by surprise. Here we were all dressed in civilian clothes with long hair, beards, and all dressed differently from one another, and there they were, all six hundred of them, recruits, who had gotten there a few weeks ahead of us. All dressed in blue dungarees, and every head shaven. A phrenologist would have a field day here. With what seemed like all six hundred shaved heads, white ones, black ones, brown ones, all turned towards us, and began to whistle and taunt as we filed in and were led to the serving line by the head chaser.

"Fifteen minutes people, and no talking."

All we were given was a pint of milk, a small box of cereal, and an apple. There was a reason for it of course, but we did not know at the time. Never before had I wanted to be shorn and out of those clothes as much as I did then. The whole point was to subject us to a massive ridicule in a state of confusion, and then feed us only a mere tidbit in the chow line while we could plainly see the full trays of our gleeful tormentors. We did not belong yet, we were not like them, we could not blend into the mass of baldheads and blue uniforms, and at this moment, we could not wait. The navy had begun its teamwork conditioning. After the fastest fifteen minutes on record, we were ordered back outside two abreast, and marched now in the pouring rain to the barbershop where four barbers stood ready to quickly shave our heads and then it was back outside under the portico one by one until all fifty or so guys had been peeled. The next stop was the shedding of our civilian clothes, and the issue of dungarees, and (boondockers) navy issue shoes. Our former clothes were put into the Salvation Army bin, or mailed home. With our now stowed sea bags slung over our raincoat covered shoulders, we were marched back outside. The rain was now only a sprinkle, and there was a slight wind coming off the bay. By this time, it was now chow time again so back to the chow hall we went only this time looking quite different from that morning. It was a relief to look like everyone else. On this trip through the chow line, we were accorded the same trays of chow as everyone else. There were no taunts or harassment this time around. Because of the tension-filled day, I had a huge appetite and inhaled the meal in no time.

"That's it people, on your feet," barked the chaser.

He led us past a row of shit cans where those who had not cleaned their trays of food dumped them into cans, and stacked them one atop another by the scullery where sweaty recruits on service week hustled them into the humid mist to steam them clean. After we were marched back outside, I noticed whole companies of about sixty men assembled on the grinder in front of the chow hall. One man in front of each company held a flag bearing that company's number on it. With the chasers now sorting us out tallest to the front and shortest to the rear, we were then marched over to the stenciling room of the outfitting building. There we finished stenciling the rest of our dungaree uniforms under the hard to understand English of a Filipino Chief. He seemed to be looking for a recruit named Richard Brett for some reason. When he approached one recruit or another, he would ask him:

"Dick Brett?" The recruit would then come to attention.

"No sir, recruit Jackson." He would then ask another,

"Dick Brett?" The kid came to attention and replied, "No sir, recruit Norman."

It seemed strange considering that we had, by this time, all stenciled our last names above our left breast shirt pocket. It was not until the chasers started grinning at yet one more request about the elusive Richard Brett, that we became aware that the chief was not asking us anything at all, but rather calling everyone 'dick breath' in his Filipino accent. After he ensured everyone had a properly stowed sea bag, we were marched back over the Humpty Dumpty Bridge to the chow hall for the evening meal. After another short meal, it was back to the grinder with our sea bags over our shoulders to formation. The rain had stopped now and we would not see it again for the rest of basic training. We were marched to the barracks we were to occupy for the first four weeks of Intensive Training. We were assigned to the second floor of a wing facing harbor drive and San Diego bay. In this compartment as it was called, were two rows of steel racks in the form of bunk beds, and a long picnic style table down the center. In between the racks were steel lockers where we were told to place our sea bags. We were then told to line up in front of the racks where upon the lead chaser then announced:

"Worms, you are about to get born!" After a brief pause, he then said even louder yet, "Company 083, attention on deck!"

There was a sense of urgency as everyone snapped to attention as best we could, staring across the center table at their new shipmate, when through the heavy fire doors strode two men dressed in dress whites. One was younger than the other and was wearing glasses. He was wearing a coil of blue nylon around his left shoulder, along with three diagonal stripes on the same side. The other man was shorter and more compact with a red goatee. On the left sleeve of his uniform were three chevrons with an insignia of the boiler rating above them, and a "crow" above that. This man had an air of authority that made the chaser look like a babysitter. He would be our Company Commander for the next nine weeks. Over his left breast were numerous ribbons and medals but it was the look of determination, rather than the braggadocio of the now vanished chaser, that got our attention. The two men made their way down one aisle and then up the other aisle to the head of the room. They paused to survey what they had to work with. With absolute silence in the room, the man with the red goatee spoke for the first time.

"I am Petty Officer First Class Hood. You people will refer to me as Mr. Hood or Sir. Is that clear?"

"Yes Sir," answered the room in unison.

Then, introducing the other man, he announced, "This is my Assistant Company Commander, Mr. Mann. You will refer to him in the same way. Do you understand?"

"Yes Sir," Answered the newly shaven group once again.

"Mr. Mann was the outstanding recruit of my last company, and that's why I chose him for this job. He should be on his way to the fleet by now but he chose to accept my offer to help kick your asses. He is one of the most squared away men on this installation, and you should be glad to have him in your face for the next nine weeks."

Mr. Hood alluded to Mr. Mann again. "This man is going places in my navy. It all starts here people, from Submarine Commander, to Fighter Pilot, to Navy Seal, to the Joint Chiefs of Staff. They all had to get squared away first and they all had to get past people like me to do it."

"The navy is the smallest branch of the military, so that makes me proud to be part of an elite group," he said. "Sea duty is not for everyone, so therefore I'm going to give you all a little quiz as to how lucky you are to be able to come here. Does anyone know the current population of the planet?" he asked.

There was a moment of uneasy silence due to the intimidating presence before us. A recruit raised his hand somewhat sheepishly. As he was about to answer, Mr. Mann sprang forward and grabbed the kid by the lapels of his dungaree shirt, and jerked him straight up.

"Anytime you open your mouth, you come to attention first, nut," he ordered. The suddenness of it came as a shock as Mr. Mann released his grip on the terrified recruit, and Mr. Hood then stepped up to him and asked, "What's the current population of the planet recruit?"

"About four billion, Sir," he answered.

"OK Mr. National Geographic, what's the current population

of the United States?" he asked further.

"About two hundred million, Sir," answered the recruit.

"Excellent," said Mr. Hood. "That makes America pretty special, doesn't it?"

"Yes sir," answered the recruit.

"And how many of that two hundred million are trusted to serve in my navy?" he asked.

"Right now I count fifty-seven of you," he said. "By the time nine weeks are up there'll be less than that. People, this phase of training will separate those of you who want to be sailors from those of you who just want to go boating. You have been accepted into an elite branch of the armed forces. Not many people are cut out for sea duty," he continued.

"How many of you men are married?" he asked. Only four hands went up due to our young ages.

"You joined the wrong branch of the service," he said. "Marriage and sea duty don't mix." The Company Commander then ordered those men who had just raised their hands to fetch their sea bags from in front of their lockers. When they had complied, he ordered them to empty them on the deck.

"Do any of you people see your wife?" he asked.

"No Sir," they answered.

"That's right, because she's not navy issue. She will not be going with you when you report to the fleet. She will become what's known in the fleet as a West-Pac Widow, and chances are she'll be humping someone else when you're bumping around in the six footers off the coast of some godforsaken island group. That's the skinny on navy marriages, people. That'll give you something to think about for the next nine weeks."

Mr. Hood went on about what he expected from us as far as watch standing, conduct and such, before ordering everyone to the head for the evening Shit, Shower, Shave routine.

"You people will shit once a day at the end of the day, and at no other time. Is that clear?" he asked.

"Yes Sir," we answered.

When the allotted fifteen minutes for all three events had passed, everyone assembled in front of their racks in our newly issued skivvies to be instructed on how to make up our racks the navy way. When that was over, Mr. Hood then assigned a 'watch bill' and turned it over to Mr. Mann.

"Taps is at 2100 hours, reveille is 0500 hours, don't be caught sleeping!" he warned.

I was awakened at 0200 for the 2 to 4 watch by the guy coming off the mid watch. There would be a constant watch now twenty-four hours a day. The recruit I was assuming the watch from handed me a green web belt, a white chasers helmet, and a flashlight with which to perform my rounds about the sleeping room. After my two-hour fire watch was over, I awoke my relief and handed over my watch gear that had been given me and hit the rack. No sooner had I drifted off to sleep, the overhead lights came on at 0500.

"Everyone up, get dressed, make those racks, and muster below," bellowed Mr. Mann.

He and Mr. Hood were already overturning the racks of sleepy-headed recruits that were not rising fast enough to suit them. The second day had begun as the first, only this time there was more order along with a sense of urgency. When we had assembled in the courtyard below, Mr. Hood asked who was a cheerleader in high school. When no one answered of course, he pointed at someone. "You look like you would've made it if you tried. C'mere," he ordered. When the kid stepped up and came to attention, Mr. Hood handed him the company flag with the numbers 083 in boldface.

"From now on you march at the head of everyone else," he said.

He then pointed at the tallest guy in the company, a blond kid from West Virginia who quickly assumed front and center. After glancing at the kid's name over his left shirt pocket, he stood back for a second.

"Quackenbush? What the hell kinda name is that, recruit? It's a seriously fucked up name, someone up there does not like you. Bet you had to whip a lot of ass in school with a name like that," he said.

"Made my share of corrections, Sir," he answered.

"Well, you look like you could make some here."

The Company Commander then addressed the rest of the company:

"I'm going to make Quackenbush here the R.C.P.O. and for your information, it stands for, Recruit Chief Petty Officer. You will obey him as a higher-ranking recruit until he fucks up and is replaced. Understand?"

"Yes sir," answered the rest of the company.

"After chow you mutts will receive your shots and be issued your dog tags. When that's complete, then you're going to learn to march."

After chow, we were marched over to the dispensary, and received our shots along with the start of our shot record that would remain with us for the rest of our time on active duty. We then received our dog tags, and were ordered to wear them at all times. We were becoming more rhythmic now in our marching as we headed over to the armory to receive our rifles. These rifles were surplus, bolt action 1903 Springfields that were issued only for drilling purposes. They weighed nine pounds and we would soon feel it. From then until the evening meal, we would learn the fundamentals of drilling with the Springfields to the tune of "Pop Goes the Weasel," coming to parade rest at the end of the tune. The rest of the week was spent learning how to march in close order, drill without taking someone's head off by turning the wrong way on the command "to the rear march." It was amazing to see how many people did not know their left from their right, and a couple of recruits were hit by the barrels of the Springfields that first week.

One hot day on the grinder, Mr. Hood became exasperated with one recruit who just could not seem to get it together. He ordered the man to double time it back to the barracks and fetch the stamp book that we had all been issued on that first week. In the meantime, he ordered the rest of the company to halt in front of the mailbox at the edge of the grinder. When the recruit had double timed it back, Mr. Hood ordered him to attention, took the stamp book, and gave the command, "Company 083, right face!" We were all now facing the recruit standing at attention next to the mailbox. Mr. Hood said to him:

"Nutt! Either you are gonna put out the eye of the man behind you or he's gonna shove that rifle up your ass sometime soon. Either way, you're starting to piss me off!" He growled. "Since you cannot seem to square your ass away, I'm mailing you home."

With that said, he began licking stamps and with his thumb, began pressing to the hapless kid's forehead. When he ran out of room there, he began sticking them along the kid's jaw line until his face was covered with stamps.

"Company 083, right face, forward march!" he ordered.

The company then marched off around the grinder, leaving the kid standing next to the mailbox with his face all covered with stamps. After an hour of close order drills, Mr. Hood stopped the company in front of the mailbox again and addressed the hapless recruit:

"Well it looks like the post office isn't interested in you either," he said. "It looks like I'm stuck with you, Nutt! It's like this recruit..." he began, "you get back in formation and we're going to try this one more time. We're going to do left oblique, right oblique, and on the order 'To the rear march.' If you even think about turning the wrong way, I'm going to let the man behind you Davy Crockett your skull, got it?"

"Yes Sir," was all the humiliated recruit could muster in a wavering voice. Mr. Hood then gave the order "forward march."

He then ordered, "left oblique hut," then "right oblique hut," "left shoulder arms," then, "right shoulder arms." He then allowed the company to march about twenty paces before giving the stamp covered recruit the acid test. "To The Rear March," came the command. The entire company wheeled in unison—everyone but the kid, that is. The man behind him ducked for the third time that morning, so Mr. Hood stopped the company as Mr. Mann rushed forward and hauled the kid and his Springfield rifle out of formation.

"Cheerleader!" bellowed Mr. Hood

"Cheerleader reporting as ordered, Sir," said the recruit upon coming to attention in front of him.

"You and the mailman here trade places," he ordered. Mr. Hood figured that the only thing he could do was to make him the Guidon Bearer, or the man that carries the company flag up in front of the company.

"I don't trust you with a rifle. You from L.A.?"

"No Sir, Canoga Park," came the answer from the stamp covered youth.

"Close enough," he said. "Let's see if you can fuck this up!"

With the kid at the head of the company, we marched off to the evening meal. Halfway across the grinder with Mr. Mann alongside the new stamp-covered flag bearer talking in his ear to distract him, Mr. Hood got between the flag bearer and the rest of the company, and with his forefinger pressed to his lips, quietly signaled for the company to halt. Meanwhile, the kid continued to march off alone across the grinder with Mr. Mann still in his ear, until he too peeled off to let the kid continue across the grinder alone.

"Hey nut!" yelled Mr. Hood as the recruit came to a halt and did an about face. We could see his head drop ever so slightly once he knew he had been had.

"Get your ass back here!" ordered Mr. Hood. When the recruit had double-timed it back across the grinder, Mr. Hood said to him, "This company can't march without a flag. What are you doing all by yourself over there?"

"I…I," he began to stammer.

"You what?" asked Mr. Hood, "You mean you didn't hear me?" he asked mocking incredulity as he waved his hand towards the rest of the company.

"They all heard me, why not you?" he asked. Mr. Hood then bore down on him.

"Look nut, you passed a hearing test when you took your physical, which means you're not deaf, correct?" he asked him. "Well then maybe you think that just because you're up front with the flag that your hot stuff. Isn't that right recruit?"

"No Sir," answered the kid.

"You think you can just march off all by yourself, recruit?"

"No Sir," answered the kid.

"Then why the hell did you do it?"

"I don't know Sir," came the reply.

"Well I know," Mr. Hood answered. "Nut, the rest of the company just jumped ship."

"Sir?" asked the recruit, puzzled as hell.

"That's right; it seems that they'll be dammed if they're going to follow some goofy looking fuck with stamps all over his face." By now the poor kid was about to break from all the abuse being heaped upon him.

"I told you all at rifle issue that you were going to learn to march, didn't I?" he continued.

"Yes Sir," replied the kid.

"As you can tell, I mean it, don't I?"

"Yes Sir," he replied again.

"Now get those stamps off your face and square your ass away," he ordered.

The kid had just under gone a transformation from screw up to A. J. Squared away as it was called in the fleet, and his harassment was not lost on the rest of us. It impressed upon the rest of the company to always be on the alert at all times. After the company had marched across the grinder to evening chow, it was one welcome meal now at the end of our first week. The tops of my ears were burnt from the San Diego sun. I was a North Country boy that was emerging from five months of winter, and the sun was creating blisters on the tops of my ears that stuck out from under our issue ball caps. After chow it was back to the barracks for the evening 'Shit, Shower, Shave' routine, final instructions, and then lights out.

Reveille at 0500 was becoming smoother now that we knew what was expected of us. There was less yelling in a general sense from the company commanders, but when they did, it was more personal. There was a point to be made in the squaring away of a recruit. The second week was spent on the obstacle course next to the estuary going through the paces we were also introduced to an exercise known as eight count body builders. The course was not designed to defeat recruits, but rather to see if the local recruiters are doing their jobs as far as the recruits' potential was concerned. The Navy washed out more than one recruit during this phase of training. The primary reason for physicals at the induction centers was to determine if a recruit was able to withstand the rigors of boot camp. When they passed there, the rest of it was up to them, as far as wanting to be a fleet sailor is concerned. We were run through the course twice, and then broken up into teams to enhance the natural competiveness of young men. It also served to release some of the tension of the first week, and although we were dragging when it was over, there was a better company cohesion now as we marched off to chow.

After chow, it was back to the grinder for more close order drill, then off to one class or another. There was water safety where we learned to make flotation devices from our dungaree trousers, first aid classes, knot tying, and so on. The next two weeks passed under the springtime sun with the company becoming fairly used to the long days, and strict regimentation.

After the first four weeks were over, it was time to cross the Humpty Dumpty bridge from the Worm Island side to the N.T.C. side in order to free up our former barracks for a new batch of civilian 'worms.' It was also time for our first big disappointment as far as our second issue was concerned. The first issue was only our dungarees, skivvies, knit watch cap, rain gear, and 'boondockers.' The navy figured that some recruits would lose or gain weight from all the physical activity and three squares a day during the first four weeks at Worm Island. The moral crushing blow came in the form of the dress blue, and dress white uniform. Where we were all expecting the regular "crackerjacks" of old, we were now confronted with a change to the old uniform. The difference was the absence of the jumper tops, and thirteen button, bell bottomed trousers. In place of the Dixie cup hat, we were issued a chief's white hat with a black bill. The dress blues that utilized the same hat were designed to look like an airline pilot with non-bell bottomed trousers, and a tie in place of the square knot neckerchief. Everyone was wondering what the hell was going on because when we had enlisted back home, all the recruiters were wearing the traditional style crackerjacks.

"You can thank Admiral Zumwalt for this," offered Mr. Hood. He went on to explain that since Saigon had fallen the week before, and there was no more draft, and along with race relations being at an all-time low, the navy needed a new tool to attract better recruits. Admiral Elmo Zumwalt, Chief of Naval Operations, and had approved of the uniform change.

"I disagree with the good Admiral," he said. "As far as I'm concerned, this is a big mistake. None of you joined to look like a milkman. None of you joined to look like an airline pilot either. You joined to look like sailors, and sailors are what you should look like, which at the present moment you don't."

It was easy to see that he was pissed off about the new uniforms. He did not care to see his company of recruits dressed in what were being called 'salt and peppers,' that is black slacks, and white shirt, open at the collar along with the white chiefs hat with black bill. We were stuck with an absolutely stupid looking uniform at the behest of an admiral who should have known better. Another surprise we found was the navy's unique tact concerning race relations between recruits that could not seem to get along. When that happened, the company commander would send for the salt and pepper team, so named because it consisted of a white chief, and a black chief. The idea was formed after the race fights on the *U.S.S. Kitty Hawk, Oklahoma City,* and other ships of the fleet. The navy decided to nip future problems in the bud during basic training. The way they went their jobs was sometimes funny, and they did it in front of the company, to be a lesson to all. The black chief would bear down on any redneck types, while the white chief would handle any Black Panther types. A typical exchange went something like this:

"So what's this I hear you said about white people, son?"

"White people smell like wet chicken? Is that what you said?"

"Yes sir," answered the black recruit with a problem.

"We may smell like wet chicken, but at least we don't walk like 'em".

It was a clear reference to the ghetto bop. The offending recruit would then assume the position, which was the push-up position, and would be left there until his arms started to shake from exertion. There was a black chief Carter, and was known as Killer Carter according to Mr. Hood. He was a career navy man and felt strongly about squaring recruits away on preconceived attitudes of race. He so tormented one recruit from Texas that the kid demanded to see the base chaplain. An appointment was set up the next day and Mr. Hood told Chief Carter the time. Just before the recruit showed up, Chief Carter told the chaplain that the old man wanted to see him about one thing or another, and then remained in his office. When the recruit showed up, he saw none other than Chief Carter sitting behind the chaplain's desk, with an open bible.

"You're not here to break any commandments are you?" he asked him.

"No sir," answered the very surprised recruit.

"Then why are you here?" asked the chief. "You're here to break one of the Ten Commandments, aren't you?"

"No sir," answered the surprised recruit.

"Would you like me to read it to you recruit?" the chief asked.

"Sir?" replied the now quite nervous kid.

"Thou shalt not bear false witness against thy neighbor," he read. "That's the one you came here to break, now isn't it recruit? You came here to be a bearer of tales, didn't you recruit?" he asked.

"No sir," answered the recruit.

"Bullshit!" thundered the chief into the kid's face.

"You came here to bitch about the big, bad nigger that's kicking yo' ass, and you know it," he replied to him.

"Sir, you are a little rough on me," replied the recruit.

"Rough?" asked the chief, "Have I punched you yet?"

"No sir," he answered.

"But you punched Washington in the back of the head, right?"

"Yes sir," he said

"And why was that?"

The recruit became flustered because he knew what the chief already knew about the fight in the showers that week.

"It was about that pencil you call a dick right?" he pressed.

"Sir, there was no hot water, and I was the first to be showered. You know how that affects it." replied the kid.

"I know how it affects you people, yes," responded the chief.

"Well sir, Washington made a comment, and I just swung I guess."

"Boy, how old are you?" the chief asked.

"Nineteen Sir," answered the young man.

"At that age you don't know how to swing anything, you get me?"

"Yes sir," he replied.

"What makes the measure of a man is the size of his heart, not the size of his cock, you read me recruit?" he asked him directly.

"Yes sir," he answered the chief.

"Assume the position, and think about it," ordered the chief.

"When your arms start to give out, you just think about the size of your heart, and not the size of your cock, understand me?" He finished.

"Yes sir."

"In the meantime I'll call Jesus back, and you can tell him that you would rather be a sailor, and not a complainer."

"Yes sir."

"Don't fail me, Honky, I'm counting on you, until then, you remain in the position until Jesus gets back."

"Yes sir," came the heartened reply from one who had just been enlightened. What Chief Carter had just done was nothing more than his job as far as the 'Salt and Pepper' team was supposed to do. It was another day of squaring away boots. On the other hand, the boot would never forget the day he was squared away that late May afternoon, after what he figured would be the easy way out. Men like Chief Carter and Mr. Hood were professionals when it came to direct logic as far as a captive audience was concerned. They understood that a young buck needed to be tested, and pushed to their physical and mental limits in order to find out about their capabilities. They also wanted to see if they could be turned around about preconceived attitudes.

The next three weeks passed with more close order drill, classes on a variety of subjects, and endless uniform inspections. The last week was spent in competition with other recruit companies where I was on the rope climbing team, and we did very well due to the teamwork we had learned the last eight weeks. We were coming close to graduation day, and so were drilling on Preble field because that is where we would be passing in review on that coming Friday. When that day arrived, Company 083 passed in review on Preble Field in the mid-morning mist of June 10, 1975. We had made it. We then marched off the graduation field, along the estuary, to the armory where we turned in the Springfield rifles we had drilled with the last nine weeks. It was back to the barracks to prepare for our first liberty in nine weeks. The married guys wanted to see their wives, of course, and the single guys all wanted to go downtown to see the sights and play tourist. Mr. Hood gave us firm instructions not to go alone because we were wearing our dress whites, and the hustlers, and con men could not help but spot us.

"Another thing, don't be messing with any dopers. There's nothing that you can buy from them that'll fuck you up quicker than the U.C.M.J."

With that advisement, he went on about his own career of how many ships of the fleet he had served on thus far, and about all the wild liberty to be had around the globe. Everything from the campfire girls of Naples, Italy to the first time he crossed the Shit River Bridge in Olongapo City, Philippines. After a while, he asked no one in particular if we believed the sea stories we had just heard. When no answer was offered, he explained the difference between a sea story and a fairy tale.

A fairy tale starts out, "Once upon a time."

A sea story starts out, "This is no shit!"

"I haven't shit you once in nine weeks, and I won't start now," he said.

"A word to the wise, people, the Salt and Pepper Team has been known to go downtown on graduation Fridays to look up old friends, if you know what I mean." He smiled as he looked at the black kid, and then at the kid from Texas.

"You two are shipmates now, and your civilian world is gone," he said. "You've got each other's backs now, and you damn well better cover that man. Liberty call is secured at 2100 hours, so if either one of you returns here without the other, you're going to be in a world of shit with the rest of the company."

"You will be seen as untrustworthy, undependable, you want that?"

"No sir," they answered in unison.

"The low-life in downtown San Diego have been preying on boot camp graduates since the first company passed through these gates way back in 1923," he began, as he addressed the entire company. "Where you are makes no difference, you cover your shipmate."

"Let's hear you people say the word SHIPMATE," he ordered.

"Shipmate," answered the company altogether.

"Sounds like you're hitting the beach with your sister!" he teased.

"Who you hitting the beach with? Your sister or your shipmate?" He asked again, searching for an answer that carried conviction.

"SHIPMATE!" Roared the company in deafening cadence.

He then looked at Mr. Mann and asked if the company was ready for liberty, and he assured him that we seemed clear on the concept. With that, Mr. Hood then spoke to the whole company again. "Company 083, attention on deck!"

The company came to attention as sharp as we ever had as he looked us over like a proud father for a moment, before telling everyone what we had waited nine weeks to hear:

"COMPANY 083, HIT THE BEACH!"

With that long awaited order, 54 newly minted, freshly scrubbed boots of company 083 rushed to the grinder downstairs to catch taxi cabs that lined up every Friday to ferry boots to downtown San Diego, or 32nd Street naval station, or Balboa Park if they did not have someone meeting them. We would be looking to unleash nine weeks of pent-up energy in celebration in what was for most of us, our first real accomplishment in life. Three of us piled into a cab and headed to downtown, Gary from Iowa, and Cliff, from San Jose. We had become fast friends during basic training, and they had received orders to school at Treasure Island along with me. Downtown San Diego was just as Mr. Hood had described it with titty bars, tattoo joints and one person about seventy years old who preached, told stories, and sometimes scolded passerby in front of the Balboa Theater. He was an eccentric to be sure, and his sermon was a mixture of his life's philosophy, religion, and standup comic. He was neither drunk, nor disheveled, and I believed him when he said to all around that he was born in the year of our lord, nineteen ought six. He had by his own admission been advisor to every major politician in the last thirty years, and went on to further state that he was a 100% California patriot. In a way, he seemed to be a "hawker" as he possessed people skills. On the other hand, there seemed to be sincerity in the way he spoke to people. The man seemed to be a paradox, a sure sign of eccentricity, but he was interesting considering we had just come from nine weeks of forced logic. We soon left him there as he went into yet another topic, and another frame of mind. Since none of us was twenty-one yet, we decided to get yet another cab, and head to the 32nd Street enlisted club where under age sailors could be served 3.2 beers. The name of the place was the Scuttle Butt. It was located at building #45, just off pier 3 on the naval station. The place was full of fleet sailors from the war ships moored nearby, and there was an abundance of pretty waitresses, a fact not lost on us. We all sat down at one of the tables, and a tawny skinned, light boned Filipina came over to take our order. After about a full fifteen seconds of us drinking her in, she smiled at us knowing that we were just out of boot camp.

"Can I get you something, guys?" she asked.

We all composed ourselves, ordered Coors beer, as she took the order, and wiggled off to the bar with us watching her every sway.

"Damn, you see that?" asked cliff as he starred at her.

"Yeah, she's married," said Gary, much to our astonishment because that's not what the two of us were looking at.

"Always look for the ring finger, boots, because if she's wearing a gold band you're wasting your time," he said.

"You can screw her fingers all you want dude, I'll screw the rest of her, besides, we just might be looking at a bona fide West-Pac widow." She soon returned with the beer, and placed them in front of us in such a way to allow a little cleavage to show. Damn, she smelled good too! I thought as she collected our money and returned to the bar area with that same sway as before.

After a few more Coors went down, we began to relax for the first time in nine weeks, and found ourselves having a good time. Then out of nowhere, there appeared a sailor in summer whites and Dixie cup. He was deeply tanned and lanky, and was a first class petty officer with what I noticed was a pair of fouled anchors between the crow and set of three chevrons on his left shirt sleeve. He was a bosun mate. On his right sleeve was a black armband with S.P. in white letters. A green pistol belt around his waist held a black billy club as he approached our table and stood for a couple of seconds before speaking.

"What are you supposed to do?" he asked somewhat tersely.

We all looked at each other for a split second as we jumped to our feet at attention. We could not imagine what we were doing wrong, and so were caught off guard by the suddenness of it all.

"Wrong!" He laughed as he dropped the other shoe. "You're supposed to doing just what you're doing, so have a seat, and let ole' boats buy you guys a beer," he laughed again.

We had been so accustomed to jumping at the first sign of authority that he knew we would do just that. He was breaking our balls on what he knew was our Friday graduation. He then motioned to the pretty Filipina who had been serving us, to set us up with three more Coors. He then grabbed a nearby chair, and joined us.

"First of all, you don't have to salute me or call me sir," he began. "I'm enlisted, just like you, but since I drew shore duty tonight, I guess you have to do as I say," and then added with a tap on the billy club, "Get a belly full a beer, and grab some ass."

We all laughed a sigh of relief as the waitress came to the table with another tray of beer while the bosun mate slipped his arm around her waist and said to us, "Like this L.B.F.M. here." He grinned at us. The three of us, and her gave him a quizzical look as he added, "You'll find out later." As the waitress left the table with that sexy sway we had been lusting after all night, we consumed the beer, and the man said that he had to make his rounds, but could point us in the right direction, which was across the room at a couple of women in their thirties talking at the bar.

"There are the West- Pac Widows, I can spot 'em every time," he said. "And there looking for guys just out of boot, good luck."

"Actually," offered Gary, "we were looking at this one." He nodded at the waitress.

"Oh, her?" Asked the bosun mate as he touched his left hand ring finger. "That's my wife!" He grinned as we laughed at the statement.

He was a stinker, and we wondered how many more there were like him in the fleet. There wasn't much we could do about the two at the bar since the time was getting late, and our liberty was secured at 2100 hours, so we got a cab back to the barracks a half hour early just to be on the safe side. The next day everyone dressed in dress blues for the trip to the airport either to take leave, or to report to their next duty station. After turning in our bedding, we marched back to the barracks and milled around saying our goodbyes, and each one of us shaking Mr. Hoods hand before boarding the bus to the airport. As the bus pulled out, I noticed a new company forming up on the grinder in front of the mess hall. They were all longhaired and scruffy looking. I thought about how far they had to go in order to be squared away. It was with great satisfaction that we cleared the gate of N.T.C., and pulled out onto Rosecrans Avenue, and to the airport. Boot camp was over, and now we were all looking forward to two weeks' leave before going on to our next command.

Chapter 2
Treasure Island, Naval Station

The two weeks' leave with the family passed all too soon before it was time to don dress blues for the trip to San Francisco, and the beginning of Hull Tech School. The plane touched down around 8 p.m. and I took a cab to Treasure Island, reported to the Master at Arms desk in the lobby, and presented my reporting orders to the M.A.A. at the desk. After giving me some bedding, he directed me to an empty room and gave me the key. After stowing my sea bag, I went in search of Cliff and Gary. After looking around the barracks to no avail, I returned to the front desk and asked the only question left to ask:

"Where's the club?"

The M.A.A. on duty pointed me in the right direction soon enough and I found them both at the bar. After some backslapping, and a brief exchange of news they ordered up some more beer. We would be starting our A-School that Tuesday. It would last about two months and would cover basic firefighting, damage control, and chemical and radiation detection, and later at San Diego, welding and compartmentation, and other aspects of shipboard life. We stayed at the club until the 11p.m. closing time, and then headed back to the barracks where there was a beer machine in the lobby that cost thirty cents a can. I went up to my room and fetched my empty sea bag back down to the lobby where we stuffed another three six packs in to it, and then it was back to my room for the duration. This room had a perfect view of San Francisco, all lit up two miles across the bay. The barracks sat opposite of Avenue of the Palms, the main drag after you entered the base. The scenery was just outstanding.

The entire city blazed away in its brilliance with the Oakland Bay Bridge to the south, and Alcatraz Island to the north, all dark and mysterious now except for a navigational lighthouse. The next morning they showed me over to the base chow hall for breakfast before morning quarters. This chow hall was quite different from the one at boot camp as it was filled not only with those of us attending A-School, but with many fleet sailors as well. One old salt in particular drew our attention, as he seemed to be much older than anyone else was in the room. He was wearing a full dress blue uniform, with the rank of Master Chief Petty Officer. On his left sleeve, there were no less than eight gold "hash marks," with each one representing four years of service in the fleet. This being 1975, a little quick math meant that eight hash marks equaled 32 years' service. This old sea dog had been riding the Grey Ghost since 1943! One of the few W.W.II sailors still left. I noticed a pair of fouled cannons under the crow, and knew it to mean that he was a gunner's mate. We figured that since he was the only one sitting at the four-seat table, maybe we could sit down also. After nodding in the affirmative and sitting down, Gary asked a question that as soon as he asked it, he knew it sounded silly.

"So, you were going to school here?" he asked.

He asked it in the way a waitress does when you have your mouth full. The old salt bit off the rest of the toast he was eating, and washed it down with some coffee before leveling his eyes on Gary, who was now starting to blush.

"Yeah, they're gonna teach me how to be a civilian," he answered. "That's why I'm all squared away." He raised his left arm and rested an elbow on the table. We could not help but notice how many other heads turned on that simple gesture. Any one of the one hundred or so people in the chow hall could have made that same motion, and it would have gone unnoticed, but then no one else carried that much rank, and the eye-popping amount of gold hash marks as he did.

"You see, today marks a special milestone for me," he began. "Repose and a rebirth all in one."

With that, he sipped on the coffee once more as his eyes seemed to look clear us. "I'm shorter than hair on a bug's ass." The term 'short' we knew to mean that he was to discharge soon.

"I retire at noon today, medical, 2400 hrs actually, but there giving me an early out," he said. "I also celebrate fifty years on the planet today."

"Happy birthday Master Chief O'Farrell," we said as we noticed his nameplate on his left breast above all the medals, and ribbons that included the unmistakable Purple Heart. The old salt knew we were wondering about the circumstances of the Purple Heart, and so rolled into it modestly enough.

"Longshaw, Fletcher class can, May of 45' Okinawa" he began. "I came aboard in January of 44' fresh from boot, and spent the next fifteen months steaming in the forward areas almost nonstop. In April we were assigned to task force .58, under Admiral Bull Halsey's command for the invasion of Okinawa.

"We spent about a month conducting harassment fire, and trying to take out Jap shore batteries, and fending off kamikazes until one day we got to close to the southern end of the island, and ran aground. We were stuck fast, and within easy reach of the very position we were trying to take out," he continued.

"We spent the better part of the day trying to get pulled off the reef until two, or three rounds from the Japs hit us in the port side. Killed a lot of men, knocked out all power, we had to abandon ship with all our dead on to an L.C.I. Our own forces sank her later that day; she now rests off Ose reef."

"Thirty years now," he finished, as he stared hard at the coffee he was holding as if he were searching for answers in the black liquid. "She was just short of her second birthday, and most of us were just shy of our twentieth," There was a short silence at that time as the Master Chief composed himself.

"Well, To the *Longshaw*, and her crew," he announced, as he lifted his coffee cup, and drained it. He then rose to reveal a six-foot frame, and admitted somewhat jokingly, "Damn, I'm gonna miss navy chow."

With that, we stood as he donned his chief's hat, and left the chow hall after finishing what was certain to have been his last chow hall meal. The rest of the meal was spent wondering how he got his purple heart since he did not elaborate on the specifics of it, and we did not want to press him on it out of respect for him. When we went back to the Master at Arms desk for morning quarters, as we had not yet begun schooling, the M.A.A. told us to don our dress blues so we could attend a retirement ceremony at 1100 hrs.

"That's got to be O'Farrell," Gary said, and then went on to tell the rest of the boots about the Master Chief we had just met at the chow hall.

"He's fifty years old today as well," he added.

The ceremony was held at fleet headquarters, Treasure Island, and all the heavyweights were there. It was the first time we had seen this much gold presence all in one place, and it was quite impressive to behold. After all assembled had been called to attention, the commanding officer of the base addressed the crowd as to why we were here, and informed everyone as to the history of Chief O'Farrell's career. The Master Chief was resplendent in his dress blue uniform with all his ribbons and gold hash marks down his left sleeve, as he stood at attention behind sunglasses while the C.O. read his life's career to all assembled.

"May 18, 1945, U.S.S. *Longshaw* {DD-559} wounded in action at Okinawa, ship sunk."

Shore duty San Diego, R.T.C., Company Commander, Twice.

U.S.S. *Brush* {DD-754} Korean War, ship hits rouge mine, 13 killed, ship survives, four battle stars Korean service.

U.S.S. *Hornet* CVS- 12, Air strikes, Republic of Vietnam, Recovery ship for APOLLO 11, and 12 moon missions.

Shore duty San Diego, R.T.C. requested.

U.S.S. *Theodore E. Chandler* {DD-717} three deployments of fire support, Vietnam. *Chandler* Decommissioned 1975." He finished.

"Which brings us to a salient point; it seems that Master Chief O'Farrell has worn out more ships than I have automobiles." There was a round of chuckles at those words reflecting O'Farrell's thirty-two years in the fleet. "For that matter, he's worn out more sea bags than I have socks!"

That one bought the house down not to mention relieving some of the stress the Master Chief must have been feeling at the emotional milestone he was facing for all to see. The C.O. then presented him with an award for distinguished service to his country and the navy, while the Marine Corps band launched into "Anchors Aweigh." The senior officers and enlisted alike shook the Master Chief's hand. Usually at a time like this, you expect someone from the retiree's family to be in attendance. But there was no one present on his behalf, no one at all. It was the strangest thing because it was not every day that someone retired after 32 years of a career like his. Why was that? I wondered,

In the next few months I would find out for myself. We began our first phase of school the next morning, and for the next month learned compartmentation, Damage control, Flooding, and Firefighting. The flooding, and firefighting phases were the most memorable of all. In the latter phase, we had to don an O.B.A. {oxygen breathing apparatus}, and fire gear to battle a real oil fire in a mock up ship's engine room It was hot, dirty work, and we were kicked in the ass by the instructors until we got our teamwork together.

The real teamwork evolution was known as "save the ship." This involved descending into a mock up compartment with shrapnel holes in the bulkheads, and the overhead. We were given a P-250 water pump, along with rubber patches, plugs of various sizes, some lumber, and damage control tools. Then the cold waters of San Francisco Bay began rushing in on us. We were told that this compartment was crucial to the survival of the ship, so we must hold back the water, or lose the ship. Needless to say, that if this had been the real thing our class would have gone to Davy Jones Locker. We kept at it until the cold waters of the bay were up to our necks. Finally the instructors let us out of the top escape hatch.

"OK Boots, back tomorrow, and every day, until you get your collective shit together."

Back we were the next day much more focused than the first. We saved the ship on our second time around with the water level only at our knees this time. Monday bought us into the second phase of our school: Chemical, Biological, and Nuclear. The instructor was a horse's ass named McIntosh from somewhere in California. I took an instant dislike to the man. On some days, he was OK and on other days, he seemed to act like a half a fag. In addition, we noticed that his ears were pierced as well. He was a miserable man from the start, and was not respected by any of the students, and not too many of the other instructors liked him either. That along with a personal grudge against me led me to fail the last part of the course. The course as presented was not very difficult; it was that a jerk like McIntosh was giving it. He was the type of guy that sucked up to those who out ranked him, and was a tyrant to those he outranked. The deciding clash came on a Friday night after returning from the enlisted club with a belly full of beer. The M.A.A. told me that I would have to take the mid-watch {12 to 0400} because the man who was supposed to have it was U.A. {unauthorized absence}.

"Smith, I've been at the club all evening, I can hardly keep my eyes open," I protested.

"To bad boot, you have the watch," he said, and then gave me the green duty belt and flashlight, and told me to change into dungarees. When I had reported to the Master at arms desk, he told me to keep at least one of my eyes open for the Phantom Shitter. The {PHANTOM SHITTER} as he was known on

Treasure Island was someone who had a skeleton key in which to access unoccupied rooms at the three different barracks. He would then lift the mattress, and proceed to take a shit on the box spring, and then replace the mattress over it. It would not be discovered until a new student was issued bedding, and then began to make up his rack only to discover a yearlong pattern.

"So that rules out those going to school," he told me.

He handed me the passkey to the vacant rooms, and told me to check all the box springs every hour in order to establish a time frame. After three hours of sound security and box spring watch, I grew drowsy due to all the beer I had consumed that evening, not to mention the peacefulness of the three story barracks because most everyone was on the beach for the weekend. When I had returned to the empty lobby, I sat down in one of the big leather chairs; big mistake. I was soon fast asleep, and was awakened by the gentle probing of the fingers of my right hand. When I came to, I saw a pen being seesawed between my fingers by another hand. When I focused my eyes, I saw none other than McIntosh with his coke bottle glasses and his greasy smirk. He held up a report chit all typed up, and ready for me to sign.

"Rise and Shine fireman wise ass." He grinned. "Sleeping on watch, tsk tsk."

It dawned on me that he had seen me dozing, and instead of kicking the chair, he had decided to get even by placing me on report. Before I could pull myself up from the chair, the on-duty M.A.A. came into the lobby, and before he could protest to McIntosh that it was one of those circumstances, the prick held up the report chit, and announced, "I caught this man sleeping on watch, and I'm writing his ass up under the U.C.M.J. He's gonna meet the man for Dereliction of duty." This meaning I was going to Captain's Mast, which was the equivalent of appearing before a municipal court judge, rather than a superior court judge. It was bad enough to be sure, because the 'old man' as commanding officers were known, had complete power over anyone unlucky enough to find themselves in front of them. That day came one week later when I and several others, who had been written up for various offences assembled at fleet headquarters, and lined up in the hallway to await our turn. I was number four on the list as it turned out, when one of the Marine Guards stepped into the hallway and announced:

"Fireman Hall, report, all witnesses to the charge report."

The first man called was the guy that had been U.A. that Friday night when I had been forced to assume the mid-watch. What I also noticed was that Mac had entered along with the man that he had also written up. They were in there about ten minutes when the Marine Guard stepped into the hallway followed by Hall and Mac. The student then surrendered his Military I.D. to the Marine, and left.

"Fireman Wingo, report, all witnesses to the charge report."

The second man called entered along with Mac again, and the Marine Guard closed the door after them. After another fifteen minutes or so, the door opened, and the three of them stepped into the hallway where the same drill as before took place as the student surrendered his military I.D., and then left.

"Fireman Gardner, report, all witnesses to the charge report."

Once again, the student, along with McIntosh, and the Marine entered the room, and closed the door. Once again, the same routine repeated itself as they came back out into the hallway, with yet another military I.D. finding its way into the hands of the Marine. There was now only myself and Smith, who was there to try to help as best he could.

"Fireman Riley, report, all witnesses to the charge report."

McIntosh entered ahead of Smith, and I, and the M.A.A. then turned to me, and remarked, "Busy bastard, isn't he?"

When the Marine had closed the door, I noticed the C.O. standing behind a podium with the navy seal on the front of it. There was a blue carpet with a small piece of white tape about four feet in front of it. To the C.O.'S left was the fleet headquarters flag, and to his right was the American flag. The Marine then told me to toe the tape, and report.

"Fireman Riley, reporting as ordered Sir," I said, nervous as hell.

I held my hand salute until the C.O. told me to uncover, at which time I removed my cover, and bought it down alongside my trousers while remaining at attention.

"Fireman, you have been charged with 'dereliction of duty', under the uniform code of military justice. Do you have anything to say in your defense?" he began.

"No Sir, the charge is true," I replied.

With my terse, yet respectful reply, the C.O. was somewhat surprised by my candor.

"And that's it?" he asked. "Just like that?"

"I just sat down for a second, I must have dozed off Sir," I replied.

"OK Is there anyone who wants to add anything?" he asked knowing that Smith wanted to speak in my behalf.

"Yes Sir." Smith nodded. "Sir, I bear some responsibility for what happened here," he began.

"How's that?" The C.O. questioned.

"Sir, I had just assumed the mid watch on the date of infraction, and my Sound and Security watch was U.A. He was just in Sir," he began.

"Riley here was just coming off the beach Sir, and he informed me that he had consumed alcohol, and was tired."

"And what did you say to him, Petty Officer Smith?" the C.O. asked.

"Sir, I told him that there was no one else due to the fact that the original watch was U.A. I was overly concerned with catching the person that has been destroying government property."

"You mean the Phantom Shitter?" he asked, to chuckles all around.

"Yes Sir," Smith frowned.

"Yes, I'm curious myself as to his name, rather prolific I hear."

"Yes he is sir, damn lucky too, been going on for a year now Sir."

"Sir, Fireman Riley only had another fifteen minutes to go, and I was checking up on him, but Mac got to him first and held firm."

"I hardly see the point, Petty Officer Smith," the C.O. responded.

"Sleeping on watch is sleeping on watch, is it not?"

"Yes Sir," responded the M.A.A.

"Is there anything you wish to add Petty Officer McIntosh?" he asked.

"I think you have everything you need sir," Mac responded.

"Fireman," he said turning his gaze at me again, "I take watch standing very seriously. Had a fire broken out, you would have been expected to sound the alarm. You know the eighth general order, don't you?" he asked me.

"Yes Sir," I replied.

"Luckily there was no fire. Did we lose any box springs, fireman?''

"No Sir," I replied.

"Well fireman, it's like this, I'm not going to take any money because you owned right up to the charge. First one today I might add," he said. "However, I must have some of your time because of the importance of the charge, I hope you understand."

"Yes Sir," I replied.

"The sentence is twenty days restriction to the base, and twenty days extra duty, starting as of now. You will surrender your I.D. to the Sergeant at arms when you leave. Do you understand?".

"Yes Sir." I answered.

"Pay attention on watch fireman, lives may be counting on you."

"Yes Sir."

"Attention on deck. Cover…, two!" he called as I came to attention, and replaced my hat.

"Dismissed Fireman." I turned with an about face, and left the room followed by Smith, Mac, and the marine guard who promptly collected his fourth I.D. that morning, and told me that I could pick it up in twenty days.

"Thanks Smith," I said as we walked back to the barracks.

"Forget it," he replied. "I'd do it for anyone, Mac's a prick."

"Listen, since you're going to be restricted for a while, I want you to help me out," he said.

"How's that Smith?" I asked.

"I'm almost certain that McIntosh is the Phantom Shitter," he said.

"You're kidding," I gasped.

"Wish I was, Riley. But everything about him fits the profile, I've been in this man's navy fifteen years now, and I've come to know certain things about people," he began.

"The person that's doing this has an obvious character defect, and Mac's full of them," he added.

"You see how he sucks up to those above him, and is a total tyrant to the students below him."

"Yes, I know," I said.

"I also noticed his reaction when the C.O. bought up the subject."

"What do you mean?" I asked.

"Everyone seemed to have an honest laugh about them," he began. "Not so with Mac, he seemed to have a sly grin like he knew something that no one else does. Writes up students for trivial reasons thinking that he's clever."

"I'm surprised that no one's taken a swing at him yet."

"Not only that, but he's been here about a year now and

everything seems to coincide with the time frame of occur-
rences."

"So what do you need me to do?" I asked.

"I'll give you a radio just as soon as you are finished with
your extra duty, because I can't be everywhere. I need another
pair of eyes. I'll also give you a pass key to the unoccupied rooms
so you can check them before, and after his watch," he said.

"So when was the Phantom's last bowel movement?" I asked.

"About two months now," he answered.

"Figure he's due?" I asked.

"Any time I'm sure."

"OK Smith, I'll talk to you later, thanks for everything,"

"Forget it kid; just cover your ass from now on, he's watching
you."

The rest of the course went by with Cliff and Gary going on
to San Diego for the welding part of the school. My attitude sunk
to an all-time low because of an instructor I could not stand.
McIntosh was even more of an asshole now that he had me on
the run because of Captain Mast, He knew I was busy with extra
duty assignments and was finding it tough to handle the course
load and him at the same time. As fate would have it, I flunked
out of the course, and would now be sent to the fleet non-rated.
What that meant was that any division chief who got to the quarterdeck first could grab me for that division. That usually meant
deck, or engineering. In the meantime, however, I would have a
month in transient billeting awaiting orders. The twenty days'
restriction and extra duty, along with my keeping an eye out to
help Smith went by with no sign of the elusive defecator. The
one good thing about flunking out of the course was that I did
not have to deal with the instructor anymore. I spent most of my
time doing maintenance duties around the base painting rocks,
fixing windows, stripping, and buffing the decks in the barracks
and that type of stuff. One day at morning quarters Smith told
me to report to the personnel office because they had something

for me. When I arrived, the man gave me my long awaited orders.

"You got a ship, Riley. You're going to the fleet pronto," he said.

My waiting in transient billeting was now over I had just received orders to a grey ghost. I looked at the ship's name: U.S.S. *Juneau LPD-10*. Tokyo, Japan was where I was to meet the ship.

"Hope you like Marines, Riley," said the man behind the desk.

"How's that?" I asked.

"She's a gator ship, Amphibs, a workhorse if ever they made one."

"And to think you're going aboard as a non-rate too," he added. At noon chow, I looked up Smith at his usual table, and gave him the news.

"An L.P.D.? Yeah I know her, definitely amphibious."

"What can you tell me about her?" I asked.

"Well, she can carry 900 Marines, and all their gear, plus two CH53 helicopters. All kinds of boats too, plus an LCU landing craft."

"She's fair-sized, about 17,000 ton's full load, Tokyo, you say?" He asked.

"Yes, that's what the orders say, with five days leave attached," I said.

"That's strange, there's no naval base there. There's Yokosuka, about twenty miles south. That must be where the ship is now. Well kid, this is what you've been waiting for. Time to steam on a Grey Ghost, and not hanging around here painting rocks outside H.Q. So when do you ship out?" he asked.

"Any time in the next five days," I answered.

"Make good use of that liberty kid, from now on it will be a precious thing indeed," he advised.

"Thanks Smith, I'll heed your advice," I replied.

"Take care Riley, and thanks for the help, even if we failed to catch the phantom," he said as we shook hands.

From there I headed back to the barracks to square away my sea bag and go over my orders yet again. I was at last going to do what I joined to do. 'Join the Navy, and see the world' as the recruiting posters had promised. I went to the personnel office to retrieve my pay records, shot records, and then to Disbursing to cash two paychecks that I had saved up. I had a pretty penny and five days to spend it. After that, I donned a pair of sweat shorts and sneakers and began to run around Treasure Island in an effort to calm my mind. I ran south along Avenue of the Palms, made a left on California Avenue, then another left on Avenue N., on the opposite side of the island, running north along the quays all the way to the firefighting school, and around the base housing area, and back to my starting point at Halyburton court. I repeated it again for a distance of about three miles then went to the barracks beer machine and pur- chased three cans of Coors that I took to the pier in front of the barracks to enjoy the San Francisco skyline along with the com- ing and goings of the merchant fleet. The fog was starting to burn off, and the sun was breaking through. I had five days leave before shipping out to my ship or "Grey Ghost" as it was known in the fleet. Time to play tourist in one of the great cities of the world. The time passed with visits to Fisherman's Wharf, and the Balcuthla sailing ship that was a beauty to behold. The San Francisco Maritime Museum, and Coit Tower, was also on the list of visited places. Time passes quickly when one is having fun, and my time was no different as the four other days soon elapsed, and I found myself on the bus to the airport. As of the first week of October 1975 when I left, the Phantom Shitter of Treasure Island had yet to be caught, and I never heard anything more of it.

TRANSIT TO THE FLEET

After the ten-hour flight over the Pacific Ocean landed at Tokyo airport, I located my sea bag, and began looking for the military information desk to no avail. I walked outside the terminal, spotted a Japanese police station marked by a revolving red cherry, and went inside to see if they could give me any information concerning my ship. After some sign language with me moving my hand in an undulating manner to signify "navy," they were able to put me through to the Master at Arms desk at Yokosuka naval station. Smith was right.

"What are you doing up there?" asked the voice on the other end.

"My orders say Tokyo," I answered.

"There's no naval base up there," he replied.

"So I've been told. I'm letting you know that I'm lost before you mark me down U.A.," I said.

"OK, there's a cab stand so get a cab, and the navy will reimburse you for the ride," he instructed.

An hour later, the cab arrived at the gate of the Yokosuka naval station where I presented my military I.D. along with my reporting orders, and was saluted through by the Marine sentry. Following the sentry's instructions, the cab let me off in front of the Master at Arms office, and gave me a receipt for reimbursement. Upon entering the office, I handed my reporting orders to the M.A.A. on duty, and he turned around to look at the roster on the wall of all the navy ships presently in port. He read it over carefully. The *Juneau* was not among them.

After informing me that he was at a loss for an explanation, he had one of the S.P. guys show me to the transient billeting for the time being.

"Muster here at 0700, and we'll see if we can locate your ship."

"Fine, I can use some decent sleep," I offered.

The next morning after chow when I had returned to the Master at Arms office, he informed me that the *Juneau* had just left Pearl Harbor for Kwajalein Atoll.

"She's just starting a West-Pac. You're going to Okinawa to await her arrival, but you can't get there from here," he said.

"How's that?" I asked.

"You have to fly out of Yokohama air force base, to Kadena air force base on Okinawa," he explained. You'll be a guest of the Air Force for the time being. Grab your sea bag, and don your Salt and Peppers."

I left for Yokohama air base about two hours later, and spent the night in their transient billeting. The next morning about ten or twelve of us lined up on the flight line, and were made to empty our sea bags on the tarmac to ensure that no contraband was going to Okinawa. When the dogs had gone over everything, we were allowed to board the C-130 transport by way of the rear ramp. After everyone was strapped in, the loadmaster gave the thumbs-up signal, and the C-130 lifted off. It was a rough, loud, and cold flight that brought us to the tarmac of Kadena air base. However, we were greeted with a balmy climate upon arrival. Once again, I was directed to yet another transient barracks where there were three other sailors besides myself. Two of them were boots like me, the other one was returning from three months A.W.O.L. We were all going aboard the *Juneau* once she moored at White Beach. That was not for about two weeks though as it turned out. In the meantime, it was back to painting rocks white, this time for the Air Force. As different as the branches of the military were, the one thing they all had in common was that all rocks had to be painted white. The rest of the duties were pretty much the same as I had been doing at Treasure Island: fixing windows, trash detail, buffing floors, etc. Then one morning at quarters we were told that the *Juneau* was in, and to don our salt and peppers, and stand ready to be picked up by the ship's van. This was the day I had been waiting for since that first rainy day at boot camp. I was finally going to sea! About noon, a grey navy van pulled up out front, and a black guy sitting shotgun says, "*Juneau* sailors come see daddy."

The driver of the van looked to be a boson mate due to the deeply tanned face, and arms. After stowing our sea bags in the rear, we hopped in the front. From there it was about a fifteen-minute ride to the White Beach pier.

U.S.S. JUNEAU [LPD-10]

When we had cleared the White Beach guardhouse, we found ourselves on a winding switchback road heading down hill. At certain intervals I could see the turquoise waters of Buckner Bay, named after LT. General Simon Bolivar Buckner, U.S.M.C. who had been the highest-ranking U.S. Military man killed in the battle of Okinawa thirty years before, the same battle that Master Chief O'Farrell had taken part in. We then saw two ships of the same class moored on opposite sides of the pier.

"The *Juneau's* on the right," announced the black guy. The other one is the *Denver*. She's going home."

As we pulled up to the brow of the *Juneau*, I noticed that the entire ship was a beehive of activity. There were many sweaty Marines and sunburned sailors all engaged in a massive working party. They were hauling up mountains of stores from the pier with the ship's giant boat and anchor crane, and depositing them just aft of the starboard quarterdeck where the officer of the deck stood resplendent in a pair of dress whites. When we had climbed the brow to the catwalk, we then went up a short ladder to the quarterdeck, turned aft to face the in port ensign fluttering in the breeze on the fantail, and saluted it. One by one, we each turned and saluted the O.O.D. and held the salute as we then announced, "Request permission to come aboard Sir."

"Permission granted. State your business," he replied.

"Reporting as ordered Sir." I replied, and handed him my reporting orders. He then repeated the same drill with the others until he came to the A.W.O.L. cook.

"Well, well, if it isn't the Boogie Man back from the beach,"

"The crew has been missing your cooking Boogie, welcome back."

"Thank you Sir." Responded the A.W.O.L. cook. The O.O.D. then told the enlisted man on watch with him to pass the word for the duty Master at arms to lay the quarterdeck. When the M.A.A. passed through the hatchway to the quarterdeck, I noticed a glimmer of recognition on sighting the A.W.O.L. cook.

"Well look what the tide washed in, and just in time," he said.

"Hey C.T., How you doing?" responded the newly returned cook.

"C.T., Escort the Boogieman to the brig if you will please," ordered the O.O.D.

"Yes sir, let's go boogie," said the M.A.A. as they disappeared through the hatchway. As the cook was escorted to the brig, the O.O.D. had the quarterdeck watch pass the word over the ship's 1MC for the duty Bosun mate, and the duty B.T. to lay the quarterdeck. This was what I had feared. I knew that if you reported aboard ship non-rated, you would be up for grabs by the two divisions that were always hard pressed for labor: Engineering and Deck division. About two minutes later, a rather large Chief petty officer emerged from the hatchway and crossed the quarterdeck to speak with the O.O.D.

"First come, first serve. Take your pick, Chief," said the O.O.D.

The Chief stood all of six foot five inches tall as he walked up to the two of us that were now left, and looked us over for a full minute before speaking to the man next to me first.

"You look like a deck ape," he said to him, as he then looked at me, looking wide-eyed at him.

"So do you for that matter, but I think I can fix that. You're the newest member of Bravo Division, follow me," he commanded. The O.O.D. just grinned, and shook his head at the big Chief's method of selection. I picked up my sea bag and followed him into, and across the mess decks, down a ladder into Damage Control Central where several dirty dressed sailors with headphones were standing in front of a large chart board marked with grease pencil. They were in the process of refueling the ship after having been at sea for so long. As I stood there wondering what to expect next, a little guy popped into the room and asked the chief what was up. The chief nodded my way, and said, "New boot, get him a rack, and a locker, square him away. After that take him down to the forward hole, and turn him over to Scratch, start breaking him in."

"Follow me, Boot," the sweat-soaked sailor said.

He led me down a passageway into the main well deck, and across to the port side of the ship. We went through another small compartment with a head, into Bravo division berthing where I was assigned a rack on the very top and a box locker to stow my sea bag. After switching out of those stupid looking salt and peppers, and into dungarees, he led me once again across the well deck to the starboard side of the ship to an open hatch way that emitted a steady blast of hot, humid air that went up in noise, and heat the farther we descended the steep ladder. Upon entering the engine room, I noticed about a forty-degree temperature increase, along with the much louder noise level due to the forced draft blowers. As we passed the blower room, I noticed the snipes had painted the door of the room with a large red devil holding a burner barrel superimposed over the boiler rating. Over the red devil's head were the words, WELCOME TO HELL.

"That's where you are now," yelled my guide with a cupped hand into my left ear. We then went down another ladder to the fire alley where there was a burner man on the boiler front. To my right was a gauge board with all kinds of gauges, and standing in between two fuel oil service pumps was the fire room Topwatch, boiler tech second class Scribeci. This was Scratch. The fire alley was about twelve feet long and about five feet wide. Right below the gauge board were two cylindrical shaped booster pumps. Right behind the gauge board were the main reduction gears that revolved the shafts that propelled the ship through the water. Scratch looked me over coolly before handing me a readings clipboard, and instructed my guide to break me in on readings. My new guide was a messenger in the forward fire room under B.T.2 Scribeci, or 'Scratch' as the other snipes called him, due to his no nonsense way of running his watch, along with a proclivity to mix it up with anyone who crossed him whether on the ship or off. I was shown where to get the readings on all the gauges on the main feed pumps, fuel oil pumps, forced draft blowers, and the like. He pointed out main generators, evaporator, and D.A. tank, on the upper level along with the throttle deck where there were three men: a Topwatch, throttle man, and a messenger. From there we went back to the lower level and he showed me the main feed booster pumps, burner barrel rack, and the big scoop injection tube; a huge brass tube that vented under the hull, hence the name 'scoop.'

"This is where we take in sea water. From there it goes to the evaporators to boil off the brine to make fresh water," he said.

"After that it goes to the D.A. tank to remove the oxygen so that the inside of the boiler tubes don't get oxygen pitting." Pointing to the burnerman on station at the boiler front he said, "We're only running two burners now, hotel steaming with size 32 sprayer plates, lights and hot water. The after fireroom is in cold iron status."

He took me back up to the upper level and showed off the steam drum, water level gauge glass, and the big main steam manual cut off valve. Pointing out the big main steam valve, he added, "In the event of an emergency this valve must be secured pronto. Scratch holds the record at 93 seconds, the guy standing burners is second at two minutes flat, and that's only because Scratch had his foot up his ass," he added. "They work well together because he's the fastest burnerman in the division. They call him Billy Burners."

Burnerman Billy Lutz was a Nebraska farm boy whose chiseled jaw line and blond hair bespoke his Teutonic ancestry. He stood about 5 foot 5, but was solidly muscled—built like a fire hydrant is more like it. At his waist was a polished brass belt buckle embossed with the boiler rating of a 'heroes boiler' with one end blowing steam up, and the other end blowing steam down. It was known in the fleet as a Flying Asshole, and because he had earned it during the ship's last refresher training, it was known as a –steamer-. It had been presented to him by Scratch, the previous owner.

Scratch had come aboard in '72, and had earned it from one of the original ships company, one of the first burnerman to steam on the *Juneau* since its commissioning on July 12, 1969. She was now six years old. Billy Burners would retain that belt buckle until the ship's next refresher training evolution, or reftray, where up and coming burnerman such as myself would have a chance to best him in speed, and skill on the burner front. He had retained that belt buckle for a year and a half now. The only other way he would have to surrender, it would be when he made pumpman, in which case he could award it to the next best burnerman in the division. Such were some of the traditions of Bravo Division. There was another tradition that Scratch was to spring on me later on watch. It was the tradition of showing a new boot like me just who was in charge of the fireroom.

After two hours of taking readings, Scratch's messenger figured that I had them down enough to take them on my own. The only tough part was checking the oil in 1alpha blower room.

Instead of an automobile style oil dipstick, the forced draft blower had a threaded screw-in type. In order to reach it you had to negotiate an insulated root steam line, and reach down under the rotating turbine to the oil sump to unscrew it. It was about 140 degrees in that part of the blower room, and not a place to linger. By the end of the watch, I decided to skip that oil level check because there was no oil on the deck, and it was a pain in the ass to reach it. Scratch was waiting for just that move. When I had returned to the fire alley after my last readings of the watch, and set the clipboard down, Scratch asked to see my hands.

"Put, em out, palms up," he commanded. When I had complied, Scratch looked at them and snarled, "You didn't check the oil on 1alpha blower."

No sooner had the words escaped his mouth than he hauled off and drilled me square in the chest. The blow knocked me to the deck plates, an audible hiccup escaping from my chest. It had been a good shot, and it surprised me plenty. I was quite shocked, and embarrassed to be flat on my ass. Scratch then turned to Billy Burners and said, "Keep an eye on the water for a second Billy." Then looking down at me he said, "Come here, boot."

I hauled myself up from the deck plates, and followed him up the burner front ladder to 1alpha blower room. When we had entered the hot, loud area, Scratch orders me to unscrew the oil sump dipstick. When I had retrieved the oil stick, he tells me to look at my right hand, as that was the hand I was holding it in. My hand was stained at the fingertips with a dark blue ink.

"I had Moe smear some Prussian blue on the back of the t-handle to see if you were checking the oil every hour. Moe told you to check it every hour, didn't he?" demanded Scratch.

"Yes he did," I admitted, thoroughly humiliated. Scratch stepped up to me and said, "The next time it'll be in the chops boot, and you won't be getting up any time soon, don't test me again... got it?"

"Yes, I understand," I replied.

"Good, go talk to Moe, there's other things to explain before your relief gets here."

When I went back down to the fire alley, I saw that everyone on watch got a kick out of my first lesson in watch standing under Scratch. I did my best to not to make eye contact with anyone, as I was still upset with Scratch's bullying tactic.

"Everybody goes through that, even Scratch when he first came aboard, there's a reason for it though, so get over it," Moe said.

Our watch was relieved at 1800 by four other snipes. Topwatch, pumpman, burnerman, and messenger. After each watch stander had informed his relief of the status of the fire room, we all left up the long ladder, and across the well deck into the berthing compartment when Scratch turns to me and says, "Go up to the mess decks and grab some chow, and make sure you shower before you hit the rack. We may sweat like pigs, but we won't tolerate any in Bravo division."

"No problem, Scratch," I replied, and then went up to the mess decks for my first *Juneau* meal. I stood in line with a bunch of other snipes that I saw from the forward fire room. They were Machinist Mates from the upper level. I picked up one of the metal trays and silverware as I approached the serving line, and watched as a large black man in his twenties doled out portions of food to those before me. This was Toungie, so named by the other black guys because he had no upper front teeth, and his tongue flicked every now and then at the corners of his mouth. It seemed to be a nervous tic of some kind, and he seemed to be of a good nature as the snipes teased him.

"Yo Toungie, I hear the boogieman's back."

"Bout mutha fuckin time too, boy done pissed me off wit dat A.W.O.L. shit, gonna boil his Boogie ass when he gets out da brig," he declared.

As the chow line moved up to where I was next, Toungie looked at me and could tell that I was a new boot.

"What's you want boot," he asked.

"Same as them I guess," I answered.

"*Juneau* steak, comin' right up FO da boot," he said.

With that, Toungie doled out roast beef and mashed potatoes, and I went over to sit with the other snipes.

When I had finished chow and deposited the metal tray at the scullery, I decided to explore my new surroundings. I walked out to the flight deck along a hanger and surveyed the 168ft. distance to the fantail. From there I crossed to the port side of the flight deck, and observed a 26ft. motor whaleboat hanging in the davits on the catwalk. I also noticed a small helicopter control station next to the after stack. From there I climbed up another ladder to the port side boat deck where four boats were held in large brackets. Two of them were flat bottomed with a ramp in front, known as mike boats, and the other two appeared to be captain's gigs.

From there I climbed up to the after gun deck where there were two mounts of twin 3 inch, 50 cal. Mk.33 mounts. One on the port side and one on the starboard side. Each held four rotating racks in which could be stored rounds of three-inch ammo. From there it was up yet another ladder, and then yet one more to the 04 level where the ship's mast was bolted to the deck in a tripod configuration. On yet one more level and all to itself was the signal shack. I went forward on the 04 level, and gazed down at the forward gun deck where two additional twin three-inch mounts were located, port and starboard. From there going forward was the ship's foc'sle where two large black painted anchor chains disappeared through hawsers into the deck. The sun was now low over the western side of the island, and I noticed that the *Denver* had since pulled out to head back to San Diego after a seven-month Wes Pac where she was involved in the recent evacuation of Saigon. The *Juneau* had just relieved her, and was beginning a Wes Pac of her own. I noticed sailors in twos, and threes heading down the quarter mile pier towards the White Beach enlisted club, which was about all White Beach had to offer as far as liberty was concerned. I hung around and enjoyed the breeze off Buckner Bay for about a half hour before returning to Bravo division berthing to shower, and hit the rack. As I lay on the third and topmost rack, I listened to snipes coming, and going to, and from the beach, the announcements over the ship's 1mc address system, and just staring at the rows of piping about a foot and a half above my face. This would take some getting used to I thought to myself. After sweepers were called to give the ship a clean sweep down fore, and aft, came taps.

Taps, Taps, all lights out, keep silence about the decks.

The smoking lamp is out, now taps. Someone secured the overhead compartment lights, and the din of the compartment began to settle down somewhat. After a while, I started to drift off to sleep, and it was not long before we were awakened by the sound of a violent scuffle taking place in the dark, the sound of a fist making contact with a face was unmistakable. A drunken voice then commanded, "Get up asshole, we're on!"

There was a second of silence before someone from another part of the compartment yelled, "Fire 'em up Hensen. Fire'em up." Then Scratch's voice called out of the lifer locker, "Knock it off Hensen! Now!"

"Fuck you Scribeci!" Came the reply. The sound of a fist impacting a face was heard once more as the fight was on. The compartment overhead lights were turned on to reveal a man sprawled out on the deck, and Scratch knocking hell out of a tall wiry man in jeans, and cowboy boots. The tall man started to rally for a moment before Scratch delivered an overhand right to the taller man's jaw, and he sagged against the aluminum lockers. Scratch then forced him up against the lockers police officer style, and then grabbing him by the topknot with one hand,

and putting his knee into the small of his back, bent him over backwards until I thought his back would break. Instead, Hensen swallowed his tongue. He started to gag as much as he could considering he was only half-conscious. The man Hensen had hit was beginning to stir with some assistance from someone else.

"Aw hell, that's all I need, gimme a pencil with an eraser quick," he said. Moe appeared with the pencil, and Scratch used the eraser end of it to probe deep down the man's throat, and dig his tongue up far enough to grab it with his other hand. Hensen's face began to lose the crimson color as he sucked in much needed oxygen. In the meantime, the quarterdeck watch had been alerted, and the call went out over the ship's 1mc.

"Duty corpsman, Duty master at arms, lay Bravo division berthing."

The third class corpsman bounded through the port side passageway just as the duty M.A.A. entered from the air dales berthing compartment. The master at arms looked first at the man Hensen had hit, and asked Moe what happened.

"Talk to Scratch," was all he would say.

"You snipes never fail," he said to himself as he walked up to Scratch to find out what was going on.

"He fucked up," Scribeci replied.

"Who's that?"

"Case," replied Scratch nodding towards the man Hensen had hit.

"How's that?"

"He's been talking shit ever since we left San Diego, had it coming the last three weeks, Hensen just picked the wrong place is all."

"Well then why did you hit Hensen?" he asked.

"Cause he sassed me," Scratch replied in a tone of voice that let on that he could not believe that he had just been asked a dumb question.

"OK, OK. This is between you snipe types, Chief Morgan will sort it all out at morning quarters, in the meantime however, Hensen's going to the brig until he sobers up," he said.

"You'll have to detail a man to stand brig watch of course," he said.

The whole time this was going on, I had been observing everything from the top rack not believing what I had been a witness to. Scratch then looks up at me, and I knew it was coming.

"You're it boot, get dressed and follow C.T.," he ordered.

I climbed down from my rack, and donned my dungarees, a fresh pair. Scratch then explained his reasoning to me.

"We light off #2 boiler at 0400 so we can secure #1 boiler and bottom blow. Hensen was supposed to stand burners, but he is too screwed up to trust. All you must do is sit outside the cell and make sure that he does not puke, and choke on it. The Boogieman is right next door so you will have someone to talk to while you are there. I'll send your relief at reveille." He finished.

I followed C.T. and the corpsman, which had Hensen propped up between them to the ship's brig, where they laid him down on the deck of the cell face down. They then shut the steel door punctuated with two-inch holes, and C.T. locked it. The A.W.O.L. cook began to stir in the next cell, and inquired about the new neighbor.

"Drunk hole snipe Boogie," answered the M.A.A.

"Aw shit, he's gonna barf and stink the whole place up," he warned.

"He just might cookie, he just might."

C.T. then instructed me on the rules of brig watch, and said that the roving sound and security watch would be by every fifteen minutes to make his rounds. There was a compartment phone on the bulkhead in case of any problems concerning the two men. I was left alone with the sober cook.

"Sure hope he don't blow Toungie's cookin' all over the

place." He drawled with a Texas accent. The cook and I began to talk about this, and why he went over the hill three months before the *Juneau* got underway.

"I met this girl back in Dallas the last time I took leave," he began. "Nice girl too. She wrote the ship later on and said that she was pregnant, I guess I freaked out. Anyway, I figured my responsibility lay there, and not here sloppin' the hawgs," he said. "One day I got pulled over by the cops, and they ran a check on me, found out I was U.A. so they sent me back to square up."

"Why do they call you Boogie?" I asked him.

"My folks ran a greasy spoon back in Dallas, and I grew up as a short order cook. When I came aboard *Juneau*, I was cookin' for a thousand people, Marines, and Ships Company. You really gotta hustle at chowtime. I was a real hustler, faster'n hell, everyone said I really boogied, it kind of stuck I guess." There was a slight pause.

"I'm the best, a real pro." He said it with conviction.

We talked for another half hour before he said that he wanted to get some shuteye before reveille sounded. It sounded soon enough. It began with a Bosun's whistle and then: "Reveille, Reveille, all hands heave out, and trice up, the smoking lamp is lit in all authorized spaces, now reveille." Fifteen minutes later breakfast for the crew was called. It was October 30, 1975. My first day aboard JUNEAU had been a trip. Moe soon arrived to relieve me, and told me to get some chow then to muster with the rest of Bravo division in the well deck upper vehicle storage area due to the fact that it was raining topside.

"How will I know which is Bravo division?" I asked Moe.

"Easy. They're the grubby looking ones," he replied.

After some breakfast, I went into the well deck and saw all the divisions lined up port and starboard, and sure enough there was Scratch and some of the others from the forward hole that I recalled from the day before. Upon falling into formation with the rest of the division, I noticed the big chief in a pair of khakis. There were two first class petty officers standing on either side of him. One had a sandy colored beard and a slight beer gut. He was the Wolfman, so called because of the uncanny resemblance of his voice to that of Wolfman Jack, the famous radio disc jockey. The other man was a little taller, and I could see that both hands and a portion of his neck had been burned at some time in his life. This was Smitty. Smitty was senior enlisted man in the forward engine room, and the Wolfman was senior enlisted aft.

I learned by listening to the Wolfman telling the chief that Hensen had gotten as far as the White Beach enlisted club, proceeded to get smashed, and started throwing knuckles at everyone in sight. Most of them wearing shiners were his friends, except Case of course.

"He'll never finish the cruise," said the chief. 'He's a good man on burners, but he's gonna get himself killed on the beach with that kind of horseshit."

"I hope not, we need all the burnermen we can get," replied Wolfie.

Most of the division had alcohol breath and bloodshot eyes, including Smitty, and the Wolfman. They had gone on a tear after three weeks at sea. It had taken *Juneau* that long with only a refueling stop at Kwalijien atoll to reach Okinawa where she embarked 900 first division Marines. As the Wolfman read the ship's plan of the day, I learned that JUNEAU would be getting underway for the Philippine coast in two days for amphibious operations. This was what she was designed for. She would be operating in the Orient for the next eight months. The chief then made the announcement:

"We're gonna cross the equator this cruise, sailors. I suggest that all you pollywogs start soaking your asses in salt water, toughen it up a bit," he added. Only about half of the division cheered the chief's remarks. They were shellbacks, the rest like me were pollywogs, and they simply had been aboard *Juneau* longer. After quarters were secured, Scratch, and Moe showed me how to bottom blow the now secured forward boiler. They had me fill the boiler with water using the emergency feed pump, and the last of the steam pressure from the boiler, then open the blow down valves under the deck plates to flush out the water drum, or mud drum as the snipes called it. The boiler was then refilled again, and the mud drum was flushed out a second time. "We'll stay cold iron till we get underway, so until then we repack valves, and clean," he said.

It was still warm in the forward fire room, but not like before. The only sounds were that of the ventilation system, and one fire pump running to supply fire main pressure to the ship. The loud forced draft blowers that fed air to the boiler were now silent. I noticed that the water in the bilge was somewhat high, and Moe explained that we would pump them out once we were at sea. The rest of the day was spent repacking valves, scrubbing deck plates, and tracing out the main steam system. Smitty then told me that I would be standing the 2000-2400 watch in the after fireroom in order to learn that system as well. The after fireroom was pretty much the same as the forward space, except that the starboard shaft ran through the length of the latter. There were different people here this time, and the after boiler Topwatch was a second-class petty officer named Deadeye. His messenger showed me where to get all of the readings along with pointing out the pumps, blowers, and such. The two boilers of the *Juneau* were the same 600lb. D type Babcock and Wilcox, while other ships of the class had Foster-Wheeler. Other than the nameplates on the front of the boiler, they were the same type. Toward the end of the watch, I noticed that my fingers were once again stained with bluing. Deadeye was taking no chances on me not checking the oil. Our relief soon arrived and the watch was relieved after talking over the status of the plant. After showering, I hit the rack and hoped that I could get some decent sleep. It had been a hectic two days, and a culture shock to remember as

I got about six hours before the 1MC blared:

"Reveille, Reveille, Reveille, all hands heave out, and trice up, the smoking lamp is lit in all authorized spaces, now reveille." Fifteen minutes later came breakfast for the crew. After breakfast came the order to muster for quarters. It had stopped raining now so the division mustered on the port fantail with M-division on the starboard side. Once again, the Wolfman read the plan of the day in his Wolfman Jack voice. When he had finished, the chief said to Scratch, "You light off #1 boiler at 0300, Lutz, I want you on burners."

"Everyone does, chief," answered the cocksure Lutz.

"Boot, you'll be there too, in the meantime sailors, make preparations to get underway," he finished.

Part of those preparations included cleaning the sprayer plates used on the burner barrel tips. There were three sizes of sprayer plates that the *Juneau* used. The smallest were size 64, regular light-off were size 32, and regular underway steaming were size 16, the largest. Because #1 boiler had only been down two days it was still warm enough to light off with size #32 plates. The size #64 plates were only used when the boiler had been down more than a week. The idea being that you wanted the firebox brickwork to expand slowly, and evenly. I was shown how to assemble the burner tips for 2 size#32 burners, and 5 size#16 burners for underway steaming. After final preparations were made for light off at 0300, I was given a tour of the port and starboard shaft alleys. The shaft alley was where the shafts ran along a bilge after it left the engine room. There were three large bearing caps clamping down on it at thirty-foot intervals before it ran through the hull of the ship and connected to a three bladed screw. The roving sound/ security watch was responsible for checking the oil in all the bearing caps while the ship was underway. It was very important.

"That's why Scratch slugged you," said my new guide. "There's no room for half steppers underway."

I was beginning to understand just how important and dangerous the engineering department could be.

"Boogie and the Wild man are getting out of the brig once we get underway. You'll get a chance to meet Robert once he's sober, and the rest of us will be rid of Toungie's cooking." He grinned.

"Is that the guy Scratch hit?" I asked.

"Yeah, he's a good hole snipe, just can't drink is all."

"In fact, he's in the running for Lutz's steamer buckle; he came close last ref-tray, but no cigar," he said.

"That good, is he?" I asked.

"Light off isn't tough, wait until we start getting bells from the bridge, when you see how Billy Burners scrambles on the boiler front then you'll understand."

"There's not much more to show you so grab some chow, and turn in, light off is at 0300, so you'll be on station at 0230." He finished.

I went up to the mess decks and grabbed some chow, then showered, and hit the rack   I was awaken at 0200 by the after fireroom messenger along with the rest of the light off watch. There was Scratch as topwatch; Moe was pumpman, Lutz was on burners, and I was the newly broken-in messenger. When the boiler had been filled with feed water to the proper level, Moe started up one of the forced draft blowers to provide air for light off. He then began recirculating one of the fuel oil service pumps, and one of the main feed pumps.

"You're good to go Scratch." He said with thumbs up.

"Main Control, Bravo one, request permission to light off #1 boiler."

"Permission granted Bravo one." Came the reply.

"Fire it up!" Said Scratch to Lutz. The burnerman then lit the light off torch, and it leaped with yellow flame. He opened an air register and thrust the torch into the firebox alongside #1 burner, then pulled down the fuel oil handle to the on position and backed away. After bringing the volume of air to the proper percentage, Lutz then opened the root valve on the burner manifold to release the fuel oil through the #1 burner. WHOOSH! Went the sound of the fires being lit, and the torch was forced back from the register about a foot due to the pressure.

"Fires lit!" yelled Lutz to Scratch. He then spoke to the throttle deck, or Main Control, as it was known.

"Main Control, Bravo one. Fires lit #1 boiler."

"Fires lit aye," came the reply. There was not much to do now except wait for the firebox to warm up enough to switch to the size #32 sprayer plates in about an hour.

"We'll bring the boiler on line in three hours. I need exact readings boot, don't get yourself punched," he said to me. "When we start getting bells there may be a casualty, and we might lose the boiler. If that happens, make sure you stay out of the way."

At 0600 reveille sounded, and then breakfast for the crew. At 0700, the word came over the 1MC.

"Now set the special sea and anchor detail."

By this time, the boiler was on line with main steam cross-connected, and size #16 burner barrels in place.

UNDERWAY

The engine room was soon fully manned, and I thought to myself that I was now going to sea. In fact, I would be part of the very process that made a ship move through the water. At the bottom of the gauge board, there were two gauges, Ahead, and Astern. The bell came from the bridge to the throttledeck, and was then relayed to the burnerman as to the speed requested. The burnerman then cut in or cut out the burners as needed. If he received an all stop bell, he would have to scramble to kick out four burners before the boiler safeties lifted from excess pressure. On the other hand, if the bridge sent down a full back, he would have to scramble to cut in the four burners before the throttleman sucked the boiler off the line. The man standing throttles was named Cox, and he was the best M division had. There was a rivalry between him and the man they called Billy Burners. Cox would give Lutz a look that said "You're all mine." Lutz would just pat his belt buckle with the 'flying asshole' insignia, and grin back at him.

"You'll never take it, Cox. You'll never take it," he would say.

The shrill blast of the Bosun's pipe was heard over the 1MC, followed by the word every sailor longs to hear, UNDERWAY! It reminded me of the term we had been told back in boot camp.

"A sailor belongs on a ship, and a ship belongs at sea!" The bells started coming down from the bridge. Clang! One third back and Lutz increased air pressure to the firebox, and cut in a third burner. CLANG!, two thirds back, as Lutz again increased air pressure to the fire box and cut in a fourth burner. The forced draft blowers were fairly screaming now although it would not be for long. CLANG! All stop. Lutz, using his whole body closed the overhead valve that controlled steam to the blowers, and kicked out #3, and#4 burners. All while maintaining main steam pressure at 650psi. The declining whine of the blowers sounded like a jet engine being throttled down. We had been backing away from the pier all this time the ship was now turned around with the bow pointed seaward. CLANG! Two thirds ahead. Once again, Lutz sprang into action increasing the air pressure much more quickly this time. WHOOSH... went #3 burner; WHOOSH... went #4 burner. The *Juneau* held that speed until she cleared Buckner Bay, and I felt the swells of the open ocean begin to gently heave her back and forth. CLANG! Ahead full, came the final bell. Lutz increased air pressure of the forced draft blowers to their maximum speed of 8000rpm's, and cut in #5 burner. There was a great deal of noise now as all of the machinery was going full blast. Eighteen knots would be the ships steaming speed until we reached Mindoro Island in the Philippines.

When the engine room had settled out some, the light off, and sea detail watch was relieved. After Scratch's watch left the engine room, I walked up to the starboard quarterdeck. The Bosun's mates were busy stowing the hemp mooring lines, and stacking the line rat guards amidships behind the hanger bay. It was a bright sunny morning as I watched the southern end of the island of Okinawa become smaller in the distance. After almost seven months in the navy, I was finally where I was supposed to be, at sea! I walked out to the fantail and saw two fantail watches. One port and one starboard, wearing sound powered headphones. The white foamy wake of the *Juneau* stood out in contrast to the cobalt Pacific. As it was the start of the workday, I returned to the fire alley to be instructed on how to pump the bilge. Billy Burners was now off sea detail and so he showed me how. The pump we would be using was the highest volume pump in the engine room at 4000 gallons per minute.

The bilge was soon sucked dry enough for him to tell me to grab a pen and paper, get down in the bilge, and walking a sort of 'duck walk' style, begin to trace out the main feed piping system. Down into the bilge I went, pad and pen in hand. I worked my way over to the main feed pump area making sure to mark down any valves I encountered along the way. I encountered many. It was an obstacle course there under the deck plates, and I soon began to cramp up. When I reached the main feed booster pumps alongside of the boiler, I could then stand to relieve the cramped leg muscles. The deck plates came even to my chest, and I leaned against it as the ship began to roll a little more now that the sea conditions had changed. I noticed a different man sitting on the rag can under the ventilation duct where the pumpman stood his watch. He just nodded in a way that let me know that I was not being picked on. I got the feeling that everyone went through this. "Name's Fred," he offered. "How ya doing?"

"Fine, but a little cramped at the moment," I answered.

"Take a left at the emergency feed pump, from there you'll see how it comes to a check valve, follow it under the fire alley around the boiler. From there it goes into the economizer, and then into the steam drum," he advised. "Thanks Fred, I owe you one." I replied. When I climbed out from the bilge an hour later and handed my schematic of the main feed system to Lutz, he looked it over closely, and seemed pleased. "Looks good, take a break boot."

I went back over to the pumpman's station to resume my conversation with Fred, and he informed me that this was also his first deployment. Fred too was a pollywog. "Been aboard about seven months now, right as the *Juneau* came off her last Wes Pac, what do you think so far?" he asked.

"It's been a trip," I shouted back at him.

"Wait'll you cross Shit River; we got two days' liberty after we land the grunts on Mindoro." He said. "We're headed to Subic after to refuel.

"After that we pick the Marines up, and we're off to Okinawa, then to Japan for more operations," he said. The next day passed much the same with me tracing out the main steam system this time, along with the lube oil system, and the fuel oil system as well. I was then shown the sequence for changing burners underway from Lutz. On the morning of the third day, *Juneau* arrived off the coast of Mindoro.

The tropical air was thick with humidity, quite a contrast to the subtropical balm of Okinawa. The two big Sikorsky CH-53 Marine helicopters were warming up their three General Electric turbo shaft engines on the flight deck. They were the largest heavy lift helicopters outside of the Soviet Union. They had about a 160m.p.h. cruising speed, and could carry fifty troops at a time. Marines that were now good to go. The huge Marine-laden Sikorsky's lifted off the flight deck one at a time trailing thick black exhaust in their wake as they headed for the thick lush jungle of Mindoro. They returned, and again until Battalion Landing Team, first division ninth Marines were all ashore. By this time, of course the X.O. had heard all about the brawl in Bravo division berthing. Hensen was on report by the Master at arms, and was now out of the brig along with the newly returned cook. Boogie was back at work in the galley much to the delight of the crew. The X.O. decided that now would be a good time to set up a smoker on the boat deck.

In the course of long periods at sea, tensions sometimes ran a little high. In order to release that tension between two sailors, a boxing match, or smoker, would be set up on the boat deck. The Bosun's mates would lay down the canvas mats, and there would be sixteen-ounce gloves for the contestants, along with headgear and mouthpieces. It was regular Queensberry rules just like regular boxing. The two men simply went at each other until one was either winded, or had his bell rung enough to call it quits. There was one custom, though. If upon watching the action someone were to point at you, then you had to accept the challenge, or leave the boat deck. It was the fleet code of machismo in an all-male environment. There was no dishonor in losing a match, but if you were asked, then you had to accept, or leave. There were two real slugfests that day that had the boat deck roaring, not to mention making some side bets on the contestants. One was when Hensen showed up, and began glaring at Scratch on the other side of the makeshift ring that was formed by standing sailors. Scratch nodded agreement, and began removing his dungaree shirt. This was to be a grudge match, the best kind. Hensen was sober now, but still sported a small lump on his jaw where Scratch had dropped him three days before. They strapped on the headgear, and then had their oversized 16oz. gloves laced up.

Hensen spoke first. "Gonna be a different story this time, Scratch."

"We'll see Robert, We'll see," replied Scratch.

After the men had touched gloves, the fight was on. There was no fancy footwork, no flurry of jabs that marked a pro fight. It was all brawling and wild haymakers. Toe to toe slugging that in its intensity was made more so by the roar of the men assembled on the boat deck, and just above on the port gun deck. By now, both men were blowing blood down their heaving chests from having been tagged on the nose. Their eyes were beginning to swell shut, but still they fought on. Slap, slap, slap, came the sound of leather against flesh until Hensen opened himself a little too much. Scratch delivered an overhand right to Robert's jaw, and his mouthpiece went flying into the crowd. Hensen was out on his feet as he threw one last swing. Scratch simply side stepped it and Hensen sprawled face first on the thick canvas mat.

"That's it fellas," said the Bosun. "Enough." Scratch held out his gloves and someone untied them. He spit out his mouthpiece into the water bucket and removed his headgear. Hensen had been helped to his feet by now, but was still a little dazed.

"I got him, Boats," Scratch said to the Boson. The applause from the assembled sailor's was heartfelt as it had been a test of wills, and both men were winner's as far as the crew was concerned. With that, Scratch draped one of Hensen's sweaty arms around his shoulders, and helped him from the scene. The two of them made for quite a sight as they crossed the mess decks, with both their bare chests spattered with blood. By now, two other men had been laced up for combat. One of them was the Machinist mate Cox, from the forward throttle deck.. The other man was shorter, but stocky. He was also an officer, the only one of the day. In addition, he had done the choosing. Cox, true to the custom, had accepted. L.T.J.G. Schott was division officer for the electrical department; he also loved a good fight.

"Once we touch gloves I'm an opponent, not an officer," he said.

"Yes Sir." Answered the Machinist mate.

Once more that day, men stripped to the waist went toe, to toe in honorable combat. Once more, the roar of the crowd pumped them full of adrenalin as they engaged in individual tests of wills for all to see. L.T.J.G. Schott drew the first blood from Cox's nose, and after a brief rally, the Machinist mate managed to score a mouse under the officer's right eye. The short L.T.J.G. proved to be a good infighter, inflicting punishing abdominal blows to Cox's mid-section. After a while, Cox could not catch his breath and had to call it quits. Once again, the boat deck erupted in a roar of approval for yet another slugfest. Once again, two evenly matched opponents won respect in this most male of environments. Sinewy, sweat-dripping men, testing their manliness against the lush green backdrop of the Philippine jungle. The smoker lasted until evening chow when the Boson ordered the mats rolled up and stowed. Back in the berthing compartment Scratch and Hensen were now showered, and cleaned up. The *Juneau* would be getting underway for Subic Bay now that the Battalion landing team had been put ashore for their two-day evolution. There was much laughter, and mutual admiration on the mess decks that evening as twenty or so sailors bore split lips, swollen eyes, and various nicks and cuts from the days sparring. The bout between Scratch and Hensen had been the only real bloodbath of the day, and they both showed the swollen effects of it. Upon seeing them at a table crowded with other snipes, the Master at arms just shook his head.

"Hope we can have a peaceful cruise now guys," said the M.A.A.

"No sweat C.T.," responded Hensen. "He learned his lesson."

"Not now, Robert," Scratch said, thereby giving up all hope of convincing him that he had been beaten honestly. After chow, the sea detail was set, and the ship raised the anchor. The *Juneau* then got underway for Subic Bay. She arrived at sunrise and once again, it was Lutz on the burner front doing his thing with grace, and speed. As soon as the ship was tied up, and the brow put in place, the announcement went out over the 1MC for an all hands working party to muster on the pier, and port quarterdeck. Bravo division began refueling the ship, as the ship's giant boat and anchor crane began hauling up stores from the pier. The forward boiler was secured in order to bottom blow, then lit back off in order to secure, and bottom blow the aft boiler. After refueling was over, and the all-day working party secured, it came time for knock off ship's work at 1630hrs.

"Commence liberty call," came the long-awaited announcement.

Those who did not have to stand duty section were busy changing into civilian clothes and heading down the brow. Magsaysay drive was their destination. First, however, they had to clear the Marine guard at the beginning of the bridge, as they were ever alert to check navy people for haircuts.

OLONGAPO CITY, PHILLIPINES

It was dusk now as Lutz, Moe, and I cleared the Marine guard, and for the first time began to cross the bridge that spanned one of the Orient's most fabled stretches of water. The odor of the chocolate brown sewer known to all who crossed it was unmistakable, and it was aptly named. This was the infamous "shit river" of Olongapo city. A canal separated the navy base from the city of Olongapo. The level of the water rose and fell with the tides. The span of the bridge ran about seventy-five yards, and on the right side of the bridge, we noticed several dugout canoes. In the forward section of the canoes stood little girls of what seemed to be all of ten years old. They were wearing white cotton dresses below the knee, and red tops. There were about seven or eight, one to each dugout. The surface of the brown water was about fifteen feet from the road of the bridge, and in their outstretched hands, they held reed made "Peso catchers" of a conical shape. They were known as "cherry girls." In the rear of the dugout were boys of around the same age that were dressed only in shorts that I noticed were wet. They were in fact beggars with a twist. Where the cherry girls would resemble colorfully dressed miniature statues of liberty holding aloft their reed peso catchers, the swarthy, spirited, 'slickey boys' would motion for passing sailors and marines to throw a peso in front of the dugout where they would dive after it. It was customary, however, to carefully drop a peso or two into the reed peso catcher held aloft by one of the lovely cherry girls. The boys would dive in after a coin broke the surface of the brown liquid, and a moment later the little diver would resurface with the peso, a "thank you Joe," and a smile. The girls, on the other hand, would retain their composure, and their doe eyed appearance.

Upon crossing Shit River, we had gone from "the world," as American's referred to the U.S.A., to the glaring poverty of the third world. They played by different rules in Olongapo. We were now entering the Dodge City of the Orient. The main drag was Magsaysay Street, named after a Filipino hero that was executed by the Spanish just before Commodore Dewey gave his famous order, "you may fire when you are ready Gridley!" Resulting in the smashing the Spanish fleet in Manila bay. There was a long line of colorfully decorated jeep's that were left over from World War 2, and remodeled to carry six, to eight passengers. There were also a number of Honda motorcycles with a side car attached called "bikies" that stood ready to ferry sailors and Marines to wherever they wanted. We decided to walk and take in the sights. Not more than a block into Olongapo, a shoe shine kid approached Lutz, who was wearing leather shoes. He bent down and lightly grabbed his trouser cuff and asked, "Shine Joe, shine?"

"No thanks, kid," responded Lutz, and the shoeshine kid,

noticing that Moe and myself were wearing sneakers, went off in search of other customers. The street was alive with all kinds of venders hawking all sorts of things. On both sides of Magsaysay Street were neon lit bars with a tout stationed at the front door trying to tell sailors how much better their bar was in contrast to the one next door. We decided to check out one called the Friendly bar #1. It was air conditioned, as that was an absolute must in the tropics if any bar wanted Yankee dollars. We went in and sat at the bar and ordered San Miguel beer. It was the national beer of the Philippines so we stayed with that for the time being. We stayed for about three beers then headed out to see the other clubs.

The next place was called the Carrier Bar. We entered to find a bargirl in a bikini and knee-high white go-go boots dancing in a cage behind the bar. A large neon aircraft carrier was lit up on one wall. Again, it was a round of San Miguel beer for the three of us, only this time we were hit up by bar girls to buy them drinks—iced tea, not alcohol. After a while of drinking, and bull-shitting the bar girls, we went to the Cavern, the Off Duty, and then ended up at one of the raunchier bars called the New Jolo Club. This bar was legendary among the fleet for the "snappers" who worked the tables—waitresses in miniskirts and nothing underneath.

They were called Snappers because sailors would stack four, or five Pesos on the corner of the table, and one of the more vaginally talented girls would approach, lift her mini skirt ever so slightly, and pick up the coins with her pussy. She would then walk away without dropping a single coin.

At about nine p.m. the real show began. After the M.C. got the crowd drinking freely, which was not hard to do, he would ask a volunteer to lie on his back on the stage. A peso would be placed on his forehead, one on his nose, and one on his lips. The snapper would descend once, twice, and thrice, neatly picking the coins off his face. At eleven p.m. the bar would announce the approaching midnight curfew which meant that everyone had to be off the streets. Magsaysay Street had a human tide of its own. At 1630 hrs, sailors and Marines would stream across Shit River into the red lights of Magsaysay; an hour before midnight, thousands off service men would stream back across the bridge to the base. The cherry girls would still be there as this was in fact their high volume time of night. The little slickie boys would still be going after coins that went wide of the peso catchers. It struck me as odd how not only could they see in that brown water, but at night at that. The answer to that came from the Wolfman once we got back to the ship. Wolfie explained that they had strung a green military parachute under that side of the bridge so that any coins going into the water would hit the chute about six feet under. The slickie boys would then run their hands along the chute, and retrieve the coin.

"You didn't think they could see in that shitty water did you?"

"I was thinking there had to be a trick," I answered.

The Wolfman then looked down at Lutz's brown leather shoes, and asked him if he was offered a shine this evening. When Lutz replied that he was, but declined, the Wolfman asked him which shoe the slickie boy approached first. "The right shoe, why?"

"Roll up the cuff." Wolfie said. When Lutz rolled up the cuff, he found there was brown shoe polish on the inside of the trouser leg.

"You throw those in with the rest of the wash, and the whole load is coming up brown," he laughed.

"Why that little shit!" exclaimed Lutz. The Wolfman explained that these were street kids that had to survive on their own, and so they lived by their own rules. He explained that what the average sailor spent in one night whoring around town could feed one of them for a month. If you refused the shine, you were seen as cheap. If you said yes, the shoe polish went on the shoe, and they got the shine of their life. Anytime you refused, the shoe polish went on the inside of your cuff. "The only way around it is to take the shine, or wear sneakers. Besides, it's only a buck, the kid needs to eat."

The Wolfman laughed as he told us that they were not called Slickie boys for nothing. He had made eight Wes-Pac's thus far, and pretty much knew the tempo of Olongapo city. "Consider yourself lucky that it's only one pair of pants and not the whole damn load."

"You guys are gonna need a Sea Daddy," He teased. "I'm headed over tomorrow night, follow me. I'll show you where to get the best meal, the coldest San Miguel, and the hottest blow job in all of P.I., and you can thank the Slickie boy's for it too."

"How's that?" asked Lutz.

"These kids live by their wits," responded Wolfie. "They know everyone there is to know, good or bad. You name it and they can get it for you. The cleanest girls, the coldest beer and the best prices. You gotta pay them, but it's still cheaper than doing it on your own."

"You treat them right, and they respond in kind. Treat them wrong, and they slit you deep, and wide. Life's cheap over here, guys." The Wolfman was giving good advice. It was what the chief meant when he said that Hensen would probably get himself killed on the beach in a port like Olongapo. Some twelve-year-old street kid could have a butterfly knife at a drunken sailor's throat in a split second; it had happened before.

The next day there was to be an import Captain's Mast held on the navigation bridge. Hensen, all dressed in tropical whites and freshly beaten up from the smoker two days ago was there along with Boogie, and four or five others that had been written up for various offenses. Hensen received another three days in the brig on bread and water, plus 45 days' restriction, and 45 days' loss of pay. The Boogieman received the same, although he was spared the brig time because Toungie was overworked without him. After knocking off ship's work at 1630, liberty call was announced. We showered and followed the Wolfman down the brow and across Shit River into Olongapo. Lutz was wearing sneakers this time. We walked down Magsaysay Street to where the Seaman's club was located and entered the front door. It was a rather plain building and not all lit up and garish like all the other clubs on the strip. He led the way upstairs to a plain, clean dining area. There was a bar with a well-dressed Filipino man behind it talking to a merchant seaman, and a couple of conservatively dressed Filipinas who were servers. The Wolfman advised us once more, pointing to the bartender first.

"He's a barkeep, not a pimp, and they're waitresses not whores, mind your manners and let's eat," he said. We were served some local dishes along with rice, and of course the coldest beer in the P.I. When we had finished the meal and retired to the bar to drink some more San Miguels as cold as he had promised the night before, he said, "Well, that takes care of two promises."

"And the third?" asked Lutz.

"We gotta get a jeepny to Subic City," Wolfie said.

"Why Subic City?" Asked Lutz.

"You want the best head in the P.I. right?" he asked. "Pay for the jeepny guys." Upon leaving the seaman's club, we took another six-pack along for the ride of five miles to Subic City. Along the way, the driver stopped to let one off here, and pick up one there and we soon arrived at a two-story building on the waterfront. It had a main bar downstairs. The sign over the front read "Marilyn's Club," and just underneath "the place with the face." We went inside and of course ordered more San Miguel beer. We sat around on the back veranda under a full moon overlooking the thatched umbrella type sunroofs over picnic tables next to barbecue pits. After we finished our first beer, a young prostitute walked out on the veranda and leaned on the railing. She looked us over and set her gaze on the Wolfman because he was older, and therefore was in possession of more money than we non-rates were. "Well now, aren't you a pretty little cock-sucker," he said.

"Mmhmm," she replied with a sultry look.

"Come scratch Wolfie's belly, make his leg shake," he said.

"We go now fur face?" she asked.

"Yeah, we go now, me so horny," he said, mocking the very line the whores used. They disappeared through the doorway and went upstairs. Soon Lutz, and then Moe, succumbed to the other whores in the place and went upstairs, leaving me alone at the bar. I was repelled at the hardscrabble life of these girls, that for a few dollars would put their dignity, yet their very souls into the rough, uncaring hands of men that would steam into Subic Bay from a hundred ships, and from all points of the globe. My thoughts were interrupted by a long howl from upstairs. It was the Wolfman howling at the full moon from the second story veranda. He then came downstairs and out on to the back veranda where the freshly blown Lutz was now enjoying an-other San Miguel. "Where's Moe?" he asked. "Upstairs I sup-pose," said Lutz.

"OK. As soon as he's done we gotta get a jeepney before cur-few."

"We have light-off on #2 boiler at 0400," he said. The grinning pumpman emerged shortly and we grabbed some more San Miguel for the ride back to Olongapo. We made the Shit River Bridge just after 2300, headed for the ship, and turned in. Light off was in five hours, and since I was new on board, the Wolf-man said I needed to learn the after engine room as soon as pos-sible even though I was still assigned to Scratch's watch. The light off watch was awakened at 0300. I felt somewhat hung over as I got dressed but figured that all would soon pass as soon as I got some cold water from the condensate coil of the D.A. tank. Wrong move! Just before they lit the torch, I felt a loosening of the bowels in the most urgent of ways. As I stood at the bottom of the fire alley ladder, it soon hit hard. There was nothing I could do except cross my legs, and squeeze. "Boot, start taking readings."

"Just a second." I replied, somewhat embarrassed.

"Wolfie, cried Deadeye, "Boots got the San Magoos" he said. The Wolfman walked over from watching the gauge glass water level, and asked me accusingly, "Boot, you gotta shit?"

"In the worst way Wolfie," I assured him.

"Well what are you waiting for?" he asked loudly.

"I'm not going to make it all the way to the head," I answered.

"Well you're not shittin in my bilge, grab a bucket, and use that."

One of the other snipes fetched up a bucket and gave it to me. I was still squeezing my legs together earnestly trying not to shit my pants until the abdominal cramps passed enough for me to go behind the boiler to let loose into the pail. I picked up a rag along the way, and all was soon over. Afterward, I hauled the pail out of the engine room, and with about thirty feet of line that Deadeye gave me, I launched it out of the side port and rinsed it clean. This is what Deadeye meant when he referred to the national beer of the Philippines as San Magoo. It tasted good the night before, but my system was paying for it now. I felt like hell, and wondered just how long this was going to go on. The boiler had been lit-off in my absence and so I now resumed my messenger duties. I felt like hell for the rest of the watch, and was glad to be relieved for breakfast. A good meal made all the difference and I felt much better by the time quarters was called. After quarters, sea detail was called, and Scratch's watch took over the fire alley up forward, while Deadeye's watch took over aft.

The *Juneau* was soon underway to Mindoro where she would be steaming figure eight's in the channel between Mindoro, and the main island of Luzon. When Battalion landing team, first division ninth Marines, were all aboard the *Juneau* headed north at eighteen knots for Okinawa. Two days later, she stood into Buckner bay to unload the Marines, and refuel. There was a non-rated working party to replace all the chow the Marines had consumed and it took the better part of the day to do it. There was to be three days liberty in the meantime so I figured it to be a good time to don swim trunks, and check out the turquoise waters surrounding the ship. About 500 yards from the pier there were some small islands just off the enlisted club beach that I snorkeled over to. The waters of Buckner bay were clear, and warm. There was much life on the reef despite all the damage it had received during the enormous battle there when the bay was called 'Nakagusuku wan' by the Japanese.

Colorful fish were abundant, and I even spotted a Moray Eel among the coral. On the other side of the small islets I saw a couple of blue sharks, about five feet long silently cruising in deeper water that faded into gloom. After an hour or so, I decided to swim back to the beach and dry off in the sun. Upon returning to the compartment, I found a new boot standing in his "salt and peppers" talking to the recently released from the brig Hensen. Unlike me who had the misfortune to report aboard non-rated, this one was fresh out of B.T.A. school at Great Lakes. He would be working in the after engine room under Deadeye. Later that day another ship moored on the opposite side of the pier. It was a guided missile Frigate; U.S.S. *Brooke* [FFG-1] there was a rumor that their engineering department wanted to play the *Juneau* snipes in a game of football. Bravo division's chief Morgan had accepted the challenge, and came down to the compartment to inform everyone that did not have the duty section, to muster on the pier. All the animals from Bravo and Mike divisions are assembled on the pier and began to taunt the quarterdeck watch of the *Brooke* to hurry.

Scratch was there as was Deadeye, Smitty, Wolfie, and the chief and even L.T.J.G. Schott still sporting the shiner he received from Cox was going to play. When we reached the playing field just above the beach, the chief points to me and the new kid I had met down in the compartment, and tell us to look for an empty shit can to put all the beer, and ice into. Everyone began donating money into my ball cap until I had almost thirty dollars. The new kid and I then went towards the package store to purchase what everybody wanted which wasn't hard as they were all yelling, "The Bull, The Bull," aka, Schlitz malt liquor.

We found an empty shit can, packed it full of beer and ice, and then lugged it back to the playing field. By this time the *Brooke* snipes were starting to arrive in twos, and threes. The *Juneau* snipes were starting to grab the bull by the horns so to speak, as the *Brooke* crew plotted their game. Chief Morgan told everyone to remove their dungaree shirts in order to be "skins" so we would be harder to hold onto. "And put your dog tags in your pocket or you're gonna get hung."

I got a feeling that this was to be full contact football without protective gear of any kind. The way the bull was going down this was not going to be a football game as much as it was going to be a football "smoker." As it turned out, that was exactly what was going to happen. The Wolfman went "odds or evens" with one of the *Brooke* sailors, and they were to receive the kick off. After receiving the ball, the *Brooke* ran it half way up the field until L.T.J.G. Schott took him down. After they had lined up against the fat lips, and shiners of the *Juneau* crowd, I could not help but notice that they seemed amused by their appearance, while some of them seemed somewhat intimidated. The chief had called for an all-out charge leaving only two guys to cover their receivers. The suddenness of it came as a shock as their defense was bowled over, and the quarterback began to back pedal, eyes wide with surprise. The onslaught came so fast that all he could do was go down on one knee to save what they had just gained. He should have run it as the full *Juneau* line hit him anyway with everyone piling on the hapless quarterback with delight. When they had all risen to their feet, the *Brooke*'s quarterback just lay there groaning. This flagrant foul bought about a protest from the *Brooke's* team captain, but Chief Morgan just shrugged it off with a remark about forward momentum, or something of that nature.

After a few more such plays, it became clear that the *Juneau* crowd was out to play rough, and it was sure that something was going to blow. The *Brooke* was on their second quarterback by now, and even he was getting sore enough to call it quits. It came time for us to receive the kick off and Deadeye caught it. We all blocked pretty well but one of the *Brooke* sailors held back as Deadeye ran it up the sideline, and was starting to charge him in a way that threatened to cut him in half. Deadeye was only twenty or so yards from a full field touch down, and was not going to be cheated out of it.

When the *Brooke* sailor got close enough, Deadeye simply punched him on the side of the head. *Smack.* The blow only stalled him for just the time Deadeye needed to cross to a touch-down as the *Brooke* sailor continued to chase him into the end zone, and beyond. Everyone saw the punch and began running after the two, the *Brooke* sailors after their man, and the *Juneau* sailors after the *Brooke*. It started with by trying to separate the two, and ended with a short-lived brawl before Chief Morgan, and L.T.J.G. Schott restored order.

It was clear to see that the game was over, so Scratch began tossing cold ones to the *Brooke* sailors, and things settled down and no one was hurt. As the *Brooke* sailors headed down the pier to their ship, the *Juneau* snipes finished the rest of the beer and lolled about in the sun that whole snipes rarely get to see. That night there was to be a U.S.O. show at the White Beach enlisted club. There were to be eight Miss America contestants giving a show. It was also Nov. 10, 1975. The Marine Corps' 200th birthday.

All the grunts were going to be there wearing their 'Charlie's' uniform of green trousers, and tan, short sleeve shirts. After everyone was showered, and changed into civilian clothes, we headed down the quarter mile long pier to the enlisted club where we entered a long hall way at the end of which was a large ballroom. On the left side of the hall way was a barroom of good size with a sign over the doorway that read:

"HE WHO ENTERS COVERED HERE, SHALL BUY THE HOUSE A ROUND OF CHEER!" It was a serious request to remove one's cover.

"Name's Landon," he offered. "Been aboard long?"

"About two weeks, I'm a boot just like you, just got back from Subic."

I told him that he would be working under Deadeye and the Wolfman, and that while they were OK on the beach, they were all business in the fire room. I did not elaborate on how they knew whether you were checking, or not checking, the oil. I figured that everyone deserved to find out the same way. Lutz and Moe arrived a short time later, and joined us at our table. Deadeye came over from the bar where he was making up to the *Brooke* sailor that he'd punched by getting him royally shit faced on shots of Wild Turkey.

"Pay attention tonight guys, Deadeye advised. "You won't see any more round-eyed women until we hit Pearl."

After an hour, the ballroom began to fill up so we went inside to secure good seats. There must have been close to a thousand men in the White Beach enlisted club that night just to see eight Miss Americas perform their show. They were not average women though, but big blue-eyed specimens of the best America had to offer. They clearly felt the testosterone in the room as they turned on the crowd with pretty smiles, and jiggly breasts. They had complete control over every man present, and they knew it. The grand finale came when they announced that they were not here for a contest, but a U.S.O. tour, and therefore should be treated equally. A general roar went up at that suggestive statement. After they disappeared for a moment, they emerged for what everyone hoped to see… The swimsuit contest! The big difference was that they were not swimsuits, but rather full-fledged bikinis.

The house went crazy when they asked if anyone wanted to be pen pals. All the Marines who were wearing their 'Charlie's' began bringing up their dog tags, and out of the duo they were issued, removed one and threw it up on to the stage. Hundreds of single dog tags were hitting the stage at the women's feet as they danced their routine. The women would lock onto a single thrown dog tag, catch it, and then she would provocatively hold it in one hand, pull her bikini panty out ever so slightly, and drop the tag in. The place was sheer sexual energy now as the women blew kisses to the lusting sailors and Marines at their feet. It had been one hell of a Wes Pac thus far, and it was only two weeks old. How many of those guys ever received letters from the Miss America's is anyone's guess, but I am sure they wrote their share of letters to lonely G.I. Joes.

The *Juneau* would be getting underway with this new batch of grunts for Numazu beachhead in Japan, where after putting them ashore, would embark yet another Marine amphibious unit for the return trip to Okinawa. Once again, I was assigned to Scratch's sea detail watch, and once again, it was Billy Burner banging away on the burner front. This time the landings were to be amphibious instead of airborne. When the *Juneau* had steamed to the middle of Buckner Bay, the bridge sent down an all-stop and set condition one alpha. That was where the ballast tanks were allowed to take in seawater and flood the lower well deck while the stern gate was lowered to accommodate the *Juneau's* duck. This was in effect an L.C.U. landing craft. The craft had a large ramp up forward, and a smaller one aft. This permitted it to be a drive-through craft. It also had a small starboard bridge or pilothouse over the crew quarters. The mast was designed to fold down to permit the craft to enter the stern of the ship. This L.C.U. could carry up to 190 tons of gear and 350 troops at a time.

When all the Marines and their gear were aboard, the *Juneau* blew the ballast tanks, raised the stern gate, along with the anchor, and got underway for Japan. After sea detail was secured, I went up to the well deck to inspect this neat-looking craft. On the port, and starboard side of the craft I noticed the hull number, 1629, was the hull number of the *Juneau's* duck. As the ship headed north along the green coast line of Okinawa at sixteen knots, the regular shipboard routine of watch standing and meals fell into place. By the end of the first day, the wind turned blustery, and the sea began to kick up white caps. The weather turned much colder on the second day as the *Juneau* steamed into the broad bay at Numazu under the majestic gaze of Mt. Fuji. The 13,000-foot mountain was rumored to be visible from any point on the island of Honshu. The conical summit was capped year-round in snow, and it made a pretty backdrop for conducting landing operations. The bosun's mates were now wearing heavy navy sweaters and knit watch caps along with green foul weather jackets.

"Now set condition one alpha," blared the 1mc.

The stern gate was lowered, and ballast tanks flooded so the L.C.U. could be floated off the wooden deck of the lower well deck. L.C.U. 1629 was packed chock full of helmeted Marines as it made its way out of the well deck, and into the choppy, white capped driven seas. It backed out about one hundred feet, then made a starboard turn and headed for the beach. The Marines jammed shoulder to shoulder were getting a heaving ride as L.C.U. 1629 plowed through the heavy swells of Numazu bay kicking up geysers of foamy spray in the process. It returned three more times until Battalion landing team 3/9, and all their gear were put ashore. When that was completed, the *Juneau* then embarked a Marine amphibious unit, or M.A.U. as it was known for the return trip to Okinawa. When all were aboard at the end of the day, and the *Juneau* had recovered her landing craft, she blew the seawater from the ballast tanks, raised the hook, and steamed out of Numazu Bay into the darkening Pacific for the two-day transit to White Beach. After another day, the topside crew switched from the foul weather jackets and watch caps to t-shirts and ball caps. The troops this time would simply walk down the brow to the pier upon arrival. There was the standard working party to replenish stores, while Bravo division refueled the ship. The *Juneau* could hold around 700,000 gallons of naval distillate fuel when fully fueled, and it was standard practice to maintain a 70% readiness at all times when deployed. The Marines returned to Camp Schwab, Hansen, or wherever they were billeted, and since *Juneau* was the only ship at the pier, we had the enlisted club all to ourselves. The large ballroom was strangely quiet now compared to a week ago when the roar of the troops had shaken the ceiling during the U.S.O. show.

We would be in port for two days, and then get underway for Pusan, S. Korea on the southeastern side of the peninsula. We would be conducting underway casualty control drills in route. These drills concerned everything from engine room shut downs, to firefighting, to damage control, to man over board drills'. I was going to get a chance to best Scratch, and Lutz on the big main steam valve. What I did not know, was how many times I would get to try. The first drill the ship underwent proved to be the most hilarious, the man overboard drill. During such a drill, a bona fide navy-issue dummy named OSCAR, complete with a dungaree uniform, and orange kapok life vest is thrown overboard from the bridge to see if the port, and star-board fantail watches are paying attention. If one of them sees OSCAR drift by, he calls it in to the bridge, and then releases a white smoke marker, and throw's it over whatever side he's on as close to the dummy as possible. The reason for this is that it takes *Juneau* roughly a thousand yards to turn around at sixteen knots. The smoking sea marker gives the helm something to bear on upon its return run. Of all that sea, if a man were truly in the water only his head would be visible, and thereby nearly invisible to spot in a choppy sea. It also gave the engineering department a good drill in shutting down one screw, in this case the starboard screw, with an emergency all stop, along with after steering going to hard starboard rudder. During such an evolution, all hands not on watch were ordered to man the rails around the ship in the hopes that one of them will spot OSCAR, and alert the bridge, or in case of danger sound the shark alert. There are Gunners Mates posted fore, and aft for just such a scenario. Meanwhile the Boson Mates begin unlimbering the 26ft. motor whaleboat in which to affect the rescue.

"Starboard fantail to bridge, man overboard starboard side."

"Repeat, man overboard starboard side," said the fantail watch.

The O.O.D. on the bridge gave the response and the order. "Bridge aye, man overboard starboard side, all stop starboard screw, hard starboard rudder."

The throttleman in the forward engine room stopped the starboard screw a split second after giving the burnerman on # 1 boiler an all stop bell. The burnerman knocked out four of the five burners to not lift safeties on the boiler.

"All hands not on watch, man the rail," said the bridge O.O.D.

The *Juneau* heeled to port as the port screw continued on its own without benefit of rudder. By ordering hard right rudder, it created a drag on the starboard side of the ship, and the port screw simply drove the ship in a circle. When the ship had almost completed its circle, the O.O.D. sent orders to the engine room: "Ahead full, Rudder amidships."

The *Juneau* steamed towards the smoking sea marker and the search for OSCAR was on. The starboard bridge wing soon located the orange clad dummy, and announced that there were shark fins in the water around OSCAR. It was only a drill as far as the sharks went, but the word was passed to the fantail watch through the sound powered headphones, who in turn passed it to the Gunners Mate with the M14 rifle. By this time, the *Juneau* had come to a gently rolling halt, and the Bosun's mates had lowered the motor whaleboat to the surface of the ocean.

The general idea of protecting a man from shark attack is to shoot as close to the dummy as possible in order to scare the sharks away. The Gunners mate chief then tells the third class petty officer to fire away. The man wrapped the sling around his left arm, braced his left palm on the fore stock of the M14, and began firing away. The 7.62mm rounds kicked up quick geysers of spray from twenty yards out as he worked his way towards the orange clad dummy supposedly being attacked by sharks. POP, POP, POP! The last half of the twenty-round magazine hit uncomfortably close to OSCAR as the motor whaleboat headed around the fantail of the ship, and for the dummy. After the last round, the rifles bolt locked open, and he removed the magazine and returned it to its pouch. The Gunner's Mate then slung the M14 over his shoulder and watched as the motor whaleboat closed upon the orange vested dummy. One of the boat crew hauled OSCAR to the boat, and the men manning the rail on that side could see that they were laughing to themselves. The Boson mate in the bow of the boat lifted OSCAR out of the water and held him high as the boat idled in the chop. A cheer went up on that side of the ship as everyone could see that the shark guard had succeeded in blowing off one of OSCAR's dungaree legs! The chief turned to the rifleman with a hearty laugh and said, "Lay the armory, and secure the weapon."

He trotted forward along the flight deck with those along the starboard rail giving him a good-natured ribbing, "Hey guns, I'm not worried about Jaws, I'm worried about you." The cheer of harassment continued as he jogged the gauntlet past the starboard quarterdeck to the hatch that led to the mess decks. The boat crew returned to the ship and began hoisting back to the catwalk. Everyone on the flight deck now converged on the motor whaleboat station to inspect the one-legged OSCAR. The bosun's mates had recovered the lower half of the leg that was shot off below the knee. Just for the hell of it, the Gunner's mate chief told the fantail watch to pass the word to the bridge that OSCAR needed medical attention. After the man passed the word to the bridge, the ship's 1MC. blared away:

"Duty corpsman, lay the flight deck on the double." When the corpsman arrived, the bosun's mates cried, "Shark got OSCAR." Unaware of the overzealous sharpshooter, the corpsman looked at the dummy and thought that a shark must be rather aggressive to attempt feeding on an inanimate object. The chief said to the corpsman, "Well, you gonna fix his leg? It's part of the drill you know."

"Yeah, yeah," responded the chagrinned corpsman as he pulled out a rubber medical hose and applied it to OSCAR's leg. Someone retrieved a metal Stokes stretcher from the now unoccupied troop spaces to carry OSCAR to sickbay; normally during a man overboard drill, the boat crew would retrieve OSCAR and that would be the end of it. Now that he had become a bona fide –shark victim, the whole process from rescue to first aid, along with a stretcher ride to sickbay, would ensue.

"Secure from man overboard drill," said the 1MC. The engineering department was next up now for casualty control drills. "Boot, grab a pair of gloves and a crow's foot," ordered Scratch. A crow's foot was a two-foot piece of pipe with two, three-inch pieces of the same size pipe welded to it. It was used to break loose stuck valves the same way a pipe wrench would. The guys in Repair welded them up in the H.T. shop. The guys in Bravo and Mike's divisions referred to them as "fresh air snipes," or "turd chasers." They were every ship's jack-of-all-trades. Welders, plumbers, carpenters, fire party chiefs, damage control men—you name it and they could improvise it quick. They welded up a number of crow's feet for us in various sizes for different size valves, and one eight-inch crow's foot in particular became a favorite of the after fire room topwatch who used to twirl it pistol fashion all watch long. This was how Boiler tech second class Denton, became known as Deadeye. I put on the gloves, and grabbing a crow's foot, stepped up on the metal stool that was bolted to the deck just underneath the main steam valve. Smitty stood at the entrance of the throttle deck and tapped his watch.

"93 seconds boot, 93 seconds," he said, referring of course to Scratch's record in closing the big valve, but first the two engine rooms had to be split so as not suck each other off the line. When all was ready, the throttle deck reported to the bridge that in turn gave the permission needed to secure a boiler. Scratch then yelled into the sound powered phones, "Low water # 1 boiler, secure fires, secure fuel pump." With the boiler fires out, and the forward generators off the line, all lights and ventilation ceased in the forward fire room.

"Hit that valve boot!" boomed Scratch from the fire alley below. With only the fixed battle lanterns providing light in the forward engine room, I laid into the main steam valve for all I was worth with the crows foot to break it free, and then it was hand, over hand until both arms became heavy, and the muscles tight with exertion. The sweat began to pour out of me, as there was no longer any ventilation. Again and again, the big valve turned, the long threaded stem disappearing into the valve body. Breath came in short gasps now as the muscles in my arms, and back began to scream from lack of oxygen. I could hear orders shouted in the dark from the throttle deck, and the fire alley below. The Machinist mates had secured steam to the starboard shaft to maintain as much pressure as possible for light off, so the rest was up to how fast I could secure the main steam valve. "Any fuckin time, boot!" yelled Smitty, tapping his watch.

"You shittin me, boot? Three whole minutes?"

Three minutes and I was still working on the valve. I had

about four inches of valve stem left now, but I was going much slower so I reverted to the crow's foot for better leverage until it was finally secure. Afterward, I sat down on the stool in the dark to catch my breath. After the casualty drill was evaluated, permission was soon granted to relight the boiler fires.

Again, the sweat poured from my face as I labored to reopen the big valve. I was using the crow's foot with my whole body although there was not the same sense of urgency as in closing it. The boiler fires were relit, and lights and ventilation resumed. There would be a short breather while the after engine room went through the same evolution as soon as the starboard screw was re-engaged. I headed over to the de-aerating tank, also known as the D.A. tank, to siphon off some of the fresh water that not so long ago was part of the Pacific Ocean. It was cold and refreshing going down. As soon as the after engine room had gone through its evolution and been re-lit, and back on line, it was time to cross connect the two fire rooms for a combined loss of main feed water casualty to make the *Juneau* lose all power through out the ship. This was so A-gang could start up the emergency diesel generator located under the M- division-berthing compartment. Until that time however, the *Juneau* was rolling in the open ocean swells in a condition known in the fleet as Hot, Dark, and Quiet. Hot because of no ventilation, dark, no power, and quiet, because all shipboard machinery was secured. After about five minutes, the distant hum of the generator was heard, and the ship's lights came back on, along with the ventilation. When the combined drill was evaluated, both boilers were brought back on line, and the two plants were once again put into a-split- condition, which meant that both boilers operated independently of one another. The *Juneau* was once again underway. I had hit the main steam valve six times in the process of securing and reopening it for light off.

I wondered how Landon had fared aft under Deadeye because he was the new boot back there. I drew another coffee cup of water from the D.A. tank, and went down to the pumpman's station where there was a vent to cool off under. Each fire room aboard *Juneau* had two steam powered feed pumps that fed feed water to the boiler. They ran on line at 750psi because the boiler line pressure was 650psi, and the feed water coming into the boiler had to overcome that pressure in order to feed it and maintain the proper water level. A second pump ran at 350psi in the standby mode. This pump ran on the by-pass part of the Leslie regulator, re-circulating feed water while the online pump fed the boiler. Sometimes though, the top part of the regulator would fail and the pump would race out of control, the pumpman would have to take control quickly to secure the root steam valve that permitted the steam to run the pump before the pump lifted its safeties and filled the fire room with hot, stinging, steam. He then had to bring the other pump up to speed in order to keep feeding the boiler with water so there was not a low water casualty.

We had been conducting drills all afternoon, and now the forward fire room was about to experience the real thing in a very dangerous, and frighteningly way. Fred, the pumpman who had given me advice that day I was under the deck plates, was up on the generator deck shooting the breeze with the generator man. I was over in front of the boiler talking to Lutz about this, and that when all of a sudden #1 alpha feed pump, the one on line, began to take off with an aircraft engine-like pitch.

The pump safeties had already lifted to the bilge, and that part of the engine room was now enveloped in hot, face stinging steam. A loud banging in the area meant that the pump was about to shake itself to pieces, and it was happening incredibly fast. Scratch now had to make a decision of whether to secure fires in the boiler without permission, and order everyone up the ladder, or try to regain control of the runaway pump. The only way to do that of course was to secure the root steam valve, and shut the damn thing down. Where was Fred? Scratch threw down the sound powered head phones that he was wearing, and started past the wide-eyed Lutz on burners with me close behind. We only got so far when the hot steam turned us both back. Scratch was almost ready to order Lutz to pull fires when the high-pitched squeaking steam began to subsist. Now we knew where Fred was. He soon emerged from the cloud of steam, and we could see how he could stand it: He was wearing overalls over his dungarees. It was that extra bit of insulation that had kept Scratch and I from getting too close to it. Fred's face, and hands were unprotected though, and he was wearing the makings of first-degree burns on his face, and second-degree burns on his hands from closing the root steam valve without benefit of gloves.

"Scratch, bring up bravo feed pump!" he yelled, his face beet red and contorted in pain. Scratch was able to enter the subsiding cloud of steam and bring Bravo pump up on line pressure at 750psi in order to prevent a low water casualty on the boiler. Lutz meanwhile maintained plant pressure on the burner front. The throttledeck by this time had slowed the starboard shaft in order not to drag the boiler off the line. When Scratch returned to the fire alley, and notified main control that everything was back to normal, the throttledeck put the starboard shaft back up to speed with Lutz cutting in the other two burners to make up for the lost steam. Fred was a hero that day in sticking with that hand blistering root steam valve.

"The harder that pump shook, the faster I moved," he said.

Fred's hands were a wreck, and he was in considerable pain as he sat on the deck plates in front of the emergency feed pump.

"Hope you weren't crying about that main steam valve boot," he said.

Fred's relief soon came down to the hole to take over on pumps as Fred headed off to sick bay to get his hands looked at. Scratch had me help him up the engine room ladder to the upper well deck, and across to the port side of the ship where sickbay was located. I tried to cheer him up as best I could by telling him that at least he still had all his limbs unlike poor OSCAR. Fred stopped in his tracks and looked at me.

"Do you have any idea what would've happened if that root steam valve had snapped at the flange like it was about to!" he asked me.

Fred was furious over what he thought was a cavalier attitude on my part. Until the feed pump took off, I had thought that I was being toyed with in having to open and close the main steam valve so many times back to back.

"What you see here," he said as he extended his palms, "comes only from the valve without gloves. This," he said, gesturing to his face, "comes from saturated steam, the nicest kind.

"If that pump had snapped that flange the way it was going to, we would have been looking at 600psi steam. We'd end up like lobsters, and quick. No one would've made it out of there."

We were now at sickbay so I left Fred and returned to the fire alley. Scratch waved me over, and said that had I fully understood the pumpman station and would be in a position to get to the root steam valve quicker. "I got Topwatch, Lutz has burners, and you're a free agent. Fred's relief is going to go over what happened with you. Pay attention, it could be your ass someday," he advised.

"Now you know why we put you through the paces on the main steam valve right?" he asked.

"Yes, I guess I do now," I answered.

"Every man's important down here, all jobs overlap," he continued. "It's Fred's fault for not being on station. Instead he was bullshitting the generator man about all those Pusan whores he was gonna meet. Got his mind on his cock instead of his job."

The new pumpman was a black guy from Mississippi, and at first, I had a hard time understanding him. I looked at his name on his dungaree shirt, Danshaw, and when I introduced myself, he just looked at me with pearly whites, and informed me that I was "Nuffin but a boot, dat's all you is." I could see that I still had a long way to go in being accepted by the salts in Bravo division. Danshaw took me over the two main feed pumps and explained the high and low pressure drains, the exhaust valve, and the sometimes undependable Leslie regulator that had just failed open, and caused the pump to take off on its own. That pump was now shot and would have to be rebuilt at Yokosuka in about a week. Until now, I had just checked the oil, and main line psi, but that would no longer be good enough. Danshaw told me that after a while, I would develop an ear for every piece of machinery, and would be able to tell if something were amiss the minute I entered the engine room.

"Lotta steamin do it 'fo ya," he said.

PUSAN, KOREA

It grew quite colder now as the *Juneau* approached the Korean peninsula and the port of Pusan. There was to be four days liberty of which I would have duty the first day in port. The forward fire room would go "cold iron," as it was known when the boiler was secured. This time I would be messenger under Deadeye in the after fire room. Hensen would be on burners and Case was on pumps. He had given Hensen a wide berth since the fight in the compartment on the *Juneau's* arrival the previous month, and Hensen had ignored him in turn. There is a saying in the fleet that if a port smells like sewage upon pulling in, your money was sure to go further than if not. Pusan was one of those foul-smelling ports.

The city was surrounded by steep mountains that trapped brown air just above the city landscape. It had a fair sized harbor that bustled with Merchant vessels. Once the sea, and anchor detail was secured, the *Juneau* found herself across the pier from a fair sized merchant ship. The name on the bow read the ship's name: *Ning-Po, Shangi.* After coming off the 8-to-12 watch, I noticed that half the racks in the berthing compartment were empty. It was a sure sign that most of the men in Bravo division had found one of the whores in every port, probably down on Texas Street. It was the Magsaysay of Pusan, Korea. Every port had one.

I showered and hit the rack, soon falling fast asleep because there were no late night drunks coming aboard due to most of the snipes having secured a "longtime," which is an overnight, with one of the local prostitutes. After reveille and morning quarters on the fantail, it was a routine workday until liberty call at 1630hrs. Down in the now secured forward fire room I was shown how to perform what was known as a lock out, tag out, on the burned up main feed pump as per navy regulations. When *Juneau* pulled into Yokosuka, Japan in about eight days, the Japanese yard workers would tear it out and rebuild it. There was the usual planned maintenance routine along with the scrubbing of deck plates, and swabbing out of the blower rooms. All the burner barrels had been steam cleaned of any leftover fuel oil, and placed on the railing of the emergency feed pump for ready use the next time sea detail was called. The sprayer plates were also cleaned. The fire room was now all squared away, so the conversation turned to Texas Street and the lures it held. We had been warned at quarters that morning by the Chief engineer not to mix it up with any local boys because most Koreans had at least a modicum of tae kwon do training from their school days, and could most likely kick your ass.

The Koreans themselves differed greatly from the other Orientals I had seen thus far. They were the largest in stature and girth, their faces were rounder and flatter than the Filipinos', and the Japanese, and they were considered the hardest and toughest. Generally, they were a gracious and handsome people. Greatly disciplined, and respectful of age and wisdom. They seemed friendly, and open to Americans, unlike the Japanese who did not much care for the big, loud, boisterous, military types they met. At any rate, our money was sure to go farther in stinky Pusan, than sunny, lush, Okinawa. Chief Morgan came down to the hole to inform every one that his replacement would be waiting for him when we hit Yokosuka.

"Whole bunch'a guys coming aboard," he said. "Including a shave tail ensign. We are also getting two third class B.T.'s," he added.

"One bona fide oil king from the *Midway*, [CV-41] and a plank owner from the *Oriskany*, [CV-34], Ensign's gonna be division officer."

The *Midway* was home ported at Yokosuka, and was the only American carrier stationed as such. It was also the oldest carrier in the fleet, being commissioned just eight days after the Japanese surrender aboard the *U.S.S. Missouri*, on Sept. 2, 1945. The *Juneau's* new Oil King would have carrier experience. The other third class would be coming off another carrier almost as old, and presently decommissioned, hence the title of 'plank owner'. Chief Morgan was up for two years' shore duty, and so was being replaced by a man that had made Chief only six months earlier.

"He's a tin can sailor from the real navy, *U.S.S. Hull*, DD-945" he said.

"I wonder how he's gonna like the Gator Navy," he mused.

Where Destroyers were known as "tin cans" and carriers were known as "bird farms." Ships like the *Juneau* were referred to as 'gators' due to their amphibious roles. The deck division had even painted the *Juneau's* seal on the back of the flight deck hangar facing the boat deck. It had the city of JUNEAU, ALASKA. Against a backdrop of mountains flanked on each side by two alligators with the words PRIDE OF THE GATORS written above it. There would be four men coming to Bravo division with only one of them yet untested, the boot Ensign. The other three were Salts.

Smitty and Wolfie, had organized a farewell party for the chief at one of the Texas street bars known as the Florida bar, as that was where he would be serving his shore duty at Mayport, Fla. There were many bars on Texas Street named after American states with many of them decorated in the theme of that state. It was just up the street from the California bar. After liberty call was sounded, all those snipes that were not on duty, headed down the brow, and on to Texas Street for the party. The Florida bar had been informed about the upcoming farewell party for Chief Morgan, and so lots of food was on hand, along with lots of booze. There were about fifty snipes from Bravo, and Mike division's, along with the *Juneau's* Chief Engineer. The waitresses served up lots of Kim Chi, Kobe steaks, potatoes, rice, and an assortment of other dishes. It was toast, after toast, to Chief Morgan, and the booze flowed freely. Chief Morgan was not one for shore duty, though, but was only accepting Mayport in order to save his marriage of fifteen years. It seemed strange that the little woman would now boss around a man like him after working regular hours and dealing with civilians who worked at the naval base at Mayport.

"I hate civilians," he would moan. "I belong at sea, dammit!"

Like many lifers, Chief Morgan had no use for civilians. He considered them undisciplined and unorganized. Unfit and undependable. He considered them to be of a lower social order. The Chief was closing on twenty-seven years in the fleet, and for the most part, it was the only life he knew. He could retire now, but it was not in his nature to join the unfit, unwashed masses in civilian life. He knew that in Mayport, he could never get together fifty people like those assembled now at the Florida bar. It still amazed me how these guys changed when not on watch down in the fire room. Aboard ship they were all 100% no-nonsense, no grab assing, no skylarking, all business. When they were on the beach, however, it was another story altogether. They were a hardworking bunch all right, and could be hellraisers on occasion.

They would not be tonight, however, because Hensen was restricted to the ship. That did not bother Chief Morgan one bit as while he could drink any one of them broke, he had no use for a drunk. He did notice that two of Henson's asshole buddies were getting loose with the mouth. Eddie and Hector were damn good hole snipes, and both were qualified pumpmen. Hector was the Mexican kid I had seen with the fat lip on my first muster that day in the well deck after I had been relieved from brig watch. One of the things Hector was known for was the ability to put his whole fist into his mouth, much to everyone's amusement. It seems that he had broken his jaw as a child, and it did not heal properly. He could click the lower jaw over and insert his whole fist and had won a lot of money in bars in his days in the fleet with that one. They had reported aboard in '73 and were promptly squared away on watch standing under Scratch. They respected Scribeci as a Topwatch, and sailor, but disliked him because he did not get loose with them on the beach. Scratch kept his own counsel. They were also the ones that had prodded Hensen into challenging Scratch on the boat deck that day only to see him be decked again for his efforts. They were known troublemakers in their own right even without Henson's presence. Eddie was the tougher of the two and Chief Morgan spoke to him first.

"Easy on the help Eddie, kimchi won't look good on you," he said.

It was a reference to keep his hands off the waitresses that were catering the party. They were outside help, not bargirls, although troublemakers one, and two could care less now. Neither one would dare to take on the chief even if it was someone else's' party. Chief Morgan simply packed too much ass on his 6 and a half foot, 250-pound frame for either one of them to handle. Hector muttered something under his breath to Eddie, and there was a five-second delay where you could hear a pin drop. Chief

Morgan half turned around in his chair and with one word said it all: *What?* The silence hung in the air as Hector would now have to explain himself, or run the risk of the chief asking 'What' once more. Hector was quick witted enough to raise his glass, and say to all assembled, "I said here's to the best hole snipe that ever lit off a boiler, or ever led a division. Going to miss ya chief," he said.

"Hip hip, hurrah! Hip Hip, hurrah! Hip, Hip hurrah!" chorused the snipes.

It had been a tense moment, and Hector handled it well even if it had sounded under duress. Chief Morgan then stood and made a little speech about how he would miss steaming both at sea, and ashore with the snipes. "Been riding these Grey Ghosts since '48," he recalled. "I was screwed, blued, and tattooed, before most of you were even born. I'm gonna miss you guys too," he admitted.

"You snipes are steamers, and you'll be getting one for your next chief from what I see of his paper work. Can't go wrong with a tin can sailor, I'm sure he'll be a steamer as well," he added.

The mood was one of good cheer now as yet one more toast, and one more after that, was given to the Chief on his last steaming night out with the *Juneau* hole snipes. The party continued around the upcoming two-week upkeep in Yokosuka, and of course, the four new replacements, and whether or not, they had their act together. The three salts would not be a problem, and all agreed it was the shave tail Ensign that commanded the most speculation as to whether he would try to act the hard ass, or give the snipes their due as far as seaman's ship was concerned. The Chief Engineer also being an officer, had been acting Division officer since the ship left San Diego, and was welcoming the new Ensign's arrival. He too, was somewhat apprehensive about an untried boot Ensign, and how all the salts in the engine room, Scratch in particular, would receive him.

"Just another ass to beat on Shellback day." He shrugged

It was the truth as far as he was concerned. Even though Scratch adhered to naval customs, and manners as dictated by rank, he had a detached, almost regal way of meeting you in the eye. It was not a look of arrogance, or pride, but of supreme confidence in his ability as Topwatch, former belt buckle holder on *Juneau*, and boat deck ass whipper. The times when officers came down to the engine room other than the Chief Engineer, and L.T.J.G. Schott, who got along with him famously, they pretty much stayed on the throttle deck talking with Smitty who also noticed a faint look of confusion on their faces upon descending the ladder into the engineering spaces.

All new officers had to acquaint themselves with various spaces on *Juneau*, and down here was the last place they cared to be. The notorious "greasing" incidents that occurred from time to time down there were well-known in the fleet. The heat, the noise, and the faces of men that had been below decks too long made the younger officers feel that rank meant nothing in the "hole." It was the most complex part of the ship, and was known as "hands off" as far as spit and polish was concerned. Snipes had been known to secure the hot water to officers country before in protest of former shave tails antics, and onetime Deadeye, who had been late for mid-rats, and was told tough luck, secured the steam line to the mess cooks berthing compartment and the ship's galley. He even removed the valve wheel and TAC welded the stem to the valve body.

The first Hull Tech that was sent to the hole to cut the weld was promptly thrown to the deck plates and greased. It took the master at arms, along with an apology from the mess cooks chief in order for the after fire room to relent from their mid-rats mutiny. Chief Morgan had backed Deadeye all the way, even excusing himself before the hapless hull tech was greased. The hole snipes were a crew all to themselves, and those who dared to enter the engine room took their chances doing so. From then

on, Boogie, and Toungie made sure to give the hole snipes special attention during mid-rats chow underway. There are all
kinds of politics in the world; it is just that on a warship they
tend to be a little more colorful, if not eccentric. The party for
the chief recalled all those memorable times along with half a
dozen more before closing time rolled around, and everyone
headed back to the *Juneau*. Bravo and Mike divisions made for
a fair amount of racket as they climbed the brow of the ship and
requested permission to come aboard. Fifty-plus men descending the aluminum ladders made for an early revile for the duty
crew.

We still had a couple of days left in Pusan, so after liberty call
the next day a few of us tramped up Texas street to check out
the California, and New York, bars before getting a meal, and
doing some souvenir shopping. I bought a silver pocket watch
for twenty dollars, wound it, and stuffed it in my front pocket.
It was Lutz, Landon, and I this time out, so after walking the full
length of Texas Street we settled on a little bar upstairs overlooking the strip. It was a local spot with some local Korean men sitting at the bar with no bar girls around. It suited us just fine for
the moment not to be bothered by bargirls trying to pry drinks
from us. Twenty minutes later Deadeye and Wolfie strolled in
and seemed surprised to see us in a respectable place.

"How'd you guys find this place?" Wolfie asked.

"Luck of the draw I guess," answered Lutz.

There were now five of us sitting around drinking the local
beer and talking. One by one, the Koreans peeled off to go about
their business leaving just one of them at the bar. He seemed
about thirty years old, and seemed to be quite drunk for so early
in the evening. When it was my turn to get the next round, I
made sure to stand at the opposite end of the bar from him. As
the Korean barkeep fetched the beer, the other Korean saunters
down towards me grinning like a fool. At first, I figured he was
headed out until he stopped about an arm's length from me, and

his grin disappeared from his face to reveal a hard-looking man. There was about a five-second lapse before he spoke.

"American pussy!" he said in an even tone, not too loud. I just looked at him, remembering what we had been told about tae kwon do being the national sport, so I did not say anything back. I was clearly outclassed. I shot a furtive glance at Deadeye, who along with the rest of the table had noticed the body language of the Korean drunk.

"Mudda fucka pussy!" he said louder this time.

At that, the Korean bartender started to berate him in Korean as the table of snipes rose on my behalf. The guy pushed me against the bar to drop the challenge, as Deadeye and company started across the room towards him. They were waved off by the bartender who had rolled across the bar and begun to spar with him. It was extremely quick hand action that I noticed was done with his open palms, and not his closed fists. The drunk was no slouch in the speed department either, but the bartender was faster as he forced the drunk out the door with a flurry that sent the drunk against the wall in the hallway. The drunk simply waved him off, and left as the five of us exchanged glances in humility at the speed, and grace of the two men.

"OK G.I. No problem, my place?" he asked us.

"No problem chief," said Wolfie. "Thanks a bunch."

We stayed for two more beers in order to give the drunken Korean time to amble off somewhere else. The bartender was also the owner who had an interest in taking good care of paying sailors. We assured him there was no harm done, and thanked him for intervening when he did.

"Ain't that right, boot?" Wolfie teased.

After a while Wolfie and Deadeye talked Lutz into going out whoring around with them leaving Landon and myself sitting at the bar. There was no one else in the place when the bartender excused himself for a moment. When he reappeared, and brought us another beer, I could tell why he had excused himself. A faint odor of marijuana hung about him so Landon asked him if he had any more.

"You like maybe?" he asked. "Maybe," answered Landon. "Men's room, behind radiator," he said. We walked into the men's room and found half a joint behind the radiator. We lit it, sucked in a hit, and passed it back a couple of times until it was gone. After returning to the bar, we noticed that he had set us up with a fresh round of beer. The stuff was good, and we thanked him for his hospitality.

"You likea more maybe?" he asked as he put forth three fingers to indicate a baggie. "Twenty fi dolla," he said.

It was still just us in the bar so he retrieved a baggie out of the rear drawer, and showed us a green fluffy three fingered bag. It was all shake without seeds or stems, yet not to fine, excellent for good joint rolling.

"Same, same," he said referring to the joint we had just smoked.

"You got a deal," said Landon as he pulled out twenty-five bucks and handed it to the bartender. We left the bar.

"They might be throwing dice on the quarterdeck," I warned.

"I know, but I have a plan," he answered. In certain ports that were considered contraband risks, the quarterdeck O.O.D. had a card table set up, and laying on it were a pair of dice. When you returned to the ship from a night of liberty, you were given the choice of calling odds or evens, and then rolling the dice. If the roll did not go as you had called, then you had to empty your pockets and get a pat down. Sometimes the O.O.D. would throw the dice for you if he recognized a known crap-shooter like Cox, or some of the black guys that Cox threw dice with in the Anchor windlass room on paydays at sea. Whatever the choice, it was not worth being busted for it, and then be suspect for it in every port after that. "How's your throwing arm?" Landon asked.

"Good, why?" I responded. Landon walked over and

reached down in a trashcan and pulled out a brown Kirin beer bottle. Once we were concealed behind a parked car, he produced the bag of shake and began stuffing the weed into the empty beer bottle. It was full, and still he crammed more and more until the baggie was empty.

"Find me a cap or something," he said. After securing a used beer cap for the pot=filled beer bottle, we talked up a plan. The deal was for me to hang back about ten minutes behind his arrival on the quarterdeck so he would have time to roll the dice and undergo a search if need be, and then go down to the berthing compartment and get into a set of dungarees. Landon would then head through the empty troop spaces and emerge on the starboard catwalk where the fantail watch stood when the ship was underway. It was important to get out of civilian clothes so as not to raise questions about what you were doing there in that mode of dress. It just would not seem right. He would have a sock with him in which to transfer the weed once he had broken the bottle that I would be throwing a distance of forty feet from the pier.

I hung back, keeping time on my new pocket watch. We had planned on him losing the dice roll, which of course he did. When Landon finally appeared on the catwalk, I drew up until I was directly underneath. I slipped the bottle out of my jacket after looking around the pier so as not to have any witnesses, and then cocked my right arm for the throw to Landon. I was startled at the broken English that I heard next. It came from above and behind me. "Mudda fucka pussy, fucka G.I. Joe."

I brought the pot laden bottle down to my side and spun around only to see the drunk Korean from the bar leaning on the foc'sle rail of the NING-PO. I could hear Landon start to break out laughing as this absurd turn of events unfolded.

"Don't let 'em rattle ya Riley," he admonished. "Get that bottle up here before he attracts attention."

I recocked the throw and threw just a little high. Landon

caught it easy enough. He went into the troop space to crack the bottle open and stuff the sock full.

"Fucka Broadway too," the man sneered in what I took to be a reference to Broadway Joe Namath, the way I corkscrewed the beer bottle to my receiver. A mixture of satisfaction at mission accomplished, and extreme annoyance at the timing, not to mention the insult from this asshole, I figured it was time for some back talk. With me on the pier, and him on the foc'sle of the NING-PO, I felt safe enough to let loose with a stream of nationalistic fervor. With my right hand extended with the single finger salute, I began my revenge.

"Up your ass you flat faced, slope headed, fuck! If it weren't for G.I. Joes, pie faces like you would be speaking North Korean, instead of South Korean," I yelled at him. "Your kimchi sucks too pie face, but not as hard as your sister does."

With that last insult, along with me rubbing my crotch, the Korean made a dash for the brow of the *Ning-Po* as I made a dash for the brow of the *Juneau*. The quarterdeck watch was now alert from the loud nature of my insults, and was watching my mad dash for the safety of the quarterdeck as the *Ning-Po* sailor came rushing down the brow of his ship just as I made the brow of the *Juneau*. I hauled ass onto the quarterdeck with the Korean in hot pursuit. The O.O.D. yelled to the bosun mate with the sidearm, "Lock and load!"

The boson mate drew his .45 and racked a round into the chamber just as I ran past him. With the O.O.D. putting his hand out for me to stop, the sailor held the .45 at port arms in case the fool failed to heed the O.O.D. command to stop. The Korean stopped at the catwalk, and returned down the brow to the pier. The O.O.D. and the now relieved bosun mate, breathed a sigh of relief at not having to shoot him. I explained how the guy had started a fight at a bar on Texas Street earlier, and just happened to see me again on the pier.

"He started in again so I just told him off," I explained.

"Well it almost got his ass shot dammit!" the O.O.D. said.

"I'm sorry sir; I did not know he was crazy," I answered.

"Go below," he said.

"Yes sir," I responded. I made my way to the berthing compartment and changed into dungarees, then headed for the after engineroom to hook up with Landon. The after fireroom was in a cold iron status, and only one man was on cold iron watch in order to monitor the fire pump, and the bilge water level. Since we were both boots, we told the watch that we needed to familiarize ourselves with the blower rooms aft. We headed into Bravo blower room now quiet, and cool. There was an exhaust ventilation duct by the hatch that led to the outer stack uptakes. Landon already had a joint rolled as we entered the uptakes.

"I've got some news, and a proposition," he said.

"Yeah, what's that?" I asked.

"Wolfman says that I'm going to the Oil Lab under this new oil king were getting when we hit Yokosuka," he said.

"No shit?"

"Yeah, I'm getting out of the hole for a while." He grinned.

"No more underway watches either."

"How'd you manage that one?" I asked him.

"Beats me, someone figured I had the aptitude I guess."

"OK what about this offer?" I asked.

"Ever hear of a slush fund?" he asked.

"Yes, why?"

"What do you say about getting one going in engineering?" he offered.

"Sure, how do we go about it?"

"We lend 20 for 25, 30 for 38, 50 for 60 but no more than 100 to any one man," he explained. "That's the limit. There's no sense in letting the other slushers pluck our pigeons. We'll undercut em in engineering, and compete fair, and square with the rest of the crew. So what do you think?" he asked.

"Sounds good, I'm in," I said. We shook on the deal, and

there in the forced draft blower room in Pusan, Korea was born our slush fund enterprise. Landon told me all about the in, and out, of the lending business, and also went up to the disbursing office and opened a bank account, actually just a safe deposit locker for the profits we expected. There would be some action soon because many of the crew were broke after four days on Texas street. The crew would be paid at sea on the way to Yokosuka. What that meant of course was that the big poker games would be held down in the mess cooks berthing compartment, and the dice would be rolling up in the Anchor Windlass room, courtesy of the deck division. Those two were for the serious money; however, there was sure to be dozens of smaller games around the ship as well. It was all part of paydays at sea. The Master at arms would be making his rounds of course, and while it was illegal to gamble, it was not illegal to play a friendly game of cards.

As far as the dice went, they threw dice on the quarterdeck, did they not? The way the rules went on the *Juneau*, was if the Master at arms came through a compartment, and saw money on the blanket, then it constituted gambling, and could be confiscated, and the players placed on report. Therefore, the players kept their money in their shirt pocket with only a pad, and pencil on the blanket. Everyone knew the score and there was rarely a bust. Since we worked in different engine rooms, Landon gave me my half of the weed wrapped in a piece of notebook paper. It would be good to have a little smoke after getting off watch, and off watch, it would be. I had no desire to cross Scratch. Like many lifers, Scratch did not much care what someone did on the beach as long as it did not overlap into the fireroom. We both had duty on the last day in port, and it was just as well because #2 boiler had to be lit off in preparation for getting underway. When we did, I was assigned to stand smoke watch this time in order to acquaint me with that watch as well. What that meant was that I stood on the 04 level with a pair of sound powered headphones, and watch both stacks for excess smoke. I would then call down to the respective fire alley, and the burner man would speed up, or slow down the blowers in order to regulate the combustion in the firebox. The Bosun's pipe came over the 1mc. and the *Juneau* was once again underway as she pulled away from the pier. It would be a three-day steam to Yokosuka at sixteen knots with payday on the second day.

Landon and I had some homework to do in order to ascertain who the high rollers were, and we knew of two in engineering, one of whom was Cox, from M division who shot dice mainly with the black guys up in the Anchor windlass room. The other was Hensen, who was a poker player anytime the offer presented itself. Hensen however, was in somewhat of a jam because he had been fined so much at captain's mast. It would have to wait until I was secured from smoke watch though. The *Juneau* headed to the harbor entrance where the harbormaster's gig picked up the pilot. The ship got underway again, and just from the puffs of smoke coming from the stacks I already knew the bells that were being sent from the bridge to the throttle deck, and then onto the fire alley burnermen. One third ahead, two thirds ahead, ahead full. The *Juneau* stood out of Pusan, and set a course for south, by southeast as I was secured from smoke watch. The sea was calm although the air was cold which made for easy watch standing in the fireroom's. Fred had his hands looked at while in port, and was told there was nothing to do except let them heal. Danshaw, and Hector, would be standing what was known as port, and starboard, meaning six hours on, and six hours off until the new man came aboard in Yokosuka. Fred, in the meantime was put out to pasture as the snipes called it, meaning that he would be in charge of the berthing compartment, and head. I found Landon up in the oil lab with Chief Morgan showing him how to test feed water, fuel oil, and going over a chart that showed the location of the ship's fuel oil holding tanks. I handed over the headset, and returned to the forward fire alley where scratch handed me a paintbrush, and can of aluminum boiler paint. "Were getting a new skipper when we hit Okinawa"

"Gonna have a change of command ceremony, I want this place looking sharp, start in back." He said. I walked around to the back of the boiler where the super heater was located, and started cutting in with the heat-treated silver boiler paint at the boiler air casing. It was not too hot due to the November air coming down through the ventilation ducts. The present captain was a rulebook skipper, and we assumed that his replacement would be the same as well. I painted behind the boiler until chow time where I ran into Landon sitting with one of the Filipino's from the after engine room. Landon introduced him as Efren Cruz, from San Felipe, about thirty miles north of Olongapo city. Efren was a machinist mate from the after engine room. There were about twenty Filipino sailors aboard *Juneau* with three in engineering, and all of them as Machinist Mates. They were known as good sailors who got along well with everyone else because they seemed to be of a good disposition, and were remarkable in that in training them, you would only have to show them once, versus the average American kid who sometimes had to be prodded. The reason for this as Efren explained to us was that the competition to be accepted to boot camp in San Diego 7,000 miles away was so stiff that the navy was sure to get a top-notch recruit. Filipino's could not vote in American elections, and were not bona-fide citizens, but could join the U.S. Military under a strict quota system. It was well known that the average Filipino was a twenty-year man, which was why you never saw them at Captains Mast. They were squared away. Since flip-flops were the national footgear of the Philippines, Efren Cruz at nineteen years old had yet to try on his first pair of leather shoes until that first issue of 'boon Dockers' once at basic training in San Diego. Efren stuck his leg from the table and said, "These are only the *second* pair in my entire life!"

"The whole plane was full of us Filipinos, and not one of us was wearing regular shoes when we went over the Humpty Dumpty Bridge to Worm Island," he continued. "When we graduated, we were all just beaming at each other because we had made it, and would be going back to the Philippines as a success."

"When Papa saw me in my whites for the first time with my Boon Dockers all shined up, he was so proud." He smiled.

"I gave him that first pair from boot camp, and he keeps them for anyone to see when they visit." "He tells them, "My son is in the U.S. Navy! He is a success."

I could understand it now that I had crossed Shit River, and seen with my own eyes the poverty, and despair that bred a fire in the gut determination to do better. The third world was social Darwinism at its purest form. Since I did not want to let any of our slush fund business out in front of just anybody at the table, I kept the conversation about work for the time being.

"So how's the Oil Lab?" I asked.

"Gonna be a handful, but I like it already. It makes for odd hours but what's sea duty but odd hours anyway," he said.

Landon had an aura of luck surrounding him, I thought. Here he was, a new boot, and already in training for assistant oil king. The job was very important as far as the operation of the *Juneau* went, but was not as regal as the title sounded. It meant being awakened at all hours of the day, and night to transfer fuel oil, test for salinity in boiler feed water, add chemicals, and contend with an ornery Topwatch from time, to time. He also had to present a daily fuel, and water report that had to be on the money. At any time, the Chief Engineer could shadow his day, and come up with different soundings of fuel tanks, different levels of salinity in the feed water, different output of fresh water, or he could observe him from the generator deck as he worked the half dozen valves on the fuel oil transfer rack below. That was one of the most important evolutions of the assistant oil king job because he had to balance the tonnage of fuel oil be-tween port, and starboard side evenly. It was essential to the ship's stability in rough weather that could arise in the Orient at a moment's notice. Any slacking on his part would be his ass at Captains Mast for dereliction of duty.

We finished our trays, told Efren we would see him later, and deposited them at the scullery window. We went up to the boat deck to discuss Hensen and how to handle in the safest manner, any request he might make for a loan. Hensen had been earning money by taking standbys for snipes that had the duty that par-ticular day. He charged the going rate of twenty dollars per standby because he was restricted to the ship for 45 days, and so figured why not make the best of it. He had earned enough money to get into Boogies opening round of poker down in the mess cooks berthing compartment, but if he were losing, then he would come looking for a loan that he just might lose again. He would not have any money on the books for at least another month because of his fine at Captain's Mast.

The risk came in the form of his friendship to Eddie. If Hensen stiffed a couple of boots out of fifty bucks, what were they going to do about it anyway? I explained to Landon what I had seen that day on the boat deck, and told him that it could get tense if we were to pressure him on any delinquent loan.

"That's where the Flips come in," he answered.

"How's that?" I asked.

"As you know, they stick together like one big family," he began. "Anybody hassles 'em, and they spread the word in Taga-log"

"When it comes to the offending parties pay records, shot records, dental records, even personnel records, they can all of a sudden become misplaced, if you know what I mean," he added. "It can cause someone a big headache. We don't have to resort to muscle; the Flips will make 'em a non-entity overnight."

"Is that what you were talking to Cruz about?" I asked.

"Not exactly, just cultivating alliances, not only that, but the Flips are serious card players. They'll know who won, or lost big tomorrow night."

"So what's the deal on Hensen?" I asked.

"We trust him until he proves otherwise."

The ship's 1mc blared again, "Turn to, continue ship's work."

I headed back down to the fire room to resume painting the boiler while Landon made for the oil lab to study the ship's fuel charts, and take soundings on the tanks. We did not refuel at Pusan, but still had plenty of fuel for the steam to Japan. The rest of the day soon turned to night with me standing the 8-12 watch in the forward fire room under Scratch, Lutz, and Danshaw. At quarters the next day, the Wolfman read the ship's plan of the day, and informed us that payday would be held at 1300 hrs on the mess decks after noon chow was over. All the slushers would be there with their little black books to collect on the loans they had made in Pusan and White Beach before that. After drawing our pay, Landon and I hung around the H.T. shop just off the mess decks, and watched who was repaying whom. There seemed to be only three or four slushers besides us so it was not as if we had a lot of competition to reckon with. We noticed some engineering guys squaring up with a slusher from deck.

"That's what we have to put an end to," Landon remarked. "That's our money he's getting, and from one of our guys too."

Soon Eddie came over and repaid forty, and soon after a few more snipes did the same. Those acts were not lost on the other slushers who were now checking out the new guys on deck. When it was all squared up, we had $130 dollars for our first profit. The balance would be loaned back out in Yokosuka for the two weeks' upkeep. I took the profit up to the disbursing office, and checked it into our little –bank deposit- locker. After that, it was back to the fire room for the rest of the workday. As soon as knock off ship's work was sounded at 1600hrs, it would be chow time, and then the cards and dice would begin in earnest. One would be clandestine. It was so because it was made up of engineering lifers from Bravo, Mike, Repair, and the chief from A-gang.

One of the lifers had a bottle of vodka he had bought aboard in White Beach in a netted laundry sack with his freshly laundered clothes from the laundry room next to the club. White Beach was not known as a contraband port, so he was not made to roll the dice on the quarterdeck. The card game was to be held down in the port shaft alley where there was an abundance of privacy because one had to descend a thirty-foot ladder to reach the now rotating port shaft that came from the after engineroom. The lifers called it a "hot bearing" card party because if ever C.T. or any of the other Master at arms went down there, one of the chiefs would take out his Zippo lighter, and heat up one of the shaft bearing cap temperature gauges, and declare a "hot bearing" that had brought them all down there.

There were all kinds of ways to bullshit someone, and these lifers knew all the ways to do it. The lifers made a point to enter the shaft alley at 2000hrs when the roving sound and security watch took over. The A-gang chief had one of his men for that watch that could be trusted to be discreet, so the important thing was to make sure the empty bottle made its way over the side when it was over. The lifers choose vodka because it did not give off an odor the way whiskey, or Bourbon did. An odor that could be detected in the sterile, steel environment aboard ship could quickly give a man away. Landon, who was now off the regular watch bill due to his new oil lab duties would drop in on the big games in the mess cooks berthing compartment, and in the Anchor windlass room to see if he could determine who the big winners, and more importantly, who the big losers were. They would be playing poker and blackjack for fifty bucks a hand with Boogie, and Hensen trying to make up for their Captain's Mast fines.

We were wishing Hensen well in his quest. Chief Morgan could not make the –hot bearing- card party in the shaft alley because he was standing Throttledeck Topwatch up forward. He knew about it though from the scuttlebutt in the chief's quarters. He had attended many shaft alley card parties in his three years aboard *Juneau*. Upon getting relieved at midnight, I went up to the messdecks where those men going on watch were being served mid-rats chow, and ran into Landon. He told me that Hensen had fared well enough in the mess cooks' card game to not be a problem for a while. He said that they had started out at fifty a hand until only a few guys were left. Hensen was one of them along with the Filipino mess cook chief. Robert wisely got out when he was ahead $400. The rest of them continued at 75 bucks a hand. Cox had cleaned out the Anchor Windlass room to the point that no one could touch him. The black guys up in deck were calling him "golden throw."

Landon had kept a coded list of names in his little black book of losers, and therefore potential borrowers for the two week up keep period in Yokosuka. They would not have any money since payday was another two weeks away, and would be at sea on the way back to Okinawa. It would be a great time for the ship's slushers to ply their trade since no one wanted to be stuck in port broke for two weeks. He kept their names encrypted in case the Master at arms got hold of it, in which case he could not make heads, or tails of it. After mid-rats were over, I walked out to the fantail to gaze upon a billion stars, and soon struck up a conversation with the fantail watch once my night vision was adjusted. What a contrast to the screaming engine room to hear nothing but the ship's luminescent, frothy wake. The fantail watch and I discussed the various ports the ship had been to thus far with Subic Bay being his favorite due to all the L.B.F.M.s that were to be had. That was the second time I had heard that term with the first being when Gary, Cliff, and myself were in the enlisted club at 32nd street, in San Diego on our boot camp liberty. So just what did L.B.F.M. stand for anyway?

"It stands for Little. Brown. Fucking. Machine," the fantail watch said.

"You don't think those little cherry girls stay that way, do you?"

"No, I suppose not," I replied.

"Pusan was great too," he said. "But Yokosuka's gonna suck, Japs got too much money, and they don't much care for Americans anyway. Nothing to do except drink unless the Wolfman shows you where the standup bar is."

"You mean they have one of those in Yokosuka?" I asked.

"It's called Tompopo's, it's run by the Yakuza," he said.

"What's the Yakuza?" I asked.

"Jap mafia, a real disgusting place too," he said. "But it's all there is as far as getting your horn scraped."

After returning to the berthing compartment, I showered and hit the rack to read some before the gentle rocking of the ship began to catch up the way it did. I turned off my rack light to drift off to sleep. We would be pulling into Yokosuka the next morning, and I would be messenger in the forward fire room as Billy Burners did his stuff on the burner front. Cox, flush with cash from the Anchor Windlass room dice game would be on throttles. Scratch told me to get ready to learn burners because it was only a matter of time before I would be called on in an emergency. Everyone still had the feed pump incident fresh in mind so Scratch was preparing for any contingencies that might arise. We had the 8-12 watch, and so were already on station when sea detail was called. I had watched Lutz scramble on the burner front many times pulling into, and out of various ports, but this port was to be something else again. Scratch told us that Yokosuka was so close to Tokyo that the merchant shipping caused a burnerman to earn his pay. The naval base was locked into a tight corner of the harbor that the Japanese shared with the seventh fleet ships.

"Yokosuka's a royal headache. It's good to double up on burners."

"That's where you come in boot," Scratch said. He had Lutz fill me in on just what to do, and when to do it. The one thing Lutz drilled into me was that when he gave an order, I was to execute it quickly.

YOKOSUKA, JAPAN

The smoke watch called down to the Topwatches in both engine rooms that there were considerable merchant vessels in the shipping lane approaching port. Some were going to Yokosuka, and some were going to Tokyo, about twenty-five miles further north. The first bell came down to the throttledeck, and was relayed to Lutz:

"Clang," back one third, [from two thirds ahead].

"Clang. All stop!" the smoke watch informed the Topwatches that the harbor pilot was coming aboard. "Clang," one third ahead.

Usually, the root valves on the burner manifold were kept closed until that individual burner was needed where upon the air register, fuel oil handle were engaged to the –on- position, and the valve wheel was manually opened allowing the fuel to gently spray into the firebox being ignited by the flame of the burner next to it. This was because the fuel oil service pumps fed fuel to the burner manifold at 350psi. They did not want a solid stream of fuel to ignite off the red-hot brickwork of the firebox. It was not because of great risk, but only to reduce wear, and tear on the brickwork. Scratch was not taking any chances on losing the boiler.

"Open 'em up," he ordered Lutz.

"You serious?" said Lutz with a toothy grin.

"We get a full back, and throttleman's gonna suck us off

the line."

"There's always a full back in Yokosuka," Scratch replied.

"If Scratch says bang 'em, then we bang 'em." Lutz told me, referring to the low *boom* that resulted from fuel oil rushing into the red-hot brickwork.

The dreaded "full back" usually came when the ship had a very tight maneuver, and one screw had to pivot the ship around at just that crucial moment. The bells came with usual regularity of the other ports for the time being, and Lutz went about his usual speed. Even when the bells came faster he kept to himself as I leaned against the railing of the emergency feed pump that was slowly reciprocating up, and down with a full prime ready to feed the boiler in the event of a low water incident. The bells came faster now, and Billy Burners was living up to his nickname in fine form as he –banged- the burners he needed to make up the urgently needed steam. Lutz worked the blower valve with a smooth brutality that was called for only because Cox had tightened down on the packing gland nut in a clandestine effort to trip up the legendary Billy Burners. Lutz was adamant that the man they called "Golden throw" was not going to even come close. Lutz was proud of his "Flying asshole" belt buckle, and felt that he could defend it under any circumstances, even sabotage. The smoke watch called down to the fire alley of both fire rooms that the *Juneau* was closing the pier, and that the tugs were roping on to the port side of the ship. She would be backing in starboard side to the pier.

"Get ready Lutz, here she comes!" yelled Scratch

This would be when one screw was either shut down, and the other screw used to pivot the ship into position, or one screw given a flank, and the other a full back in order to effect the maneuver more urgently. It depended on the circumstances, and the skipper as to which way the call would be made. Scratch forward and Deadeye aft, both knew this. They had been through Yokosuka before.

"Clang, back full," came the bell from the throttle deck.

Lutz lifted his short, compact body off the deck plates, with one swiveling motion turned the blower valve 360 degrees, and with a second brutal thrust, 180 degrees more. The blowers screamed in response as he then opened the air register handles, and bought the fuel oil handles down on numbers#3, #4, and #5, burners. BOOM, BOOM, BOOM, came from the firebox each time as a burner was cut in. He had the fuel oil ball valve opened to the 12 o'clock with the full force of the fuel oil rushing through the burner barrels to produce the urgently needed steam being sucked away by the Throttleman pushing the starboard screw in reverse to its utmost. There was a tense moment as the plant pressure began to drop, until the smoke watch called down to let the Topwatches know that the *Juneau* was closing the pier.

"Prepare for all stop!" Scratch warned. "You lift safeties, Lutz, and you're gonna wire brush, and paint 'em."

One of the other traditions of Bravo division was that if a burnerman let the pressure of the boiler exceed 678psi, and the boiler safeties lifted, then he would have to don his Navy issue pea coat, climb up on a hot boiler with a can of silver, heat treated paint, and wire brush, and repaint the blown safeties. There were four safeties on the top of the steam drum, and usually only one safety lifted because they were set to lift one at a time instead of all at once, however, it was 150 degrees on top of a steaming boiler. When a safety lifted, the escaping steam rushed up a pipe that vented at the outside of the top of the stack, and made a mess of the Bosun's mates fine paint job, not to mention the Captain's gig on the boat deck if it were in the right wind conditions.

"Clang, All stop," came the bell from the throttle deck.

Again, Lutz was up in the air on the blower valve wheel spinning it, and him in the opposite direction this time and quickly knocking out four, of the five burners, and closing the air registers so as not to blow out the one remaining burner with excess air pressure. The plant pressure had climbed to 670psi before it began to drop back down to the normal 650psi. It lingered for a couple of moments, and then began to drop until Lutz had to cut in #2 burner in order to maintain pressure. The dreaded Full Back bell had been met and handled well by Lutz as Scratch gave him the thumbs up. The *Juneau* was now moored starboard side to the pier and in a few minutes would be hooked up to shore power so that the boilers could be secured for a bottom blow, and complete cleaning of the boiler tubes.

She would be in port for two weeks for general upkeep, so there would be plenty of liberty for the crew. It would also be a good time to make some slush money. As soon as Scratch was given the word from Smitty, he raised the water in the steam drum gauge glass ten inches above the N.O.W.L., or normal. Operating. Water. level. Scratch then drew his forefinger across his throat as the hand signal for Danshaw to secure the main feed pump, and Lutz secured fires in the boiler. I was instructed to remain behind in order to bottom blow the boiler with Danshaw watching over me in case I got the sequence wrong. After that, the boiler would be allowed to cool for twenty-four hours, and then be drained and opened up for inspection, and cleaning, or FIRESIDES and WATERSIDES as it was known in the fleet. Danshaw and I went through the evolution remaining in the fire room for about two hours. We were just about to secure when we saw Chief Morgan descending the fire alley ladder followed by another pair of khaki covered legs that held the body of a black man. It was his replacement, and Bravo division's new chief.

"Fellas, this here's Chief Craddick," he began. "Chief, this here's Danshaw, and a new boot." We both shook hands and the new chief looked us both over. He was about thirty years old, and had a pencil thin mustache with a slightly receding hairline that was graying at the temples. He seemed to have an easygoing manner, and quick smile. Chief Morgan resumed taking

Chief Craddick on a tour of the spaces. After chow there wasn't much for the hole snipes to do since the boilers had to have time to cool, and be drained before being opened up for cleaning. The Chief Engineer granted early liberty in the meantime, so all the snipes not on duty changed into civilian clothes, and headed for the Yokosuka strip.

We hooked up with Cox, and Smitty along with some of the Machinist Mates from the after engine room as we headed down the pier. A busy four-lane street separated the naval base from the sailor's strip, so we had to wait for the light before we could cross. After crossing the busy street, we took a right onto one of the most crass, and garish sailor's strips anywhere to date. Where Okinawa had gate #2 street just outside Kadena air base, Olongapo had Magsaysay Street, and Pusan had Texas Street, Yokosuka had something altogether different. The Japanese had a copycat flair for everything in American culture. There was the Zigzag bar complete with a large sign containing the same logo of the rolling papers Zigzag man all lit up in neon, probably intended to attract people like myself. Farther on was the Dumb-shit Okie, a country and western bar, still yet there was the Dance-yo-ass off, which was geared towards black servicemen, with Kool and the gang blasting from the inside. In front of one of the other bars was a sign that promised BIG TITS.

That was almost sure to attract those who just had to see for themselves whether any Asian women could fulfill that advertisement. It was early so the BIG TIT show would have to wait, even if there was anything to behold. Having walked the full length of the strip, Lutz, and I decided to check out the DUMB SHIT OKIE only because of the stupid sounding name. Cox was trying to get Smitty to join him at the soul brother bar that was blasting Kool and the gang. Smitty was protesting that all he wanted now was a quiet beer, and was not interested in doing the –Bump- with a bunch of black guys. Cox gave up trying to convince Smitty to go with him, but did convince Deke, one of the after engine room Machinist Mates to try it. Where there were black servicemen entering any of the various clubs on the strip, rarely, were there any white people that wanted to enter the clubs that catered to black servicemen. Cox was an exception to that unwritten rule. Cox was known as a reverse Oreo, or a "Wigger," as it was known. His mode of dress, his speech patterns, even his physical mannerisms were more black than white. He even walked with a "bop" the way the blacks did, but he did refrain from that swagger known among the whites as 'swatting flies' as the movement was known , referring to the way some blacks passed their hand over their ass with fingers pointed downwards when they walked. Cox had his trusty pair of dice cupped in his hand, and was blowing into them as he, and Deke entered the bar. Smitty and the other snipes joined Lutz and me at the DUMB SHIT OKIE.

In the meantime, Smitty was taking on all comers on the pool table. That is until Cox, and Deke came in. It seems that the Brothers had some pool action going on instead of dice, so Cox chalked up and played pretty good until a "sleeper," that is, someone who holds back, gets you to up the bet, and proceeds to lift your scalp as he did to Cox. He was looking to make his money back from the DUMB SHIT OKIE crowd. He would have to be the same kind of sleeper that had just taken $200 bucks of him at DANCE YO ASS OFF. The bar was starting to fill up now that it was liberty call for the rest of the ships in port.

We had moved to one of the tables near the pool action that was getting underway so we could watch Cox work his hustle, which was sure to happen any time there was a buck to be made. There were several quarters lined up on the table indicating those awaiting their turn. Cox had a gleam in his eye as he surveyed this roost of pigeons just waiting to be plucked. When his turn came he would play for a beer like everyone else, and after winning two or three beers, would claim to have had enough beer, so suggested a couple of bucks instead.

He would be sure to stay tantalizingly ahead of his opponent, just out of reach of everyone he played. He would also ignore his opponents to make them feel slighted which he knew would lead to their biggest mistake, their ego. He played them like a musical instrument, plucking a chord here, a chord there, while picking up ten here, twenty there, and so on. He made sure to keep the games close enough to make the other person think that Cox was just having a lucky night. With what seemed like annoyingly lucky wins, the level of agitation rose among those who had lost, or were about to lose.

"The guy's such an asshole too," muttered one to another.

"Fuckin Wigger's what he is," replied the other. "I bet if I lay down some real money, he'll fold like the bullshitter he is."

It was just what Cox wanted to hear. He had fished this kind of pond so many times before that he knew when they would bite at the bait, he kept dangling before them. Cox played his part to the hilt.

"Let's shoot some real pool, showboat," said the one.

"Let's shoot for a Franklin," he said as he laid a hundred-dollar bill down.

Cox pretended to be flustered for a second as he searched his pockets of all those tens, and twenties, he had been collecting all night, knowing that this would be the person's last game if he lost, and of course, he would. Cox broke the rack wide open, and easily ran the balls down to the eight ball. Instead of taking the closest pocket, he called a side pocket, and double banked it in. Cox had pulled off the 'sleeper' perfectly as he palmed the person's money from the table, and stuck it in his pocket. Instead of getting mad at having been hustled, the guy congratulated Cox on his game, and offered to buy him a drink.

"Let's you and me talk some serious business friend," he said.

"What business is that?" asked Cox.

"The hustle business, what else?" laughed the big guy.

Cox and the big guy moved to a corner table, and were soon immersed in a low conversation about a pool hustle that the guy had in mind for the Soul Brothers over at DANCE YO ASS OFF. Unlike Cox, who had found out about the sleeper the hard way, the big guy knew him well.

"Were both here on shore duty," he said. "I've staked him several times against the Jap."

"Who's the Jap?" asked Cox.

"His name is Mr. Kihara, rumored to be with the Yakuza. He travels with muscle, if you know what I mean. Plays a lot of Snooker mostly, he's just starting to learn nine-ball," he said. "These smaller tables tend to crowd his stroke. I've noticed that he tends to over draw a lot. You shoot a smart game Cox, you might have a chance. How long are you in port for?"

"Two weeks' upkeep," replied Cox.

"Tell you what, show up at the base recreation center, they have a pool room there, my sleeper will be there too," he said. "I want you and Alfie to play straight up, no bullshit. I want you and Alfie to play nine-ball. I have to tell your true speed before I stake you. Make sure that you're not just another grocery player," he finished.

"I'll need a better cue than this ramming wood," Cox advised.

"We'll set you up with one. 1800 hrs. sound good?"

"That'll be just fine," Cox replied.

Cox and the big guy shook hands and said good night. Meanwhile Cox continued to play nine-ball by himself because he had worn out everyone else by now. There was a fresh gleam in his eyes as he sensed easy money. He would have to get past Alfie, though, in order to get a game with Mr. Kihara, reputed to have his finger in every pie on the Yokosuka strip as a member of the Yakuza mob.

Alfie was good, he thought to himself. He played every day because he was assigned to shore duty. This was the first time

Cox had touched a cue since leaving San Diego two months ago. He felt certain that he could regain the muscle memory for the fluid stroke he possessed. He would find out tomorrow at 1800hrs. In the meantime, four, or five of us decided to begin bar hopping on the strip to see what else Yokosuka had to offer a sailor with a pocket of Yankee dollars. We ended up at the Zigzag bar at the bottom of the strip around seven p.m. It was decorated in somewhat of a hippie theme, and had several areas that were semi private. Rugs adorned the walls, and the place smelled of incense.

In keeping with the theme, the bargirls wore bell-bottomed pants, with flowers in their hair. The Grateful Dead came out of the speakers mounted on the wall. Each bar on the strip was a microcosm of some part of American culture or another. Redneck bar, Disco bar, Hippie bar, they seemed to cover all the bases. The Zigzag bar was so comfortable that I could even see rolling a joint at one of the tables although I did not dare. The Japanese drug laws were Draconian and we were warned against testing them. The way it worked on the strip concerning American sailors was that if there was trouble that from time, to time happened when to many ships were in port after long periods at sea, and the police were called, if in responding to a call the Japanese police got there first, then you fell under Japanese law. If the shore patrol got there first, then you fell under the U.C.M.J.

After reveille and chow, the next morning, Bravo, and Mike divisions mustered on the Fantail for quarters. The sky was cold and gray as I gazed around the bay at some of the other navy ships in port. There was the old carrier *Midway* [CV-41], from where our new oil king had come from. It was home ported permanently in Yokosuka. Moored on our port side separated only by a large 'doughnut' which was used as a holding tank for bilge water while in port, was the ammo ship *Mt. Shasta* [AE-33]. Across the small bay were the guided missile cruiser, and seventh fleet flagship U.S.S. *Oklahoma City* [CLG-5] one of the few WW#2 Cleveland class cruisers still left in the fleet. She was one of only six such cruisers left in a class that produced 40 such vessels. Alongside another pier was moored the U.S.S. *Tripoli* [LPH-10], a helicopter carrier, and fellow amphibious troop ship. An assortment of frigates, and destroyers were rafted together on the opposite side of the pier from the *Tripoli*.

Once everyone had been head counted, Chief Morgan and the Wolfman came out flanked by the new chief and the two third class petty officers. The oil king was the chubbier of the two, and I noticed that Lutz had been right about his description of the other third class. He was not so much taller, as he was bar-rel chested, and thick armed. He had an easy smile that belied enormous strength. When they had arrived in front of the divi-sion, the chief introduced them to all assembled. "Snipes, I've got three new steamers I'd like you to meet. This will be your new chief," he said as he nodded to his replacement. "This is Chief Ted Craddick, from the HULL DD-945. Chief, welcome to Bravo division."

Chief Craddick thanked Chief Morgan as the snipes nodded hello to him. Turning to the big third class, the chief paused for a second, and then said, "And this side of beef is petty officer third class Swenson, from the *Oriskany*, Swenson, welcome to bravo division."

"Thanks Chief," answered Swenson. Turning to the new oil king, who seemed to be wearing a "cat got the canary" grin, mixed with an early morning cup of Irish coffee, the chief said, "This is petty officer third class Pruitt, from the *Midway*. Pruitt, welcome to Bravo division."

"Well hot dawg!" drawled the oil king in his Carolina accent. "Fellas, go ahead and fall in," he said.

The new men took a place in the ranks while the new Chief remained in front of the division. The Chief continued, "As you know we are getting a new division officer. He's a boot Ensign, so he's going to need your help. Be sure he gets it. The Chief Engineer will introduce him shortly."

There was a general chuckle amongst the salts as they kidded each other. I understood why as they were curious as to the Ensign's temperament, and whether or not they would have to play hardball with him. They would not look kindly on a boot Ensign that was all spit, and polish, and book bound, trying to force his will on the wildest division on the ship. They had all kinds of tricks up their sleeve if that were the case. In the meantime, the Wolfman read the ship's plan of the day in his gravelly Wolfman Jack voice. When he had finished, Chief Morgan took over once more.

"After quarters, start opening up those boilers, I want to get one last look for old time's sake. Pruitt, you'll be checking the water side of the tubes."

"Aye, Chief," responded Pruitt, knowing that in doing so, he could tell by any excess scale on the inside of the tubes whether the boiler had been properly treated with Phosphate when it needed it. The boilers had to be opened up for cleaning every 1800 steaming hours, and it just so happened that it occurred at a scheduled upkeep period. Soon the Chief Engineer came down from the 04 level where the ship's officers held Officers call every morning with the new Ensign at his side. When they approached the fantail, Wolfie called "Attention on deck," and the division came to attention as the Chief Engineer introduced him.

"I would like you to meet your new division officer, Mr. Benson, welcome to *Juneau* engineering," he said.

"Thank you Sir, I'm looking forward to the cruise."

The new Ensign had a look of false toughness, as he was slightly built, but seemed to be sucking in his belly in an effort to make his chest swell out larger than what the Lord had given him. Ensign Benson then asked the chief if he minded if he conducted a general dungaree inspection of both Bravo, and Mike divisions. Chief Morgan seemed amused at the request, but consented out of protocol. After calling the two divisions to attention, we were ordered to uncover. With the order to remove our ball caps, the new Ensign began his haircut, and overall dungaree and shoe polish nit-pick. He went down one row, and up the next, picking out a frayed trouser cuff here, a hole there, along with a number of snipes that he felt needed a haircut. There were side-glances, and some slightly held back smiles at Ensign Benson's attempt to make a manly impression upon the salts. The Ensign had Smitty follow him on his inspection, and write down the names of the snipes with whom he'd found a discrepancy. Smitty gave Chief Morgan an annoyed look as he took a small pad, and pen from his shirt pocket, and tried to look serious. As the Ensign approached Deadeye, he noted that his trouser cuff was somewhat frayed. "Somewhat unbecoming for a second class wouldn't you say?"

"Would you like the truth Sir?" Deadeye replied.

"Of course," answered the Ensign.

"In ten minutes we are about to begin the single, most filthy job on the ship which is why we are not all spit and polished as you can see," Deadeye told him.

"Firesides and Watersides, I presume," said the Ensign.

"Yes Sir, you do presume," answered Deadeye Cooley, knowing that the boot Ensign had yet to crawl into a steam drum.

"There's no sense screwing up good dungarees for such a task as Engineering takes quite a toll as it is Sir."

"I see," the Ensign said, sensing that he had just blown his first chance at intimidating the division. Deadeye had scored one on him by wording a simple answer the way he had. The Ensign was out of his league, and now knew it, so instead decided to concentrate on those snipes who he felt needed haircuts. When he had finished his inspection, he returned to the front of the division, and read off the list of names of those men that he felt needed haircuts. When the names had been announced, he ordered them to report to the Log room to await his arrival.

"Attention on deck! Dismissed!" he said, and quarters was over.

The snipes that had not been cited went to their respective fire rooms and began tearing the boilers apart. The firebox, the Desuperheater, Economizer, steam drum, mud drum, and so forth. It was an all hands effort to extract the Desuperheater coil from the Steam drum in order to remove the cyclone separators, feed pipe, dry boxes, and finally remove the belly plates to get at the Generator bank of tubes.

It would be three days of hot, dirty work until the job passed inspection from the Chief Engineer. In the meantime there were Japanese yard workers tearing out the burned up main feed pump that Fred had stopped from killing the entire watch that day on the track to Korea. Outside of cleaning the boilers, there was much other work to be done on leaking valves, and the Machinist Mates had to inspect the main reduction gears, and flush the lube oil system. That job involved sending a man into the lube oil sump tank clad only in a pair of skivvy shorts, and a small bale of rags that had been carefully counted out beforehand. It was imperative that every rag he went into the sump with, he also came back out with, or he would be back into the sump to find it. The slightest bit of debris could interfere with the smooth synchronization of the main reduction gears. Clearly a million dollar job if they were damaged.

After the desuperheater coil was removed, I was assigned to crawl into the steam drum, and begin unbolting the cyclone separators, and dry boxes. The belly plates were removed last in order to access the rows of generating tubes for 'punching' with a small brush attached to a pneumatic hose. I noticed Chief Craddick crawling into the steam drum in a pair of green coveralls holding a flashlight as he crawled my way. "How you doing, boot?" he asked.

"Fine Chief, how about yourself?" I responded.

"Let's have a look at some of these tubes over here," he said as we changed positions in the cramped space. He peered at several rows of tubes with his flashlight for about five minutes, and seemed pleased at what he saw meaning that the good condition of the inside of the tubes meant that the chemicals added to the boiler had been of the right amount, and timing. He gave me a smile. "Looks pretty good, gonna be easy punching."

It was my first time in the boiler so the new Chief explained the whys, and hows of tube punching. In the next three days of much needed schooling, Chief Craddick took me all through the D- type boiler from the bottom boiler air casing, to the top of the economizer, and into the stack uptakes. He explained the functions of all the different pieces of machinery along with the dangers, and what he expected from me as far as watch standing was concerned. He did so in a patient way pausing now, and then to be sure I was clear on the subjects covered. He also told me that I would begin learning the burner man's station on the way back to Okinawa.

"A messenger is a standby burnerman in my fire room," he said.

"Speaking of Okinawa, I wonder what kind of skipper we'll get."

"Who knows?" answered Craddick. "A steamer I hope. Someone to reign in this boot Ensign," he added. "I though you Chiefs ran the ship"

"We do, it's just that this young pup don't know it yet," Craddick said.

"Wait till we get underway, fire room's gonna scare the hell out of him"

By the fourth day, both boilers had passed inspection from the Chief Engineer, and were reassembled. The rebuilt feed pump was now back in place, and we were ready to hydro test the boilers for any leaks as far as the steam drum, mud drum, and super heater hand hole flex gaskets were concerned. After the hydro test was secured, the Chief Engineer was satisfied, and we began an overall scrub down of the fire room and by 1600, the spaces were all clean, and squared away. The *Juneau* still had another week in port so the Chief Engineer granted early liberty to the snipes for the rest of the stay in Yokosuka.

This was to prove to be a windfall for our slush fund enterprise. Business was already brisk, so now with the extra liberty the need to borrow until the next payday was increased. Landon, and I had nearly a thousand dollars shelled out thus far, and would be in for a tidy profit when the crew was paid again at sea in another seven days. The extra time also allowed Cox to train at the base rec. center with Alfie. The big guy was quite impressed with his stroke now that he could practice against a good player. Until Alfie arrived however, Cox practiced drills, and fundamentals. Cox knew that a solid game rested on mastering the one, two, and three, of fundamentals rather than trick shots, and fancy banks. He had showed off a week ago when he had purposely double banked the eight ball instead of taking the closest pocket to win the $100 dollars. He did not dare do that against Alfie in practice because not only could Alfie make him pay for any mistakes, he would also allow himself to drift away from the cardinal rule of money players: sinking the money ball in the closest, pre-planned pocket. After an hour of solid drills that included rail shots, draw shots, force follow, and throw shots, which were known as the gear principal when two balls were married together, Alfie and the big guy would show up, and they would shoot nine balls until closing.

The guy staking Cox was certain that he was ready to play Mr. Kihara, and so he set up a match for the following night at Dance yo ass off. It would be for $2000 with the format being the best three, out of five games with a 70/30 split if Cox won. The next morning at quarters, however, was to throw a wrench into Cox's plans in the form of one Ensign Benson. Ensign Benson decided that since all boiler work had been completed, and the engine rooms were squared away, that there was no excuse for dungarees that were out of order. Cox was hit on a frayed cuff, and told along with four other snipes to report to the Log room after quarters. The little Admiral then told them that his edict was not to be ignored without repercussions. Ensign Benson was going to make an example.

"You will surrender your I.D., and *Juneau* cards," he said.

"Your liberty is cancelled for two days."

The *Juneau* would be underway on the morning of the third day for Okinawa anyway so what this meant was no more Yokosuka liberty, and in the case of Cox, no chance to play Mr. Kihara. There was nothing he could do but surrender both cards to the skinny Ensign. The *Juneau* card was the ship's I.D. card that all ships company were issued to show the quarterdeck that you were indeed assigned to that particular ship. Cox was one mad hole snipe when he came down to the engine room that day.

"I'm gonna grease his ass the first time I catch him down here," he fumed. As Cox went on about his lost chance to make some easy money, I got an idea to help him out, but kept it to myself until I spoke with Landon up in the oil lab an hour later. I found him and Pruitt going over the fuel oil charts, or at least that is what they pretended to be doing.

After Landon assured the new oil king that I was alright, Pruitt grinned wide and said, "Well hot dawg, 'nuther rebel to the cause."

The cause I noticed was a large can of orange HI-C, which he was pouring into washed out coffee cups. "Take a snort of this," Pruitt said.

Lutz had been right on that call as well. The new oil king was a definite wild card. Pruitt had brought what appeared to be an innocent looking can of HI-C past the quarterdeck watch because both ends of the can were sealed, just like at the store. It looked exactly like it was, a can of orange HI-C.

"How'd you work it?" I asked.

Pruitt then looked at Landon, who assured him that since we were already slush fund partners, I would be willing to embark on another moneymaking enterprise. The bootlegging business. When we both assured Pruitt that we had liberty at noon, he said to bring about 400 bucks with us. "Gonna raid the base package store, and then retire to my partner's apartment off base. It takes a while, but it works, hot dawg it works," he crowed. "What do you need to see me about?"

"New Ensign pulled Cox's liberty card, his big game is tonight, and he'll miss it," I said. I felt wise to keep quiet about the contraband we had thrown up to the catwalk in Pusan, so I winked when I referred to the after line handling room.

"What do you say about Cox going hand, over hand down the fantail mooring line?"

"Depends, how bad does he want his game?" he asked.

"Real bad, he's steaming mad as we speak," I replied.

"Any Flips on quarterdeck watch tonight?" he asked.

"There's one on now, he'll have the 8-12 again tonight," I said.

"I'll talk to Cruz, see what he can do. Tell Cox to come see me later, maybe we can work something out," he said.

I swallowed the little bit of vodka Pruitt had given me, and returned to the fire room to relay the message to the still raving mad Cox. In the meantime, however, it would be interesting to learn how Pruitt got the vodka into the can of HI-C. Both ends were factory sealed, and one look told the observer that they had not been tampered with. I found Cox near the coffee station on the generator deck and told him that Landon may be able to solve his problem about getting off the ship that evening. "Gonna lend me a pair of wings is he?" he asked.

"No, just work out a plan is all. What can it hurt to hear him out?"

Cox just shrugged, and said OK then went up to the oil lab.

He already knew that Landon was a sharp character when it came to thinking on his feet. When he arrived, he found Cruz from the after engine room laughing with Pruitt, and Landon. Cox was soon filled in on the plan to get him to his big game that evening. The plan involved Cruz talking to the Filipino sailor who had the 8-12 watch to not be so observant at say, 2030hrs or so. Cox would don dungarees over his civilian clothes, and go hand, over hand, down the fantail mooring line to the pier. The only problem was being able to get around the mooring line 'rat guard', If he could not, he would have to return, or drop into the drink. "Think you can handle the rat guard?" Landon asked. "Yeah, I want this game so bad I can handle anything." He said.

They explained that when he was ready to go, Cruz would give the Filipino on the quarterdeck the nod, and then he would take a bag of trash to the dumpster on the pier. It would be dark by then so Cruz would tarry a bit, and make sure the coast was clear as far as foot traffic coming down the brow. When Cox got the signal from the pier, he would then crawl through the line handling port on top of the mooring lines, and then work his way down to the next obstacle; the rat guard. The rat guard was a metal cone shaped device that came in half cone pieces that the Bosun's mates lashed together on the mooring lines when the ship was tied up in port. It was designed to thwart the large wharf rats along with other vermin from gaining access to the ship via the mooring lines. The rats could only go as far as the conical cone before being halted. The mooring lines were set so that there were three lines that wrapped around a Bollard on the pier, and then wound their way back up to the line handling room. The Bosun's mate on the pier attached the rat guards, and then the line handling party wound the line up so that the rat guards were pulled up about six feet from the pier to hang in midair. Any rodent trying to gain access to the ship could only go as far as the guard, and then have to turn around, or drop into the water. Cox spent about ten minutes in the after starboard line handling room studying the logistics of the plan before telling Cruz that it would be a go at 2030hrs. Sharp. Cox was a gambler all right. He was willing to risk disobeying a direct order from Ensign Benson in order to gain $600 bucks from Mr. Kihara. His 30% share of the two grand provided that he won. If everything went well he would have to re-negotiate the mooring line rat guard once again on his late night return. With the several lines that were pinched together by the rat guard, it would be tricky at best, but possible by someone who was determined. The device was meant to deter short-legged rodents, not long armed, and long legged humans with $600 bucks on their mind. After knock off ship's work was sounded for midday chow, Pruitt, Landon, and myself headed for the mess decks. Pruitt told us that he had shipmates from the MIDWAY who had an apartment just off the Yokosuka strip. Since his former ship was home ported in Yokosuka, many sailors rented apartments off base in order to get some private time away from the old carrier. It would be at one of these apartments that the HI-C trick would be shown to us. We wished Cox good luck on his game, showered, changed into civilian clothes, and headed to the rented apartment of one of Pruitt's old MIDWAY friends. Landon had withdrawn $400 dollars from the profits of our slush fund enterprise so that the three of us could raid the base package store on base, and purchase as much vodka, and Gin as the money would buy. We also bought about fifteen cans of HI-C from the base commissary. Pruitt hailed a cab, and we drove to his MIDWAY friend's apartment.

"Key's under the third rock." Pruitt said as we walked to the side door of the place. I opened the door and let us into the kitchen where there was a table, and four chairs, a fridge, stove, and a large double sink.

"Stuckey won't be here till five, he won't mind though, 'jest another rebel he is."   "Riley, how are your nerves boy?" he

asked. I held my hands out palm down wondering what the oil
king had in mind now, as he reached into a drawer of the silverware, and produced a razor blade.

"Well hot dawg, we got nerves of steel, Doctor Riley, you get
to peel these cans."   Pruitt instructed me on how to peel away
the wrapper of the cans to be able to replace it afterward. After
I had finished the one can, Pruitt took hold of it, and with my
buck knife tapped a hole on both sides of the can directly in the
concave furrow. He also tapped another hole next to the first
hole to allow air to escape when it was refilled afterward, placed
the can into the sink to drain out the HI-C, and then went into
the other room before returning with a solder gun, and some
solder wire. He plugged the cord in and set the solder gun on
the counter top. "This part takes a spell." He said as we cracked
open a bottle of single malt Scotch so Pruitt could give a toast to
his ancestors. "Here's to the house of Pruitt, and how we do it."
Then said "HOT DAWG" as Landon, and myself gave a "HOT
DAWG" of our own. The three of us drank Scotch, and played
cards until the HI-C can was fully drained. Pruitt dried off the
can, and then soldered one of the holes shut while smoothing
the solder even with the furrow. By doing it in one of the fur-
rows, it allowed the bead to be even with the outside of the can,
and not leave a-bump- under the wrapper that might provoke
closer inspection from an observant O.O.D. on the quarterdeck.
He then placed the can into an oblong Tupperware container so
they would not roll. That left the top of the can with the other
two, side-by-side, holes ready to fill with one hole allowing air
to escape. With a freshly opened bottle of vodka sitting on the
countertop about a foot above the can in the sink, Pruitt produced a small length of clear hose, and stuck it to the bottom of
the bottle of vodka. He then sucked on the other end to prime
the hose, and stuck it into the can in the sink as we watched the
level in the bottle begin to decrease, and fill the can. It took a bottle and a half to fill one can of HI-C before it started to over flow

at which time he stuck it into another newly opened can to catch the rest of the bottle. With the first can ready to finish, Pruitt dried it off, soldered the two remaining holes shut, and replaced the HI-C wrapper with a touch of glue. There it was, an innocent looking can of vodka filled HI-C, perfect!

"OK, snipes, there's one down, $15 bucks here will get you $50 bucks at sea." He crowed. For the next four hours, we drank, played cards, filled HI-C cans, and replaced the wrappers. A little after five, Pruitt's friend arrived at the side door of his kitchen.

"Hot dog how's things on that Gator boy?" he asked as he entered his kitchen, and noticed all the cans of HI-C, along with the bottles of vodka on the counter. "Aw man, you done gave away the secret"

"It's still all yours on the *Midway* Stuckey, but I'm on the *Juneau* now partner, got a whole lotta Wes-pac going on." He grinned. Stuckey only pretended to be disappointed knowing full well that his buddy he referred to as –Hot dog- was sure to carry on with the scheme even after he was assigned to another ship. Stuckey was presently making some good money on the *Midway* after being let in on the trick two years previous by Pruitt. "One chair open old' stick, 'cop a squat."

Stuckey joined the cards, and Scotch as one can after another was dried off, soldered shut, and re-wrapped. After about five hours, all were full of booze, and marked in a very simple way. The cans holding vodka, were dented at the top of the can, while the cans holding Gin, and were dented at the bottom of the can. You only had to look at the label right side up in order to tell which, was which. The subtleness of the dent was something you encountered at the store all the time and thought nothing of it. Shoppers were strange however, as they would never buy a can that was dented, even slightly. What that meant was the store could not sell it, and it would sit on the shelf forever until the store put it into salvage so they could get credit for it, or it would have to be sold at half price in order to get rid of it. Pruitt would have two cases of dented, salvage HI-C to bring aboard ship tomorrow morning.

The crew had often brought foodstuffs aboard for that three-month period that Boogie was A.W.O.L., and Toungie had been overworked to the point that every meal was pretty much half cooked. There in Pruitt's old apartment was born our wholesale liquor business. This one would not require any book keeping either. "Wonder how our man Cox is doing?" Pruitt mused. Cox had done just fine as it turned out, and had stripped off his dungarees to reveal his civilian clothes underneath. He had scaled the fence at the naval base and headed over the busy street, and over to Dance-Yo-Ass-Off to meet up with the big guy who was staking his game. He met up with him easy enough, as he was the only other White person in the place. Cox mentioned the trouble with the Ensign, and the mooring line monkey business as he ordered a drink, and began to loosen up on the pool table in order to find his stroke. He wanted to be focused when Mr. Kihara showed up.

"First man to win three out of five games wins," the big guy said. "You just might play all seven games, Cox."

"I doubt that it'll come to that," Cox replied.

"I hope not. I have a spread of you winning 5-3," the stake horse added. "But then this is nine ball, anything can happen."

Cox could tell by looking around the room that the Brothers would be making all kinds of bets from what they had heard from Alfie about the way Cox could stroke a ball after he had had some practice. Cox responded to the guy in his best Black English, "You pays yo' money, you takes yo' chances."

"You just win the match my friend, that'll do," he answered. It was a little after nine p.m. when Mr. Kihara, and a large, rather hard-looking Korean man showed up at the bar. "That's his muscle for any tight spots if you know what I mean. The black guys call him Odd Job. He's bad."

"Mr. Kihara's on the level, Odd Job ensures you are too," he said.

"Hey, I'm just here to shoot pool," Cox responded. Cox ran off the rest of the balls while Mr. Kihara removed his coat and handed it to Odd Job. The Korean was squaring away everything with the man he knew well from the previous matches with Alfie. Mr. Kihara screwed together his cue stick, laid it down on the freshly cleaned pool table, and went into the men's room to wash his hands. There was something about the way Mr. Kihara gently placed the cue stick on the felt that drew Cox's attention to it. Cox approached the table and asked Odd Job if he could inspect it closer. "No," replied Odd Job. Right about that time Mr. Kihara returned, and knowing Cox was curious about the cue, told him that he could look but not touch. Upon closer inspection, he could see that it was inlaid with Mother of Pearl in several places, and had a fine Irish linen wrap on the butt. The tip was a LePro leather type preferred by money players, and had to be carefully fitted. She was a beauty, that was for sure, and then he saw it down at the very base of the cue: G.B. Cox knew those initials to belong to none other than George Balabushka, the famous cue stick maker of the early twentieth century. "This for real?" he asked.

"Yes," replied Mr. Kihara, "it's a real Bushka. You like it, yes?"

"Yes, but not as much as you do, I'm sure." Cox said. Upon walking back to where the big guy was standing, he asked Cox what was up with the cue. "That isn't no regular cue dude," answered Cox.

"The worlds full of violins, but there's only a handful made by Stradivarius right?" he asked. "That Balabushka he's holding is worth about $3,000 because there's only so many in the world."

"I'd be interested to learn where he got it," Cox said. The big guy then advised Cox not to extend his hand to Mr. Kihara either before or after the match. "Nothing personal, it's a Japanese thing, and a Yakuza thing all wrapped in one. You're not his equal as he sees it."

"Game time will tell, along with that Bad Ass cue he's got."

With that said, Cox and Mr. Kihara stepped to the end of the table to lag for the break. That was when each player tapped a ball at the same time to the far end of the table to rebound, and come back down the table in order to get as close to the cushion as possible. The man whose ball was closest to it won the right to break the first rack.

Cox won the Lag, and those who had money on him smiled slightly. It was important to be able to break first. Money players knew that the break was one of the most important shots of the game. Odd Job racked up the balls, and Cox inspected the rack with care to ensure that it was good, and tight. He then set aside the cue the big guy had loaned him, and using a broad tipped house cue, blasted apart the rack. The one and the six balls fell before the rest of the balls came to a halt. The nine ball was stopped square in the jaws of the side pocket with the two ball about eight inches dead in line with it. Cox smiled at this most lucky of circumstances. A simple combination of the two into the nine, and the first game was over.

Nine ball could be that way. Odd Job racked up the balls again, this time for Mr. Kihara, because they were using alternating breaks in this format. Mr. Kihara used the broad-tipped house cue to break apart the rack so as not to deform his perfectly fitted LePro leather tip on the Balabushka. After dropping the four ball, he proceeded with a flawless run out to take game two. The first lucky game could happen to anyone, the run out during the second game showed the room what kind of speed Mr. Kihara possessed. Odd Job racked again, and Cox broke with no balls going in. Mr. Kihara stepped to the table, surveyed the lay out, and neatly ran the rack to take game three. Cox noticed that his opponent used proper English on the more difficult shot's. He even knew about –cut shot throw-, the secret of ninety degree cut shots.

The rest of the match went one for one, with Mr. Kihara leading into the final game. As he broke the rack, the balls fell about the table in such a way that even a novice could manage a textbook run out. Cox cast his eyes down after a glance at the big guy who found himself about to pay Odd Job one more time. Mr. Kihara worked his way around the table with ease, but when he shot the seven ball, he over drew the cue ball out of position for the eight. The big guy just smiled at Cox, who had remembered being told about his opponent's tendency to overdraw on certain shots. Kihara was now faced with an off angle cut shot or a bank shot. He chose the latter.

The problem was that he shot it too hard, and it jawed itself square in front of the corner pocket. It was now child's play as Cox tapped in the eight ball, rebounded slightly, and tapped in the winning nine ball. He had been given an extremely lucky break by his opponents overdraw. Nine ball could be that way. It had gone seven games after all, and Mr. Kihara had proven himself a worthy opponent. Cox nodded, and congratulated him on a good game, knowing it could have gone the other way. Odd Job paid the big guy, and he and Mr. Kihara talked for a minute before they left the bar.

"About time he paid *me* for a change," he said to Cox.

"Here ya go buddy, here's $600," he offered.

"Thanks, pleasure doing business with you," Cox replied. "Hey listen, I gotta get back before they change the Flip on the Quarterdeck at 2400hrs."

"OK Cinderella, look me up next time you're in port," he said.

"You got it. See you in a couple months at best," Cox replied.

Cox hurried down the strip in order to get back to the *Juneau* before the change of the mid- watch. After scaling the fence of the naval base, he located the dungarees, and ball cap he had stashed behind a dumpster, and put them on over his civilian clothes. He then made his way back to the pier, and after watching the foot traffic for a while began his return back over the rat guard, and up the mooring line to the line handling room, and hauled himself through the portal. Mission complete. He had beaten the new Ensign at his own game.

Cox made his way down to engineering berthing, and hit the rack $600 dollars richer. The next morning at Stuckey's apartment, everyone picked himself up off the living room carpet, put their shoes on, and rubbed their bloodshot eyes from all the Scotch, and cards the night before. On the kitchen table, there were two cases of salvage HI-C ready to be placed into inventory. Landon was in a hurry to get back because he had to come up with that day's fuel, and water report. Stuckey offered us a ride that made a big difference in time. We thanked him for the ride, and trotted the contraband right up the brow, and onto the quarterdeck. The O.O.D. opened each case and Pruitt told him that he had gotten them for half off because they were all dented, and they could not sell them before the expiration date. After being saluted aboard, Pruitt, and Landon, headed to the oil lab, and I headed down to change into dungarees, and then went up to the messdecks to get chow. The *Juneau* would be getting underway for White Beach tomorrow so today would be spent in a massive working party to replenish stores, while Bravo division spent the morning taking on fuel oil. The ship would undergo a change of command ceremony at Okinawa where we would be getting a new skipper. The last two weeks of upkeep had put the ship in good shape so the new captain was sure to be pleased.

After quarters, Scratch told me that I would be breaking in as a new burnerman once the ship cleared port. Once at sea, standing burnerman was mostly comprised of staring at the main steam gauge, and maintaining plant pressure. Since White Beach was considered an easy port to enter, he wanted me to handle burnerman for sea detail. It would be my first test.

Smitty, and Wolfie, would be showing the new chief, and the new Ensign the ropes as far as refueling the ship while the Chief Engineer would be showing Pruitt the location of the fuel oil tanks, and the over flow pipes. Pruitt was already a top-notch oil king so he caught on quite easily. Pruitt and the Chief Engineer would be in the Log room where they would command the refueling process. The rest of Bravo division was dispersed on the port, and starboard side of the ship in the troop spaces where the tanks were sounded by tape measures with a brass plumb bob attached. The snipes had a piece of oval blue chalk they scuffed across the tape to mark wetness as the level of fuel oil rose. When the fuel reached a certain level, Pruitt called down to Landon in the forward hole where he was manning the fuel oil rack, and he would then switch tanks in order to balance out the tonnage. The refueling was to last until 1300hrs so Toungie would bring the snipes on duty box lunches from the galley. He had them all packed in a sea bag slung over his shoulder as he made his rounds of the troop spaces, and handed out half cooked Roast Beef on Rye. *Juneau* steak on a bun, just what we wanted.

"Boogieman's busy on workin party, sorry snipes," he said. After the tanks were topped off, and the sounding watches secured, everyone reported to the oil lab to stow their sound powered headsets. After that, they returned to the catwalk to unbolt the refueling line, and lower it to the pier. The massive working party was wrapping up and all preparations made to get underway first thing in the morning. Both boilers were to be lit-off at 0200, and come on line at 0600. I would be on light-off watch on the forward boiler with Scratch, Lutz, Moe, and the new chief. The Japanese yard workers had re-installed the feed pump, and everything looked rather nice. Craddick, however, was skeptical.

"Just don't trust overseas rebuilds, they had that packing gland tighter than a two-dollar watch," he would say. When I had come up from the fire room, the last thing I had done was assemble some size #64, sprayer plates for light-off, size #32, for the warm up of the recently repaired firebox, and size #16 barrels for underway steaming once sea detail was called. It was important to heat the firebox evenly now that the boilers had been down two weeks. Light-off was to be at 0200 the following morning, and we would come on line at 0600 at the latest. I then went up to the oil lab to see Landon about where he and Pruitt had stashed the booze. Landon pulled out a panel under the sink counter, and told me that they stashed back behind the chemical test bottles. Since Pruitt, and himself were the only two that had a key to the panel they would be well guarded. The Chief Engineer, along with the Bravo division chief, had spare keys to the oil lab proper, but not to the under sink panel.

"Check this out," he said as he pointed to the back of the oil lab door. Pruitt had made up a sign that seemed innocent enough to those not knowing what we were up to:

OIL LAB BAR AND GRILL

BEER, WINE, SPIRITS,

H. D. PRUITT

PROPRIETOR

"He's not thinking of hanging that out, is he?" I asked.

"There's no telling what he'll do next. He's born to do business," he answered.

"I've got light-off in eight hours, talk to you later," I said.

Upon entering the berthing compartment, I noticed one of the snipes showing off a brand new stainless steel Gerber, folding clasp knife to some of the other snipes. It came with a nice brown leather snap down sheath. There were many men that wore Buck knives on their belts when they wore dungarees aboard ship, and they came in handy for all sorts of uses. The Bosun's mates to a man, all wore one, as did much of Engineering. I happened to be in the right place at the right time as he offered to sell his other perfectly good Buck 110 clasp knife for ten dollars. Everyone was pretty much broke this close to payday so I spoke up and he showed me the knife. It had a perfectly sharpened edge with a hardwood handle, with brass ends. The sheath was well-worn black leather that he'd Mink oiled to make it pliable.

"It's a steamer boot, had it three wes-pacs now," he said. "But I can use the money so it's yours for a sawbuck."

"You got a deal, Stewart. Thanks," I said.

"Naw, you're the one who got a deal. Enjoy," he added.

I gazed at the Buck knife and could tell that it had been around. How many miles had this knife steamed in the last three wes-pacs? How many wires had it spliced, how many gaskets had it cut out down in the fire room? How many cans of beer had it opened on the beach? How many cans of Marine Corps C-Rations had their contents liberated by this Buck 110? If this duty hound knife could talk! I felt that I had just purchased something sacred, like a Rembrandt that is found at a garage sale.

This Buck 110 had made three wes-pacs already, and countless foreign ports. It had crossed the Equator with its former owner, and both had gone from Pollywog, to Shellback together. Now Stewart had allowed his eye to roam to another knife. He had betrayed his trusty companion for the gleam of a stainless steel upstart. How would this untried knife handle its first packing gland dig out? It's first can of stolen U.S.M.C. rations. This new Gerber was all shiny, and the sheath was all new and stiff. It was a good knife to be sure, but it was still a novice, unproven, his new Gerber was still a boot! My second hand Buck 110 was a salt, a steamer, it had character! I would give it a worthy home, and new life in the fleet. The next time the Grunts and all their gear were aboard, I was determined to purloin a can of Pound cake for it to lance open for me. Since most of the division would be on light-off watch and sea detail after that, the compartment lights were secured, and silence kept about the Engineering berthing compartment. Most of the crew was glad to be putting to sea again because Yokosuka had drained their wallets. They had borrowed from Landon and me to the tune of a thousand dollars in the two weeks we were in port.

Payday would be at sea on the way to Okinawa again so it would be easy to find those who owed us money. After all, everyone had to make an appearance on the messdecks sooner, or later in order to eat. Our schedule called for a change of command at Okinawa, then three weeks of –grunt runs- between Okinawa, and Numazu landing beaches for Amphibious operations. After that, it would be a liberty call at Subic Bay. It would be at the end of the three-week period that Pruitt's bar, and grill would be open for business. After the light-off watches were on station, the boilers were lit-off with the size #64 sprayer plates, and allowed to warm up slowly due to the new refractory that Scratch had put in the week before. I was wearing my Buck 110 steamer on my web belt where it would remain ever after. Since the boiler had a ways to go in order to make steam, the watch just hung around the fire alley and shot the breeze.

Chief Craddick said he wanted to bring the new feed pump on line only after we were at sea in case his hunch proved correct. It would idle at 350rpm, in the standby mode for the time being. Around 0400, the pressure was up enough to upgrade to the size #32 sprayer plates. "Boot, you'll be standing burners once were underway. You're taking her in when we hit White Beach," he said.

"White Beach is easy; we slow to two thirds when we enter Buckner Bay, then one third when we close the pier," he said. "We'll get an all stop, and then the tugs rope on, and bump us in. Real easy."

This was to be my first real test as something other than a messenger and general coffee boy, so I was eager to prove to the rest of the salts that I had what it took to be one of them. I wanted to be as dependable as my salty Buck knife that I wore openly like everyone else. I asked Lutz when the last time anyone had lifted safeties was.

"Hensen, the day we left San Diego, him, Eddie, and Hector, all went down to Tijuana the last night in port, and got the worm out of the bottle. Royally shit faced, lifted safeties alongside of the pier, and hadn't even got a bell yet," he said. "Scratch threw him off his watch, and I've been here since. That's what the fight was all about between him and Case on your first night aboard. Case teased him all the way across the pond and you know the rest."

Until then I had never asked what Scratch meant when he told C.T. that Case had been talking shit for the last three weeks that the *Juneau* had been transiting the Pacific. Scratch was a man of few words to be sure. Concise and to the point. Scratch exuded an air of authority, no half stepping allowed, word had it that he'd already stared down Ensign Benson. He had told the Chief Engineer that he would consider him as just another boot if he crossed him in the fire alley. It was well known that some of the snipes had plans to get even once Ensign Benson began standing Throttle deck watches underway.

Cox had come up with a twist to the bluing trick I had learned on my first watch, and could hardly wait to spring it on him. Another hour passed, and the boiler was ready to come on line now, as main steam was being cross- connected between the fire rooms. When that was done, Chief Craddick would relay word to the Throttle deck, who in turn would relay it to the Bridge that they were good to go. The new Chief was going over the new feed pump intently checking exhaust pressure, lube oil temperature, and making sure that the packing glands were not too tight, which of course they had been.

Chief Craddick eyed the packing gland for a moment before asking Moe to fetch him an inch, and a quarter breaker bar. The Chief then told me to have Scratch come over to the now suspect main feed pump. In the meantime, Craddick had placed one end of the bar over a bearing cap, and placed his ear to the other end of the bar. He did not stick the end of the breaker bar in his ear, but rather placed the upper cheekbone ear lobe onto the end of the bar in order to seal that ear. That way he could tell the different vibrations by the low pitch rendered by the upper ear lobe acting as a buffer. He then placed his other hand over the other ear to act as a sonar man of sorts.

Scratch knew what he was doing, and figured that Craddick had asked him over for a second opinion. The Chief listened for about a full minute before handing the breaker bar to Scratch who in turn demonstrated the same technique on the pump. Scratch listened intently, and then lifted his head in agreement with the Chief;

"Tojo fucked up on clearance. This pump's out of balance," he said.

"Just as I thought," Craddick said. "We'll keep her in standby for now."

At that moment, the ship's 1MC. called for the special sea and anchor detail to commence. "Put those gloves on boot," he said. "Get ready to secure this pump if need be."

Craddick went up to the throttle deck to inform the Chief Engineer of the faulty workmanship on the rebuilt feed pump, and that if the pump went out then main feed would have to be cross-connected, or the forward boiler would have to be secured. The *Juneau* steamed once at sea, in a 'split' condition, meaning that the fire rooms steamed separate of one another so that if one boiler went off line, it would not drag the other boiler with it. The fire rooms were now 'cross connected' for sea detail only. Craddick convinced the Chief Engineer that if the replacement parts could be flown to the ship, he could rebuild the feed pump back to operational standard. It was essential that the fire room had two feed pumps during underway steaming, as the *Juneau* would be underway non-stop for the next three weeks. The Engineer knew this of course, and admitted to Craddick that we now had little choice. He promised that he would bring it up with the new Captain after the change of command ceremony in two days. The Chief Engineer told Craddick that the new skipper had an engineering background, and would be sharp on the subject. In the meantime, the pump would run at only 350psi in the standby mode to not take any chances. The Bosun's pipe came across the 1mc. again, "Underway". The bells started coming down from the bridge now as the *Juneau* began pulling away from the pier. There was no need to turn around this time so the ship headed out of Yokosuka harbor at one third ahead. After a while, the smoke watch called down to say that, we were now in the shipping channel as Lutz received a 'two-thirds ahead' from the throttle deck. When *Juneau* had cleared the main channel, he received an ahead full, and the ship stood out to sea at eighteen knots. The weather was still cold, and gray, and the sea was rough with white capped four footers as the ship plowed through the water. Unlike sleek hulled Cruisers, and Destroyers, that had a tendency to –knife- their way through the swells, the flat-bottomed hull of the *Juneau* tended to plow through due to her broad beam, and stability. When the topside smoke watch had been secured, Scratch called me over to the fire alley and put me on burners. Lutz explained the various gauges to keep an eye on with Blower air casing pressure, and Main steam gauges being the most critical. In pointing out the main steam gauge, he said;

"If it drops below 630psi, cut in another burner, if it goes above 660psi, cut another burner out and adjust the air pressure as it calls for."

"Keep her at 650psi, it's real simple once we are at sea, sea details where it gets tricky," he finished. I stood my first burner man's watch uneventfully that first day at sea just cutting burners in, and out as necessary while Lutz looked on. Scratch told me later after I was relieved to go up to the Tech Library, and see Chief Craddick.

"You, and Swenson are gonna help him rebuild the feed pump,"

"It'll be good training for you," he said. I reported to the Tech Library, and found Craddick leafing through the Worthington feed pump tech manuals for the information he needed. Swenson showed up behind me as I entered the cramped tech library stuffed with all kinds of volumes of every piece of machinery on the ship.

"You want to see me Chief?" I asked.

"Yes, have a seat Boot," he said as he gestured to the both of us. "I've been going over your paperwork, and I see that you were supposed to be a fresh air snipe."

"Yes I was. I flunked out of A School at Treasure Island." I answered.

"What brought you to the engine room?" he asked.

"Chief Morgan," I answered.

"Yes, of course, so what do you think so far?" he asked.

"It's hot, loud, and scares the hell out of me, 'Why? I asked.

"Ever tear apart a car engine before?"

"No, I can't say I have."

"Feed pumps not much different really, just like putting an expensive model together," he said.

"How about you Swenson? Car engine, or feed pump?" Swenson asked.

"Either one I guess.Lots of car engines, but no feed pumps to date," answered Swenson.

"Well, I'm going to need some help once we get all the parts flown in. We're going to rebuild the pump underway." He said. "Time is of the essence, 'It's going to be long, hot, hours but it's got to get done, 'we can't go steaming around with only one feed pump."

The Chief had us stay up in the tech library to study the feed pump schematic to get an idea just what the operation would entail. He gave Swenson a list of special tools we would need, and told us to round them up before we hit White Beach. One of the hardest things that we would have to cope with during the job would be the heat of the feed pump area. If you were directly under a vent, you at least had a steady supply of outside air to cool you somewhat. Just a few feet away from the ventilation vent however, the temperature was 130F. That was bad enough standing there idle, but when you were busting knuckles, and using a chain hoist to lift a bearing cap, it could become unbearable. Just crawling around under the deck plates that one day was salt depleting. Swenson and I went from one shop to another in search of the tools we needed as per Craddick's written list. By mid-day, we had signed out, transported to the fire room, and secured what we would need for the job. After chow, we headed up to the tech library to confer with Craddick, and discuss the general game plan. "New Captain might get a little nervous with only one feed pump." "It'll give Bravo division a chance to shine if we come through." He said. "Don't expect any problems do you Chief?" I asked.

"Depends how bad Tojo screwed up on the clearances, you find those tools OK?" He asked. "There locked up forward." I answered.

"Good, I'll inventory the lot of them tonight." He said as Swenson handed him the key, and told him not to lose it because he had signed his life away in order to be loaned the tools.

"Relax heavy duty, I didn't get to wear a chief's uniform by being absent minded." He assured us. As a fire room chief petty officer, that was a definite understatement. It took a hell of a lot more than just hanging on to a key to be entrusted with a high-pressure boiler, and the lives of thirty other men. I spent the 2000-2400 watch standing burners with Lutz, who would resume the watch while I took my readings around the fire room every hour. We would be arriving at Buckner Bay at sunrise, and set the sea detail. When I had been relieved by the mid-watch I went up to the flight deck and let my eyes adjust to the darkness before looking at a billion stars in the black night as the *Juneau* serenely made sixteen knots. I made my way to the fantail, nodded to the fantail watch, and looked at the green phosphorus trailing the ship in its foamy wake. My mind was on the sea detail tomorrow and how would I do on my first test as burnerman. The thought of showering steam, and hot water that resulted from condensation all over the boat deck, and the fresh paint job that was just rolled on at Yokosuka was enough to make me have a stress nightmare that night. In the dream, I was standing at the burner front, and the bridge sent down the dreaded 'fullback'. I reached up to open the valve that controls the speed of the forced draft blowers, and it broke off in my hands. Scratch began yelling to cut the burners in anyway, and as I did, they too broke off in my hand. The smoke watch called down to say that, I was filling the Wardroom with smoke due to improper combustion in the firebox. Then the bridge sent down an all stop, and I could not cut the burners out because they had all broken off when I had opened them. The safeties then lifted, and the smoke watch said that the Boat deck looked like Old Faithful had just erupted and the new Captain was mad as hell about his Captains gig being covered with boiler water, and wanted to know who was responsible for it. Scratch sent me up to the boat deck to face the music and when I arrived, I saw the smoke watch talking to none other than Captain..., McIntosh! Standing there in his dress whites holding up a report chit all ready for me to sign while giving me his old greasy smirk   "I'm writing your ass up under the U.C.M.J." I'm so mad I could just SHIT!" he was saying. It was with an audible sigh of relief that I awoke with sweat on my brow, and realized that it had only been a dream. I hopped down from my rack to get a drink from the scuttlebutt, and after a second or so, began to chuckle to myself about how absurd the dream had been. It was strange how the sub- conscience worked when you were under stress about an upcoming event. At that point, I was not worried so much about having to climb on top of a hot boiler in my peacoat, and wire brush the blown safeties as much as I was worried about failing my first test as burnerman, and having everyone thinking of me as incompetent. I noticed that Pruitt's rack was empty, and knew it to mean that he was busy mixing chemicals to add to the boilers. I got dressed and headed aft to the oil lab bar, and grill in the hopes that he had some loose vodka handy so I could calm my nerves, and get some sleep. Pruitt was just finishing up as I knocked on the oil lab door;

"If it isn't a rebel to the cause, isn't no cause to be here." He answered. "It's me Hot Dog," I said, "Open Sesame." He unlocked the door, and I entered and sat down on one of the stools. "I didn't by any chance miss last call, did I.?"

"Good Lawd Boy, you look like you just seen a ghost!" he said.

"Yeah, the Ghost of Treasure Island, 'A Phantom to be precise, 'I could use a belt Pruitt, how about it?" I asked. "You look it." He said.

Pruitt moved some chemical bottles, and headphones out of the way, and reached back to pull out a can of HI-C with a dent at the top rim of the label meaning that it was vodka, not gin. He washed out two coffee cups, opened the sealed can, and poured for the two of us.

"Can't stand to see a man drink alone, 'Here's to the newest Flying Asshole recipient," he said in reference to the belt buckle that Lutz so proudly wore. "We'll find out tomorrow I'm sure." I said.

"Don't sweat the load Riley, 'Half a cup of this stuff and you'll sleep like a baby."

Calvin Pruitt would most certainly be a barkeeper had he not been currently at sea in the Navy, although with the HI-C trick, he did not see why he could not set up shop anyway, keep it low key with a few trusted lifers as customers, and it could be a profitable, and pleasant side job. The way Pruitt saw things; he was providing a service to the Chiefs that pretty much ran any Navy ship. The lifers were all experienced drinkers with many years sea duty behind them so Pruitt did not have to worry about someone getting puke sick at sea, and blowing his good booze all over the berthing compartment. In the sprit of supply, and demand that is the cardinal rule of economics, he would wait until the ship had been at sea a good long time before providing that very welcome service. I soon finished the vodka, and thanked Pruitt for opening a can early, and he suggested that since he had done so, he would keep it for late night snorts to calm the nerves underway. "Jest us three rebels to the cause you understand," he said.

"You got it Pruitt, thanks. See you on the beach," I replied.

We locked up the oil lab and headed back to the berthing compartment where I was soon fast asleep. We would be pulling into Buckner Bay at sunrise so the 0400-0800 watch woke us up earlier than usual ahead of reveille because Scratch and Dead-eye's watches always stood sea detail. We began getting dressed in the dim red glow of the compartment red-lens, and started filing through the passageway to the Well deck on our way to our respective fire rooms. The 1MC. came over the ship's speakers:

"Reveille, Reveille, Reveille, all hands heave out, and trice up. The smoking lamp is lit in all authorized spaces, now Reveille."

There was a short pause before the 1MC. resumed:

"Now set the special sea, and anchor detail."

Since I'd first come aboard *Juneau*, I had always been glad to hear those last announcements. It meant either going out to sea, or pulling into some Far East port. Either way it had always been an adventure of sorts. Now however, it filled me with apprehension as Scratch sidled up alongside me while crossing the Well deck.

"It's show time boot, hope you paid attention. Cox is on

throttles so you better step lively."

He entered the starboard side hatchway ahead of me. One thing I remembered to bring was an eight-inch crescent wrench with me and loosen the nuts on the valve wheel-packing gland so that I would not have trouble turning the valve wheel. Cox had tightened down on them once when Lutz was banging burners, and it almost caused him to lose his rhythm. I was nervous enough as it was, and did not need any jokers adding to the upcoming confusion. The act of cutting a burner in, or out, was no big deal since I had been doing it on the way to Okinawa the last two days. The test would be when the Throttleman began opening, and closing the large Ahead and Astern steam wheels that fed steam to the turbines.

I in turn would have to cut in burners to make up that steam, or cut burners out in order not to lift safeties when Cox throttled back. The difference in the sequence was that during sea detail it all happened so fast. As a burnerman, I also had to be ready to secure fires in the event of an emergency. When I had relieved the watch, I counted three burners with the yellow handles pulled down into the ON position, and the other two ready for instant use that they would soon be getting. The two-forced draft blowers were reading out at 5,000 rpm's while one Alpha fuel oil service pump was online, with the other one turning over on ready standby. The emergency feed pump was slowly pumping up, and down in the event of a low water casualty. The smoke watch had been detailed up to the 04 level forward of the starboard stack, and was screwed into the sound powered circuit to the two fire rooms. Scratch called up to the smoke watch to inquire where the ship was in relation to Buckner Bay. "Just passed Henza Shima Island," he replied. "We're coming up on Tsugen Island now." Just south of Tsugen Island was the entrance to Buckner Bay, and I could expect my first, -one third- down from two thirds at that point. We were still running at sixteen knots according to the throttledeck where Ensign Benson was standing with the Chief Engineer, Smitty, Cox, and the Machinist Mate messenger. About ten minutes passed before the smoke watch called down to say we were now past Tsugen Island, and could see the break to the bay.

"Get ready for one third." Scratch advised. No sooner had he said it than the throttledeck sent it down. I cut out # 3 burner, and closed down on the blower valve wheel to 3,000rpm. To my relief neither one broke off in my hands. I grinned to myself as I thought about last night's dream, and how it had shook me up.

"Whadda you grinning at boot?" asked Scratch. "Pay your ass attention dammit!"

We were now entering the bay at twelve knots under sunny, warm skies. Another ten minutes passed before I received an all stop, then another four, or five minutes went by as the *Juneau* slowly glided to the pier. 'One third back' and I cut another burner in, and brought the blowers up to 5,000rpms. After about twenty seconds I received an –all stop-, and cut the burner back out, and brought the blower speed down to 3,000 rpms. The tugs roped on, and pushed the ship to the pier with a slight 'bump' as the Bosun's mates were throwing the heavy hemp mooring lines to the pier, and tying up the ship. "Moored, Secure the special sea, and anchor detail."

I had passed my first test as underway burnerman, and felt relieved, and somewhat proud of myself. Lutz shook my hand, and Scratch gave me the thumbs up gesture, but again warned me;   "This ain't nothing; wait till we hit Singapore. Hong Kong's a workout too," He warned.

THE NEW CAPTAIN

Scratch allowed the boiler water level to rise almost to the top of the gauge glass before drawing his forefinger across his throat to signal securing fires in the firebox, and the securing of the main feed pump. When the fires were out, I let the forced draft blowers run until they wound down on their own due to the loss of steam in order to purge the firebox, and economizer section of any lingering gases. Chief Craddick, and Swenson began tagging out the faulty pump while Scratch began rigging the chain hoist over the bearing cap end. As soon as the system cooled down, we would drain the steam line to the turbine, and begin tearing the pump apart. Smitty came down from the throttle deck to tell us that the Chief Engineer, Ensign Benson, the Captain, and the new Captain, were on their way down to check out main control. It seems that the new C.O. had an engineering background as Smitty was telling us. "Good" replied Craddick,

"He'll get us those parts twice as quick, engineering C.O.'s know the skinny down here,"   "I'm starting to like this Gator after all." he added. The four of us continued working around the pump spreading a Navy blanket, and using the top of the large rag can as a make shift table to spread out the feed pump schematic, and manual. I soon noticed several pairs of khaki-covered legs descending the burner front ladder, and I called Attention on deck as we ceased doing what we were doing, and came to attention. The Chief Engineer began introducing us to the new skipper with him shaking hands as we were introduced. The Engineer then came around to Scratch, and introduced him as head Topwatch in the forward fire room.

"Captain Petrowski, this is petty officer second class Scribeci."

"SCRIBECI!" Exclaimed the new skipper in mock alarm; "You mean you trust this place to a Pollack?" he said as he pumped Scratch's hand in good-natured ribbing. They connected right away with the both of them grinning at the Captains use of the term "Polack."

"You must be Scratch. Am I correct?"

"Yes Sir," replied Scratch.

"Well I'm pleased to meet you Scribeci." The new Captain

then inquired as to the status of the feed pump, and Craddick told him about the faulty job in Yokosuka, while the Engineer related the story about how Fred had saved the watch that day when the previous pump had taken off and damn near shook itself to pieces. We had a three-week underway amphibious deployment ahead of us so we had to correct the problem ourselves. The parts would have to flown to the ship at sea. The *Juneau* would be in port only two days in order to refuel, and take on stores.

The change of command ceremony would take place in Numazu bay where the former skipper would be helicoptered off to Yokosuka where he could then catch a flight back to the states. After some small talk Captain Petrowski, and his entourage moved on to the generator deck and met some of the other snipes. Captain, William- wild bill- Petrowski U.S.N. was a career naval officer with twenty years of service behind him, and many more ahead of him as far as he was concerned. He had served on everything that the Navy had allowed to float. As an Ensign, he had been the Engineering officer aboard the U.S.S. QUAPAW [ATF-110] a fleet tug of the Cherokee class as his first duty station. From there he went to the minesweeper U.S.S. PUCK [MSO-464] As Chief Engineering officer for a three year tour before going into a Destroyer Squadron as Executive Officer [X.O.] of U.S.S. JOHN W. THOMASON [DD-760] where he earned his moniker of 'Wild Bill', during an incident at Cam Rahn Bay, in '66 when the area came under fire from a mortar battery.

The Captain was on the beach at the time of the attack, so X.O. Petrowski ordered the mooring lines cast off, put the crew at General Quarters, and proceeded to –back- the THOMASON at a double full back across the bay in order to engage the mortar battery with its five inch forward mounts. The Destroyer fired over 100 rounds during the engagement before air strikes from an aircraft carrier steaming in the Tonkin Gulf arrived to take over, and smash their positions. Petrowski's quick thinking, and bold initiative, although somewhat unorthodox in the way he traversed the bay in reverse, earned the Destroyer a unit citation. Since that time, he had served his share of shore duty after which he became Commanding Officer of *U.S.S. Ramsey* [FFG-2], a Brooke class guided missile frigate.

In his second command of a warship as C.O., the *Juneau* would also be the largest ship that he had served on to date. At 17,000 tons full load, the *Juneau* was twice the displacement of anything he had served on before. Perhaps it was the reason that he was so open at first meeting. He was used to serving with a small ship's company therefore he thought nothing of the easy familiarity with the crew unlike some Captains that kept a professional distance from the enlisted men. At 435 crewmembers, the *Juneau* would be almost twice the crew of anything he had ever served on before.

I worked for another two hours on the feed pump with Craddick, and Swenson, before it was time to bottom blow the boiler, and then we lit back off so the after boiler could secure, and do the same. Pruitt was in the log room directing refueling operations over the sound powered headphones while snipes sounded the port, and starboard tanks. Boogie was handling the massive foodstuffs working party, while Toungie made his rounds of the troop spaces with the sandwich laden sea bag. The ship's giant boat and anchor crane swung supplies up from the pier, and deposited them on the quarterdeck.

We were embarking 900 Marines and their gear at the same time. The *Juneau* was in the same beehive mode of activity as I had found her the day I reported aboard. When I had been relieved from watch, I went up to the compartment, showered, changed into civilian clothes, and headed to the White Beach enlisted club. There were a couple of tables of snipes downing beer, and arm wrestling for money as I walked through the doorway. There were some Bosun's mates and some Airedales as well. It would be three weeks before the crew could relax again at the clubs of Olongapo, or White Beach so the crew was making the most of it. I grabbed a beer, and joined the festivities, which were interrupted by the Okinawan bartender ringing a brass bell, and thereby turning everyone's attention toward the bars entrance-way. The room fell silent for a split second before someone called attention on deck. The room full of sailors all rose to their feet as Captain Petrowski strode through the doorway clad in khakis. He smiled as he remembered the edict posted over the door;

'HE, WHO ENTERS COVERED HERE, SHALL BUY THE HOUSE A ROUND OF CHEER'. The new Captain had been a West-Pac sailor all of his career, and so knew about the enlisted clubs custom.

"Damn if I don't keep forgetting to uncover, barkeeper, set 'em up. As you were, fellas," he smiled, and then asked, "You guys sneak out of working party?"

The working party and refueling detail had already been se-cured, as he already knew. He was just breaking balls to make everyone feel at ease now that he would be our new Captain. The bartender was busy with pen and paper writing down all the beers, or drinks for the assembled group of about thirty sailors, and totaling up the cost that must have exceeded fifty dollars. Many of those present had already met the new Captain, so he engaged in small talk with a table here, a table there, before excusing himself to go to the top of the hill where the officers club overlooked Buckner Bay.

The sailors seemed quite pleased with the easy going manner of the new C.O. that made the upcoming three week operation that much more bearable. The *Juneau* would be put through her paces during this evolution that included every surface problem known to the fleet that fell within the ship's capabilities. One of them called for what was known as a Power Run, where the ship's boilers and main engines were pushed to their utmost to affect maximum speed. The *Juneau's* maximum speed was rated at twenty knots full load, and twenty-two, when empty. Because the new C.O. had an engineering background, Deadeye, and the Wolfman came up with a plan to increase the ship's speed by another four knots, and by doing so hoped to enable *Juneau* to set an Austin class speed record of the eleven ships of that class.

The plan was somewhat unorthodox, so they would talk to Scribeci about it first since the new C.O. could be expected to visit the fire alley on a regular basis. It would also involve the oil king. They had already figured Hot Dog Pruitt for the good time Charlie that he was, and knew that he could be counted on as a fellow rebel to the cause. The snipes were discussing the plan and the various ways to put it into effect as they went over the engineering specifics that would have to be taken into account. The *Juneau* was rated at 24,000-shaft horsepower with two screws, which was not a lot of power to propel a 12,000-ton ship when empty, much more than the twenty-two knots it was rated for. Deadeye wanted to try to make twenty-five knots on the power run so if he had to cheat some, then so be it. Until then however, he kept Pruitt's involvement between himself, and the Wolfman.

The rest of the afternoon was spent downing sixteen ounce-pounders- of Schlitz malt liquor, and enjoying the time off. At quarters the next morning, Craddick told Swenson, and me that after sea detail was over, we would be taken off the watch bill and belong to him for the duration of the pump rebuild. After I had arrived on station for sea detail, I checked all the burner nozzles for the proper sprayer plate size, and tightness. As soon as the mooring lines were pulled in, the Bosun's pipe sounded,

"Underway" came the announcement. "Clang, one third back" as I increased blower air pressure, and cut in a third burner. The ship backed away from the pier, and out into the bay before I received my next bell. "Clang, all stop!"

The tugs were now turning the ship around as I cut the third burner back out. We received a one third ahead, then two thirds ahead, until she stood out of Buckner Bay, and into the Pacific where we received ahead full to come up to sixteen knot standard. We were bound for Numazu beachhead in Japan, to land the Marines of Battalion landing team third division, ninth Marines. From there the *Juneau* would steam in concert with other ships of the Seventh Fleet.

We were to engage in make believe surface problems with our three inch gun mounts. After that, would come more shipboard drills with an emphasis on damage control, and firefighting. We would also refuel from an oiler at sea, and replenish stores, and ammunition from a CH-46 Sea Knight helicopter in what was known as a Vertra-Rep. Sometime or another, we would conduct our power run. Off our starboard side about a thousand yards out was the Anchorage class ship, *U.S.S. Fort Fisher* [LSD-40], an almost identical troop ship to the Austin class *Juneau* except newer by four years. It had the same overall capabilities with the same engineering plant, and the same twin mount three-inch guns.

The *Juneau* however, drew about five feet more draft due to more displacement. We would be competing with *Fort Fisher* for overall ship readiness with our aircrews against theirs, our gunnery division against theirs during surface problems. Our deck apes against theirs, during the UNREP, and of course, our hole snipes, against theirs during the power run. Capt. Petrowski wanted to come on strong during each evolution, and was about all the departments spreading good cheer, and encouragement as the old skipper escorted him about the ship. Capt. Petrowski proved to be a quick study of all the departments he toured, and he toured them all.

The first day out found the *Juneau* tracking F-4 Phantom jet fighters from Yokota air base that would buzz the ship at the speed of sound right at the 04 level. It was something to be gazing out to sea, and suddenly see an air craft silently zip by. The

F-4 would then disappear into a red dot before the sound of its passing would roar by all of itself. One of the Gunners mates was on the port side three-inch mount using the hydraulics to pivot the mount around as if to engage the now vanished aircraft. A minute later, the F-4 flew along the opposite side of the ship in the same fashion. Because the *Juneau* had no missiles of any kind, the obsolete three-inch mounts were woefully out classed by the speed of the jet. As the electronics suite along with the Gunnery division tracked the jet, the fire parties simulated damage control.

The ship was kept busy the next two days as we arrived at the entrance to Numazu bay to off load our Marines. We set condition one alpha, and flooded the well deck. The Grunts and all their gear were taken off in three consecutive loadings, and deposited on the beach. When all was complete, the crew was ordered to don their dress blues, and report to the flight deck for the change of command ceremony.

The skies were still as silky gray, and over cast as the last time, we were here, but it was a calm sea we rested on this time around, as the crew formed up all around the flight deck. There was a general sense of excitement about the new Captain as while the outgoing C.O. was every bit a professional, and competent naval officer, he lacked that aura of shenanigans that gleamed in the eyes of Wild Bill Petrowski.

The outgoing C.O. began by highlighting the career of his relief, and pretending disappointment at having to return to the U.S. which all assembled took with a grain of salt because for one, the U.S. was not considered a bad place to be, and for two, the Gator Navy was –not- considered the choicest duty to be had. Even then, Pruitt, and Swenson, considered a Gator ship better duty than that of aircraft carriers they had each come from. The ceremony undertook the usual accolades and ended with Capt. Petrowski at the podium promising the crew a memorable Wes-Pac cruise. The event ended due to the approaching

Marine helicopter that was to take the outgoing C.O. to Yoko-suka's Naval Base after delivering a load of mail, and the precious feed pump parts for the rebuild.

After the Airedales recovered the mail, and the pump parts, Craddick motioned for Swensen, and I to change into coveralls and meet him in the fire room. The new Captain saluted the outgoing Captain as the Boson piped him off and the CH-46 Sea Knight Marine helicopter lifted off the flight deck and headed north across Numazu bay with a Thump.. Thump... Thump... of its twin rotors. When Swensen, and I had reached the fire alley, I noticed Scratch, and Wolfie pouring over the fuel, and water holding charts that Pruitt had loaned them as fellow conspirators in the plan to break the ship's top speed of twenty-two knots on the upcoming power run against the *Fort Fisher*. Scratch looked up at me as I inquired what was up, and pointed to the feed pump area.

"You got work to do, boot. Turn to," he said as he motioned with the first two fingers of his right hand in the peace sign, and then twisted his wrist twice, which was the sign language of the fleet for "Turn To," or commence ship's work.

I left him and joined Craddick, and Swensen at the feed pump. We began disassembling the top part of the pump in the moist heat down to the shaft itself for inspection.

Craddick pointed out where the shaft had been scored by the faulty installation of the bearing caps, and why it was now useless, along with the caps themselves. He showed us how to set the bottom part of the two-piece bearings into the block, and then set a thin piece of solder wire smeared with Prussian bluing compound, and then set the new shaft onto it and the bolt the caps back in place. We then took it all back apart down to the bottom bearings to inspect the crushed bluing covered solder wire for uniformity. This was done to measure how much of the Babbitt to scrape from the new bearing to ensure proper clearance. Craddick then used a micrometer tool to set the amount of Babbitt to be removed. We repeated the entire process in the 120-degree heat before taking a cold water and coffee break under the ventilation vent by the big brass salt-water scoop injection tube when the Machinist Mate messenger came down from the Generator deck and asked to borrow the tube of bluing for a minute.

"Cox wants to measure the clearance from Mr. Benson's ear to the earpiece on the phone." He grinned. Cox had decided that it was time to have a little fun at the Ensign's expense. He would wait until Ensign Benson was on the throttle deck, and then Smitty and the messenger would find something to do all of a sudden leaving just Cox, and the Ensign alone for a moment. Before leaving with Smitty, the messenger would very lightly smear the bluing around the earpiece of the black throttle deck phone. Cox would then look down at Lutz on the burner front and nod. Scratch then dialed the throttle deck phone, and when Ensign Benson answered the phone, Scratch would simply hang up the fire alley phone. "Main control" answered the Ensign,"Main control" he repeated. When he realized that there was no one to talk to, he hung up the phone and shrugged;

"Wrong number I guess," he said. Cox played it straight pretending to look at the gage board, and not at the blued ear that the new Ensign would now be wearing around the *Juneau* for the next three days. That was how long it took it to wear off my fingertips after the blower room incident on my first watch. When the Ensign went to get a drink of water from the D.A. tank, Cox removed the bluing from the phone with a rag. Mission completed. He glanced down the fire alley ladder at Lutz, and grinned like a fool as Lutz grinned back. Once again, Craddick, Swensen, and I tore into the feed pump in the sweltering heat to measure how much Babbitt had to be scraped from the bearing. The Chief could only scrape small amounts at a time to ensure that he did not take off to much of the precious Babbitt thereby rendering the new bearing as useless as the old one. He had convinced the Chief Engineer to allow him to undertake the rebuilding of the pump, and could not afford to make an expensive, and not to mention, embarrassing mistake. We spent a total of sixteen hours in the engine room before retiring for the night to grab some chow, shower, and get some rest before getting back at it eight hours later. In the meantime the *Juneau* and *Fort Fisher*, were getting ready to refuel at sea from the fleet oiler *U.S.N.S. Mispillion* [T-AO-105]   The oiler would refuel both ships at the same time with one on each side of her. Our deck department would be rated against theirs for overall efficiency, and speed during the refueling operation   Landon came down to say hello as he took up station with a set of sound powered head phones that he plugged into the 2JZ circuit at the valve rack so he could balance out the fuel oil at Pruitt's order.

About that time, we took another break so I went over to shoot the breeze with my slush fund partner. "How goes the pump?" he asked.

"We're making good progress. We'll turn it over soon enough." I answered.

"Chief taught us some interesting stuff the last two days."

"You see the Ensign's ear?" I asked.

"No, but I heard he wasn't at quarters."

"Don't blame him though; it's got to make him feel foolish."

"He has to know that it was Cox by now."

"Must have been a sight up in the wardroom. I'll bet Wild Bill got a kick out of it."

Meanwhile the *Juneau* was pulling alongside of the fleet oiler *Mispillion* just as the *Fort Fisher* was coming up on the other side. The three ships were steaming at fourteen knots in two-foot chop. The deck departments of the two Gator ships stood ready to receive the monkey fist shot lines from the MISPILLION. The competition would begin when the lines were fired across the fifty-foot distance from the oiler. The 1MC spoke:

"On the *Juneau*, stand by for shot line. On the *Fort Fisher*, stand by for shot line."

The shot lines were fired across, and landed on the flight decks of both ships as the Bosun's mates began to haul the refueling line across the fifty foot distance. The 100ft. refueling line was supported on the oiler by a winch topping lift that included an inboard, and out board saddle both connected by a whip line to make the line resemble the two humps of a camel. The signalman ran up the red refueling Bravo flag to let the other ships in the screen know what evolution was underway as the off watch snipes stood ready with wrenches, and flex gaskets ready to bolt the refueling line to the flange. When all was ready, our fuel pumping station began to suck the fuel oil across the way as *Fort Fisher* did the same. We would be receiving about 100,000 gallons of fuel with *Fort Fisher* receiving the same.

The entire evolution only took about twenty-five minutes due to the high volume pumps each ship had. When the fleet oiler had turned on her pump in order to suck the remaining fuel from the line, we unbolted the flange, and sent the line back a mere two minutes after the *Fort Fisher* had done so. The *Juneau* had lost her first round. As the MISPILLION dropped back to return to Yokosuka, the signalman aboard *Fort Fisher* began to signal by light;

"J-U-N-E-A-U A-P-E-S S-L-O-W- P-O-K-E-S"

"Damn," muttered Wild Bill under his breath at having lost the first round. "Oh well. We'll get em on guns tomorrow. Mr. Jensen, how many rounds are we going to fire tomorrow?" he asked.

"Two hundred Sir," replied the Gunnery officer. "Fifty rounds per mount Captain," he added.

"Do we have any artists in 3RD division?" asked the C.O. "

I'm sure I could find one Sir. Why?"

"Mr. Jensen, I want a pair of eyes painted on every round that leaves this ship tomorrow," he began. "Tell the men that they can paint any other nose art on those rounds they wish, but they have to have a pair of eyes on all two hundred rounds."

"Yes Sir," replied the gunnery officer. "I'll have the Boson un-
lock the paint locker so they can get started right away."

The rest of the bridge watch just grinned in silence remembering that he was not known as "Wild Bill" for nothing. Landon
remained in the fire room after balancing out the fuel oil was secured to let me in on a little secret. Deadeye and the Wolfman
had come up with a way to both lessen the *Juneau's* deadweight,
and increase boiler combustion at the same time. The first involved Pruitt as oil king, and the second involved getting Scratch
to go along as head Topwatch in the forward fire room. They
had already enlisted Pruitt's help for the fresh water part of the
plan, now they had to convince Scratch as to the burner barrel
part. If they could convince him, and they were sure they could,
then he would be instrumental in convincing the Chief Engineer,
and the Captain. So trusted by officers, and enlisted alike,
Scratch's word was considered the straight dope as far as the fire
room went.

"So that's what they were talking about," I thought, remembering how Scratch had run me off with the "turn to" hand signal.

"What do they want Pruitt to do?" I asked.

"Dump about 100,000 gallons of fresh water," he said.

"100,000 gals... Are you serious?" I asked.

"Do you have any idea how much 100,000 gallons of water
weighs?"

"Not really," I replied.

"Try about 400 tons," he responded. "It's mostly reserve
water for the Marines that were not floating right now. We keep
enough on hand for emergency use in the boilers and the evaporators can make up the balance in two days' time."

"Pruitt's got it all planed out does he?" I asked.

"Hell, that's the easy part, you ever hear of steam assist?" he
asked.

"No," I replied.

"It's simple. You mix steam with the fuel as it goes through the burner barrel in what Deadeye calls –inside mixing- to break up the fuel oil so it becomes a finer spray, thereby burning hotter than it normally would on its own." he explained.

"Sounds easy enough," I agreed.

"It is," Landon, said. "The tricky part is that Deadeye wants to drill out the underway sprayer plates to twice their normal size in the process. Gonna be fire hosing fuel into the firebox so there has to be enough steam to break up that amount of fuel."

"The three of them were up in the oil lab all last night working out the details, and the physics of it all, Wolfie, and Deadeye are adamant that it'll work, and they said they'll stake their Crows on the outcome," he added.

"The Chief Engineer just may take them up on that." I said. "How do they plan to mix steam in the burner barrels?"

"They're going to drill, and tap the top rear end of the barrels with a threaded fitting, and then make up a steam rack with five steel hoses that connect to the end of the burners. The emergency feed pumps high pressure drain valve is higher than the 350psi from the fuel oil service pump so it acts as a pusher to the fuel oil as it mixes," he said. "Not only that, but they already tested it for the Engineer on the mid watch last night when we slowed down to blow tubes."

"You mean they've already got a working model?" I asked.

"It seems that the Hull Tech Chief from Repair division let them do their burner barrel work up in the H.T. shop on condition that they promise not to grease any more of his men when they venture down into the engine room."

"Period! Deadeye promised?" I asked.

"No shit. He's quite serious about his plan," he answered. "They're going to bring the steam rack up forward on the mid watch when they change burners, and blow tubes, so they can demonstrate it to Scribeci. If the Engineer gives the green light,

Deadeye just might get his Austin class speed record. At any rate, we have two days to get it together before the power run."

"Shake-a-leg boot," Craddick said, "Time to turn to."

"OK buddy. Thanks for the scoop, gotta run," I said.

It was time to get back to the hot work at hand with Swensen and Craddick over the feed pump. We went through the routine one more time, and after three more hours, we were ready to put the feed pump to the test. Just before Scratch's watch was relieved, Craddick ordered Moe to bring the newly rebuilt pump on line at full 750psi, and drop the online pump down to 350-psi standby mode. So far so good. The new feed pump hummed along smooth, and quiet considering the overall noise of the engine room. Craddick told us to get cleaned up, and hit the rack. The hard, hot, knuckle busting was over, and we had won.

After I had showered, and changed into clean dungarees, Landon invited me down to the oil lab for a snort of vodka with Pruitt. It felt good to be clean again, and in possession of some good vodka in an air-conditioned compartment. We talked about the loss to the *Fort Fisher* on the refueling part of the trials, and how much fun the Gunners Mates were having painting eyes, and god only knew what on the 200, three-inch rounds being ready to fire tomorrow. Pruitt raised his cup of vodka and said; "here is to a great plan snipes" we all touched cups of vodka in a toast to Deadeye's idea of hot rodding the two boilers. Not only that, but to dump 400 tons of fresh water could mean putting the crew on water hours for about two days after. After finishing the vodka, I headed back to the berthing compartment to turn in. When the fire room messenger woke Scratch's watch for the mid watch, I decided to go down even though Craddick had given Swensen and me an extra grace period for our work with him on the feed pump. My curiosity about the modified steam assisted burner barrels had gotten the better of me, and I was eager to see it in action. When we had finished mid rats on the messdecks, and arrived in the fire room,

I saw that Deadeye, and Wolfie, already had their steam rack contraption rigged up to the high-pressure drain on the emergency feed pump, and the five altered barrels ready for use. There were five steel wire hoses emanating from an improvised –steam chest- like some kind of hydra headed creature. Each one had a fitting on the fore end in which to screw onto one of the barrels that had been drilled, and tapped to accept a threaded fitting.

"Take a look at these," Deadeye said as he opened his palm to reveal five size # 16 sprayer plates that had been drilled out to a larger diameter to allow for increased fuel oil volume. Each sprayer plate was about the size of a nickel, with a typical size # 16 underway plate having a hole about fifteen percent of the plate itself. Deadeye had drilled them out to twenty five percent of the overall plate.

"Gonna push some fuel through these boys," he assured. Scribeci looked them over carefully, and inspected the steam assist device with an approving nod. His inquiries were logical, and matter of fact. Deadeye, and Wolfie, answered his questions with authority, after all, Deadeye had even promised not to grease any more fresh air snipes from Repair division on the rare occasion they entered the domain of the hole snipe. Scratch trusted them both as fellow boiler men as Wolfie was even his superior at rank as a first class petty officer. As the machinery roared away, and the *Juneau* pushed along at sixteen knots, Scratch inspected the five custom made barrels, and gave his approval to a test run when the ship slowed down to blow tubes. This he just had to see for himself, so with a grin on his face he spoke into the headphones he was wearing;

"Bravo One, to main control," he said. "Main control aye." Came the reply. "Request permission to hot rod # 1 boiler?" he asked.

"Permission granted, 'Hot rod # 1 boiler," came the reply.

I assisted Lutz in changing one burner at a time, and inserting one of the newly tapped burners, and screwing on one of the five steel hoses until all five burners had been in place, one at a time with the enlarged sprayer plates in the nozzles. There was a slight hissing sound as the steam ran through the barrels into the firebox. Scribeci peered through the inspection port glass, and noticed that the fires were still burning bright yellow. He knew that if there was too much steam mixed with the fuel that there would be an Orange glow to the flames at the burner nozzles.

"So far, so good, the real test comes when we blow tubes." "Got it covered Scratch, 'You'll see" assured Deadeye. After about ten minutes, Scratch notified main control he was ready to begin blowing tubes on the boiler. The *Juneau* started to slow speed as I began pulling on the chains that operated the various soot blower valves. This was done every twenty-four hours underway on the mid watch to clean the Economizer tubes of soot build up. It used high-pressure steam around the tubes that carried the excess soot out the stack in a kind of chimney sweep steam cleaning. The steam assist device worked perfectly as the ten-minute soot blowing operation concluded. The *Juneau* held off resuming speed until Lutz, and I changed back to the regular burners, and normal sized sprayer plates. As the duo wrapped up their Rube Goldberg invention, they awaited Scribeci's nod.

"We go to the Engineer in the morning after quarters, leave the steam chest here. Congratulations, you guys did a great job," he said. The biggest of hurdle number one had been cleared with Scribeci's approval of their invention. Now they had to convince the Chief Engineer to give the ship the added racing edge of dumping 400 tons of fresh water in a clandestine manner over the next two days. That would be hurdle number two, and that was where Pruitt's expertise would come in.

Each engine room had an evaporator that could distill 3,000 gallons of fresh water a day to replace the dumped water before the ship returned to Numazu bay to pick up the Marines. Pruitt

had figured out how long it would take the evaporators to replace at least half the fresh water the crew and the Marines
would use before returning to White Beach where the ship could
replace the rest with shore water from the pier hook up. With
the only water being used for drinking, and emergency boiler
use, the crew would only go without fresh water showers for
two days before things returned to normal. The snipes considered it a small price to pay in order to gain a class speed record
in the process.

After quarters the next morning Scratch, Wolfie, Pruitt, and
Deadeye met with the Chief Engineer who would bring them,
and their well thought out plan into the Wardroom to meet with
Capt. Petrowski. On the way up the Gun Deck ladder, they saw
the port and starboard after gun mounts being prepared for that
days firing exercises against the *Fort Fisher*. All the three-inch
rounds had been wildly painted the previous day with a pair of
eyes on the head of every projectile. Some had been painted to
resemble Sharks, some had Dobermans, some had the Confed-
erate stars, and bars, some had the Copperhead flag with –don't
tread on me- along with the snake of the same flag. There was
"From Juneau with love, Speed demon, Rock and roll, Fort
Fisher Finder, Marilyn's Club, Buy me Drink, Me so
Horny,Where you go now?"

Every term known to the crew had gone onto the projectiles
just behind the eyes ordered by the Captain. In looking at the
gunners mates loading the rounds into rotating racks just below
the guns, Deadeye figured that they should not have a hard time
convincing Wild Bill. A small Destroyer escort would be towing
a target about a half-mile behind her for the ship to shoot at.
Each ship would be graded on how many rounds they could get
out of their barrels, and on target in the shortest amount of time.
They reached the Wardroom just as the mess cooks were clearing
the last of breakfast from the twenty five-seat table.

"I'll find the Captain. Pruitt, start laying out your charts."

"Yes Sir," answered the oil king. They had each prepared themselves for the questions they were sure to encounter from the Captain as to the feasibility of the plan, and felt confident that they had all the bases covered. Everyone knew better than to waste a Fleet Captains time with mere suggestions without benefit of a plan to bring it to fruition.

A few minutes later the Chief Engineer returned with the Captain. "Attention on deck!" The men stood at attention as Capt. Petrowski entered the wardroom.

"Have a seat Fellas," offered the C.O. "I understand you're not satisfied with the *Juneau* design speed, that you have a plan to increase it."

"Yes Sir, and set a speed record for its class as well." Replied Wolfie. "OK, "Run it by me." Said the C.O. Slowly, and clearly, the Wolfman explained the steam assist principle combined with the higher volume of fuel oil through the drilled out sprayer plates, even going as far as to produce Polaroid pictures of it in use when they tried it out in the after engine room. Wild Bill grinned as he studied the five steel hoses attached to the customized burner barrels. They were aware that the C.O. came from an engineering background, and knew a thing or two about boilers. After taking, the C.O. through the plan he stood silent for the questions he knew would be forthcoming;

"Scribeci?" asked the C.O., looking at scratch,

"I tested it myself sir. The plan is sound. If we dump the deadweight, I'm sure we can squeeze at least four more knots out of her," he said.

"What deadweight?" asked the Captain as Scratch looked over at Pruitt, with the ship's fuel, and water holding tanks spread out in front of him. "Fresh water Sir, all the excess tonnage," replied Pruitt.

"How much tonnage, Petty officer Pruitt?"

"About 400 of em' Sir, give or take a few."

"400 tons? We can dump that much?"

"Yes Sir. Most of it is bulk storage for the Marines; the ship's company would never require that much."

"We keep enough on hand for drinking, and any boiler emergency that might arise, and the evaporators will quickly make up the rest," Pruitt replied.

"What's the status of the evaporators?" he asked.

"Both were rebuilt before we left San Diego Sir. They're good to go Sir," Deadeye said.

There was not a single question the Captain asked that one of them did not have some sort of expertise. He grilled them on their answers, and got even more relevant information in return. "What happens if we have a low water incident?" He would ask in a direct fashion to Scratch.

"Emergency main feed will be cross- connected between the fire rooms, either feed pump can feed either boiler instantly," replied Scribeci without missing a beat. "Main feed is the only thing we should leave cross-connected Sir. Both plants will remain in the split underway steaming condition as usual Sir."

"Are the boiler superheaters going to have to compete with this thing?" he asked Wolfie, knowing that the superheaters had to have a positive steam flow of at least 25% at all times to prevent overheating and warping of the tubes. Superheated steam was used in the main engines because it was a drier steam than saturated steam used in the rest of the engine room machinery.

"No Sir, the steam comes from the high pressure drain on the emergency feed pump so it's saturated steam Sir," Wolfie replied. "It's out of the superheat loop Sir."

With that, Deadeye gave the C.O. the last month's readings of the engineering log that detailed how many gallons per hour both evaporators were producing, along with salt-water intake, and average hourly temperature. "I'll have Landon balance out the fuel oil tonnage so we maintain an even keel to offset the empty water tanks, and it'll be a walk in the park, Capt. Sir," Pruitt said.

"What's your opinion, Screws?" he asked the engineer.

"My opinion is that you've got the best engineering depart-ment in the amphibious group Captain," replied the Chief Engineer.

"Wish I could say that about my deck department," mused the C.O. Wild Bill was still disappointed about the critical lapse in teamwork that had cost the *Juneau* the first day's competition.

"Pruitt, how much fresh water do we presently have on board?"

Pruitt handed the C.O. a copy of that day's fuel and water report. Wild Bill looked it over closely, and then handed it back to the oil king. "Keep 15%, Dump the rest."

"Yes Sir," replied the beaming Pruitt.

"Scribeci, I want to observe this thing in action after the gunnery exercises."

"I'll have it ready Captain," said Scratch. Just then, a messenger from the bridge watch entered the wardroom to inform the C.O. that the target towing destroyer escort-VANCE- was about three thousand yards off the starboard bow, and the gun mounts were manned and ready. "I'll be on the bridge shortly," he said.

"Gentlemen, we've got us a race," he said.

"Thank you Sir," they replied.

"Get started building another steam chest, and Pruitt, I want you to keep at least 15% on hand."

"Aye, Aye, Sir" answered the oil king. The quartet left the wardroom, and headed down to the H.T. shop to start building the second device while the Captain headed to the bridge.

"Captain on the bridge," announced the Helmsman as Wild Bill arrived.

"As you were," said the C.O. "Mr. Jensen, what is the target position,?" he asked the O.O.D.

"Range, three thousand yards Captain," he replied. "The *Vance* is ready when we are Sir."

"Mr. Jensen, you have the conn. I'm going up to the 04 level to watch the show." He grabbed a pair of earmuffs that he knew he would need. "Captain off the bridge," announced the Helmsman as the C.O. left for the 04 level.

After going odds or evens amongst the four mount captains, it was determined that the starboard aft mount would be firing first, and the mount captain was standing between the gun barrels, and up high wearing a battle helmet over a pair of sound powered headphones while the four other helmeted members were loading the three-inch projectiles into the mounting breeches. The rounds were about three feet long, and the projectile weight was seven pounds. The guns had a maximum range of 14,000 yards at a 45-degree elevation, but since the target was only three thousand yards away, they would be firing straight out.

A good gun crew that worked together could fire fifty rounds per minute through the twin barrels of the guns. That was what Wild Bill wanted to see as they noticed him looking down at their mount. The gun mount captain gave him the thumbs up signal that they were ready, and good to go. Wild Bill gave the mount captain the 'turn to' hand signal Scratch had given me earlier, and the gun crew placed their hands palms down on top of the breeches cover plate to signify that they were –hands clear- of the moving parts of the gun as the mount captain requested permission to fire. Ka-boom, Ka-boom, Ka-boom, Ka-boom, came the roar of the guns as ten rounds burst from the muzzles with red tracers disappearing into the ocean grey distance.

The gun crew then hustled another ten rounds from the rotating racks, and quickly reloaded the guns. "Clear hands," shouted the mount captain as once more they placed their hands palms down on top of the breech plates. Ka-boom, Ka-boom, Ka-boom, Ka-boom, went the guns as another ten rounds with attendant red tracers disappeared into the grey distance, and the crew hustled more rounds from the racks, and reloaded the guns.

"Clear hands," shouted the mount captain as another ten rounds slammed into the target. Twice more they performed the task as fast as possible until their allotted fifty rounds were expended. Captain Petrowski peered through the signal shack pair of -big eyes- at the target, and was pleased by what he saw. He was impressed by the speed and fluidity of the mount crew. The crew had taken just under a minute to off load fifty rounds with about twenty or so hits on the target. Not bad considering that the ship and the target were rolling along at sixteen knots.

Wild Bill returned to the bridge wing to observe the forward starboard side mount in action once the destroyer escort VANCE had hauled in the target, and replaced it with a fresh one. As the first gun captain had given him the thumbs up signal, so did the second one. Captain Petrowski responded with the "turn to" signal as before, and the mount requested permission to fire. With the forward part of the ship shaking with every salvo, both engine rooms had been forced to set what was known as "Circle William," which meant that forced ventilation in the engineering spaces was secured due to all the rust, and other loose particles that were shook loose during firing, and blew all over the fire alley, and throttledeck area.

I arranged to get myself loaned out to Deadeye for the day, and ferried five more burner barrels up to the H.T. weld shop just off the messdecks where I assisted him in drilling out, tapping threads into, and fitting the steam hoses onto the burner barrels to ensure that all matched up ahead of time while the Wolfman was busy welding quick closing ball valves onto the units chamber. It was a rather simple device after all once I saw how they had worked it out. Wolfie measured off the different lengths of steel hose that the distance of each burner would require from the original pattern, and fitted each one with a coupling at each end.

After four hours, the new unit was ready to be given a trial run for Captain Petrowski's inspection. The *Juneau* had completed her firing exercises with all four gun mounts expending their allotted fifty rounds. The starboard aft mount, the first to fire that morning, held the shipboard record with twenty-two rounds on target. The other mounts had scored 16, 19, and 12, rounds respectively for 69 hits out of 200 fired. It was a disaster. The *Fort Fisher*, using the same type guns fared much better with 93 hits out of 200 fired. The VANCE had reported the tally, and pulled in her targets and headed to Yokosuka.

"Signal light from *Fort Fisher* Sir." Reported the wing lookout.

The light from the *Fort Fisher* flashed across the three thousand yard distance as the signalman copied it down, and gave it to the C.O.

J-U-N-E-A-U- G-U-N-N-E-R-S-   MR. M-A-G-O-O- S-A-M-E- S-A-M-E-

It was a clear reference to the blind character of Mr. Magoo fame.

With helo operations, and the power run still to be conducted over the next two days, Captain Petrowski had the signal shack send the following message in return'

I-T- A-I-N-T- O-V-E-R- Y-E-T-

A-G-R-E-E-D- came the response, O-U-T-

"Oh well, we'll get em tomorrow on Verta reps," the C.O. said.

The chief Engineer then notified the Captain that the second device was ready to undergo trials in the after fire room, and that he should be on hand to witness it. The two men descended to the after fire room and Deadeye proudly showed off the day's work and got permission from the throttledeck to begin the barrel change. One by one the burners were all changed out, and the steam cut in until all five were ready to go. Scratch's watch up forward got permission to do the same, and Wolfie began hooking that one up as well. The C.O. went up to Main Control, as the forward fireroom was known to supervise the trials.

"What's our present speed?" he asked the Throttleman.

"Sixteen knots Sir," he replied.

"Bring her up to ahead full."

The Throttleman informed the bridge as to the Captain's order and sent the bell down to the burnerman who responded in the usual way by cutting in four burners and quickly reaching twenty knots. Usually it would take all five burners to reach that speed so the snipes were sure on to something he thought to himself. The C.O. rang up the after fire room. "Deadeye, how many burners are you running?" he asked.

"Four burners Sir," Deadeye replied. "Twenty knots and power to spare. It's looking Screws," he said to the Engineer.

"Shall we go to flank speed Captain?" asked the Engineer.

"Negative, we'll wait till the power run when we've shed all the dead weight."

"Yes Sir. The *Fort Fisher*'s in for a surprise," he concluded.

"Bring her back to sixteen knots, Throttleman."

"Aye, Sir. Sixteen knots." Each burnerman went down to just two burners in each boiler, so Deadeye aft, and Wolfie, forward, secured those idle burners steam quickly, closing at the steam chest. The Captain stuck around the fire alley to shoot the breeze with Scribeci, and Lutz about the upcoming power run while they assured him that the fire room's machinery was in tiptop shape, and good to go. "How's the feed pump running?" he asked.

"Runs like a scalded dog Sir. Craddick did a great job, damn modest about it too," Scratch said. "Where is the Chief anyway?"

"He's up in the tech library Sir," answered Scratch.

"I think I'll pay him a visit," Petrowski said.

Before leaving the fire room, the Captain had both fire rooms change back to the regular burners, and noticed that they now had to have three burners to maintain sixteen knots instead of the steam atomized two. He felt a great deal of satisfaction with the whole snipes of Bravo and Mike divisions.

"Hell, if they could only shoot too," he mused. "They'd probably figure out a way to hot rod the guns too."

Upon entering the cramped tech library, the C.O. found the chief pouring over manuals, and schematics of the fuel oil service pumps, and knew that it had to do with Deadeyes steam assist device. "Double checking 'em Chief?" he asked.

"Oh, there squared away all right Sir," replied Craddick. "Just seeing what I can get out of that fuel pump as far as volume increase, and I think I can increase it in conjunction with the steam chest."

"And?" asked the C.O. Craddick took the C.O. over the fuel oil system schematic, and pointed out valves here and there that were safety features by the contractor that sold the system to the naval planners that designed the ship. They were anti-lawsuit features designed to protect the contractor, but if skirted by the snipes here, and there, could produce more fuel oil volume at the burner front. The only problem was that they could tamper with everything except the forced draft blowers that could only supply the air pressure at the eight thousand r.p.m.s that they were rated at. There was simply no way outside of replacing the blowers themselves that they could come up with increased air pressure. "Just thought we could Sir," he said.

"Good man Chief. I just want to thank you and your men on the feed pump rebuild job," he added. "I'm fast learning that I've got quite an engineering department."

"Yes Sir, They'd make good tin can sailors," he smiled.

"Agreed, this your first Gator Chief?" he asked.

"Yes Sir, and you?"

"Yes as a matter of fact, the biggest ship yet."

"Tell me Craddick, 'Do you think we can pull it off against the *Fort Fisher*?"

"Well Sir, if we don't then it won't be because we didn't try everything we could. There's only one thing that can possibly foil the plan, Sir."

"What's that Chief?" he asked.

Craddick then pulled down a book of all the ships in the American fleet, turned once to the Anchorage class ships of which the *Fort Fisher* was one, and then to the Austin class ships to which the *Juneau* belonged. The C.O. compared the statistics of the two classes of Gators.

Juneau —23 ft. draft.   *Fort Fisher*—18 ft. draft

The *Juneau* not only displaced more tonnage, but also was pushing more water under her hull. "That's why we have to cut corners, Captain."

"We already have, Chief; do you know that we just made twenty knots on only four burners per boiler? Those two steam chests worked perfectly."

"Well Sir, I guess we'll find out tomorrow."

"We will at that Chief. We will at that," he replied. "I just want you to know Craddick, that if you run into any problems I can fix, the Chief Engineer has been instructed to bring you on up, OK?"

"Thank you Sir, but I think we've got all the bases covered," Craddick replied.

"OK Chief, I've got some ass to kick up in fire control, I'll let you get back to business."

"Good day Captain," replied Craddick, and the C.O. left. Another routine day at sea was shaping up off the coast of Japan, and the weather was crisp, and clear. The Air Department was busy doing dry runs on the flight deck in securing helicopters to the deck for the next evolution. We would be undergoing vertical replenishment of stores, and ammunition from the supply ship *Mt. Shasta*. The *Fort Fisher* was proving to be a tough opponent so Captain Petrowski was most interested in the air department's dress rehearsal. In the meantime, Scratch informed me that I would be standing burners underway at a regular pace to condition me to the post. They had dogged the watch bill so one watch would not have to stand the mid watch all the time. I would still be assigned to Scratch's watch. The 4-8 watch made for a long day because once you got off watch at 0800hrs. You had chow, then mustered on the fantail for quarters, and then returned to the fire room for an eight-hour workday. Right around knock off ship's work at 1600, you went right back on the 4-8 watch for a sixteen hour day. If the ship hit any kind of rough weather, then it was goodbye to a good night's sleep.

In looking around at some of the older crewmembers, it was revealing to see forty-year-old men that could pass for fifty easily. A life in the fleet and its constant demands took a physical attrition that few other occupations could match. Sea duty was not for everyone, that much was sure, and I had already noticed the different breed of men that made up the amphibious group. Some were career naval men like the Captain, and the Chief Engineer, that had wives, and families back home. Many like Deadeye, Smitty, and the Wolfman, were also career naval men but that was all they had. They had no friends other than each other, no families waiting for them when the ship returned, and outside of a hooker in every port, no normal relationships with women. They had sex, but not relationships; the seagoing life they cherished simply would not permit it. They were not the type of men that fit well in normal society because most people did not care to be around them after they had a few drinks in them. When ashore, men like them were more at home in a biker bar than around the average civilian. They did not mean any harm, it is just that they were incorrigible miscreants unless they were steaming a screaming boiler, tearing down a pump, or riding out a typhoon. They were exactly the kind of men the Navy needed to man the ships, and so many of their shortcomings tended to be overlooked.

Actually, many things tended to be put by the wayside when it came to eccentricity. One of these was a crewmember who was a dental tech that was known as the 'tooth fairy' because he was rather effeminate in his mannerisms. He was a nice enough guy as everyone agreed, but could care less that he was obvious as hell. He did not seem to have any problems so the crew did not give it a second thought. He was seen as just one more member of the world stage that Shakespeare wrote about, one more symptom of the human equation within the steel-hulled microcosm of American life that was plowing through the cold waters of the North Pacific at sixteen knots. At quarters the next morning on the fantail, we could see the *Mt. Shasta* coming up between the *Fort Fisher* and us with a Marine CH-46 double rotor helicopter warming up on its fantail flight deck. The Airdales were all dressed in either yellow or purple jerseys that signified their respective responsibilities in the upcoming helo verta-rep evolution. The ships would be receiving foodstuffs first and ammo second, so Boogie had a working party standing by to quickly retrieve the foodstuffs from the cargo net once the Sea Knight helicopter dropped them on the flight deck.

It would take most of the day to replenish the food the crew had consumed as of late, and what the now deployed Marines had consumed before that. Once that was secured, the ammo handling party would stow the balance of the three-inch ammo that had been expended the day before. Back and forth came the Sea Knight as tons of foodstuffs were delivered to both ships, and their respective working parties hustled them from the flight decks, and down to the reefers. The Verta-rep lasted most of the day, and when it was over, the *Juneau* had tied the *Fort Fisher* in speedy recovery of food, and ammo. We were back in the game!

Captain Petrowski thanked the air department on a job well done along with Boogies working party in the way they hustled the foodstuffs quick enough to enable the ammo handling party to retrieve the balance of three-inch ammo. The last evolution would be the power run back to Numazu bay to pick up the Marines. It was set for eight a.m. the following morning when almost all the fresh waters 400 tons would be pumped overboard. Outside of the forced draft blowers that we had no control over, the snipes had done everything conceivable to squeeze as much speed out of the ship as possible. Landon sounded the fresh water tanks at 0400 that following morning, and reported 15% on hand as per Petrowski's order along with the regular fuel oil report. Pruitt ran it up to the Chief Engineer, who delivered it to the Captain at officer's call on the 04 level.

"Were about as light as we can get, Captain," he said. "It's up to the snipes now."

"Thanks Screws, I think we'll take em," he answered. The *Fort Fisher* was about 500 yards off our port side now as both ships' engineering departments made final preparations for the power run to Numazu bay. The sea was calm, and the sky was overcast as Wild Bill ordered the *Juneau* to an all stop with the *Fort Fisher* following suit. Both *Juneau* fire rooms changed from the standard burners, to the steam assisted customized barrels with the drilled out sprayer plates. Both fire rooms went down to only one burner as the ship rolled slightly in the calm sea. Captain Petrowski spoke into the T.B.S. system (talk between ships.)

"Ready when you are *Fort Fisher*," he said.

"Let's go *Juneau*," came the reply.

Wild Bill turned to the Helmsman and ordered Flank Full, sent to both engine rooms. Each Throttleman opened up the ahead wheel, and the burnerman cut in all five burners, and raised the blowers to their 8,000rpms maximum speed. All machinery was running at full blast as the *Juneau* began churning white foam in her wake. Ten knots, twelve, sixteen knots, eighteen and climbing, as the two grey ghosts matched each other's speed over the calm Pacific. Twenty knots and the *Juneau* began to pull ahead as she crested twenty-two knots, and her funnels began to emit a light brown haze. Twenty-three, then twenty-four knots read out on the throttle deck shaft revolutions gauge. Wild Bill called down to the forward hole to ask Screws how much more we had left.

"Twenty four knots, and still making way Captain," he said.

"Pour it on, Main Control." The C.O. cheered. Everything

had been opened all the way as now we just waited for the *Juneau* to reach whatever speed she was going to reach. The empty lower well deck was vibrating like crazy as the ship reached twenty-five, and then topped out at twenty-six knots. A new class speed record had been set, and at the same time, the *Juneau* was leaving her tormentor in her frothy wake. Both stacks were now emitting light brown smoke as the C.O. of the *Fort Fisher* called over to inquire as to the circumstances.

"No problem, just thought we'd slow down, and blow tubes on the boilers," joked Petrowski.

"You can't be blowing tubes at twenty-six knots, it's not possible for your class of ship," responded the *Fort Fisher* C.O.

"*Fort Fisher*, I give you my word that there is steam going into the fire boxes of both boilers," Petrowski chuckled. There was a moment of silence until Wild Bill wrote down a message on a piece of paper, and handed it to the signalman. After promising the man that the spelling was correct, the signalman began to signal *Fort Fisher* by signal light. "Signal light from JUNEAU Sir," alerted the bridge watch of *Fort Fisher*. The bridge wing lookout copied down the message from the *Juneau's* C.O.

O-L-D- F-A-R-T- F-I-S-H-E-R- S-L-O-W-P-O-K-E-

S-E-E- Y-O-U- N-U-M-A-Z-U- O-U-T-   The C.O. of the *Fort Fisher* conceded to his bridge that although he did not understand how they were pulling it off, the *Juneau* was indeed making twenty-six knots, to their twenty-one. The C.O. spoke into the t.b.s. system:

"Good show *Juneau*, See you in court, out."

In two hours, the other grey ghost became a mere speck on the horizon, and then disappeared. The *Juneau* maintained the unheard of twenty-six knots all the way to Numazu Bay where she then dropped the hook, and set condition one alpha. It had been a 200 mile power run and the *Fort Fisher* was nowhere in sight as the first load of Marines were brought into the flooded well deck by the LCU-1629. Only as the last load of troops was being ferried from the beach did the *Fort Fisher* appear out of the distant haze, and enter the bay. With the increased speed being held for so long, the Evaporators were able to replenish larger amounts of fresh water more quickly than at sixteen knots. The troop loading was completed by sunset so the *Juneau* blew her ballast, raised the hook, and stood out of Numazu bay bound for White Beach to drop off this M.A.U. (Marine Amphibious Unit), and embark another one for operations off the Korean coast with South Korean forces. In the meantime, however, it would be payday on the way to Okinawa, and all the gamblers were planning their games up in the Anchor windlass room, and down in the mess cooks berthing compartment. Pruitt had made our first sale of vodka to the Wolfman for the upcoming lifer's only shaft alley "hot bearing" card party. The one can went for fifty bucks, and came with a promise of future requests. Before giving the vodka to Wolfie however, Pruitt poured the hooch into spare plastic bottles with screw on caps in order to keep secret the trick of the HI-C cans. The last thing he needed was for that information to get out. If it did then everyone would be doing it, and it would not be long before a good thing was over.

There was not much to collect this time around in the way of debts because we had pretty much been at sea since leaving the upkeep period in Yokosuka two weeks past. We would be out for two weeks on this deployment with more at sea refueling, and replenishment before returning to White Beach to off load the Marines. The weather was cold that far north so it made for easy watch standing down in the fire rooms. The days went by the usual way at sea with watch standing, revolving around the three daily meals, and Toungie serving mid-rats chow to those going on the 2400- 0400 watch. Boogie had all he could handle with 600 Marines, and 435 Ships Company to feed so he detailed Toungie to dole out the mid-rats. There was a noticeable absence of hole snipes at mid-rats chow because of the fact that some of them had bribed one of the Marine guards standing watch in the well deck with some marijuana, and he had slid out a few cases of C-rations to them and they had spirited them down to the fire room. They figured that they were not going to eat Toungie's half-cooked roast beef, if for a few joints they could have a few cases of C-rations.

What they would do was fill a mop bucket with water, throw in cans of beans, franks, chicken, turkey, and such then hook up the steam assist device to the low pressure drain of the emergency feed pump, put one hose into the water to act as a steam lance, and in no time start the water to boiling thereby quickly cooking the contents of the green cans.

A case usually contained a small four pack of stale cigarettes, matches, gum, shit paper, and a can opener that the snipes called a "John Wayne." They were handy little devices, and much sought after by the snipes who would attach them to their key rings. Wolfie, and Smitty, had the little 'John Wayne's' that were fifteen years old. Real steamers, I decided that I had to have one too. As it turned out, it was Stewart, the one who had sold me his Buck 110 clasp knife for ten dollars who was reported to have bribed the Marine guard in the well deck with some Marijuana to make the transaction. He was over by the scoop injection vent picking at a can of pound cake with his new Gerber. Stewart was a Machinist mate, and so was not under Scratch on the lower level. He tended the Evaporator on the upper level coming down every now and then to shoot the breeze with the pump-man.

The lower level watch was having a feast after boiling the C-Rations, and then opening them with one of the 'John Wayne's' that every box held. Stewart was a bartering fool to say the least, on yet another occasion, I found him by the coffee station on the Generator deck honing a regulation Marine Corps Ka- Bar, style knife that he bartered yet some more weed to the same well deck Marine for. It came with a black leather sheath, and a ringed leather handle that I saw was somewhat crushed after many years in the fleet. On one side of the knife were the company's name, Camillus, New York, U.S.A. Further inspection revealed a seven-inch blade, and a stout pommel that held it all together. This knife had been in the fleet since at least the Korean War, maybe before that. It was a real steamer.

"Ain't she a beauty?" Stewart asked me.

"Looks like she's all business, that's for sure," I replied.

"What's this Grunt doing, giving away the store?"

"Sort of. He's getting discharged soon," he answered. "Hell, at this rate I'm Gonna hit him up for a .45."

"You're kidding of course, right? I asked.

Stewart stopped honing the Ka- Bar for a second, and gave me a smirk before resuming work on the blade with his favorite Arkansas whetstone. "Beat it boot, I've got work to do," he said without looking back up.

We were back at White Beach soon enough to unload one Amphibious unit, refuel, take on yet another mountain of stores, and embark another six hundred Marines for the exercises off Korea. There was no liberty granted this time around because time was short, and pressing matters were at hand. It was a busy two weeks at sea with no place for the crew to spend any of their pay. Hensen had made a killing at Boogies mess cooks poker game, but was still restricted to the ship, and therefore had no place to spend it. Landon and I were hoping that he would not embark on a slush fund of his own, and thereby give us competition in Engineering since he had so much time on his hands.

Another thing we were worried about was him finding out that we had liquor on board. We decided not to sell him any because if he got drunk, and went berserk the way he was known to do, then it was only a matter of time that the booze would be traced back to us. Neither Landon, nor Pruitt had seen him in action the way I had on my first night aboard, and later on the Boat deck with Scratch off Mindoro. If he got drunk aboard ship then it was only a matter of time that he would go after Case again, and things could get ugly. Other than that, our liquor sales were regular, mostly to Smitty, and the Wolfman, who acted as salesmen, and carefully screened the requests to make sure that only the right Lifers received any. We retained our own can for those infrequent get togethers after watch to relax before hitting the rack to doze off, gently lulled to sleep by the gentle rolling action of the ship as she steamed over the swells. Our exercises were conducted up near the 38th parallel so the North Koreans could see our commitment to the South Koreans. We were steaming in concert with the *Fort Fisher, Tripoli,* which was a helicopter carrier, *Ranger,* a Forrestal class aircraft carrier providing air support, and *Oklahoma City,* the veteran WW2 Cleveland class cruiser now outfitted with guided missiles, while a destroyer, and a couple of frigates of the Knox class ran anti-submarine patrols. It was a formidable display of sea power for the North Koreans to witness Uncle Sam showing off his dick. The *Oklahoma City* acted as flagship for the operation. We returned to Buckner Bay the day before Christmas, and would be there for New Years Eve of 1976. The crew got liberty and headed to Kadena and the red light strip of Gate 2 Street. I stood watch down in the forward fire room on New Year's Eve, and someone made up a sign complete with "flying asshole" and the Machinist Mates screw on either side of it that read:

HAPPY NEW YEAR

1976

JUNEAU SNIPES

All the snipes on the boiler level gathered behind the sign in the fire alley while one of the Machinist Mates snapped off five pictures of Scratches watch. Afterward, he had me take the sign up to the throttle deck, and snap pictures of all the Machinist Mates so everyone could receive a print to mail home once the film was developed. On New Year's Day, we received orders to put to sea because a tropical storm had developed into a full-fledged typhoon, and was headed right for Okinawa.

We were going to Subic Bay in two days anyway but did not want to run the risk of getting caught in port just in case. The typhoon was coming along the west coast of the Philippines, so Wild Bill conned the ship around the north coast of the main island of Luzon to the eastern side in hopes of avoiding the brunt of the storm. The first day out found everyone securing anything that could move to ensure that it did not. It was warm, and humid, and the skies began to turn dark as the sea turned heavy. On the second day, the seas grew to twenty feet, and the ship had trouble making sixteen knots. On the third day, the rains hit with a face stinging lateral wind, and the seas grew to sixty feet as the ship bobbed like a toy.

All normal work was called off, and the Chief Engineer doubled the watches in the fire rooms to ensure that safety was maintained because the crew was not getting any sleep due to the heaving seas. We were not carrying any Marines now so the ship was not at full load. Our fuel and fresh water tanks had been topped off at White Beach, so the only thing to do was ride out the edge of the storm and head for the San Bernardino straits in order to go around to Subic Bay.

What would normally take two days to transit from Buckner Bay to Subic Bay would now take us five storm-tossed sleepless days because of the typhoon-directed side route. On the fifth day we entered the calm San Bernardino straits with an exhausted crew so the Captain ordered what was known as a 'holiday routine', which is a stand own of sorts so the crew could get some rest. We made Subic Bay that afternoon and Scratch had me stand burners for sea detail. This time it was different, much different from White Beach. That, mixed with my exhausted state of mind led me to lift safeties on the forward boiler. The Smoke watch on the 04 level had ripped off his sound powered headphones, and hauled ass to escape the shower of hot boiler water once the steam had condensed, and began to fall all over the Captain's gig on the boat deck, and starboard rear gun mount.

After sea detail was secured, Scratch lit into me. "Boot, go up to the compartment and get your Peacoat, then get your ass back down here," he said.

When I had complied with his order, he handed me a paint-brush, and a can of heat-treated silver boiler paint, along with a small wire brush to scrub the old paint off. He then had me don my Peacoat, and ordered me atop the hot boiler to begin scrub-bing the blown safety valve. "Don't paint em till inspect em," he called after me. It was a good 130 degrees on top of the boiler, and wearing my Peacoat did not help much either. I was deter-mined to get through it because it was a custom for a burnerman to do so whenever he lifted safeties. In any event, the peacoat offered some protection in case you were to lean on an uncov-ered portion of steam line, or a hot valve. It was wicked hot, so I worked the wire brush as fast as I could to clean the blown safety valve. It took around a half hour in order to clean off the old paint enough to please Scratch, and by then the boiler had been secured in order to bottom blow. Scratch crawled up to in-spect the valve, and check on me because he knew that it was god awful hot up there.

"Looks good boot, paint her up," he said.

I remember starting to paint the valve, but that is about it. The next thing I knew, I was staring up at the overhead while snipes were pouring cold water from the D.A. tank down my crotch, and armpits in an effort to revive me. I had passed out of course, and in doing so had knocked the can of silver paint over the lip of the boiler where one of the snipes noticed it run-ning down the burner front. After a few shouted cuss words, and no response from me, they knew something was wrong, and found me lying across a steam header on my back.

The thick wool of the issue peacoat was the only thing that kept me a third degree burn on my back for the two minutes I lay there. Three of them hauled me off the top of the boiler, and over to the L.P. air compressor where there was more room to lay me out. After a few minutes, I was able to reach the sitting position and drink some water. My entire body and uniform were soaking wet from both perspiration, and he D.A. tank water they had used to cool me down.

"He's had it Scratch. He's spent," said Lutz. "Get him outta here, and put him in his rack."

Lutz, Moe, and Danshaw, carried, and pulled me up the fire room ladder to the troop spaces, and to the cool air of the well deck. The air was actually thick with moisture, and tropical humidity, but because I was so depleted, I felt a chill. They walked me around the well deck a bit until I was good enough to hit the shower, and hit the rack. Smitty stuck a late sleepers tag on my rack, and the rest of the division refueled the ship.

At quarters the next morning, Hensen was discovered to be U.A. from the ship. It seemed that Cox had let the cat out of the bag about the fantail mooring line escape route, and it proved too much of a temptation for Hensen to resist. He had won over a thousand dollars at Boogies card party, and was just itching for a place to spend it. Olongapo would be glad to part him from it. What had happened was after he went down the mooring line to the pier, he hooked up with some guys from deck, and they all crowded into a cab after downing plenty of San Miguel at the base enlisted club, and after it had gotten dark enough, passed through the Marine guard at the Shit River gate with everyone holding up their green I.D. cards, and Hensen holding up a one dollar bill folded in half that the young Marine missed.

It was a tricky way to deceive anyone in the dark when you were sitting in the darkened rear of the cab. Sailors could be that way. The problem was that when the curfew came he had gotten a room and spent the night, and was now U.A. All the next day there was no sign of him either so everyone figured that he was out for the duration of his one thousand bucks, and however long it would last. At liberty call that evening Pruitt, Landon, and myself all headed across Shit River onto Magsaysay street depositing coins into the conical reed peso catchers of the lovely Cherry Girls.

Our first stop was the Seaman's club that the Wolfman had shown us the last time we were here to grab a decent meal, and of course the coldest San Miguel in the P.I. We stayed for a while before setting out to tour the clubs on the strip hitting five, or six before the curfew approached. It was a weekend so none of us had to be back on board until 0700 Monday. We had rented rooms prior to setting out that night because they were the cleanest, and most secure. You could receive three squares, and relax in a place that did not allow hookers inside. The next morning room service came around to wake us for breakfast that was served out on the upstairs veranda overlooking Magsaysay Street.

Over bacon, eggs, and pineapple juice, and then the local Philippine coffee, we planned to head up near Subic City where there was a Marriott Inn, and hang out at the pool, swim, and catch some sun that hole snipes so seldom get to see. It was nice swimming laps in the pool, and what was nicer yet was seeing white women who were tourists because of their Aussie accents. The problem though was that they were all someone's wife, or girlfriend, and the old man was around.

It did not stop them from being extremely friendly to us so we quickly struck up conversation with them. They were very down to earth, typically Australian. Peter and his wife Linda were in their mid-thirties, and lived in Perth, on the Indian Ocean. We got to talking about this, and that, before the conversation soon turned to the local political situation, and why there was a need for a curfew the last two years.

"N.P.A.," answered Peter.

"Who's that," I asked.

"New People's Army, Communists," Peter said. "You see, Marcos was elected in 65' and 68' when Americans were pouring money into here. But a lot of people saw that he was corrupt, and he figured he'd never get re- elected in 72' so he used the N.P.A. as an excuse to declare martial law until order was restored. With martial law came suspended elections which mean he's President as long as he wants to be."

"Unless he's overthrown," said Pruitt.

"Highly unlikely Mate," said the Aussie. "The Army's in his pocket, and he's in the pocket of the C.I.A. It's only when you Americans get tired of him that anything will change," he said. "Once Washington cuts off the money he's though. Until then he uses the N.P.A. as an excuse to pillage the country."

"You should see the bust of himself that he's carving out of a whole mountain. It's the size of Mount Rushmore, and it's costing millions of Pesos where the office of President only pays him ten thousand dollars a year," he explained. "When anyone asks him where the moneys coming from, he tells them it's all from "private donations" if you get my drift. And the little tyrant says it with a straight face too. So you can understand why people are joining the N.P.A. You wouldn't tolerate Martial Law in the States any more than we would down under. You can't expect Filipinos to tolerate it either," he said.

"The reason I'm telling you guys all this is because the N.P.A. has begun targeting tourists, and American Military personnel for hard cash," he continued.

"It's purely economic guys. It's just that they need hard currency, and people like you have it. As I'm sure you know most Filipinos are very gracious to Americans in general, but the N.P.A. is angry with America for supporting the Marcos regime. Keep your spider sense alert if you're in the smaller districts where they have support. I know that it goes against human nature to roll over, but these are serious, and committed people. Stay calm, and you'll stay safe, they only want the money."

Peter proved to be a good source of information, and a damn good conversationalist to boot as he told us all the places he had been in the Orient with the Australian Navy. "You guys cross the equator yet?" he asked.

"Not yet," I answered.

"When you do, you'll have to kiss the baby's belly right?"

"Yes." I said. The "baby" Peter was referring to was usually the biggest, ugliest, Boson mate on board that was already a Shellback when the ship crossed the equator, and Pollywogs such as me were initiated into the Royal Order of King Neptunus, Rex, ruler of the raging main. Among other harassments, you were forced to kiss the belly of Neptune's baby that was smeared with grease, peanut butter, and coffee grounds.

"Well as you know, everything is a bit different down under," he began. "Our seasons are opposite of yours, and we drive on the correct side of the road, not the right side of the road," he joked. The Shellback tradition comes from ships crossing from North to South, and not South to North the way Aussies have to do it."

"What's that got to do with the baby's belly?" I asked.

"You Yanks have to kiss his belly, us poor Cobbers have to flip him over and kiss his fat ass!" He roared with laughter as he delivered the punch line with the three of us joining in on the self-deprecating humor. That is pretty much how the rest of the afternoon went there around the hotels pool. Laughter, drinking, and good-natured sparring at each other's respective countries. The three of us yanks, and this Aussie, and his "sheila," along with some other Aussie tourists that soon joined the table had that area of the pool resembling a good-natured riot. The Australians were a fun loving, big hearted, ballsey, bunch of people, and the afternoon passed all too quickly.

The next day would be Sunday, and since we already had rooms reserved back at the Seaman's club, we grabbed a Jeepney back to Olongapo after saying goodbye to our Aussie drinking friends. About four blocks from Magsaysay street, Pruitt suggests that we stop at a little place for a before lunch drink. It was a small place upstairs from the foot deep red mud of the street that we walked on a two by ten plank to get to the lower level, and went upstairs to find Case at the bar talking to one of the bargirls. He was beer drunk, and running off at the mouth as usual, but was tolerated because he was tipping well. The three of us occupied a table near the veranda overlooking the typhoon soaked muddy street, and ordering a round of San Miguel. Case began teasing me about lifting safeties on the boiler, but I sensed that there was nothing good-natured about it. It was boot this, and boot that, and I had just begun to feel normal again as all weekend long Pruitt, and Landon had been calling me by my first name of 'Tim', not to mention that the Aussies had me feel welcome like some kind of extended family, so I just turned away from him ,and ignored his taunts.

Just then, I saw Pruitt's eyes go wide, and a grin come across his face as he stared at the doorway. "Well look what the wind blew in," he said.

We turned around to see none other than Hensen entering, and making his way over to our table. He noticed Case sitting at the otherwise empty bar with the Whore on his lap, but outside of an annoyed look, paid him no mind.

"Hey Snipes. How goes it?" he asked as he drew up a chair and joined us. The rains started up again and began to rattle the corrugated metal roof with a metallic din as the humidity began to rise in the room.

"How ya'll doin is more like it," said Pruitt. "The whole division's looking for you boy, ya'll in a world of shit now," he added.

"Yeah, well I'm having a blast for the first time in three months," he replied.

"Gonna keep it up too, till I'm broke anyway," he added. "Were pulling out in three days," said Pruitt.

"You gonna be there?" he asked him.

"Not unless they drag me back by then," he answered.

"Your goin over the hill for good then, is that what you're

saying?"

Hensen turned towards Case at the bar, and said, "Hey, between assholes like him, and shave tails like Ensign Benson, I'm pretty much worn out."

"You know that after thirty days you'll be a deserter, correct?" Pruitt asked.

"I'll turn myself in on the last day," he said. "They'll give me some brig time, fly me back to the states, and discharge me... big deal. Until then I'm gonna spend some of Boogie's money, and screw everything in sight. It's my decision guys, OK?" he said.

"No problem," we all agreed.

The bartender brought over another round of San Miguel, and the conversation turned to less pressing matters before Case started in from his perch at the bar;

"Well if it isn't two of the worst burner men in the fleet, side, by side, he bellowed. With you two guys forward, and aft, blowing safeties, the Bosun's mates will never have to wash the boat deck. Haw!"

"See what I mean," Hensen said softly. "Just won't let San Diego rest. How many times do I have to lay him out?"

The rain on the corrugated roof beat a constant tattoo so that even we could hardly hear his words much less Case chatting with his whore. Every few minutes he would say something else towards the table in reference to Hensen being U.A. from the ship, and we were surprised that he just kept ignoring his taunts. Maybe the fact that it was pouring outside, and Hensen did not feel like leaving in the downpour had something to do with his perceived patience, but at any rate, he just kept up a running conversation about what he was going to do once the Navy finally discharged him.

Meanwhile, Case's whore was busy surprising him with how nimble her fingers were by coming up with his locker keys, Zippo lighter etc. until he began to whisper in her ear while glancing over at Hensen with his back to him and his poker-filled wallet filling out his jeans. Case ordered another beer from the Filipino bartender, who then retreated to the kitchen after serving him because Case was now becoming the classic ugly American with his boorish behavior. The whore slid off Case's lap and sashayed over to Hensen making doe eyes at him, and cooing things of a sexual nature in his ear all the while softly stroking his back lower, and lower still. The whore pretended to nibble on his ear as she slid her right hand down the inside rear of his jeans. She bit down just enough while rising a few inches knowing that he would have to rise with her thereby releasing the tautness of his jeans back pocket, and giving her nimble fingers access to his wallet.

What she did not know along with the three of us, was that Hensen was wise to her trick. No sooner had she palmed his wallet than he whirled around, grabbed her arm, and retrieved his wallet from her hand. Hensen put his wallet back in his pocket, and slapped the whore so hard across the face that she started to drop. He then swooped her up in his arms the way a groom would sweep up his bride, but instead of carrying her across a threshold, he carried her to the railing of the veranda, and held her over for a split second:

"Hensen... NO!" yelled Pruitt.

Hensen dropped the whore about ten feet to the foot deep red mud below... KER-SPLAT! She lay on her back with the rain pouring down in sheets, and the mud oozing in all around her, the very same mud that broke the swarthy pickpockets fall.

"Why you son of a bitch!" roared Case as he charged from his barstool at Hensen, who delivered an overhand right to Case's jaw, dropping him to the deck colder that a Seaman's Club San Miguel.

The bartender emerged from the kitchen upon hearing the commotion to find Case out cold, and the whore missing. Without saying a word, but putting his palms out in a questioning sort of way, the bartender turned his gaze towards Hensen.

"You see that guy there?" Hensen said. "He just threw your whore off the veranda!" Hensen pretended to be indignant."If this is the kind of place you're running, then we'll just go someplace else, my friend. But I suggest you find a cop, and lock this animal away before he hurts someone else." The three of us rose in agreement. The bartender ran downstairs as we followed him out the door, and past the whore who was still loopy from the slap. We found a Jeepney on the next block and hopped in as it made its way to Magsaysay Street.

"Sorry guys, but I'm at the end of my rope with that guy. He deliberately sent that L.B.F.M. over to lift my wallet. Some shipmate he is, huh?" he asked.

"Don't worry ol' stick, were on your side," offered Pruitt. "Thing is though, as soon as the whore comes around she's gonna finger you as the one, and Case's Gonna identify you as U.A. It might be wise to turn yourself over to the Shore Patrol before the Olongapo police grab you first," Pruitt advised.

"Nothing doing Bub," replied Hensen, "Not with a thousand bucks I'm not."

The Jeepney let us off in front of the Seaman's Club, and we all went upstairs to get a meal. The Wolfman and Deadeye were there at the bar as we walked in and they nodded at Hensen as Pruitt related the story about Case and his whores attempt to lift Henson's wallet all the while agreeing that Hensen was now in a jam for assault on a Philippine national. Wolfie soon had a plan to smooth things over with the bartender, and get him to drop charges. He was going to enlist the aid of a Slickey Boy.

"Why a Slickey Boy?" asked Hensen.

"Because he speaks Tagalog. He's the courier," Wolfie replied.

"Courier for what?" asked Hensen.

"Courier for money. Whadda ya think?"

"Whose money?" asked Hensen.

"Your money. It's called a bribe, fool."

Hensen and the Wolfman looked at each other for a solid ten seconds before Wolfie narrowed his eyes, and asked, "Just how hard did Scratch hit you that day, anyway?"

"Look, it's like this, you punched Case which ain't a crime in my book, but the Old Man will see it different because you're on record for it. Number two, you threw a Philippine national out the window, and that's serious stuff."

"Even if you turn yourself in to the Shore Patrol, you're still going to have to answer that charge, "They don't look kindly to Sailors beating up on their L.B.F.M.s,. You read me Hensen?" he asked.

"Yeah Wolfie, I read ya," he replied. "You're gonna sit in the Olongapo Hoosegow for about a solid month, then you're gonna pay for a lawyer you can't understand. Then you're gonna pay a fine and restitution that by that time you won't have, then they're gonna throw your ass back in jail, and you're not gonna like it. And remember, you're still missing ship's movement too. "Either way you're gonna pay. You agree?" he asked him again.

"Yeah, I guess you're right," Hensen confessed. "How much?" he asked.

"That's for the Slickey Boy to find out. He's gonna be your lawyer, and you are gonna pay him a percentage. So until then I suggest you get a room, and water the horse for a while. But whatever you do don't go strolling down the strip where you can get picked up," he added. "We'll get this all worked out tomorrow."

"Thanks Wolfie, I owe you one," said Hensen.

"Yeah well, just consider yourself lucky I'm not charging you too," he replied. That much was true. The Wolfman had just given him some valuable advice from someone who knew his way around Olongapo City, in the course of eight, Wes-Pac deployments. Hensen got his room squared away, and then rejoined us at the bar for the rest of the evening.

The next morning everyone had breakfast out on the veranda as before, only this time somewhat more boisterous. The Wolfman said that he had a kid in mind to act as translator/ courier to the bartender. The fact that his bar was off the main drag meant that he would be easier to bribe because he did not get the traffic like Magsaysay did. He was not located in the part of town known as the "Jungle," where all the black sailors and Marines went either. He was the equivalent of an off the beaten path whorehouse with only one working whore. She would no doubt be on sick call because of the slap and the fall. Not seriously hurt, but not able to command the full price of twenty dollars. The idea was to get to him as soon as possible before he lost any money because of Hensen, which of course he would claim he had. The Wolfman knew a Slickey Boy of about twelve years old who said could take care of everything, but would charge a percentage as usual. Hensen had no choice but to pay whatever it was going to be. He had a thousand dollars from Boogie's poker party so it was not as if he had worked for it, luck of the draw was more like it. As it turned out, the kid was one of the mixed race shoeshine Slickey Boys that roamed the streets of Olongapo City earning their scruffy, meager, living off of American sailors and marines that crossed Shit River every day at 1630 liberty call.

THE SLICKEY BOY

The boy knew the whistle from the upstairs veranda to be that of the Wolfman, and so rose up off his shoeshine box that he had been sitting on, picked it up with one hand, and climbed the stairs of the Seaman's Club to conduct what he assumed was shoe shine business. When he arrived at the veranda and approached the six sailors at the table, most of us were faced for the first time with one of Olongapo's more brutal realities. The

Slickey Boy had all the regular features of his swarthy prostitute mother, and the red hair of his one-night-stand American father. He was Eurasian, and he ran with all the other mixed race shoeshine boys and was an astute student of the street. He made his living as did all the other Slickey Boys from the thousands of American servicemen that streamed across Shit River every evening at liberty call.

Wolfie introduced him as Ramon. "Shine em up Ramon, a buck a foot."

We were all wearing leather shoes, and so took turns at receiving our shines, and then forking over two dollars to the young street kid. When it came time for Hensen to receive his shine, Wolfie spoke to the boy in Tagalog for a moment. He went to work with renewed vigor on this last customer. Clutching a cup of coffee in his right hand, and gazing out at Magsaysay Street, the Wolfman spoke again in Tagalog with neither he, nor the boy looking at one another. A half minute passed before the boy answered him, and Wolfie speaking softly again in Tagalog received an OK from the twelve-year-old boy.

The Slickey Boy finished up the last shine, and rose to look Hensen in the eye and Wolfie said, "Hensen, meet your new lawyer. Known him three Wes-Pacs now. He's a square kid."

Hensen just nodded at the boy who stood there impassively until Wolfie asked him, "Well, you gonna pay him or does he gotta show you how fast he is with a butterfly knife?"

"Oh yeah, sure." He fished two bucks from his shirt pocket and handed them to the boy. The Wolfman spoke to the boy in another round of Tagalog again while nodding at Hensen, and using his hands to say "no big deal" when the boy shot Hensen a glance that seem to convey that he disagreed. He spoke to Wolfie in faster Tagalog for a moment, and then picked up his shoeshine box, and headed out the door, and down the street.

"What's the story?" asked Hensen.

"He'll make the best deal he can, but he didn't like the part of her going out the window," Wolfie replied. "That could very well have been his mother, you know."

"He's gonna talk to the bartender and set a price for him to drop the charges, and that's what you'll pay," he said.

"How do I know he won't bargain him low, and charge me high?" Hensen asked.

"You don't, just be glad he doesn't know how much of Boogie's Poker money you've got on you," Wolfie replied.

"Why did you tell him about her going off the veranda?" Hensen asked.

"He's your Lawyer, he's gotta have all the facts of the case," Wolfie said. "I told him what you guys told me about her picking your pocket, and belting Case. He doesn't have a problem with you slapping her, but sailing her off the top deck was overdoing it, don't you think?" he asked.

Ramon Tuzon could have cared less whether the charges against the big American were dropped or not. He worked his way from the recently paved main drag of Magsaysay street to the unpaved side streets that were dusty red in the dry season, red mud during the Monsoon season, and foot deep red mud after a Typhoon. He hoped he could strike a deal with the bartender, and make some easy money from the American sailor. Ramon knew the bar of course, CRACK A SMILE was the name of it, and he knew that it wouldn't be located on the Magsaysay strip with all the other gaudy dives whose whores hung out front all painted up, and perfumed, and took sailors, and Marines inside to continue the age old Olongapo practice of separating them from their money.

The further removed from the main drag of Magsaysay, then the more blatant the sexual come- hither names of the bars. Regardless of the name, they were all the same him, and all the other mixed race Slickey Boys who everyone knew had been conceived in just such a place. Where the average Shit River diver, and the little Cherry Girls were all Filipinos by birth, and their parents were just the average third world unfortunates, the mixed race children of Olongapo were without a doubt the product of a prostitute, and a White man. A prostitute and a Black man. A prostitute, and a Mexican, an Arab, or whomever. Many, if not all, ever knew the name of their father because it is not as if you had to show I.D. to get a piece of ass in Olongapo, or anywhere else in the Orient for that matter. They were the human conclusion anytime an American Military base was located in a poor country, and all the cottage industries, both legal, and otherwise sprang up to serve every desire of the overfed, overpaid, Americans.

Ramon Tuzon was a hard young man at the age of twelve years old, and had nothing to grin about as he entered the front of the CRACK A SMILE and went upstairs. There were a few sailors there, one of which was talking to the whore with a slightly swollen face that she had disguised as much as possible with Rouge. The bartender was behind the bar, and said hello to Ramon who he assumed was there to pick up a few bucks shining shoes. They began to speak about the incident the day before, and Ramon told the man that the American wanted to give him $150 dollars as an apology if he would not press charges.

Just then, the whore gave the bartender a twenty-dollar bill from her new John and they left the bar. "She still makes money, now you make money," Ramon said knowingly to the man. The bartender agreed to retrieve the police report for the cost of ten dollars and have it ready to exchange to Ramon when he handed over the $150 bucks from the American. The retrieval of the official police report was the only way Hensen could be sure that he was indeed off the hook.

Ramon returned to the Seaman's club and gave Wolfie the news. "He wants 300 bucks, and you get the report. If I were you I'd take it," Wolfie advised.

Hensen counted out $300 dollars in twenties from his wallet

and handed them to the boy who then folded the bills in half and stuck them in his pocket as the Wolfman said something to him in Tagalog. The boy nodded and left. He returned about twenty minutes later and handed the police report to Hensen who breathed an audible sigh of relief. It had been stamped with the seal of the Provost Marshall, with a red line stricken through it. Now all he had to face was the Naval Brig at Subic Bay, a piece of cake in comparison.

"Thanks kid," Hensen said to Ramon. The Slickey boy shrugged, and left without saying another word with an easy $150 American dollars for his effort.

"Like I say guys, treat em right, and they'll do you right, treat em wrong, and they'll slit you deep, and wide." Wolfie advised.

We spent the rest of the day at the Seaman's club, retiring rather early in order to get up and walk back to the ship in time for breakfast before morning quarters at 0700. The early morning air was thick with humidity as the five of us headed across the Shit River Bridge onto the naval base. Hensen had decided to remain U.A. until the money ran out, and then turn himself in to the Shore Patrol. He could expect three months in the Brig under the Marine guard at Subic, and then a general discharge back in the states. Chief Morgan had been correct on that call when he stated that Hensen would never complete a full Wes-Pac. We decided to keep his whereabouts to ourselves.

The next two days went by, and still there was no sign of Hensen, so Scratch detailed Lutz to the after fire room to replace Hensen on burners and informed me that I was now replacing Lutz on forward burners with him as Topwatch.

The ship got underway that Wednesday morning without Hensen, which added another charge against him, "missing ship's movement," one of the more serious charges any sailor could face. I handled the sea detail much better on the way out of Subic than on the way in, and Scratch was pleased with my performance this time. Scratch's watch would have the 8-12 shifts on the way back to Okinawa where we would refuel and take on stores and the Marines again for our regular runs to Numazu bay. We would then head for Yokosuka for another general upkeep period, only this time it would be for our flight deck to be stripped and resurfaced. The guns would also get a going over and inspection.

We would have two weeks' liberty in which to replace our depleted stocks of vodka and gin at Pruitt's *Midway* friend's apartment. The time spent at White Beach was without liberty due to the pressing matters at hand loading all the Marines, and their gear for the Numazu run. Sea detail was a breeze leaving Buckner Bay, but then Yokosuka, and it's dreaded "full back" awaited me soon after. All the way to Numazu, Case blathered to Lutz, who as burnerman was confined to the burner front, and thus could not escape him, about how Hensen had sucker punched him again and thrown his L.B.F.M. off the veranda, purposely reversing the sequence of events in order to save some of his still swollen face.

Lutz just nodded and kept his eyes on the main steam pressure gauge's 650psi reading figuring that it was Case's story so he could tell it as he wished. We arrived at the entrance of the broad bay at sunrise, and dropped the hook, set condition one alpha, and the LCU-1629 began its troop-laden runs to the beachhead. The seas were quite choppy this time around so the Marines got a very wet ride in on the LCU. At mid-day, the evolution was complete, and the ship raised the hook, blew ballast, and steamed off to Yokosuka. We would arrive late in the afternoon so in the meantime Case had been topside telling every deck ape who would listen that a boot was on burners on the forward boiler so to stay clear of the forward stack, and boat deck during sea detail. He was setting me up for a confrontation with deck just because I had been present at "Crack a smile" when he was decked.

I was off watch now and would not go on sea detail until it

was called at 1600. I had early chow along with other snipes and Bosun's mates that would also be on sea detail, and one of them inquired as to who it was that would be standing burners up forward. Case was waiting for just such a question, and eagerly volunteered my presence by pointing at me across the table from himself. The Boson mates just eyed me Cooley for a second, but said nothing. They did not have to, their gaze said it all: DON'T BLOW SAFTIES ON MY BOAT DECK PAINT JOB! It was completely uncalled for, and one of the other snipes even said as much while the deck apes had mercifully gone back to their conversation. I remembered Hensen at the "Crack a smile" asking, "How many times do I have to lay him out anyway? I was beginning to detest Case, and at the same time, I knew that he could care less.

On the way down to the fire room Scratch gave me some advice that I knew he meant. "Don't worry about him boot, worry about your job. By the way, did you bring your peacoat?"

"Oh yeah, I forgot about that," I said.

"Hope you don't need it boot, really. "But you know the rules."

"Yeah Scratch, I know the rules," I replied. I returned to the compartment to fetch my peacoat with the burn mark across the back of it where I had laid across the steam header that day, and arrived on station at the burner front just as sea detail was being sounded over the ship's 1MC. Scratch donned headphones and reported the forward fire room manned, and ready. Yokosuka was the port where one of the fire rooms always received the dreaded full back bell, depending on which side of the ship was to be moored to the pier.

The smoke watch called down from the 04 level to report that we were now entering the shipping channel, and could expect bells to come down from the bridge at any time now. I tested the valve wheel of the forced draft blowers, and found it loose enough to not cause any problems when the time came to move fast. The smoke watch relayed that we were now in the shipping channel proper. We received a one third back, and then an all stop as the harbor pilot was brought aboard. I received a one third ahead, and then all stop, two thirds ahead, and then all stop again. Then it was another round of up and down scrambling on the burner front as the smoke watch called down to inform the Topwatches that the ship was now closing the pier

"Stand by for ahead full," warned Scratch. We got an all stop, and I cut out three burners and waited. Ahead full, came the bell from the bridge as the throttle man opened the ahead wheel, and began sucking steam from the boiler as fast as I could replace it. The main steam gage began to drop steadily even though all five burners were cut in and the fuel oil throttle valve was at the twelve o'clock position indicating wide open.

Scratch yelled into the headphones to the throttle deck, "Throttleman, you're sucking us off the line! Back off! Boot, standby for all stop," he warned.

Clang! came the bell as soon as he had said it.

I turned down the blower valve wheel with my whole body swinging on it the way a Basketball player swings on the rim after a slam-dunk. After dropping to the deck plates, I scrambled up the burner front cutting out four burners, and brought the fuel oil throttle valve to the three o'clock position. I was the minimum amount of fuel going to the single remaining burner in which to keep fires lit in the boiler. The pressure kept rising, 660, 670, 675, 678, Bang, WHOOOOSSH! Went the boilers safeties as steam rushed up from the steam drum vent, and out the stack. Once again, the smoke watch shed his headphones, and hauled ass to escape the hot boiler water shower emanating from the starboard stack. Scratch was pissed, but not at me, this time much to my surprise.

"It's not your fault boot," he said. "I'm gonna take care of it in just a minute."

MOORED, came the announcement over the 1MC. Knowing

with that announcement that we would not be receiving any more bells, Scratch shed his headphones and headed up to the throttle deck where an argument quickly erupted between him and Cox, the throttle man.

"What's he supposed to do, secure fires?" demanded Scratch. "First you almost suck us off the line, then you flood the boiler with steam, and the safeties blow!"

"If you're not working with us, then you're working against us, that's how it works Cox," he said. Cox started to protest until Scratch's eyes opened wide with the thought that he might be sassed, before Cox decided that discretion was the better part of valor. Besides, he knew that Scratch was right.

Cox knew that it was just as easy to pop the safeties, as it was to suck a boiler off the line. He just wanted to have a little fun with the new burnerman, and keep me on my toes.

"Smitty, my boot was on the ball, your man blew safeties, he's gonna scrub em," Scratch insisted. "My boot will paint em, but your man's gonna scrub em."

"OK Scratch. Fair enough," conceded Smitty, knowing full well that Scratch had a point about Cox horsing around with the steam with a new boot on burners. "Cox, grab a wire brush, and get busy."

Cox descended the burner front ladder to get the wire brush as Scratch followed him down, and came over to speak to me. "You did good boot, real good," he began.

"Then why do I have to paint safeties?" I asked.

"Because you are the other half of the team," he replied. "Cox is a good Throttleman, and knows better than to do what he did. That's why he's scrubbing em. It was his fault they lifted. The reason you were up there at Subic was because you were too slow on the bells, it was your fault. Cox gave you plenty of time then, and you weren't squared away," he said.

"I've stood hundreds of sea details boot, I know when the Throttleman is playing around with the steam. This is one of the ways you learn, you're looking good. After a while you'll learn to pre-empt him, that's what makes Lutz so good. Stick with it. And don't paint those safeties till inspect em. Make Cox scrub em right down to the quick, he's gotta learn his lessons too," he finished.

True to the code Cox scrubbed the blown safety valve until all the paint I had put there at Subic bay was now gone, and the valve was just bare metal. Scratch inspected the job, and I donned my Peacoat, and climbed atop the boiler to begin painting the valve. I had the easy part because it only took me ten minutes to paint the valve where as it took Cox an hour of furious wire brushing to clean off the previous paint job to Scratch's satisfaction. Cox was still sitting under a vent sipping some cold water when I came down from the boiler top, shed my Peacoat, and began bottom blowing the now secured boiler. After I secured from the bottom blow, I went up to the flight deck to survey the scene. I could see some of the other ships that we had operated with off Korea were also in port along with some that were new to me. One of these was the U.S.S. *Chicago* [CG-11] a double end missile cruiser with an enormous looking superstructure. It looked like it would be top heavy until I considered that it must be made from aluminum in contrast with the steel hull. The *Tripoli* [LPH-10] was back in port as was the flagship of the operation, *Oklahma City* [CLG-5] After returning to the berthing compartment, those not on the duty section were busy forming a hole snipe liberty party. There were about fifteen of them heading out to the Dumb Shit Oki, to drink, dance, slug the jukebox, and after a while, probably each other. Bravo division's resident hell raiser Hensen, was still prowling the dives of Magsaysay. Hensen was a good hole snipe, and the division was sorry that he had made the decision that he had.

The Dumb Shit Okie would be a wild place indeed in a couple hours so after Cox got loosened up a bit on the pool table, he headed over to Dance yo-ass-off, to see if he could meet up with either Alfie, or the big guy in order to set up another match with Mr. Kihara. I had duty the first night in port as it turned out, so would be standing Cold Iron watch in the forward engine room on the mid watch, which was fine with me because I would not have to deal with everyone coming back off the beach in an intoxicated state between the hours of 2300- to 0300. I used the four-hour watch to clean the sprayer plates, and wash down the fire alley until I was relieved at 0400. Upon returning to the compartment, I found the air heavy with boozy barf with one of the snipes vomiting into the compartment shit can. The man crawled back to his rack, and soon passed out. Since I was already awake, I grabbed the handle of the can and hauled it towards one of the side port doors, un-dogged the door and pushed the entire can into the harbor. There was no way I was going to clean up the guy's mess, and I was not going to let it remain in the compartment stinking to high hell.

I decided that the bottom of Yokosuka Bay was a good resting place for it. It seemed that one of the snipes had imbibed a little too much liquor known as Absinth 58 while engaged in a shot for shot contest at the Dumb shit Okie. He won the shot contest, but lost the corn dogs that were sold on the strip once he had lain down, and everything began to swirl. Absinth 58 was clear liquor that tasted like black liquorice candy and could sneak up on a man if he happened to mix it with any other alcohol.

This one form of booze caused more trouble than any other kind of alcohol known in the fleet. It caused slugfests, it caused puke fests, and it caused severe hangovers. Most of the crew stayed away from it until someone else called for a shot contest. Wild Turkey was tough enough, but Absinth 58 separated the true garbage gut from the true novice.

Reveille that morning was a riot as I watched half the division struggle to heave out, and Trice up. It had been one hell of a liberty party and the snipes looked like they got the losing end of it. Breakfast on the messdecks was in full swing with the snipes table hardly manned. As soon as I had finished with chow, I arrived on the fantail just as quarters were sounded over the 1MC. With the crew filing through the passageway from the messdecks, some of the more daring snipes decided that it was time to play pin the tail on the donkey, or Ensign Benson as it turned out. The tail consisted of a piece of two foot long red Christmas ribbon that one of the snipes had left over from a package that had been tipped with a thin copper wire in the form of a hook. As everyone passed the messdecks on their way to the flight deck, one of them deftly hooked the tail on the rear belt loop of Ensign Benson. As Ensign Benson made his way down the flight deck to the fantail, the rest of the crew assembled on the port, and starboard of the ship could not but notice how funny the young Ensign looked with his red tail fluttering in his slipstream. Mr. Benson had been forced to wear his blued ear for three days because of Cox's phone trick, and so was hip to that one.

No one would tell him of his new tail, even the other officers because they too were once a boot ensign. Kept within reasonable bounds of course, they too got a kick out of the skill, and daring it took some half-sober snipe to attach it. Chief Craddick, Smitty, and the Wolfman just grinned as the Ensign made his way down to the fantail to address Bravo division.

As he stood in front of the snipes with the three of them, he tried to sound as serious as he could. "We're missing a shit can from Bravo division berthing," he began. "I don't know why anyone would take it, but I want it back. It's Government property, so if it's not back by 1600, liberty for the entire division will be secured," he said.

Ensign Benson then gave Chief Craddick the P.O.D. or "Plan of the day," as it was known, and Pruitt gave the Ensign that day's fuel and water report so he could take it to the Chief Engineer. "Thanks Chief. Thanks Pruitt," he said before making the understatement of the day:

"I don't care where you find another shit can, but if you use your imaginations, there's no telling what you guys can come up with."

With that said and done, Ensign Benson wheeled and began walking up the flight deck with his red tail slip streaming behind him. There must have been a good two hundred ships company assembled port and starboard as he walked the Gauntlet with as much dignity, and Military bearing as he could muster. He got that feeling as one does when all eyes seem to be on you for whatever reason, and he figured that it was because he was new on board that everyone was gawking at him with those goofy looks:

"Remember your bearing, to hell with em," he thought. Ensign Benson proved to be the most dignified, squared away, example of Military bearing that ever wore a red tail, however unknowingly. The idea was to see how long he would go before he discovered the tail. Since no one had seen me dispose of the can, I said nothing even though I would not have been blamed for getting rid of the stench-filled contents, although I did feel responsible for locating another one so the snipes could have liberty. Since all the cans on board were marked with that division's name, it was not as if I could just grab one from another division. I would have to search for one on base. Both engine rooms were scheduled to have all their gages calibrated on shore at the base calibration shop, so I volunteered along with Lutz to take them over so I could scout out another shit can on base. Lutz figured that we could also squeeze in a "nooner," a reference to grabbing a couple of draft beers at the enlisted club located in front of the Calibration shop. We dropped off the two boxes of gauges, and then headed for the club checking out the rear of the kitchen where there were several trashcans with various degrees of food scraps. We decided to grab a beer first, and then empty one of the cans, and spray paint "B-DIV" on the side before returning to the pier.

"So that's what the paint was for," said Lutz, referring to the can I had in my coveralls. I decided to level with Lutz about dumping the can out the side port, and how I now felt responsible for securing another one before liberty call. The glasses of beer were drained, and the new trash can purloined, and spray-painted. Everyone was down in the engine room when I replaced the new can in the berthing area so I did not have any explanations to worry about inventing. The Ensign was informed of its reappearance and everything was fine.

Lutz and I spent the rest of the day collecting steam gauges in the boxes for the trip to the calibration shop, while the Japanese yard workers were stripping the flight deck, and preparing it for resurfacing by grinding off the old surface in a hellacious racket that vibrated the entire well deck all day long. At liberty call, I met up with Pruitt, and Landon for our scheduled liquor refueling operation at Stuckey's apartment. The first had gone so well that we were now going to bring four cases aboard instead of the previous two, only this time we would space out the cases four, or five cans at a time during the two weeks in port so as not to arouse any suspicions from the Quarterdeck O.O.D. After pulling out some money from our bank account at the disbursing office, we headed up to the quarterdeck. After surveying the ships in port, we could see the MIDWAY was not among them, so we would have Stuckey's place to ourselves. We stopped off at the meat aisle of the base commissary while purchasing the cans of HI-C to select some steaks to grill while the liquor refueling took place. At the package store, Pruitt loaded up on his favorite cigars having run out of them at sea on the way to Numazu Bay. When we had everything together, we hailed a cab and proceeded to Stuckey's apartment. The key was under the same rock as before, and we let ourselves in.

The night went as it had before as we transferred $200 worth of vodka into the HI-C cans, cooked steaks, and played cards. The next night would be another $200 of booze, this time it would be Gin instead. The third night came, and went as the other two had with steaks on the outside grill, smoking cigars, and drinking Scotch. The cans were marked as before, and brought on board a few at a time, and stashed down in the oil lab. Cox managed to cross cue sticks with Mr. Kihara one more time and lost his ass on a game of Snooker at his favorite Snooker club in Yokohama, further up the coast. Mr. Kihara took Cox out with a score of 147-63. The big guy refused to stake Cox anymore unless they played nine-ball, so they agreed to another match at Dance-yo-ass-off before the ship got underway.

The first week in February would find the *Juneau* steaming across the Equator for Jakarta, Indonesia, where Pollywogs such as me, and many others would undergo the Shellbacking initiation. The Shellbacking rites also included a traditional beauty contest where each division had to supply a beauty queen complete in drag. The only way to affect the drag was to beg, buy, or steal the items from local hookers, or L.B.F.M.s.

Calvin Pruitt, the owner of the oil lab bar and grill, had volunteered to be Bravo divisions beauty queen. His thinking was that each Shellback got one good swat on each Pollywog that passed before him on the flight deck. One of the Flips in the personnel office informed him that the *Juneau* presently had among it's salts, 258 Shellbacks from the last Wes Pac of 74'. That meant that each Pollywog would receive 258 swats on the ass by the end of the day. The Beauty queens however, were exempt. Pruitt's problem was finding women's clothing among the locals big enough to fit his portly frame.

"If I need to buy it, then I need to buy it, but I ain't getting whooped like the rest of y'all," he would say. The last time the *Juneau* had crossed the equator was when she had steamed to Australia, the stories of Aussie hospitality were legendary in the fleet, and many of the crew longed to return. The problem with Jakarta was that of the entire crew, only a handful had ever been there before. The Wolfman was one of them, and had this to say:

"Every planet has an asshole, and Jakarta is the asshole of planet Earth," he said. "That bad, aye Wolfie?" someone would ask.

"It's the real third world, guys. Sad sack city, you'll thank God you were born in the states," he added. "Jakarta's rough on the eyes, but it's good for you. Make you think about how lucky you are to be an American. You guys gotta be extra careful in this port because they have sexual cooties floating around the likes of which modern medicine hasn't seen yet. If you don't rubber it up, your gonna be riding the Silver Cadillac up in Sick Bay," he warned.

The Silver Cadillac was a long stainless steel plunger type of instrument with a probe that was inserted down the full length of the penis to the very base. It was equipped with an umbrella type tip once at its destination, which enabled the doctor to scrape the walls of the member upon extraction in order to obtain the V.D. sample. It was the best way to determine what kind of Clap some unlucky sailor had received. It was a much-feared procedure, and made most of the crew think twice, and always carry condoms.

The Wolfman's description of the upcoming port visit to Jakarta paled in comparison to what we had been hearing about Australia, and its people. There was nothing to be done about it so it would be seen as just another port, and besides, it was only for five days. The Flight deck was nearing completion by the end of the second week, and Lutz, and I had returned all the gauges to the engine room, and reinstalled them. The Oil lab bar and grill was restocked, and general preparations made for getting underway. Pruitt had made a small spectacle of himself at the Base Exchange buying large gals garments, heels, wig, and all the necessary gear that would go with being a drag babe. Everyone kidded him about it, but he was adamant that he was not going to get 258 whacks on the ass.

Sea detail was called after quarters so Scratch donned headphones again, and reported the forward fire alley manned and ready as Deadeye aft, reported the same. Since the foc'sle was pointed towards the bay, there was no need to turn the ship around with a Flank, or Full back on the respective screws. We would simply steam out at one third ahead, coming to a stop at the mouth of the bay to let the harbor pilot off. When that was done, the ship came up to two thirds ahead through the shipping channel, and once cleared of it came up to ahead full plowing along at sixteen knots to Numazu bay where we arrived at noon, and set condition One Alpha, lowered the stern gate, and sent the L.C.U. 1629 towards the beach to pick up the Marines. Loading was complete by 1600 when the *Juneau* blew ballast, raised the stern gate along with the hook, and steamed off for White Beach. The two days at sea went by as usual with life revolving around watches, drills, and the three meals on the messdecks.

We entered Buckner Bay on the third day, and set sea detail that was as easy as before. We offloaded the Marines of Second division, fifth Marines, and embarked a Battalion landing team of First division, ninth Marines for what was known as a "patrol float" because that is what the *Juneau* was designed for. It made little sense to send the ship that far south without Marines because if anything happened in that part of the South China Sea, we would have to head a thousand miles north to Okinawa in order to re-embark them. It was going to be a crowded float for all involved not to mention all the Marine ass to be had on the flight deck on Shellback day. The Shellbacks of both Navy, and Marines, had begun to cut two-foot pieces of out dated fire hose, and tape one end to form a handle. They called these improvised ass beaters "Shillelaghs" and they would be used to whack the backsides of all us Pollywogs. When all the Marines, and their gear, along with the mountain of stores were aboard, the ship got underway fully fueled under sunny skies. Our Amphibious commitments had been met so now it was time to explore some of the more exotic ports in the Orient. After Jakarta, we would hit Singapore, Thailand, Subic Bay, and then Hong Kong, before returning to White Beach and awaiting our relief.

We left White Beach on February 8, 1976 and the regular routine of watch standing, drills, and chow time fell into place. After three days, the temperature rose with the thick humidity of the tropics so much that Wild Bill allowed the after engine room to be secured, and the ship ran on one boiler so the snipes could stand four and sixteen watches instead of the regular four and eight. That meant that we would only have to stand one four-hour watch every sixteen hours because the engine room temperature had climbed to 130 degrees, and the blower rooms had soared to 150 degrees. All unnecessary work was called off and the hole snipes spent most of their time up on the 04 level with blankets spread out, and shorts on, sunning themselves under a sun they seldom saw. On that third day, we received an escort in the form of a pod of Bottlenose Dolphins that were having a great time playing just ahead of our bow wave. At least we thought they were Flipper until one of the Bosun's mates informed us that it was not so:

"There not Flipper. Flipper's all grey colored, these are common dolphins. Look at the black backs on them," he pointed out.

"Flipper's a Tursiop's Truncatus," he added rather smugly. "These black backed ones are Delphinus Delphis. One's we had off Okinawa first day out were Spotted Dolphins. Stenella Attenuata. Flipper is much bigger than these guys."

"Thanks for the education Monsieur Cousteau," said Scratch.

"Anytime snipes, say tell me, just how hot is it down there anyway?" he asked.

"140 in the hole anywhere you go," someone replied.

"How can you guys take that kind of heat day after day," the Bosun asked.

"We are a different species," Scratch answered. "Hole Snipest, the Greaseus."

"That's a good one, now one more question for the record," he said.

"Which is?" someone asked.

"Which one of you guys keeps blowing safeties all over my nice clean Captains gig? There were about ten hole snipes sunning themselves on the 04 level, and I was one of them." There was a short silence, and just as I was about to render an apology, Scratch said from behind sunglasses, "I did, sorry about that. Hate to interrupt you when you're counting dolphins, I know how hard it is to fill Cousteau's shoes," Scratch said.

There was a general murmur of laughter from the snipes because they knew Scratch was tiring of this self-appointed know it all. "What's that supposed to mean, Scribeci?" he asked.

"It means that I don't care about your boat deck, or your dolphins," Scratch replied, still sunning himself. "Engineering has a lot more to worry about than Deck does, my friend. To you it's nothing more that tying up the lines on the pier, or dropping the hook at Numazu. With us, a runaway feed pump, boiler flareback, fuel oil flash fire, or one of half a dozen other things that can go wrong can result in thirty chairs not getting filled at chow time," he said.

"We do our best, but with all things considered, we really don't care if you get distracted from watching dolphins to clean off the Captain's gig."

"You didn't blow safeties Scribeci, You're a Topwatch," said the man knowingly. "That's right, I didn't, My Burnerman did, but I'm Topwatch so it's my fault, understand!" Scratch removed his sunglasses, and rose to the sitting position visibly annoyed by now with the cheeky Bosun's mate.

"Unless you would like to continue this conversation on the boat deck I suggest that you drop it," he said. "Hey, don't get excited Scribeci," the man said.

"Quit your bitching and go back to your dolphins, we've earned our rest now let us have it," Scratch said while glaring at the Bosun's mate.

"OK Fine then, fuck you too," said the man as he walked off to the signal shack while Scratch put his sunglasses on, and reclined back on the blanket.

"That guy is the Case of deck division," he said. "Just won't let things go."

"Thanks Scratch, I owe you one," I said to him.

"Forget about it boot, you take your ass chewing from us, not deck. They don't understand what's going on down there." Scratch replied.

The rest of the afternoon was spent sunning, playing cards, smoking cigarettes, and writing letters to the folks back home. The dolphins kept up their game ahead of the ship's bow wave, and an occasional flying fish would leap from the path of the ship and cruise airborne for about thirty yards before re-entering the table flat Pacific. It was times like this that made being at sea so peaceful in contrast to the screaming engine rooms, and I even envied the deck department being able to spend so much time topside. On our way down from the 04 level, we noticed the Airdales that were Shellbacks were sewing together a thirty-foot section of canvas into a tunnel like configuration, and after every meal were packing all the leftover chow from the shit cans on the messdecks in front of the scullery. The rotting food would heat up in the broiling sun for a week before we crossed the equator, and all of us Pollywogs would be forced to crawl through the fetid mess as part of the Shellbacking rites.

The farther south we steamed the hotter it got until the Engine room handrails got so hot that they were uncomfortable to the touch. Deadeye, ever the inventor, came up with a solution. Since the burner front handrails leading to the fire alley were conviently close to the emergency feed pump, and were hollow, Deadeye rigged a length of rubber hose to one of the ends that he hack sawed flush. The other end of the hose he attached to one end of the low pressure drains that helped to prime the emergency feed pump that was kept gently reciprocating up, and down on standby in case it was needed to feed the boiler should a low water casualty occur. Deadeye cracked open the condensate valve, and the pressure from the pump filled the hollow handrail on that side.

Another length of hose went from that rail under the deck plates, and attached with duct tape to the other handrail where the pressure from the pump acted like a booster to make the condensate climb up the other rail. The top curl of the handrail was hack sawed flush at the end of the curl, and a third length of hose went from it down to the bilge. The condensate was warm, but still cooler than the otherwise hollow aluminum rails. It was just the right temperature not to make the handrails sweat. Wild Bill got a big kick out of the idea the next time he visited the forward fire alley:

"If that don't beat all. Cooling water to the handrails! You guys are the most improvising hole snipes I've ever met," he exclaimed.

These were the sort of things the snipes would dream up after spending so much time at sea. They got to know the four corners of the engine room top to bottom. It was what Danshaw meant when he said your ear could be calibrated to the vibrations of the engine room machinery after so many hours in the hole. As the ship steamed southward, the general mood of the *Juneau* was a contrast of excitement on the part of the Shellbacks, and apprehension on the part of the Pollywogs.

The dolphins were there every day and the sea remained calm. The incoming temperature through the scoop injection valve read out at 82 degrees F. Surface temperature. of the ocean, as the *Juneau* approached the Equator, and the night fall quickly enveloped the dusk as the Navigation department fixed our position at roughly eightly miles north of Zero latitude, somewhere equal with Singapore. At one second after midnight on February 16, 1976 those Pollywogs on watch from the Bridge, to the fire alley, officer, and enlisted alike, were forced to strip, and redress inside out, along with putting their shoes on opposite feet in order to make them walk like a duck.

SHELLBACKING
LONGITUDE 107-50- OE

When reveille sounded at 0600, the ship became absolute bedlam as Shellbacks dressed in all kinds of outlandish costumes rousted all the Pollywogs, and began hog-tying them into Stokes stretchers, and hauling them up to the messdecks for trial before Wild Bill and his council of Trusty Shellbacks. We were brought up on a variety of charges including being among other things:

CHARGE= Wasting water
VERDICT= Salt water bath

CHARGE= A squeaking wheel
VERDICT= Greased in armpits

CHARGE= Excess hair
VERDICT= Head shaved

CHARGE= Insulting to look at
VERDICT= Stockade pillory

CHARGE= Insulting Neptune's baby
VERDICT= Must kiss baby's belly

CHARGE= Skylarking
VERDICT= Visit royal doctor

CHARGE= A liberty hound
VERDICT= Liberty secured

CHARGE= A chow hound
VERDICT= Pollywog breakfast

The engine room received an all stop, and the ship came to a halt while the Bosun's mates lowered the motor whaleboat to go get King Neptune, and Davey Jones, his Royal scribe, who was in fact a Shellback from the personnel office to record the event in their personnel folders. King Neptune was the status granted to the Shellback who had crossed the Equator ahead of all the others. In this case, it was the ship's Master Chief Petty Officer of the Command, M.C.P.O.O.C. Who had crossed on his first year in the Navy back in 1951. They entered the motor whaleboat by way of one of the side ports, and were motored around to the starboard side of the ship where they ascended a Jacobs's ladder to the Quarterdeck. The 1mc announced his arrival with, "NEPTUNE, ARRIVING."

King Neptune would then ask Wild Bill, "Do you have a warrant to enter my domain?"

"Yes Neptune, but we are in possession of unworthy Pollywogs," replied the C.O. "They have been tried, and found guilty; we are ready to carry out punishment on your command."

"Very well Trusty Shellback. Hoist the colors," ordered Neptune.

Wild Bill then gave the order to fly the Jolly Roger underneath old Glory popping in the breeze above the halyard. Once the Skull and cross bones were aloft, King Neptune gave the order, "Let the sentences be carried out, and may the punishment fit the crime."

With 258 Shellbacks forming a gauntlet from the quarterdeck, and snaking around the flight deck, Wild Bill gave the order, "Bring em out, it's show time Wogs!"

At that moment large speakers mounted by the Boat, and Anchor crane began to boom out Glenn Miller's "In the Mood" as Pollywogs began their hands and knees procession through the gauntlet. The flattened fire hose shillieghs began to make spanking sounds against the salt water soaked rumps of all the Navy, and Marine Pollywogs. Many of us had thought to wrap rags around our knees under our inside out and backwards dungaree trousers.

We had received our Pollywog breakfast of gooey pancakes, and jelly, and then had our heads shaved by the Royal Doctor, boot camp style. Now we had 258 licks, and a few other trials to go through before becoming worthy enough to dare enter the realm of KING NEPTUNUS REX, RULER OF THE RAGEING MAIN.

Having been found guilty of being a squeaking wheel, we were greased in our armpits, and on our newly shaven heads. Then because we were now insulting to look at, we were placed into the pillory, and had our head, and face flushed with salt water. After that it was on to kiss the baby's belly in the form of the biggest, blackest, marine on board the *Juneau* that was a Shellback. A belly now covered with grease, Peanut butter, egg yolk, and yet more grease. After that, it was on to the royal doctor for a spoon full of Tabasco sauce, and then getting whacked all the way to the garbage chute filled with rotting food that was allowed to putrefy in the equatorial heat. For thirty yards, we crawled through the disgusting mess in the dark before emerging out the other end like a Turd from a colon.

It was then time to get flushed free of all the slime by being immersed into a makeshift canvas pool to remove as much slime as possible. When all the Navy and Marine Pollywogs had been through the Shellback gauntlet by noontime, we got the privilege of cleaning the flight deck free of debris in order to be ship shape for the Beauty contest that was to be held in front of the hanger bay after evening chow. Meanwhile Hot Dog Pruitt was down in the oil lab having some vodka, and some second thoughts about being all dragged up the way he was, much to everyone's amusement.

THE BEAUTY CONTEST

Pruitt was a hoot to look at with everything on except his black wig. He looked like a dolled up Honky Tonk Angel, a real bar hog, as he threw back his forth shot of vodka. Landon and I had cleaned up and changed into clean dungarees and white t-shirts, as was the uniform of the day for new Shellbacks as we joined him in the oil lab for a cup of vodka of which there was only two cans left due to the Wolfman's having arranged so many sales for us. Half the lifers on board were sure to be half in the bag by the time the show started. The Beauty contest promised to be a riot, and Pruitt had promised himself to be three sheets to the wind when he paraded before the judges, and the 600 cheering Sailors, and Marines of the *Juneau*. "How ya'll feel after all that?" Pruitt asked.

"I got a sore ass, and a red neck from the sun," I offered, "How you feeling?"

"I'm gonna hang my shingle out in a minute or two, "I'm throwing a party for the girls before we go topside, so you can kiss the vodka goodbye," he said. Just then, the Wolfman's gravelly voice was heard over the ship's 1mc, on the quarterdeck where he stood all decked out in pirate gear. "All Beauty Queens lay the oil lab." Pruitt produced a roll of Dixie cups, lined them up along the stainless steel counter top, and began topping them off with vodka. When he had filled about ten or so, he asked me to remove his shingle from the rear of the oil lab door, and place it on the passage way side. To our amusement, it was not the original sign he had made up when he first took over the oil lab. He had made up a new one just for this occasion and it read:

THE DRAGSTRIP LOUNGE PRESENTS
PETER PAN AND THE TANALIZING TINKER BELLS,
ONE SHOW ONLY   NO PASSES
H.D. PRUITT, PROPRIETOR.

Pruitt was sure into the swing of things with his wild sense of humor, and the way he was pouring vodka into his expected guests Dixie cups ensured they too, would soon lose their butterflies and put on a great show for the crew.

"Ya'll gonna have to leave now. This party is for Dragsters only," he said. "It's a cross dressing thing, ya'll wouldn't understand."

"OK Pruitt, thanks for the booze. We will be howling for ya at the show," I said.

One by one, the division Beauty Queens began to lay the oil lab for Pruitt's party as those men not on watch began to converge on the flight deck around the judges tables set up in front of the hanger bay where there were five judges with Wild Bill, and King Neptune among them. The party in the Drag strip Lounge was going strong, and the Beauty Queens were throwing back the vodka, and laughing at each other's get up. Pruitt looked ever so matronly while the Tooth fairy and a black kid from CIC were hands down favorites for the foxy face award. Most of the guys were just plain ugly with hairy legs, and five o'clock shadows mixed with water filled condom breasts. Pruitt kept the vodka flowing until the 1mc. Called for them to lay the flight deck, as the sun was low on the starboard side of the ship. The sea was smooth as glass, and the underside of the clouds were pinkish as the Tantalizing Tinker bells filed out of the oil lab and up to the port catwalk feeling the glow of the vodka, and the loony ness of the occasion as a roar went up from the men assembled on the flight deck as they climbed a short ladder to the flight deck, and made their way to the hanger bay.

"Atta girl, Hot Dog!" Cheered the hole snipes as other divisions cheered their beauty queens as well. The 40s Glenn Miller music that had been coming from the speakers before, now was changed to Burlesque strip music as the drag queens lined up to start their walk in front of the messdecks tables of judges. When the first beauty queen began his walk, his division would send up a cheer in support because that was how the winner would be decided overall. The thing was ,though, Dental only had four men plus the doctor so there could hardly be a challenge for the sixty some odd men from Deck, or Engineering, or the Air department, but then the American sense of fair play took over when the Tooth fairy began his high heels stroll before the judges tables.

He was very convincing, and everyone admitted that he looked damn good in heels not to mention being able to walk in them as well. He received a boisterous display of applause from the crew, and high marks from the judges. Engineering roared their guts out as Hot Dog Pruitt waddled his act in front of the judges' tables, and Deck gave their man an equal roar when his time came. By the time the Black kid from CIC was up, it was clear to see that the Tooth fairy had some real competition in the way the sarong-clad kid shimmied in front of the judge's tables. He was quite convincing, and the crew howled with laughter at the antics as the judges awarded the Black kid first place prize. All the other Beauty Queens took it well enough as they were completely embarrassed, and half lit from all the vodka that was now kicking in. The Tooth fairy took runner up, and Pruitt took third due to all the hole snipes yelling themselves hoarse when he waddled

About. King Neptune then called an end to the day's proceedings as the sun began to sink below the fiery horizon, and Wild Bill ordered the Jolly Roger flag hauled down from under Old Glory. So ended the *Juneau's* Shellback ceremony, a day before we made Jakarta, Indonesia. The Shellbacks kept their fire hose Shillelagh's in their stand up lockers until the next Wes-Pac line crossing, but the Beauty Queens stripped off their drag stuff, and chucked them over the side of the ship leaving them with their swim trunks on. Deadeye's watch was ordered to light-off #2 boiler at midnight so the ship would have both boilers for sea detail at 0700. Our easy 4 and 16 watch standing was coming to an end, and we would have to keep one boiler lit-off in every port to supply hotel services for the crew until we hit Subic Bay in another month or so. We had been nine days at sea since leaving Okinawa and other than the equatorial heat, the sea had been perfect for the entire track.

JAKARTA, INDONESIA

The after boiler was brought on line at 0400 and both engine rooms manned and ready when sea detail was called at 0700. The tropical air coming in through the ventilation ducts smelled worse than Pusan, Korea. The harbor was thick with tropical sewage due to all the canals the Dutch had designed more that two centuries ago, you name it, and the canal systems of Jakarta had it. All the diseases known to man lurked there and it gave the city a very high infant mortality rate. The fire alley was a broiler as sweat just poured out of you if you moved away from a vent even for a few seconds, and even under one, there was still certain clamminess to the skin. The ship came to an all stop in order to take on the harbor pilot so he could guide Wild Bill through the sewage of Jakarta bay. It was an easy sea detail this time around, and neither Lutz, nor myself had any problems. After bottom blowing the now secured boiler, I went top side to check out the new port from the 04 level.

It was almost 11a.m. and the sun was blazing away over the steaming city of Jakarta. The air was so heavy, and wet that it felt as if I could take my Buck knife, cut out a square piece of it, and wring the moisture out of it like a saturated sponge. Pruitt, and the rest of the snipes were refueling the ship, and a working party was forming up on the Quarterdeck in order to replenish all the chow the crew and the Marines had consumed.

The C.O. had some Indonesian moneychangers on board so the crew could change dollars into Ruphia, the local currency, and addressed the crew about keeping an eye out while in Jakarta by using the buddy system while ashore. After that, I had the duty section on the midwatch with Deadeye, and his crew so I used that time in between to write letters to the folks back home. The weather in the North Country this time of year would dip to 10 degrees below zero at night, and the locals would be fishing through the ice of Lake Champlain hooking mostly White, and Yellow Perch, gouging out an eye to re-bait the hook, and then sending it through the hole to hook yet another.

My brothers and their friends would have their ice shanties out between Crab, and Valcour islands with all their gear for the afternoon consisting of a skillet, gas stove, cooking oil, cornmeal, and a generous supply of Genesee cream ale. That frozen winter landscape was a world away from the steaming tropics of Indonesia. The midwatch passed hot and uneventfully enough with the Wolfman telling stories about the last time he was in Jakarta, and how he was sure that the social conditions could only have gotten worse. He warned us about giving spare change to any of the smaller children in view of the bigger ones because they tended to pounce on the smaller ones and take it away from them. "They all have it tough enough as it is, "You'll just get the little ones hurt," he advised. "You hand out money anywhere in the world and you'll draw a crowd. You're gonna see human misery on a scale you have never known before, and it's gonna shock you wise."

"This entire island is roughly the size of California, and it's got 130 million people on it," he said. "Think what 130 million people would do to California. It's an authoritarian state run by the military. No elections, at least none that are fair. No bill of rights, no social security, no economy for the expanding population, and a million mouths a year to have to keep pace with," he said.

"Place almost went Commie in 65' last time I was here," he continued.

"Johnson backed the military and bailed em out, and a quarter million people got whacked in the process. Waste of money though because it's gonna happen again. There's just too much suffering to have stability. You guys remember what the Old Man said about drinking the water because it's for real. It'll put you in sick bay before you can piss it out," he said.

The Wolfman painted a less than rosy picture of our new found port that night on the midwatch, and to further the point about personal responsibility, Sick Bay set up a table on the quarterdeck complete with condoms, and just so everyone got the message, the Corpsman had the Silver Cadillac displayed alongside the condom box with a sign that read: WHICH WILL IT BE?

The next day at noon when liberty call was announced, Pruitt, Landon, Lutz, and Myself, donned tropical whites, changed dollars into Ruphia, and headed for the quarterdeck. The O.O.D. told us to help ourselves at the condom box, and we grabbed two apiece while looking at the wicked looking "Silver Cadillac" with its long probe, and reverse plunger. It had an effect on anyone who had contemplating whoring around.

We had planned on getting a cab to the American embassy and asking the Marine guard where the good places were, if at all. The problem of language, and communication arose because the grinning, nodding cab driver assumed that we wanted to be around other Americans, and so he dropped us off about a block from where the *Juneau* crowd was drinking. He also let us out in front of a crowd of about twelve or so people that quickly accosted us for change, and wanted us to buy clove cigarettes. We were getting wise to this sort of thing because the cab driver had done it on purpose. He was probably related to some of the street urchins that now surrounded us begging, and tapping our pockets as a child with no legs below the knee sat on a wooden cart that he propelled by wooden blocks in each hand.

There was one guy that was missing his nose, and you could see into the cavity of his head. This was what Wolfie had warned us about as one of them reached up and tried to swipe my hat off my head most likely to try to sell it back to me. "Uncover guys," ordered Pruitt, as we removed our hats with one hand, and used the other hand to push our way through the sad bunch to get to the end of the block. It was a crowded street, and people were just staring at four Americans in dazzling white uniforms amid a sea of brown street urchins as we pushed our way to the entrance of the place where we had not really wanted to go. Once inside the air-conditioned building we met up with some *Juneau* sailors that were chatting up some Dutch women tourists, who at first glance did not seem too interested in wanting to know them. There was an international mixture of people that included a heavyset Aussie who seemed to be feeling the effects of too many glasses of Lager. He was a big red-faced man, with large tattooed forearms, and sat at a table all alone. He had one big fist wrapped around a fresh glass of beer, and there was an empty glass in the middle of the table turned upside down. What that upside down glass meant was that the person that had set it that way was proclaiming that he could whip anyone in the place. If no one took the challenge then the big Aussie could feel superior to all the other men. Anytime someone wanted to challenge him, they had only to approach the table, and right the glass.

"Be wise to ignore ol' red," advised Pruitt. "Looks like a hard case,"

The red-faced Aussie had a good-natured grin on his face as he nodded in our direction. "Ow ya doin, Yank?" he asked Lutz.

"Fine, said Lutz. "And yourself?"

"Little bored at present, definite lack of sportin blood 'round 'ere," he replied with a smile that revealed a missing tooth. He was fully aware of the meaning of his upturned glass. "Could gather dust in a place like this," he said referring to the glass. From the size of the man, it was easy too see why no one wanted to play tag with him. He kept up a conversation with us in a friendly tone and manner, and it seemed like the glass was just an option in lieu of conversation as if to say, "Talking's fine with me, but if you want to trade shots, then that's OK"

The place had a large pool area out back where some hole snipes had brought swim trunks, and were lounging around the pool drinking Fosters Lager from large plastic cups, and soaking up the sun. Renting swim trunks seemed like the thing to do at the moment in order to rinse off some of the humidity, and to distance ourselves from the big Aussie that seemed like he could be trouble.

"Think Hensen could whip 'ol Heavy Duty?" I asked.

"Don't know, but he'd probably try anyway," said Lutz.

"Yeah well, I'm glad he's not here because we'd have to get involved," replied Pruitt. "This ain't a place to go to jail."

The pool was refreshing, and it was not long before we started doing racing laps for Fosters Lager for the winners. I proved to be the swiftest swimmer, and so got my fill of free beer until Pruitt switched the game to belly flops that I of course could not match due to his girth. Just when he thought he could not be topped, and was enjoying his first payback Lager, the pool erupted with a huge splash that sent water spraying everywhere while the waves broached over the sides of the pool.

"Who the hell was that?" exclaimed Pruitt. Just then, the big red-faced of the Aussie rose above the surface of the pool with a Lager-laden grin. He then lifted the empty glass and poured out the chlorine water, swam over to the diving board and placed it up side down on the end of the board.

"By Crackey, I thing I've found me some sportin blood.

Whadda say Yank?"

"OK Big'un, you're on for a Fosters," replied Pruitt. The Aussie hauled himself from the pool to reveal that he had thought to bring swim trunks before jumping in. After removing the glass, Pruitt mounted the board, took a few steps and jumped as hard as he could on the end to propel himself as far as possible into the air. And came down with arms, and legs spread eagle into a belly flop. Pruitt made a good-sized geyser, his best yet we thought, and came up for air.

"To the boozer ya go Yank, fetch me that Fosters," said the giant as he mounted the board. With that, the Aussie came down so hard on the end of the board that it seemed to almost touch the surface of the water as it bent under his weight before throwing him not so much up, as out from it. Because of his size, he seemed to hang in mid air as if in slow motion before coming down in what was surely the winning belly flop. The sound of flesh contacting water made a giant cupping sound as the man splashed down followed by a KER-WHUMP, as a torrent of chlorine water erupted into a geyser.

There was no way Pruitt was going to match the Aussie. He took it well enough when he turned toward us and said with his characteristic smile. "Ya'll need anything while I'm there?"

We all raised our cups for a refill as the giant hauled himself out of the pool, and came over to fill one of the poolside chairs while straining it considerably as he settled in. Pruitt returned with a bar tray of plastic cups of Lager, and set it down in the middle of the table as we helped ourselves. "Name's Gibson, from Queensland," he said.

"Names Pruitt, South-by-god-Carolina," he replied as the two shook hands. Pruitt then introduced the rest of us as we shook hands until it came to Lutz, who gripped the Aussie hard enough for him to pause for a second, and look him in the eye. "Fine grip you got there short stop," said the giant. "Care to twist the wrist for a Fosters mate?"

Lutz calmly gazed back at him as the Aussie's forearm muscles tensed while he and Billy Burners had a little hand squeeze contest.

"High school wrestler, right?" he asked.

"And gymnast in my spare time," answered Lutz without ever breaking his gaze. This we all knew from watching Lutz work out on the main steam valve while the ship was in a cold iron status at Yokosuka for the two weeks' upkeep. The steam line was drained at the time so Lutz would practice opening, and closing the valve without benefit of the step stool mounted on the deck plates just below it. He would go through the revolutions one hand at a time with his whole stiffened, compact body in the air pulling the valve wheel hand, over hand until fully opened, then closing it in the same way. It gave him incredible hand strength as well as complete control of his body.

Bobby Burners was the only guy in the division who could do one-armed pull-ups and one-armed push-ups better than most people could do with two.

"For a Fosters then aye' Yank?" he asked Lutz. Billy Burners looked around at the rest of us before upping the bet.

"Win, or lose, it's four either way," replied Lutz.

"Deal it is by crackey. That's the sportin blood!" said he giant.

The Aussie figured Lutz was strong, but not so strong that someone his size would have much of a battle with the compact Lutz who was at least 150lbs. his junior. He figured wrong. Lutz took a wad of paper napkins from under the ashtray that was used to keep them from blowing away, and used them to cushion his elbow. They locked thumbs, and then grasped palms tightly as their forearm muscles tensed as they gauged each other's eyes. Pruitt placed his palm atop their enjoined hands, and asked if they were ready. As soon as they nodded, Pruitt removed his hand as Lutz swung his legs out tight together, and then straight up in the air while leaning back from the table. He lifted his compact frame off the chair, and was supported only by his napkin-padded elbow that acted like a ball and socket, while giving him tremendous leverage, not to mention complete surprise to his startled opponent. The more the Aussie strained, the more Lutz simply moved his legs away from the table and grinned at his opponent as if it were all a walk in the park.

It took superb abdominal control on his part, not to mention one hell of a grip as he swung his still together legs out another six inches thereby increasing his advantage as the other man began to shake with exertion. What this achieved was for Lutz to use all 150lbs. of his compact frame behind a vise like grip earned from one-handed workouts on the main steam valve, as leverage against only the upper body of the 300lb. Aussie. Slowly the Aussies arm began its downward path to the table with Lutz grinning like a fool until the back of the Aussies hand touched the table. Lutz then resumed his former posture and they separated their grip. "That'll be four Fosters mate," said Lutz.

"Right you are Yank, four Fosters, coming up. By crackey that's the blood. Yank, from now on yer money's no good. You got me tricky, but you got me. You're a strong little bastard, short stop, so be it," he laughed.

The Aussie got up to fetch five more beers as the waiter was busy at another table, and couldn't keep up with the speed of all of us at our table. We congratulated Billy Burners on his physical prowess, and guts the way he conned the giant into a game he had no chance of winning. "E're ya go Yanks," said Gibson on his return to the table with another tray of beer. He drained his in one long swallow, set it down, and then announced, "Can't lose at belly floppin. Can't win at wrist twistin. I'm off to the cemetery to raise the dead." He patted his crotch, meaning that he was headed to the place where many of Jakarta's prostitutes lived and plied their trade.

It was located alongside an actual cemetery lined with corrugated roofed hovels where whores and their extended families eked out a borderline existence in this most miserable of cities.

Lutz perked up on mention of the place, and decided we should all go and see the place we had all heard of now that the sun was setting. "Can't hurt to check it out guys." He said. We all agreed that since there was not much else to do now, that we would let Gibson be our guide for the trip to the cemetery whorehouse of Jakarta. After we had changed back into our dress whites and assembled out front, we noticed three "bet jacks" that is, pedi-cabs, alongside the curb. They were rickshaws powered by a bicycle attached to the rear. The skinny, undernourished owners motioned for our business while Gibson went back inside for a moment. When he re-emerged, he was carrying the round serving tray from the poolside table.

"With him pulling me, it's a heart attack in this heat, and this little seat's goin straight up me arse," he announced. He then placed the serving tray rim downward as his large frame straddled the bike. His enormous rump then crumpled the tray around the seat as the pedi-cab owners howled at the sight of it. "Hop on Dusky," he said to the owner. The skinny man climbed into the seat while the four of us sat two apiece in the other two pedi-cabs.

"Off we go!" said Gibson as we started down the street. Gibson was a sight as he pedaled the pedi-cab driver, laughing with the other two, at the sound of the misshapen tray crumpling as he swayed back and forth, with each revolution of the rusty sprocket. "Beat's 'avin it stuck up me arse I'll say," he grinned. After awhile the pedi-cab drivers pulling the four of us began to tire trying to keep up with Gibson who then signaled for us to halt, and suggested that Lutz, and Landon, pedal instead.

"Those whores will be grandmothers by the time these two get there," he said. Once Lutz, and Landon were seated and ready, Gibson challenged them to a race.

"No standing up though cause me arse protection might fall off."

There was no automobile traffic on the side street he led us as Lutz, and Landon strained to keep up with the laughing giant. The pedi-cab drivers figured they could not beat this particular fare because they were being paid NOT to haul the big Caucasians to the whorehouse at the cemetery's edge. It was dark now that Lutz, and Landon, had conceded the race to Gibson, and they returned to a normal pace so as not to receive a perspiration bath from the humidity. Upon pulling up to the darkened row of hovels that bordered the cemetery, we found ourselves surrounded by about twenty or so of the resident whores who quickly solicited us for business. "Don't hog all the pretty ones," said Gibson. "That is, if you can find any," he added.

That much was true, I thought as I got a closer look when they ushered us to a dimly lit room that served as the whorehouse bar. They were the sorriest lot of hookers I had seen thus far. Gone was the tawny brown of the Filipinas, and their smooth light-boned frame. Gone too was the size and beauty of the Korean women of Pusan along with the composure of their Japanese cousins at Yokosuka. To the big blue-eyed Miss Americas of the U.S.O. show at White Beach, they stood as polar opposites as they lined up around us in a desperate bid for our money. They ran in age from a little older than me, to a lot older than me. Their eyes were not as slanted as those of Korea, or Japan but more almond appearing with some of the whites of those eyes appearing yellowish due to vitamin deficiencies. They were extremely dark owing to what I figured was Malay blood in their veins. Overall, they were a sad sight to behold, and we were turned off at the prospect of using our sick bay issued condoms. Pruitt looked at Lutz, and Gibson, and shook his head back, and forth:

"Ya'll the ones that wanted to come here, so have at it. We'll spend our money at the bar," he said. "Belly up snipes, Hot Dawg's buying."

We were forced to remain to ensure Lutz's safety against robbery. As far as the big Aussie went, we could not fathom anyone going up against this roadblock on two feet, besides, we were becoming somewhat fond of this good time Charlie. His robust outlook on life appealed to the adventurous strain of our fleet sailor way of thinking. He picked two from the crowd in the room as Lutz put one hand over his eyes, and in a pin, the tail on the Donkey pantomime chose one for himself.

"Cover the nozzle on that burner barrel Lutz. That's a direct order sailor," Pruitt said.

As they both disappeared down the hallway, we sat at the make shift bar, and listened to a box radio playing Suzie Quatro while we were served warm beer with a chunk of ice in it. The beer tasted lousy as warm as it was, and we only had one because we were afraid that the ice was made of contaminated local water. Lutz, and Gibson re-emerged soon enough and Billy Burners had a somewhat pale look on his face. "Next time I'll look before I leap."

Gibson, on the other hand, seemed quite contented as he strolled over to the bar. "OK Yanks, ready to roll?" he asked.

We paid for our beer and left a decent tip to placate the house since Pruitt, Landon, and myself could not bring ourselves to partake in any of the sordid business this place had to offer. Once outside we made the pedi-cab drivers earn their fare this time around by hauling us back to the shipyard gate where the ships were moored. We bid goodbye to Gibson, who was a third mate on a scrap iron Merchant ship out of Darwin. Just as we were about to enter the shipyard gates a young woman of about twenty or so emerged from the shadows and begged us to let her blow us for two dollars apiece.

We all declined even as she persisted, saying, "Two dolla, two dolla," her hand holding up two fingers to get the price across. I felt sorry for her appearance so I fished a five-dollar bill from my pocket, and gave it to her. She was somewhat puzzled that I did not require her to perform for it, so I just told her to go home and eat something else for a change. Jakarta's sad spectacle of human misery was beginning to get to me as I turned away from the poor woman who would no doubt remain outside the ship-yard gates as more prospective clients arrived by pedi-cab to re-turn to whatever ship was in port. The Wolfman's description about Jakarta being hard on the eyes was right on the money, it was also hard on the heartstrings to see so much misery every-where on he streets.

"Forget it, boy," Pruitt advised "That Mr. Lincoln you gave her will feed her for three days. You did her a favor."

"Yeah, I guess so," I replied.

We made the brow of the *Juneau*, and rolled the dice on the quarterdeck card table with Lutz being the only one having to be searched. The inside of the ship never looked so good com-pared to the city of misery we'd just left, and it was like coming back to a little piece of America where you could drink from the scuttlebutt all you wanted, and not have to worry about intes-tinal problems. Something that simple made all the difference in the world.

I decided to remain on board ship for the rest of our stay in Jakarta in order to spare myself from having to deal with the local wretches. There was not much to do down in the engine room outside of scrubbing deck plates, and when that was done, everyone except the cold Iron watch retired to the air-condi-tioned berthing compartment. In the evenings, I would go top-side to the 04 level and look at the city of Jakarta, and count the many blessings I had as an American. I had duty section on the last day in Jakarta, and then stood burnerman for sea detail up forward while Lutz stood burners aft on Deadeyes watch. The ship was two days at sea bound for Singapore for a five-day visit, and according to Scratch, the toughest sea detail in the Ori-ent.

"It all depends on how well Wild Bill conns the ship," he said. "Up to three hundred ships have been known to anchor off the island at any given time. And since we are mooring pier side, we have to thread this ship through the lot of them. Counted forty six bells last Wes-Pac. Half of them Full backs, and Flanks too. Singapore's a real workout boot," he said. "It'll be a real test to see if you got what it takes to be a burnerman."

"It's a great city Singapore, not like that mud puddle we just left," he continued. "No Dysentery, no begging, no litter, no crime. It'll be worth scrubbing those safeties."

There was a full moon that night when I had been relieved and went topside for some fresh air, and serenity. The sea was flat and the only breeze came from the sixteen knot speed of the ship as the *Juneau* steamed north back across the Equator. The moon lit up the whole ship once my eyes adjusted to the difference, and made for a peaceful scene indeed, as I gazed out from the 04 level across the boat deck towards the fantail where I could clearly see the port, and starboard watches with their sound powered headphones on. There were ten, or twelve other sailors along the catwalks also enjoying the beautiful evening. The *Juneau* was in a condition known as –darken ship- so there could be no cigarette smoking topside even though the visibility was a good six miles, with eight miles being about the maximum on any clear day at a height of fifty feet where the 04 level was. My thoughts drifted off to all the novels I'd read by Joseph Conrad. *Lord Jim, The Secret Sharer*, etc. Set in these very waters on moonlit nights such as this. The adventure of the Orient mixed with the mystery, and the danger. How things must have been in the days when Conrad himself was a mate on the *Otay*, bound for the same city we were now steaming to. The long voyages from Europe with nothing but sun and sea for the senses, only to have those senses overwhelmed by the smells of Hibiscus, and Bougainvillea, wafting out to the ship when approaching Sumatra, and the Molucca straits.

The Singapore of 1976 would be very different from the dangerous backwater of Sir Stamford Raffles day with its exotic diseases, and pirates. As humid as the equatorial night was, it was still thirty degrees cooler than the Engine rooms that stood around 130 degrees F. God help the hole snipes should a boiler casualty cause the ship to go "Hot Dark Quiet." Without ventilation, the engine rooms would become unbearable if they did not get power back within fifteen minutes and the snipes risked dropping like flies on the Engine room deck plates. There was no alternative because they would not be allowed to leave until power was restored, and the ship was underway again.

After about forty minutes topside, I made my way down to the cool of the berthing compartment and undressed, tying my socks in a half hitch around the belt loops of my dungaree trousers as the rest of the crew did so as to be sure of getting them back from the ship's laundry. They were the only article of clothing not stenciled with a mans name, and division. When you ran out of belt loops, then you tied the rest in a half hitch around one of the socks themselves. It was the only way to get your socks back at sea. After a shower, I changed the linen on my rack and climbed in to it. We would arrive at Singapore the next afternoon, and I would get my supreme test as a burner-man. I felt more confident now than I had that first time at White Beach when I had, had that absurd dream of the Phantom, and the subsequent lifting of safeties all over the Captains gig.

Cox was sure to be on throttles so I would have to "step lively," as Scratch put it, and I looked forward to the challenge. I was feeling salty. Reveille sounded at 0600, and it was "heave out, and trice up," as was the saying, so I made my way to the messdecks for breakfast. After greetings to Boogie, and Toungie, who were working the serving line, I sat down next to Pruitt, and Lutz, and dug in to the pancakes and eggs before Pruitt asked us if we had heard the news about Deck division.

"Seems that some ol' boys in second division didn't take care of Sir Richard, so now they're leaking green, and howling when they pee," he said. "Story has it that they all wanted the same whore, so they pulled a train on her," he explained.

"How many guys?" asked Lutz.

"Four of em, and not a bag between the four. She gave it, and now they got it. Wild Bill had their division officer put them on report for, Damaging Government Property."

"Yeah they're gonna ride on that disciplinary freeway courtesy of the Silver Cadillac," he smiled.

"Thanks for grossing out breakfast, Pruitt," said Lutz, as he and I pushed away from the table and deposited our metal trays at the scullery after dumping our pancakes, and eggs into the shit can to clear the tray of excess chow.

"Son of a bitch did that on purpose," said Lutz as he headed down to the after engine room. I arrived in the forward fire room to assume the watch in time for the other burnerman to grab some chow before quarters was called.

"Stay away from Pruitt unless you're starving," I warned.

"Why's that?" he asked.

"He's telling gross out stories about some guys from deck, you'll see," I said.

In the meantime, Fred the pumpman came over to the burner front to shoot the breeze with me about how Case was once again going around to the guys in deck division and putting a bug in their ears about the forward stack being named "old faithfull" because of the safeties lifting at Subic Bay, and then because of Cox, at Yokosuka.

"He left out the part about Cox. He's putting all the blame on you. The Bosun's Mates don't understand the relationship between Throttleman and Burnerman," Fred began. "Case knows that, and he's using that to make you very unpopular up in the Foc'sle these days. As I'm sure you know by now that all that steam blowing out the vent pipe is acidic because of the chemicals that Pruitt adds to the boiler. The sulfite we use as an oxygen scavenger in feed water is the main culprit, and it can eat anything it comes into contact with. It eats holes in the tarp that covers the Old Mans Gig if they don't get it off in time. Plays hell on the paint job they do too," he added. "If you don't come to terms with Case soon, then deck will think that every time the damn safeties blow, then it was you again."

"What do you suggest?" I asked.

"Confront him the next time he starts in about it," Fred replied.

"What if he tells me to stick it?" I asked.

"Call him out to the Boat Deck, and settle it there."

"The Boat Deck? "Him and me?"

"It's either him, or twenty five Deck Apes. Some of those guys are ugly," he said. "By the way did you hear about those four..."

"Yeah, yeah, I heard it from Pruitt at chow," I replied.

"OK. Then you know what I mean," Fred said. "Singapore's the toughest sea detail on Wes-Pac.   Think what he's going to say if you blow safeties again," he said. "I don't see you as having much of a choice, Boot, there's no law that says you have to whip him. But you do have to defend your good name. You'll deal with Case only once. Twenty-five Deck Apes is another story, now isn't it?" he asked. "Look, I have to get back on pumps, Think about it."

Fred went back to his feed pump station when he noticed Scratch move his head in that way that communicated exactly what he meant. The Shaft Revolution Gauge indicated that the *Juneau's* speed was sixteen knots as I contemplated the thought of slugging it out with Case on the Boat Deck, at the next smoker at White Beach before we crossed the Pacific back to the states. Fred was right; I could not go around with half of Deck division cussing my name for the rest of the deployment, and Case was the kind of guy that would laugh in a mans face if asked for a favor. I had remembered asking him what time it was once, and he said. "Time for you to buy a watch, Boot."

The man would not even give you the time of day! After getting relieved for noon chow, I went up to the oil lab to find Pruitt and Landon discussing the four unlucky men from Deck Division who were now standing outside Sick Bay. Before I could explain my Case problem, the ship's 1mc. blared forth with Aretha Franklin's "Pink Cadillac" through out the ship. It was an obvious reference to the guys up in Sick Bay about to under go the discomfort of the Silver Cadillac, and they also knew that it was Wild Bill's sense of humor that caused it to be played, something that would never be allowed to happen over the 1mc., the ship's official channel. "Those poor Dummies won't be able to walk for a week," said Pruitt. "What with all that penicillin being pumped into their ass,"

"They'd be better off drawing straws with the loser having to supply the sample," said Landon.

"It's not up to them, it's up to the ship's doctor," replied Pruitt. "He's well within his rights to order all four to go for the ride. Besides, that sign on the Quarterdeck in Jakarta was enough warning, they gambled and lost, time to pay up."

Aretha's voice soon trailed off, and the 1mc. was silent as I explained what Fred had told me on watch.

"I got it all worked out, Tim," said Landon, much to my surprise, along with Pruitt. "You're going into training right after sea detail on how to control your wind," he said.

"How's that?" I asked.

"Going to learn how to breath through your nose, not your mouth, that's how boxers train because in the ring if you have a loose jaw, it ain't long before it gets busted," he explained. "I also want you to round up some bubble gum from the ship's Gedunk store, and start chewing it."

"Bubble gum? Why?" I asked.

"Strengthen those jaw muscles," he said. "The X.O. won't set up another smoker until we get ready to cross the pond back to the states, got about a month and a half to train," he said. "The beauty of all this is that while your running around the flight deck, or the well deck, chewing your cud with your mouth shut, Fat Boy won't have a clue as to what's about to happen when we hit White Beach. By then you'll be in shape diaphragm-wise, you'll have a month and a half of training for a three-minute event. Read me?"

"You're allowing him to think he's strong so that he'll stay complacent."

"Fat, Dumb, and Happy, is more like it."

"Fred's right, Tim. You don't have a choice, but now you have a plan," he said. "Damn good one too, boy," added Pruitt.

SINGAPORE

It was settled; first there could not be anymore lifting of safeties on my part. Subic was bad, Yokosuka was worse; Singapore was going to give three chances easy to blow boiler safeties. Lutz had burners aft under Deadeye, with Wolfman on throttles, and Ensign Benson under his instruction. The young Shave tail was proving to be a quick study, and Wolfie felt confident that he would be ready to handle a sea detail on his own in a short time.

Aft was in good hands. Scribeci was Topwatch forward with me as his Burnerman, and Messenger. Cox was on Throttles under Chief Craddick, and Smitty, while Fred was on pumps, and Danshaw was Checkman. Scratch came over and told me to open the root valves on the burner manifold. "Singapore's tricky, we're gonna bang this port," he said as I began opening the fuel oil root valves on the manifold.

Scratch was not taking any chances of me being too slow opening the valve wheels, so we were going to "bang" the burners just like we did at Yokosuka. The movements were correct, but it was my speed that needed polishing. I did not yet possess the fluid muscle memory of some of the other burnermen, and Singapore would be Wes-Pac's most demanding sea detail. It was the burnerman's ultimate trial by fire maneuvering in close quarters. Those Screws must speed up, or slow down when called for so the Throttleman and Burnerman must work like hand, and glove. Cox knew about Case making trouble for me, and had promised Scratch that he would not horse around with the steam in such a difficult port.

Scribeci requested permission to cross- connect main feed so both firerooms feed pumps could feed either boiler in the event of low water. Pruitt had nothing else to do until we moored so he volunteered to stand smokewatch for the way in. The ship slowed to one third as Pruitt kept the Throttlemen of both engine rooms aware of the ship traffic: "This place must be having a Tramp Steamer clearance sale," he drawled as he saw all the Merchant ships anchored out waiting their turn to either load, or unload, as their business called for. There were ships of every description from oil tankers, to ore carriers, rubber, steel, furniture, scrap iron, you name it, and it all passed through Singapore. Some were freshly painted, while others dripped rust, each one with its own character, and its own story of the sea. Ships manned by a hundred different nationalities with a hundred stories to be told.

The air coming down the ventilation ducts had changed from the pure ocean air to an earthly fragrance that so far did not carry the sent of open sewage the way Jakarta, or Pusan, or Subic did. "Cleanest city in the Orient," Scratch had promised. The bells started coming down as each Throttleman, and Burnerman began their routine, and the tension began to mount as I banged burner, after burner, that was coming with more frequency now. The forced draft blowers, with their up and down aircraft engine whine sounded like a plane that could not make up its mind whether to take off or not. The vibration of the main reduction gears that were located behind the fire alley gage board, rumbled right along on a full back, or Flank bell.

After an hour, the ship came to a halt in order to pick up the Harbor pilot. We ten received a one third ahead at that time as the Harbor pilot pointed the bridge watch through the screen of Merchant ships, and into the inner channel. The pilot was used to guide the ship to our berth, although the Captain had overall responsibility for the safety of the ship, and could take over at anytime if the situation called for it. After another half hour, just such a situation occurred when an Indian Freighter on our port side lost control of her rudder, and her stern began to swing out towards our bow. This was a common occurrence with single screwed ships because at slow speed, the screw blade below the shaft got more of a bite in the denser water than the blade at the top of the revolution, and it tended to push the stern sideways. This motion is kept in check by the ship's rudder, which in the case of the Indian freighter, had failed.

Luckily, the *Juneau* was at an all stop while gliding at four knots when the freighter's Claxon sounded in a long blast indicating that she was now out of control. The *Juneau's* own claxon sounded the alarm of possible collision as Wild Bill sized up the situation. If the ships were allowed to collide, the freighter's stern would hit the *Juneau's* bow, and do no more harm than crush the peak tank. The freighter would most assuredly take the worst of the encounter. The stern of the ship was swinging out at us at four knots as the bridge sent down the emergency full back bell. We had already heard the Claxon alarm, and knew that whatever was coming at us was headed towards our Foc'sle. If the *Juneau* had more room to maneuver then Wild Bill would have ordered full back on the port screw forcing the bow toward the backing screw and out of the way of the freighter's stern. He did not have that choice now, and every second counted when he ordered both screws all back emergency full. Most full back bells are sent with a sense of urgency attached, however, an emergency double full back is sent with a "Hail Mary" attached. A full double back was something I had yet to experience, and the noise was incredible. All five burners on both boilers were banged in and the blowers screamed at eight thousand rpms, as they raced to catch up with the now heavy black smoke pouring out of both stacks. The *Juneau* then shuddered as her screws bit deep, and began to move her in reverse in the narrow channel.

"Pruitt! "What's going on?" yelled Scratch into his headphones.

"Ass end of a tramp headed our way," Pruitt replied. "The tramps coming sideways,"   "We gonna hit?" asked Scratch wide eyed.

"Negative, were outta there, but I'd get ready for an all stop soon," he said.

Once we were clear of danger the bridge sent down an all stop, and soon after a one third ahead, to slow our reverse course as the bridge crew breathed a sigh of relief. "Secure from collision alarm," announced the 1mc. It had been close indeed. If the *Juneau* had been at one third ahead when the Tramp's stern began it's journey into our path then there would have been no way to avert a collision, such was the narrowness at this point in the inner shipping channel. The stern of the tramp swung around so now the ship was facing the other way. The tramp's captain ordered both bow, and stern anchor's set to keep it on the side of the channel until a harbor tug could get to her.

We stayed at one third ahead for another twenty minutes when Pruitt called down to the two Fire alleys that we were closing the pier.

"You done good this far boot, don't blow it now," Scratch said. "Ten more minutes and you get a five-day break before you do it all over again." He grinned.

Ten more minutes was no cause to relax because pierside was the trickiest time of all when maneuvering a ship. The bells came down from the Bridge, and the throttledeck passed them to Lutz and me on burners. Bell, after Bell was answered until the 1mc. announced the condition Lutz, and I longed to hear: "Moored, Now secure the special sea, and anchor detail."

Scratch gave me the thumbs up, and Fred slapped me on the

back for a job well done. It had been a sea detail to remember as I sucked down a cup of cold water from the D.A. tank. The regular watch soon took over, and it was with an immense sense of satisfaction that I climbed up the engineroom ladder that day dripping with sweat. I had met the most difficult sea detail in the Orient, along with a near collision, and had passed with flying colors.

Another dash of Salt had been added to my shipboard education. The ship's 1mc. Announced that the Smoking Lamp was secured while refueling, and to muster a non-rated working party on the starboard quarterdeck. Non-rated personnel, that is, those who were not yet third class petty officers were usually called upon to man working parties for foodstuffs when in port. Those of us in Bravo division were exempt during refueling to sound tanks and such. Those who were not needed could be found hiding down in one of the shaft alleys in order to escape the chore with the reasoning being that the hole snipes sweated all day long, and could not justify being further used as pack animals by the Messcooks division.

I headed up to the oil lab to see where Pruitt wanted me during the evolution, and he said I would be down on the pier to keep an eye on the overflow vent. He put Fred in charge of the hose crew that pulled the refueling hose from the pier up to the fuel oil flange, and bolted it on. The hose was quite heavy, and clumsy, so it took all of four men to bring it up. "The rest of ya'll find a shaft alley," he smiled. About ten snipes headed down to the port shaft alley to play cards, and wait out the conclusion of the working party as I took my headphones and headed to the starboard refueling station to screw into the 2JZ circuit, and then headed to the pier.

Once on station I called in to Pruitt at D.C. central just as Fred's crew arrived at the flange with a fuel oil drip pan they placed under the flange. I could hear all the other phone talkers calling in to Pruitt to let him know that they were manned and ready to start sounding the fuel tanks, and I could see from the pier that the signal shack had run up the red bravo refueling flag. Fred's crew hauled up the hose, and bolted it on while one of the men called it in to Pruitt, who then called me on the pier to tell the civilian workers to commence pumping.

Once refueling started, there was not much to do except keep an eye on the overflow vent, and stand by to tell the pier workers to secure pumping if need be. I looked at Boogie on the quarterdeck where he was checking off all the stores being brought aboard by the 100-man working party. Just aft of the *Juneau* another ship was being nudged to the pier. It was a good-sized freighter with a single screw, and a white superstructure that needed paint, what caught my eye though, was the American flag flapping at the ship's stern. It had to be the first American flagged vessel I had seen in all the ports we had visited thus far. The ship was full of containers on its main deck as it bumped against the mooring donut, and half a dozen Asian crewmembers threw mooring lines to the workers on the pier. It was then that I saw the freighters name on the stern, *Mayaguez*. It could not be, but it was!

This was the ship taken by Cambodian forces in May 1975 in an act of high seas piracy that prompted President Ford to send in the Marines of 2nd battalion, 9th Marines out of Okinawa in order to retake the ship at a cost of 41 American lives. The Air Force helicopters from Utapo air base in Thailand that were carrying the Marines, ran into an unexpected torrent of fire while attempting to land on the narrow beach of Koh Tang island, destroying two of them laden with the Marines of 2/9. What had just been an attempted insertion became a hell for leather evacuation by the other Air Force helo pilots to get the Marines off the island before their utter destruction by the Khmer Rouge forces closing in.

My thoughts were interrupted by snipes calling in to Pruitt to say the tanks they were sounding were now topping off, as one tank after another, was secured. Pruitt called me to tell the pier workers to secure from pumping as Fred's crew unbolted the line and sent it back to the pier. As I saluted the O.O.D. upon arriving on the quarterdeck I thought about the *Mayaguez* moored aft of us. To allow this ship to moor next to an American Amphibious vessel that carried Marines, and sometimes Marines of 2/9, seemed strange. Why couldn't that Indian tramp in the inner shipping channel have been the *Mayaguez*, and why couldn't the *Juneau* have been doing two thirds ahead, instead of gliding at all stop the way she was when the tramps stern swung out at us? To think of the poetic justice of sinking her in such a freak accident would have been! What a story for the annals of Maritime history!

After turning in my headphones at the oil lab, Pruitt said that Landon had a plan for us to go over in the berthing compartment. When I arrived, those snipes not on duty section like myself, were changing into civilian clothes, and forming a hole snipe liberty party. They had decent food, cold beer, and clean women on their agenda with Wolfie, and Deadeye, arguing about the sequence of events. I saw Landon over by the Lifer Locker where the lifers bunked talking to Scratch who had an old leather belt that he was busy punching an extra hole in when Landon waved me over. Scratch nodded us both into the Lifer Locker, as the little alcove was known, and pulled the shower like canvas curtain closed behind us for privacy.

"Take your shirt off, boot," he said.

"I'm not getting flogged am I?" I asked.

"Maybe later," he grinned.

When I had complied, Scratch placed the belt around my upper chest and cinched it tight. It was not so tight to interfere with breathing, but it was tight all the same.

"What's this for?" I asked him.

"It's to make you control your wind when you exert yourself," he replied. "Let's go to the flight deck and try it out."

When we arrived on the flight deck they had me run laps around it, and I soon found myself straining against the belt. After five laps, I could hardly get enough air even though my mouth was wide open sucking in as much air as I could. When I came to a gasping stop in front of them, Scratch said, "Just what I thought he'd be doing. Boot, you're not letting the bad air out when you bring the good air in. You're sucking too much in and your holding your breath too long, even if you don't know it," he said. "Now I want you to take another lap, only this time with your mouth shut, breath through your nose," he said. "That way you won't hog oxygen that you're not doing anything with anyway."

Back around the flight deck I went, only this time a little slower as my nostrils flared with the intake of oxygen, and the expulsion of carbon dioxide. "Two more laps, boot," said Scratch as I made my second pass in front of him and Landon. Because of the restricted airflow, I was forced to breath in a rhythmic fashion, and soon came to understand that the best to learn was to be in a position to *have* to learn quickly. I came around on my last lap, and stopped in front of them fairly spent, and flushed as Scratch uncinched the belt, and I could feel the difference respiratory freedom. "Big difference wouldn't you say?" he asked. We hung out at the port side catwalk for a while as Scratch explained his reasoning to me.

"Remember the last smoker off Mindoro?" he asked. "There was that black guy from deck that kept making that hissing sound every time he threw a punch?"

"Yeah, I remember," I said.

"Well what he was doing was letting the bad air out through a clenched jaw so he didn't end up getting winded," he began. "It was plain to see that he had some training, he kept his jaw clenched tight in case he got tagged on it. That's why we had you run with your mouth closed. Good training for you. It's the same trouble swimmers get into trying to stay afloat, they tend to gulp air, and then hold it. Ever hear of the term "Drown proofing"? The SEAL teams go through it in BUDS training at Coronado. They bind their hands behind their backs, and also their ankles together. Into the pool they go over their heads, and since they can only kick for so long, they quickly figure out that it's easier to get one breath, and go to the bottom of the pool, let it out, and then push off with their feet to the surface where they just take an easy breath and sink back to the bottom and repeat the process.

"Once they learn to breath rhythmically they can do it all day long. All the weight lifting in the world won't help you in the ring against someone who knows how to breath proper. Control your breathing, and you'll control Case."

I returned to the compartment, showered, and climbed into my rack to read some now that the Liberty party was on the beach and it was quiet. After Scratch's watch was roused for the mid-watch at 2300, we headed to the messdecks for mid-rats chow, and then made our way to the after engine room. I began with taking readings, and inspecting the fire room as was customary when assuming the watch and learned that Danshaw had to act as Checkman with a Crows foot to keep the water in the boiler at a safe level due to a faulty Copes regulator feed water valve. That meant that Fred was now called upon to act as pumpman on the lower level because Danshaw was on the upper level at the feed water valve to manually control the feed water level with the Crows foot. Later in the four-hour watch, Fred cane over to the burnerfront to shoot the breeze about this, and that before we got around to Case.

"You know boot," he said, "a lot of people want to see you whip Case because of the way he's been trashing you up in Deck. He's planning to ship over once we hit San Diego, and Deadeye has been talking to Wolfie about greasing his ass the day we pull in," he said. "That's how much they don't like him. You'll have the whole division in your corner. Just keep a low profile till then."

Our relief arrived on station at 0400, and Scratches watch left the fire room and headed up to the head to shower, and grab a couple hours sleep before reveille at 0600. That was the trouble with the mid-watch because no sooner did you drift off to the deepest part of sleep than you were forced awake again at 0600, and it tended to make one irritable. Since my body was on a four hour go, I headed up to the 04 level and surveyed all the ships in the harbor with their decks all lit up in contrast to the *Juneau* with only her two topmast red lens. There was a balmy breeze coming off the sea as the first rays of dawn arrowed their way through the tropical morning.

After awhile I checked my pocket watch and found it was about ten minutes from reveille so I made my way to the mess-decks to be the first in line for a change. When I arrived at the galley, I found C.T. and three others outside the serving line doing everything they could to keep from laughing. C.T. put his forefinger up to his lips to signal silence, and I could see that they were listening to Boogie, and Toungie, having a somewhat hung over chat about Toungie coming off the beach three hours late.

"Three whole hours, big deal," he said. "Boy, you gone three mutha fuckin months."

"Aw man, you didn't even start them taters yet," boogie chided.

"Fuck dem tatoes," Toungie replied with a shrug. "Been slicing enough o' dem in mah sleep."

"What about the eggs Toungie," Boogie asked.

"Dat's nuther thing, easy over this, sunny side there, hard here, scrambled there, shit too!" he groused. "I'm wrecking dese chickens, Dey getting em' scrambled today."

"What about the snipes Toungie?" Boogie asked.

"Already thought bout' dat, Snipes gonna get the best damn scrambled eggs in the fleet," he said. "Deadeye mess wit my hot water again, and I'm gonna whip his snipe ass. Ain't takin dat shit no mo," he muttered softly.

"Aw c'mon Toungie, the Hawgs don't mean any harm, they just got tired of Roast Beef is all."

"It doesn't make me feel any better when the snipes call it JUNEAU STEAK either buddy," Boogie added.

"God loves you too Toungie. Remember that," he said.

"I don't care if it be Sunday or not," Toungie declared. "De big man getting scrambled eggs too!"

Back and forth they went with their hangovers doing most of the talking, and Toungie cracking egg after egg and depositing them into a large galley bucket until there was two feet worth of eggs closing on the rim of the container. Reveille sounded as Boogie waded through the potatoes slicing them up for home fries as Toungie covered the large galley griddle with butter, and picked up a large galvanized pitcher as Boogie laughed a warning. "Look alive Toungie, here come those hawgs."

"Yeah well watch dis," he replied. Toungie dipped his pitcher into the egg-filled vessel and tossed the yellow contents across the griddle as it made a popping, sizzling sound. He dipped his pitcher two more times until the griddle was covered with egg yolk.

Boogie could see that he was serious about not being in the mood to cook eggs to order on this particularly hung over morning. Boogie was busy on the other griddle pouring pancake batter as the sliced potatoes warmed up along side of it. Toungie then took a straight broom from the corner, and began swirling the twelve dozen or so eggs into one big yellow mass as the crew began moving along the serving line. Scrambled eggs were the order of the morning, and Toungie could care less whether they liked it or not. Because most sailors depended on someone else to serve them either food, or alcohol, there was a saying in the fleet that the two people you never messed with was a bartender, or a cook.

As breakfast progressed, several crewmembers at a time passed across the messdecks in civilian clothes fresh off the beach from a night of liberty, and stopped here and there to impress upon those who had duty last night about all the sights of Singapore. Each conversation was the comparison of Singapore, in relation to Jakarta, and how Singapore was cleaner, and more orderly, than Jakarta. Some praised the absence of whores, while some bemoaned it.

Overall Singapore was getting rave reviews from the liberty party so the duty section could not wait to hit the beach at 1630. When liberty call sounded, Pruitt, Landon, and myself headed to one of the places Pruitt had been the night before with the Hull Tech Chief from Repair division. Pruitt said the Chief wanted to talk to me about my immediate future or some such thing. The place was one of those places geared towards Merchant seaman being close to the harbor, and there were obvious sea going types here and there, as we entered, and made our way to the bar where we saw Chief Heller from the weld shop. The Chief had swapped with the former chief on *Juneau* because he wanted to stay on Wes-Pac that the ship was preparing to begin. He had come from the *Hepburn*, a fast Frigate of the Knox class that was now in the yards in Hunters Point, San Francisco. We all settled in at the bar and ordered Singapore Slings from the Chinese bartender who looked for the entire world like Peter Lorre, from the Humphry Bogart movies. The droopy eyes and slight build were just like Joel Cairo, in the Maltese Falcon as he made, and delivered one Sling after another until all three of us had one. Chief Heller wasted no time in reminding me that I was supposed to be a Hull Tech, not a Boiler Tech, and wanted to know if I wanted to strike for Repair division, and get out of the engineroom.

"We are short a man in Repair division boot," he began. "Scratch speaks well of you, says you catch on quick. Hear you flunked out at Treasure Island, why so?"

"Had a falling out with one of the instructors," I replied.

"Which one?" he asked.

"Guy named McIntosh," I said.

"That's what I thought," the Chief said. "Got some news on that one. Mac's been relieved from what I read from one of the guys at T.I. Seems that he had a nervous breakdown two months ago, he had been acting strange by shaving his head, growing a goatee, and even showed up at quarters one day with a fucking earring of all things," he said. "One day he didn't show up for class so they went looking for him, and the Shore Patrol found him walking down Avenue of the Palms, butt naked, and trolling a yo-yo."

"You're kidding!" I gasped.

"Wish I was, kid. At any rate, the C.O. of Treasure Island had him hospitalized, and all the current students' grades were reconsidered for a full review because he failed so many for minuscule reasons. I served with him for two years on the HEPBURN, and he was always writing people up for nickel and dime shit, even people from other divisions. Mean prick, you know?" he said.

It bought to mind the day of my Captains Mast when Smith, the Master at Arms said to me before we entered the room, "Busy bastard, isn't he?"

"Everyone had complaints about him, but the division officer, a guy named Blount, would never do anything about it for some inexplicable reason," he went on. "On my last Wes-Pac with HEPBURN, some of the guys kept seeing him and Blount on the beach together in almost every port, definite fraternization no-no. Very unprofessional on Blount's part. Anyway, the Old Man figured everything out, and scuttlebutt has it that he told Blount to either resign his commission, or take a duty station in Rota, Spain in order to break them up."

"Which one did he take?" I asked.

"Don't know, but he left the ship when we pulled into Pearl. Asshole shipped over when *Hepburn* went into the yards at Hunters Point, and got two years' shore duty at Treasure Island where you ran into him," he said.

"I swapped out with the other chief so I could go Wes-Pac again," he explained. "You know, it's amazing what one man can do to the morale of an entire division if his buddy keeps him from answering for his actions. Anyway, we were glad to see him leave because in all my time in the fleet, I never met a more mean, petty, flat out despicable son of a bitch in my entire life." Chief Heller pulled a cigarette from the pack, and lit it with his Zippo lighter as he continued the story.

"And I never met a more gutless Naval officer than LT. Blount, I hope he resigned, I really do, and I hope they discharge McIntosh too, I don't need people like them in my Navy. At any rate you could be up for a pardon, boot, Craddick speaks well of you, and Scratch gave me the thumbs up."

"I know that Bravo division is short a burnerman because of Hensen, and Scratch doesn't want to let you go, but he knows that it's not his call to make," he said. "So, do you want to strike for Repair division, and get out of the hole?" he asked.

"It's all kind of sudden, Chief," I said.

"That's how it always works boot," he replied.

I sat there somewhat stunned with the tantalizing offer to get out of the hole that I had been sent five months ago after reporting aboard as a non-rated fireman. Everything seemed to fall apart after I had tangled with McIntosh. The harassment, the grade deflation, the Captains Mast, and the shock of being grabbed on the quarterdeck that day by Chief Morgan, and sent down to hell, only to then witness the brawl in the compartment in such a brutal fashion.

I remembered my state of mind at my first morning quarters when I saw all the animals with their split lips and shiners. I thought about the day Fred had saved all our butts after the

feedpump had run away, and the pain he had endured in securing the root steam valve before it shook itself to pieces. I thought
about my lifting of safeties at Subic, and Yokosuka, and the time
I had passed out on top of the boiler. All the hard steaming, all
the hot, loud watches, All the tuning of my ear to the rhythm of
the fireroom machinery, the joy of a successful pump re-build,
and the sense of a job well done. I was a hole snipe, a burnerman.
Lutz and I were the two most important men on board when the
Indian Tramp came at us in the inner channel two days ago. My
first double full back, Hail Mary style! I was there and I was
square!

I looked at Pruitt and Landon, and remembered our slush
fund and the liquor-refueling trick, and all the good times we'd
had. I remembered the excitement of the boiler hot-rodding con-
spiracy against the *Fort Fisher* and the engineroom camaraderie
that it had bred. No other division had the espri de corps that
the snipes had during that evolution. The way the *Juneau* snipes
steamrolled over the *Brooke* sailors at football that day, and what
other White man than Wolfie had I ever heard speak fluent Tagalog in order to get Hensen out of a jam back in Olongapo. The
more I thought about the last four months with the snipes, the
more I became convinced that I could never cross rate out of the
hole. They had been tough on me to be sure, but they had also
been fair, and now that I had passed the big Singapore sea detail,
things could only get better for me as far as my status was concerned.

I saw Pruitt, and Landon, looking at me as I contemplated
Chief Heller's offer, and knew then and there what my answer
would be. "Thanks, but no thanks chief, I'm a hole snipe now,
it's where I belong," I said.

"Atta Boy Riley!" beamed Pruitt.

"Damn Right!" followed Landon. "A true Rebel to the cause!"

Pruitt crowed as he ordered up four more Singapore slings
from the bartender. Chief Heller was disappointed, but re-

spected my decision to remain with the snipes of the forward hole. "Loyalty is a good trait to have, says a lot about character in a man. You're a square, boot, good for you."

"Thanks Chief," I replied. Pruitt, and the Chief began a conversation about this and that as Landon and I retired to a nearby table to discuss business, and the upcoming port visit to Thailand. Our slush fund was going just fine, along with the liquor sales so we each had some money to burn by this time. We were starting to feel more like regular fleet sailors now instead of boots, although we were still referred to as such. That was the ship's custom for a new recruit until he had been successfully "Screwed Blued and Tattooed," as the snipes referred to the making of a Salt, so we still had a few months to go. Distorted ethics they may have been, but then life in the Amphibious Fleet was not even close to life in general.

Maybe that was what appealed to men like Wolfie, Smitty, and Deadeye, and the rest of the Lifer Corps that made up the backbone of the fleet. Being able to make up the rules as they went along, versus having a nameless, faceless, society do it for them with all its rules, and constraints, all it's ever changing dictates on how to behave.

Boiler Tech, First Class Wolfe, need only follow the fleet axiom of never mess with a bartender or a cook- along with rank protocol in order to get along. Even rank itself was subject to a back burner when it came to who was right, or wrong, as Scratch had proved on many an occasion. At sea, everything was pretty much cut, and dry when it came to your shipmate. If someone had a beef, they addressed the man directly. If they could not resolve it there, then they went to the Boat deck in front of the crew. It was not hard when I thought about it, to understand people like Wolfie, and the rest that had matured in such an environment to see why they could not be civilians, lightrally fearing the prospect of it.

I remembered the party for Chief Morgan back in Pusan,

when faced with shore duty exclaimed, "I hate civilians!"

It was not the people he hated, but rather the anonymity of their lives. When Lifers like him retired, they would no longer be in charge of 37 gung-ho snipes willing to give their all in a tough sea-lane. He would become just another tail light on the San Diego freeway. The Navy allowed men like him to rise to the top based only common sense, and guts. The two most indispensable traits for leadership that made men like them so much different from civilians. The *Juneau* snipes were like one big grubby gang, and that was what enamoured me to them. Soon after, Pruitt came over to the table, and announced, "Ya'all ready?"

"Ready for what?" said Landon.

"Ready for Hot Dawg to show you boys around Singapore, that's what," he replied.

"Beats sitting here all night," Landon said. "Good, first thing we do is get some great sweet and sour Pork, and see what our fortune cookie has in store for us," he said. We bid Chief Heller goodnight, and headed to one of the taxi cabs parked at the curb where the driver soon asked us where we wanted to go in halting English.

"Yin Yin, Yum, Yum," answered Pruitt as he rubbed his belly to indicate that we wanted to go to the Yin Yin, a restaurant near the business district for what Pruitt had promised us would be our best Chinese meal ever. On the way to the place, Pruitt asked the driver if he was familiar with Boogie Street. The cab driver smiled at the request as Pruitt made an OK sign with his left hand, and then poked in and out of it with the forefinger of his right hand. Even though Singapore was known as the Orient's cleanest and hooker free city to the average tourist, sailors knew that the quickest way to the action of any port came from the cabbies. They knew what sailors the world over wanted: food, women, and beer. Some wanted the gambling that so many Asians seemed hopelessly addicted to, while others wanted the local drug scene.

Penalties for all the above were severe in Singapore, but as usual wherever there was a demand for something, there was bound to be a supplier for it. Pruitt's priorities were Food, Pussy, and one of his favorite cigars afterwards. Boogie Street in Singapore was known to the Seventh fleet sailors as the place to be hooked up with all the things the government deemed illegal, or immoral. More discreet than Olongapo, and more upscale than the slums of Jakarta, but not as openly garish as the Yokosuka strip, this small street stood in open defiance of Singapore's big brother system of government, dominated at present by Malay Muslims, in contrast to the Chinese who ran the bustling business sector of the economy. The Chinese also tended to to run most of the illegal activities on Boogie Street.

Once the cab arrived at the restaurant, Pruitt peeled off a twenty-dollar bill, and asked the driver to hang around until we were finished in an hour or so. The Chinaman agreed, sensing a profitable evening from the three Americans. There were many well-dressed locals, along with a sprinkling of Caucasians, and their wives as we were ushered to a table next to the wall. We noticed Fosters Lager on the drink list and ordered up a round as we ordered the meal. During the meal Landon informed us that Cruz, one of the Filipinos from the after engineroom, had invited us to visit his family in San Felipe, about twenty miles north of Olongapo in order to see the real Philippines instead of just the Magsaysay strip. "There gonna roast a babui for us," he said. "It's a pig roast, and we just supply the San Miguel. He wants us to meet his family, and where he's from," he said.

"I'm in, I always wanted to see the other things besides the strip," I offered.

"Fair enough to me," Pruitt replied.

"Cruz says that he's going to take us foot fishing in one of the rice paddies, whatever that means," Landon said. "All his extended family will be there too, should be quite a party," he added.

"In that case we'll raid the base package store at Subic for some Scotch before we go," Pruitt said. "Might as well go armed, right?"

"To tell you the truth guys, Stewart's planning on doing just that," admitted Landon.

"How's that?" Pruitt asked. "It seems that he succeeded in bartering for that .45 from that C- Ration Marine he got everything else from," he said.

"You serious?" I asked, not really surprised as I remembered the sly grin Stewart had given me while honing the Ka-Bar knife that day.

"Yeah, it's a real beauty, fresh back from the arsenal, all rebuilt, and refinished," he said. "New barrel, bushing, main spring, brand new."

"Cruz says that San Felipe is N.P.A. country so Stewarts not taking any chances. He didn't transact this business while the Marines were aboard did he?" Pruitt asked, knowing full well that if the pistols disappearance could be traced to when the Marines were embarked, then there would be a general shipboard search for it, resulting in every rack, locker, compartment nook, and cranny, including the oil lab bar and grill, and its horde of liquor filled HI-C cans to come under scrutiny.

"He thought about that too," Landon explained. Stewart had the guy meet him at the enlisted club the night before we steamed for the equator. "It'll be reported missing from Camp Hansen, not the ship."

"Good move on his part," Pruitt said.

"What about the Grunt?" I asked.

"His last night on the Rock, he's stateside now."

After we finished the meal and returned to the taxi waiting at the curb, Pruitt lit up one of his favorite cigars, and the aroma of the Humidor filled the cab as the driver headed towards Boogie Street, and the illicit wares it offered. We were let out in front of a plain building with a sign next to the door that carried a logo for Tiger Beer that showed a Bengal Tiger parting the Elephant grass with one forepaw, and a snarl, flanked by palm trees. That must be the one that pisses in the vats at the brewery," drawled Pruitt. "Nasty stuff."

We went inside and sat at one of the tables as one of the bargirls that doubled as a waitress approached us. "Singapore slings, babe," Pruitt said as he held up three fingers. She returned with the three multi colored slings, and we noticed that there was a tad more gin than the ones we had had earlier with Chief Heller. It didn't surprise us because it happened in every port for at least the first two drinks. Magsaysay, Texas Street, Gate 2 Street, Yokosuka strip, and now Boogie Street. They were all the same hustle. We drank for a while as some of the bar girls eyed us every now and then, and chattered amongst themselves in whatever dialect they were speaking, when Pruitt strolled over to ask how a nice American boy like him could get a date. The girls just giggled and pointed at each other in a way that made Landon and I laugh at the sight of them trying to push their hooker duties off on one another. Pruitt wasn't a bad looking guy I suppose, but then we were used to looking at him every day, and had seen his easy humor and generosity on many an occasion. One of the girls pointed to the bartender as if to imply that he would make the call. Pruitt walked over to lean on the bar.

"What's the story ol' stick?" Pruitt asked.

"They afraid right now, is bad time for them now," he said.

"Why's that?" Pruitt asked. "One girl, she go upstairs with sailor man two days ago, no come down," he said in broken English.

"No see man no more, he gone too," he said. "I check the rooms, everything same, same.   Maybe she leave with sailor man, maybe not," he continued. "The girls afraid, you must understand."

"Hey ol' stick, I'm real sorry, that's a hell of a thing, Ol' Hot Dawg just wants to get his back cracked if you know what I mean," he said with a wink at the bartender.

"Maybe you talk to them, maybe they like you, maybe not, so solly," he shrugged.

"Don't mind if I try my luck do you Hop Sing?" Pruitt said, even though the bartender did not have the slightest clue about the cook from the T.V. series *Bonanza*. The bartender motioned with a "be my guest" swing of his arm, and resumed cleaning the glasses from the previous evening that were stacked near the sink as Pruitt made his way over to the table of women to try and loosen one of them up enough to take him on for a "short time" in one of the upstairs rooms. Landon and I joined him at the table with the girls, and bought another round of Singapore slings and some tea for the women.

Pruitt settled on the one he wanted after a few minutes, and began to butter her up with some southern charm when she asked his name soon afterwards.

"Y'all can call me Sweet Daddy tonight," he said. I shot Landon a glance….Sweet Daddy? I mouthed silently, half laughing at the same time. Pruitt was on a roll with his cigar, and his snake oil charm, and from the looks of it was putting the whores at ease. It was, after all, what they were in business for, and they were sure to have "short timed" rougher looking men than the portly Oil King with the easy smile, and happy go lucky demeanor.

"OK Sweet Daddy, we go short time?" she asked. "Now yer talkin, Sweetheart," said Pruitt as he rose to walk her upstairs to one of the rooms for his long awaited short time. "Y'all hold the fort," he said to us as the girl was squaring away things with the bartender. Pruitt went upstairs with the whore as we sat at the table and drank another Sling for about five minutes until we heard the screaming coming from Pruitt's room. It was a high-pitched woman's scream, followed by Pruitt's voice yelling, "Oh my Gawd! "Oh my Gawd! "Abandon ship! Abandon ship! We jumped from our chairs and ran to the upstairs hallway followed by the bartender holding a small bar billy in his right hand. He started to raise the billy at Pruitt, who he figured was somehow tearing up his merchandise when Pruitt's whore began pointing through the doorway with one hand, and covering her mouth with the other.

"Easy Hop Sing, it ain't me," Pruitt stated. The bartender lowered his hand with the Billy and looked to where the whore was pointing.

"What the hell's going on Pruitt?" I asked. "Look see for yourselves guys," he said.

Landon and I followed Hop Sing into the darkened room as Pruitt raised the window shade to allow the fading sunlight to light the room better. We noticed the mattress on the floor as he pointed to the box spring of the bed. Crammed into the fetal position in the box spring was the dead body of the missing whore the bartender had spoken to Pruitt about.

What had happened was that Pruitt wanted a back rub first, and so was lying on his stomach when felt something underneath that did not seem right so he figured that he would just put the mattress on the floor and go from there. Once his eyes had adjusted to the low light condition in the room he made out the outline of the body. It was not until touching it that he became shockingly aware of what was going on, and who she was.

"OK Fellas, trice up, we're pulling out," he said. We started down the hallway when the bartender attempted to stop us saying that we were witnesses to everything, and so must hang around and give a police report. Pruitt's portly countenance hardened considerably, and he told the bartender flat out:

"Now you look here Hop Sing, We don't owe you a thing, we got nuthin to do with this and you know it," he said sternly. "You raise the wood to me one more time, and we'll Turn Toputtin it up yer ass. We're leavin Stick, now move!" he ordered.

The authority in Pruitt's voice galvanized Landon, and me, as the bartender, and Pruitt held each other's gaze for a couple seconds. The bartender knew that we would follow Pruitt's order to steamroll right over him in our present state of nerves, and so wisely stepped aside and let us pass.

"Let's get some distance between him and us before the cops get here, guys."

"But we didn't do anything Pruitt," I reminded him as we jogged to a taxicab and jumped in.

"Sure we did," he replied out of breath. "We solicited a prostitute, that's a crime here, remember," he said. "How am I gonna explain why I was in that room? The courts here don't mess around when it comes to sailors testing their laws. They'll whip yer ass with a bamboo stick for something like this. Y'all might be toughened up after that Shellback whuppin, but Hot Dawg likes his rear end just the way it is, thank you very much."

"Where you go now? ssked the cab driver as we got underway.

"Waterfront," said Pruitt, meaning he wanted to go back to the Seaman's club where we had met Chief Heller. The reason he explained later was in case the police checked with the cabbie, the man could not say that he took us to a particular ship where they could then make a beeline to the *Juneau*.

"Y'all didn't do any talkin to those gals about being from the ship did you?" he asked.

"No," we replied.

"Good then, the trail's getting colder."

As soon as the cab pulled up to the waterfront club, we paid the driver and went inside the club. When the cab pulled away, we left and walked back to the ship. "That's enough of Singapore, guys," Pruitt announced. "Best to stay aboard till we get underway again."

Once aboard the ship I thought about the dead woman in the box spring, and it clouded my thoughts for a long time before drifting off to a fitful sleep. "Thanks for grossing out breakfast Pruitt," said Lutz as he and I pushed away from the messdecks table where Pruitt had just violated his own edict about saying anything to anyone.

"Son of a Bitch did that on purpose," Lutz muttered as he passed Deadeye and dumped his almost full tray of chow into the shit can in front of the scullery.

"Did what?" Deadeye asked.

"You'll hear," Lutz replied as he headed to the fantail to muster for morning quarters. The crew was soon called to quarters, and everyone fell in as the Wolfman read the ship's plan of the day in his Wolfman Jack voice. Ensign Benson had the same bloodshot eyes that morning as Wolfie, and Smitty, because they had surprised him on the beach when he was shopping for souvenirs. The pair had taken the young boot Ensign under their wing on the Throttledeck, and then on the beach in Singapore.

It was against Navy regulations to fraternize with enlisted men off duty, but the young Ensign had been overwhelmed by their hole snipe sprit. He tried to placate them by protesting that three's a crowd, only to have Smitty remind him, "Only in the sack Ensign. On the beach it's the Three Musketeers, now let's go," he said.

They braced him police-officer style under each arm and walked him around the corner to the bar they had just left. The young Ensign knew that it was rules bending time, and since they were alone figured what the hell. The two Salts treated him to a good time without any shipboard politics brought up, something he appreciated, and he learned that not only were they good boilermen, but were worldly in other ways as well. The officer to enlisted rule soon faded when Smitty began to wax morose about the friends he had lost aboard the U.S.S. *Frank E. Evans* [DD-754] in the early morning hours of June 3, 1969. The Sumner class Destroyer had been plane guarding for the Australian aircraft carrier, *Melbourne,* when she somehow crossed in front of the carrier, and was cut in half between the funnels. The forward half of the Destroyer sank within ten minutes, and took 74 of her crew with her, mostly hole snipes, and almost all of deck division as well. After a brief silence, the young Ensign spoke. "You were on the *Evans*?" he asked softly.

"Yeah, I was on the *Evans*," Smitty replied without looking at either man.

"I'll never get over that Claxton a few day's ago, it's only the second time I've ever heard it." He said. "Gave me quite a start. The last time I heard it was just before the *Melbourne* came through the *Evans*. I was a third class Topwatch in the after fireroom, and the forward hole had just finished blowing tubes on the forward boilers. We were awaiting permission to start blowing tubes on the after boilers, and I had just unchained the soot blower valves," he said to the young Ensign's now rapt attention. "All of a sudden we received an emergency double full back, and then she hit us on the port side, and cracked us in half. It's hard to explain the sound of tons of steel being crushed all at once, It's a sound you can only hear once in a lifetime. When she severed the main steam line the boilers lost pressure all at once in a sound you can't believe." He looked down at his drink.

"You lose a 600 pound plant through a ten inch line, and it sounds like a bomb went off. That's the last sound the forward hole snipes ever heard. The *Evans* rolled over on her starboard side, and the sea water started pouring in, and it's what saved us from getting burned more than we already were," he said.

"So that's where the burns came from?" the Ensign asked as he looked at the burns on Smitty's lower arms.

"That's where they came from," he replied. "Anyway, we got everyone out of the after hole, and up to the fantail securing all the hatches as we went. Everyone was in a state of shock, and either burned, or banged up in some way. The sea was table flat, and I noticed the *Melbourne* was stopped dead in the water with all her deck lights on," he added.

"The forward boilers had exploded and the surface of the water was covered with steam, and smoke and I'll never forget the smell of that Sulfite in the steam. Nasty Shit, that fucking sulfite. Most of the guys were standing around in their skivvies because they were sound asleep when we got nailed. Once we got a muster going after we'd been taken aboard *Melbourne*, we found that we had lost three brothers from the same family, the Sage brothers," said the Ensign.

"Yeah, the Sage brothers," Smitty replied as his eyes began to grow wet.

"Lemme show you something boot," Smitty said, ignoring the officer status of the young Ensign as he rolled up his right shirtsleeve to reveal a tattoo. It was of the forward section of the *Evans* at the bottom of the sea with a glowing cross in place of the topmast with the words "sailor's grave" emblazed in a half moon script over the cross along with the coordinates of the sinking, 08-59. 2N -110 -47.7E. "Notice anything out of place with the hull number?"

Ensign Benson looked at the hull number on the hull just behind the anchor, and it read 74. "Sumner class cans were numbered in threes," Smitty explained.

"That's the number of men that went down with her, all the surviving snipes got this tattoo when they towed the watertight half of the *Evans* back to Subic," he said. The young Ensign was feeling quite humble by now along with feeling quite tipsy the way the two lifers were pouring drinks down his throat, as Wolfie went into a less emotional subject before Smitty lost composure. "So all this stuff about bluing your ear, and pinning a tail on your ass doesn't mean anything personal unless you take it that way," Wolfie added in his gruff voice.

"By the way, how long did the tail last?" he asked the Ensign. A big smile came across Ensign Benson's face as he remembered the walk up the flight deck after quarters in Yokosuka, and he noticed everyone grinning at him.

"I wore that damn thing all the way to noon chow," he admitted. The three men looked at each other for a second before breaking into a fit of laughter as the alcohol laden Ensign came clean. "If Wild Bill hadn't asked me if my ass was bleeding, I'd never have looked," he said as the three of them roared on with Smitty slapping the Ensign on the back. The Ensign was beginning to understand that he was not really disliked by the snipes but rather if he was worthy of being division officer of a hard charging bunch. Ensign Benson had come a long way since his first foolish attempt to intimidate these ruffians three months ago at Yokosuka.

The next morning after quarters, I headed down to the forward hole and was told to empty the fire alley shit can on the pier. After hauling it seven decks to the quarterdeck where L.T.J.G. Schott had the 0800-noon watch, I dragged the can through the passageway. What I had not seen was whom he was speaking with until I turned back around to see five Singapore policemen in uniforms, along with the bartender from last night. To the policemen I was just another sailor going about my day, until the bartender focused his eyes on me with a glimmer of recognition. It quickly came to me that even with Pruitt's dodge; the police had put two, and two, together as to our American accents, and youthful looks described by the bartender.

Since the *Juneau* was the only American ship pierside, it was only a matter of time before they arrived. The bartender quickly raised his arm and pointed at me as one of the three as I started to turn away from the scene. Two of the policemen started to move toward me before L.T.J.G. Schott ordered them to halt, and a general argument ensued with Mr. Schott telling me to stand fast as well. The policemen were telling him that I was one of three material witnesses to the discovery of a dead body, and therefore must come with them. L.T.J.G. Schott was telling them that they were now aboard a U.S. Navy vessel, and were in no position to be giving any orders on his quarterdeck. All five policemen were armed with pistols, while the quarterdeck watch, a third class Bosun's mate, was armed with a .45 automatic. The situation became tense with the policemen insisting that they be allowed to take me into custody on the spot. The Bosun's mate stared hard at Mr. Schott not knowing what to expect while the officers mind raced to control the situation. There was no way he was going to surrender a member of the ships company without orders from the Captain, and at the same time couldn't order the Bosun's mate to Lock, and Load, for fear of being outgunned five to one. He would have to activate the ship's security code. L.T.J.G. Schott picked up the mike that served the ship's 1mc. System, and calmly spoke into it: Captain Petrowski, Lay the Quarterdeck."

"It'll only be a minute, Inspector," Schott smiled at him.

In fact, it was only slightly after a minute before we saw the first of ten flack jacketed, shotgun armed members of the *Juneau's* security alert team. There were two above the quarterdeck next to the Boat, and Anchor crane, and two came up from the troop spaces on the starboard catwalk, while two more appeared from the flight deck hangar. The rest came through the passageway off the messdecks.

"Fire team Lock and Load! It's not a drill!" Mr. Schott ordered.

All ten men promptly racked shells of 00 Buck, into the chambers of the model 37 Ithaca shotguns, and held them at port arms as the stunned Inspector, and his men just stood there knowing that any furtive movements on their part may very well make the security alert team a tad nervous. Just then, Captain Petrowski emerged through the passageway holding a .45auto, with the hammer in the cocked position.

"Attention on deck," called the Bosun's mate as those of us not on the security alert team came to attention.

"What's the skinny J.G.?" he asked Schott.

"Sir, these men want Fireman Riley, and two others as witnesses to the discovery of a dead body," Schott replied. "This man here claims that Riley was one of three Americans present when the body was found, and that they threatened to assault him if he tried to stop them from leaving," he said. "They were rather adamant about taking him, so I was forced to activate the security code."

"Good work Mr. Schott. Which one of these guys is in charge?" Petrowski asked.

Schott nodded to the Inspector as the Captain thumbed down the hammer of the .45, and handed it to the cool-headed O.O.D. "From now on Mr. Schott, The entire Quarterdeck watch will be armed until we hit White Beach," he said.

"Yes Sir, I'll make an entry of the order in the logbook," he replied.

Wild Bill approached the man Schott had nodded to, and looked down on him from a full head taller. "I would ask you who is in charge here but I think you already know, don't we?" Petrowski said in order to get it across once, and for all.

"Who are you?" he demanded.

"I am Inspector Yee, Chief Inspector for Singapore, these are my men," he said.

"Well I'm Captain William Petrowski," he said as he swung his arm around. "And these are my men!" he said with a slight chuckle knowing that the sound of ten shotguns being racked full of 00 Buck was still ringing in their ears. "Inspector Yee, This ship is United States soil as far as international law is concerned, and even if it wasn't you would still get a fight from me. If questioning one of my men is all you need to do, then you may question him in my presence, and at no other time while you are aboard this vessel," he said.

"Your men will surrender their weapons to Mr. Schott, or they will have to leave at once," Inspector Yee knew that this was check mate any other way, so he ordered his men back to the pier to wait it out.

"Your Weapon Inspector," the C.O. said.

Inspector Yee handed his pistol butt first to Mr. Schott who then removed the magazine, and put it in the quarterdeck lectern. "C.T., escort these men to my inport cabin, and Mr. Schott, have the Bravo division officer meet me there as well, Riley, you stick with me."

"Yes Sir," I replied.

L.T.J.G. Schott spoke into the 1mc. an order for Ensign Benson to report to the Captain.

"Bravo division engineering officer, your presence is requested at the Captain's inport cabin."

So *that* was how Mr. Schott activated the security code! Of course! Why hadn't I caught the otherwise blasphemous announcement the very second he said it? Fear I suppose, what with all the cops, and the bartender looking at me. To the Singaporeans, Mr. Schott's request over the ship's 1mc. For the Captain to "lay" the quarterdeck meant nothing, and they figured they were going to expedite their business. What that meant to the ship's fire team was that there was something amiss on the quarterdeck, and to respond in an armed fashion. If officers from the X.O. on down are needed anywhere aboard ship, then their presence is "requested" at that location. Enlisted men on the other hand are ordered to "lay" or report, it is not a choice.

The Captain is always sent a personal messenger through the chain of command. You do not summon a ship's Captain at any time, he does not report here, or report there. Anyone, officer, and enlisted alike, would know better than to order a superior office, much less a ship's Captain, to "lay the quarterdeck," as if he were a common seaman. That was the security code Mr. Schott spoke of when Petrowski asked him for the skinny when he arrived on the quarterdeck.

Upon re-entering the passageway with C.T. and the two Singaporeans, we noticed about ten other men holding a fully charged fire hose to act as backup in case the intruders got past the quarterdeck. A full blast from a one and a half inch salt-water hose was enough to knock a man flat, or rupture an eyeball if caught full in the face. "As you were, sailors," Petrowski said as we filed across the messdecks on our way to officers country.

When we arrived at the Captains cabin with C.T. still holding the Ithaca at port arms, the Captain asked me if I would rather speak with him privately first before answering any questions from Inspector Yee. Before I could respond, the Inspector asked the bartender something in Chinese. "What is it, Inspector?" Petrowski asked.

"Captain, I am looking to speak with one man in particular, the one who found the body," Yee replied as the bartender spoke up next. "We want to talk to "Sweet Daddy," said the bartender as he looked at me knowingly.

"Sweet Daddy?" asked the C.O. with a grin at the name Pruitt had bestowed upon himself the previous night trying to impress the whores.

"Who the hell is this "Sweet Daddy," fireman?" he asked me.

"The oil king sir," I replied.

"Pruitt?" he asked.

"Yes sir. But it's not what it seems sir," I added.

"Who else was with you, fireman?"

"The assistant oil king sir, Landon." I said.

"Mr. Benson, have the quarterdeck pass the word for Oil lab personnel to lay my cabin," Petrowski said.

"Aye sir," the Ensign replied as he moved over to the Captains phone to call L.T.J.G. Schott, and relay the order.

"BT3 Pruitt, Fireman Landon, lay the Captains inport cabin on the double."   Inspector Yee, I think we'll get this situation cleared up in short order," Petrowski assured him. Two minutes passed rather uncomfortably before Pruitt, and Landon, appeared in the doorway of the Captains cabin.

"Oil lab reporting as ordered sir," announced Pruitt. "Come in gentlemen," he said. "Let's get acquainted. Pruitt, and Landon glanced at me as they entered the cabin, and I just raised my eyebrows to signify helplessness at the present situation. "This is Inspector Yee of Singapore's finest, he's here to act on a complaint from this man here," Petrowski said, referring to the bartender who was looking at Pruitt with a "my turn" sort of look complete with victory grin.

"Good morning...old stick!" said the bartender.

"Mornin, Hop Sing!" countered Pruitt quickly.

"Knock it off Pruitt," said Wild Bill. The two men exchanged glances with the bartender shrugging his shoulders to indicate that he had no idea why the oil king kept calling him by another man's name.

"Pruitt, if you want to speak with me first, then you're more than welcome."

"Thank you sir, but we have nothing to hide sir," Pruitt replied.

"OK Inspector, you may question the men now," Petrowski said.

"Thank you Captain," replied the Inspector as he stepped up to Pruitt.

"Is it fair to say that your name is not, as you say, Sweet daddy?" he asked.

"Depends on who's asking sir," Pruitt replied, as Landon, and myself cracked a smile.

"How about Chief Inspector Yee, of Singapore police?"

"Well sir, in that case I'm Calvin Lee Pruitt, Great, Great, Grandson of Festus Philos Pruitt, 4th Regiment, Carolina Fusiliers, Battle of Bull Run!" Pruitt quickly replied.

"No Shit?" asked Petrowski after a short silence on the part of the Inspector, who had no idea what Pruitt was talking about after he had stated his full name, and then explained a colorful southern history for all to hear.

"That's affirmative Capt'n Sir," Pruitt replied.

"OK Mista Poowit," interrupted Inspector Yee. "Did you find

the body of the woman?" he asked.

"Yes Sir, I did."

How did that happen Mista Poowit?" Yee asked.

"Well Sir, the day before the discovery, the three of us boys threw our backs out hauling up the refueling hose from the pier, and spent that night in great discomfort," he answered. "Anyway, we all figured we could get some relief from a masseuse down on ...Ah... Kuan Street."

"You mean Boogie Street, Mista Poowit?" asked Yee.

"No Sir, The sign I remember said Kuan Street, and Sir Stamford Raffles Quay," he replied.

The Inspector grinned knowingly before nodding. "Continue, Mista Poowit."

"Anyway Sir, I suggested to the boys here that the best way to loosen up for a massage was to indulge in some of the local beverage that Singapore is famous for. Sort of loosen up a bit," he said.

"OK Mista Poowit, so you were loose. What happened next?" he asked.

"Well Sir, There were some gals at the next table that noticed us twistin, and turnin, tryin to crack our backs into place, and one of em' offered to help me for a fee," Pruitt said.

"How much, Mista Poowit?"

"Twenty five dollars, U.S.," he replied. "So I went upstairs with her, and laid down on the bed when I felt a lump under the mattress, I figured that it would be better to place it on the floor, when I saw the outline of the body Sir."

"Did you touch the body, Mista Poowit?" Yee asked.

"Yes sir, I did, but only to make sure I wasn't seeing things," Pruitt said.

"Where on the body did you touch the woman, Mista Poowit?"

"I think it was below the knee sir, if I'm not mistaken."

"It's very important that you remember Mista Poowit,"

Yee stressed.

"Below the knee sir… It must have been," Pruitt said.

"Why do you ask, Inspector?" asked Petrowski. "There are three sets of fingerprints on the body Captain. One set belongs to the masseuse. The other set belongs to whomever touched her on the right foreleg, if that is indeed where Mista Poowit touched her, which I'm sure he did now that he has spoken," Yee explained.

"That only leaves one set unaccounted for which must be the killer's, because this man was the first one I had checked," Yee said nodding to the bartender. "The body has been deceased for two days, so I need to put the fingerprints in the proper time frame. It's all I have to work with at the moment Captain," he said.

"Of course, Inspector."

"One more question for Mista Poowit, Captain?" he asked.

"Yes Inspector, by all means," replied the C.O.

"Mista Poowit, did you succeed in getting your back cracked that evening?" Yee asked.

It was clear euphemism as to whether or not he had been laid on Singapore's infamous Boogie Street, or Kuan Street, as it read out on the city index. Pruitt figured that it was time to stop insulting the Inspectors intelligence for the first time this morning, and so said no, he had not, which was true. "In that case I believe this belongs to you, Mista Poowit." Inspector Yee handed Pruitt an envelope that was unsealed, and asked him to count the contents. Pruitt counted out twenty-five dollars in American money much to our surprise.

"Is it correct, Mista Poowit?" Yee asked.

"Yes Sir," replied Pruitt.

"Then it would seem that my business here is concluded Captain," Yee added. "Captain, if you will escort me off the ship, please," Yee asked.

"Of course Inspector," Petrowski replied. "Mr. Benson, keep

these men here until I get back."

"Aye Sir," answered the Ensign as C.T. followed the Captain and the two Singaporeans out of the cabin as was the custom anytime a ship's commanding officer moved about the ship. It was also important that the Inspector knew his place on any naval vessel, not to mention that Inspector Yee had the nerve to attempt to arrest an American sailor on board his.

They arrived at the quarterdeck to find the security alert team fanned out along the starboard catwalk all the way to the fantail watching the four policemen on the pier smoking, and chatting amongst themselves as they awaited the return of the Inspector. When Inspector Yee started to descend the brow, Captain Petrowski asked him to look to his right. The Inspector looked instead at the Captain who he found looking aft at Old Glory, popping in the wind at the fantail where she always resided when in port. "The rules are different when she's aloft Inspector," he said. Without answering, the Inspector made his way down the brow to the pier as the Captain spoke to Mr. Schott.

"Secure the fire team, Mr. Schott."

"Aye Sir."

"Now secure the fire team," barked the 1mc. Captain Petrowski re-entered the cabin where Mr. Benson and the three of us had been awaiting his return. The Ensign called Attention on deck, and we snapped to. Petrowski centered his attention on Pruitt first, and then on Landon, and then me before he spoke.

"Well, it isn't every day I get to defuse an International Incident," He began. "I can hardly believe the sequence of events here. First Riley almost gets hauled off the ship. Second, they almost get shot. And last but not least, the culprit that caused it all gets his money back!" he exclaimed to Mr. Benson. "Can you believe this guy?" he said, looking at Pruitt. "Hell, that's the easy part; the real part is what I would do with both oil kings, and my number two burnerman in the Singapore jail. We've still got three more months left on Wes-Pac you know.

"Fellas, there is no way I'm going to let them take you from the ship, but if you were to get grabbed on the beach there is nothing I could do about it," he said. "So for your own good, I'm restricting the three of you to the ship for the duration of the visit. Any problems with that?"

"No Sir," we said.

"That goes for emptying trash on the pier too fireman," he said to me.

"Yes Sir," I answered.

"Mr. Benson will turn your I.D. cards over to C.T. until we hit Thailand, where upon if you have behaved yourselves, you can hit the beach and get your ... backs cracked. Dismissed, fellas."

Once outside the Captain's cabin we surrendered our I.D. cards to Mr. Benson and he headed off to the Master at arms shack to turn them over to C.T. By this time, the whole crew had heard what had happened on the quarterdeck, and Mr. Schott had an extra Gunners Mate assigned to the quarterdeck watch armed with a shotgun. The rest of the time in Singapore saw me kept busy in the fireroom during the day, and training with Scratch, and Danshaw after knock off ship's work in the well deck. They put me through jumping jacks, push-ups, sit ups, and had me slug a rolled up rack mattress with a pair of leather work gloves. The *Juneau* departed Singapore on the sixth day, and once again, it was Lutz, and I on burners for the two-hour sea detail. Once we cleared the last of Singapore's off shore islands, she pointed her bow due north, and steamed along the east coast of Malaysia bound for the port of Sattahip, Thailand.

We would spend two days at sea before arriving to one of the best R & R ports in Southeast Asia. World famous Pattaya beach was only a short distance away from Sattahip, and many of the crew wanted to go there at first chance. Others, however, were more interested in Bangkok itself, and threw in for a chartered bus that would arrive on our second day in port.

BANGKOK, THAILAND

At liberty call that evening after we had dropped the forward boiler and refueled, Pruitt, Landon, and myself headed up to the Master at arms shack to retrieve out I.D. cards from C.T. The Master at arms threw up his hands at the request much to our surprise. "You guys have to clear it with your division officer first," he said. "Sorry Snipes, those are his orders."

We would have to find Ensign Benson and plead for our liberty cards before we could leave the ship, so we wasted no time seeking him out. We found him sitting at the Chief Engineer's desk going over the Fuel oil system that Pruitt and Landon knew so well.

"Anything I can help you with Mr. Benson?" Pruitt asked. "Pull up a chair guys, let's have a talk," he said.

It struck me from his easy demeanor that there wasn't going to be any kind of chew out on his part, so I was curious to hear what he had to say after the Captain had told us that we could have liberty if we behaved ourselves, which of course we had because once underway, there is no room for Skylarking. Work, eat, and sleep, if you can get it, are the orders of the day.

When we had all pulled up chairs, and settled in, the Ensign told us that he'd had a conversation with Captain Petrowski in the wardroom one evening while underway from Singapore, and he told him some things about his Korean War steaming days that he wanted him to relate to us so that we understood just how important we were as Engineers. The Ensign began with Bravo and Mike divisions berthing that were located just forward of the port and starboard sideport double doors. It was one whole compartment without benefit of bulkheads that ran the width of that part of the ship, and between them was Repair division berthing as well.

"Think what could happen if we received one anti ship missile, or one eight-inch shell in that part of the ship at one hour after taps some night," he began.

"Ninety percent of Engineering would be wiped out, one hundred percent of Repair division would be lost, where would we be with only a handful of snipes," he asked. "We could have almost four hundred ship's company left, and yet we would be useless without the lost 73 snipes," he said.

"Let's narrow the point a little further here. What happens if you three and fireman Lutz get yourselves picked up on the beach some night in some hell hole like Jakarta?" he asked. "You can't get to the ship, and C.T. can't get to you. Let's say there was a mission warning order, or a typhoon alert, and we had to get underway in a hurry. Where would we be without both oil kings, and two burnermen out of six? So if you three and Lutz miss the ship when we steam then we lose 100% of the oil lab, and 1/3 of the burnerman watch. As you know from Singapore that scenario almost played out, didn't it?"

"Yes Sir," answered Pruitt.

"I hate to split up the three Musketeers, guys, but the readiness of the *Juneau* comes first, from now on the oil lab will stand port and starboard liberty, and the burnerman section will stand three section duty instead of four section, as of tonight."

"Mista Poowit," he grinned to Pruitt as he broke his balls over the way Inspector Yee pronounced his name, "you, and Landon flip a coin to see who stays aboard tonight, Fireman Riley, spread the word that one of the three off duty burnermen will have to stay aboard tonight."

"Yes Sir. I'll take it myself Sir," I replied.

"OK. I'll get with Chief Craddick, and make up a new burnerman watch bill. He'll have it ready for quarters tomorrow." Ensign Benson dismissed us so we could retrieve our liberty cards from C.T. even though Landon, who had lost the coin toss with Pruitt on the way to the Master at arms shack, and myself who had volunteered, would not be going anywhere tonight.

We understood the importance of ship's readiness, and knew that the Captain was on the money concerning the worst-case scenario related to us by the now easy to get along with Ensign. When we reached C.T.s office, he was just putting the compartment phone back into the metal holder on the bulkhead after hearing from Mr. Benson to return our liberty cards.

"All clear snipes," he said. Afterward, Pruitt donned his civilian clothes, and headed to the pier where the taxicabs were waiting to whisk sailors to Utapo Air Force Base where rumor had it there was the biggest, and best enlisted men's club in all of Southeast Asia.

"I'll do some forward scouting for y'all," he promised us as he entered the waiting taxi with some of the other *Juneau* snipes. It was a Friday night so the Utapo enlisted club would have a chance to live up to its fleet wide reputation. The Navy and Marine Corps looked at Air Force people as having the best of everything in the way of food, housing, working conditions, and recreational facilities. Kadena Air Base in Okinawa was the Taj Mahal compared to the enlisted club at White Beach. According to the grinning Pruitt the following morning at quarters, the Utapo club was like going from Bravo division berthing, to a suite on the Queen Mary herself. "They even got a Playboy room and everything," he crowed. "May the Lord hand my sinning ass over to the opposition if I'm lyin. Ah had two of em' walkin all over my back, butt, and everywhere else they could fit them purty lil' feet," he grinned. "Boys, y'all gonna get your backs cracked, and that's a fact!"

"And another thing," Pruitt continued in a low voice to Landon, and me, "This place has a package store that carries some good stuff. Picked me up a bottle of twenty-five-year-old McCallans single malt for quite a reasonable price if I do say so myself. Darker than most, slight taste of Peat, Smokey like, Label read out 1951," he said.

Chief Craddick then called Attention on deck, as the Wolf-man read the plan of the day noting that the bus going to Bangkok would be leaving at 0800, so he needed a list of names to secure reservations at the hotel where everyone would be staying for the three-day excursion. When quarters broke up Scratch, Deadeye, Stewart, Wolfie, Lutz, Cox, and myself started packing gym bags with socks, skivvies, and extra shirts for the trip to Bangkok.

"This oughta be a sight to see," said Cox to Lutz in reference to Scribeci joining a hard charging liberty party. Scratch was not a real drinker to speak of in relation to three of engineering's well known elbow-benders, so it would be interesting indeed to see the other side of the stoic Scribeci. The seven of us snipes along with several crewmembers from other divisions boarded the bus at the foot of the brow, and were soon underway for the one-hour ride. The snipes commandeered the rear of the bus, and Stewart got a card game going as the bus soon rolled into Utapo air base to pick up anyone else going to Bangkok. Scratch and Deadeye used that time to raid the base package store where they each purchased a bottle of the prized McCallans single malt Scotch that Pruitt had been crowing about at quarters. After picking up some *Juneau* sailors that had stayed over on the base last night, we were soon underway into the Thai countryside in the early morning mist. Deadeye cracked open his bottle of scotch, and passed it around with some Dixie cups with an edict attached to the gesture. "Snipes only," he said. After an hour or so, the bus pulled up to the front of the hotel and everyone filed out and headed to the lobby to check in and receive their room key.

MR. CAN DO

I noticed a middle-aged Thai, dressed rather conservatively, handing out a business card to someone once they received their room key, and began looking around the place. He seemed very polite yet I also noticed that he did not miss a single chance to hand his card to someone once they had left the check in desk. When it was my turn he met my eye with a smile I did not quite trust, and handed me his card that read his services: Tours, nightlife, taxi, companionship, etc.

"You can do all this?" I asked.

"Yes, I can do, I can do for you," he replied.

"OK Mr. Can Do," said Wolfie. "Set us up with some San Miguel for starters, and give us a chance to cut the dust for awhile, and we'll get back to you for a canal tour, OK?"

"Yes, I can do for you anytime," he nodded eagerly.

As soon as I got my key, Wolfie told me to hang tight and not stow my gym bag just yet because he wanted to scope out the place first. "Oldest trick in the book for a thief is to hit your room as soon as you hit the pool. By the time you even think to take precautions it's already too late," he warned. "Did you bring a liberty wallet?"

"Yes," I replied, meaning that it was just a bare wallet with my I.D. and any money I was ready to either spend, or lose. There was no sense in bringing all the family pictures, SSN, etc. In addition, all the things that meant everything to you, but nothing to a thief out for cash. When I had checked out my room and changed into swim trunks, I grabbed my gym bag and headed to the pool where the round of San Miguel was arriving. The first couple of rounds went fast and the little Thai waitresses were kept busy as Mr. Can Do hung around like a grinning vulture at the prospect of making a good buck in providing the Americans what he knew all to well they would soon want.

Scratch in the meantime had opened his bottle of Scotch, and had the waitress fetch six or seven tumblers that he filled for everyone to sip at their own pace. Everyone swam, drank, and played cards while the hotel staff prepared food on the outdoor grills. This first day would be spent just relaxing while Wolfie arranged a canal tour complete with a cobra-mongoose fight for the next morning. After dinner poolside, the Scotch began to kick in and the mood all around began to carry a decidedly R & R scent as Wolfie recalled prior canal tours from years past.

"What do say to a canal race, Scribeci?" Wolfie asked him.

"Fine with me as long as they're both the same size engines," he replied.

It was hard to imagine Scribeci as anything other than a squared away Topwatch I was used to dealing with in the forward fireroom, the no-nonsense Boilerman whose word was law up forward, doing anything even the slightest bit irresponsible in the pursuit of having fun. There is a time and place for everything I suppose, and since this looked to be about the time, and Bangkok, definitely being the place, there was no telling what tomorrow would bring in the way of adventure.

Later in the evening, I noticed Stewart in conversation with Mr. Can Do, and did not think much of it until I noticed Mr. Can Do put his right hand with forefinger touching the thumb to his lips in a pantomime motion that could only mean one thing. He then spaced the same forefinger and thumb about five inches apart to signify length. "That's gotta be Thai Stick," murmured Cox, Stewart's fellow Machinist mate from the forward engineroom.

Mr. Can Do was offering to provide some of the world famous marijuana from Thailand's golden triangle to Stewart as so many other Americans before him had requested. Mr. Can Do could quickly procure Thai Sticks along with anything else from the Golden Triangle for that matter, for a price that was reasonable when you figured that it saved you the risk of looking for it on your own. You paid a little more but then that was the price of doing business in safety. Mr. Can Do glanced at his watch then held up one finger to signal one hour, then left the pool area as Stewart looked over at Cox, and grinned approvingly.

"Want in, boot?" Cox asked.

"Depends, how much?"

"How's a buck a stick sound?" he replied.

"A buck a stick? That's all?" I asked.

"This is Thailand, boot, guys like Mr. Can Do get them in packs of five for a dollar as long as it's American money," he explained. "He sells them to us for a buck apiece, and makes a 400% profit on a pack of five."

I figured that since my last stash from the bartender in Pusan was running low, and there was still three more months left on Wes-Pac, you would be hard pressed to beat a dollar a stick for some of the world's best Indica.

"Have to careful with this stuff though," he warned. "It's not like the sativa beat weed we get back in San Diego. Thai stick is ten times more potent. I think it's what Picasso was smoking when he fucked up all those paintings of his," he added. Stewart came over and told us to meet him up in his room later on.

"I'm going to make the deal in the hallway by the stairs just in case anyone tries to follow him up," he said. "Anything goes wrong I can say he accosted me in the hallway as I was entering. You guys see anyone else entering the building from that side once he's up there, then just pound on the inside of the door. I'm not worried about him as much as I'm worried about the cops being onto what he's doing. Wherever Americans are, they all know what we want," he said.

Cox and I gave Stewart five dollars each and went up to the room while he waited up at the hallway stairs. Soon he noticed Mr. Can Do arrive and park his car then walk through the main lobby. A minute later, he appeared on the second floor, and Stewart waved him to come down the hallway where he was guarding the exit. Stewart waited for Mr. Can Do to produce the small package and open it up. There were twenty Thai sticks pressed into a small rectangle clump. Stewart then gave Mr. Can Do twenty dollars, and a five-dollar tip whereupon Mr. Can Do produced a joint and indicated that it was laced with something

other that marijuana. "If you like this, I can do for you," he nodded in his usual eager way in reference to the joint that Stewart
put in his cigarette pack that he kept in his top pocket.

"I'll get back to you if I'm interested, Slick," Stewart said.

"OK my American friend," he replied. "You likea pussy?"

"Yeah, I likea pussy," he answered. "But maybe later OK?"

"I can do anytime for you," he said. Mr. Can Do left to go
downstairs and Stewart waited until he was gone before entering
his room where Cox and I waited keeping an eye on the parking
lot. Once inside, Stewart removed the package from the folds of
the towel and opened it. The sweet aroma of the Indica soon
filled our nasal passages as Stewart began picking the string tied
sticks apart from one another.

"I've waited all Wes-Pac for one of these," he said as he put
one to his nose, and inhaled deeply. He then took one of the cigarettes from the pack and began rolling it between his fingers to
loosen up the tobacco to make it fall out into the ashtray. He
peeled the thin strand from around one of the Thai sticks, and
stuffed the cannabis where the tobacco used to be. When the
length of cigarette paper was full, he crimped one end, then tore
off the filter, and crimped the other end as well. Stewart lit the
improvised joint, inhaled deeply, and then passed it around. We
each had a couple hits before the joint became a roach stub, but
then it was more than enough due to the Indica's T.H.C. content.

Stewart gave Cox and myself five sticks apiece, and kept the
rest for his share. As strong, as they were I was sure to space
them out for the rest of the deployment. "Canal tour bright and
early guys," he said as Cox and I headed off to our respective
rooms.

The next morning after breakfast around the pool with everyone else, the seven of us crowded into two taxis that Mr. Can Do
had arranged for us the previous night, and headed out into the
traffic to where the canal tour would begin. Our starting out
point was at the floating market place where several long dug

out canoe type boats with six cylinder automobile engines floated alongside the waters edge. The hulls were brightly painted, and roomy enough to seat two people side by side, for their full length. The market place was bustling with floating commerce of all sorts of foodstuffs, and live animals for sale or as barter, as the cornucopia of the exotic Far East overwhelmed the senses with its myriad of strange smells as the Wolfman, and Scratch, began rounding up some beer for the excursion.

"Slick, you come with me," Wolfie said to Mr. Can Do. "Scratch, you take the other one," he said in reference to which dugout they would be taking.

The two Thai boatmen sat at the rear of each dugout grasping the handle of the long stem on which the engine was mounted. At the rear of the engine was a coupling, and attached to that was about a six foot long steel pole with a small propeller on the end of it. We piled into the dugouts as the boatmen started the engines, and we were soon underway. The morning was still somewhat misty and humid, but that did not stop the Wolfman from passing out San Miguel beer to everyone except the two boatmen who politely refused. As we proceeded through the myriad of canals full of floating vegetation, there would appear small, colorfully painted models of castles in someone's back yard, or at least that is what they looked like from a distance. Wolfie explained that they were Thai sprit houses on those stilt platforms where the Human occupants of the residence would leave ceremonial foodstuffs, along with prayers, and messesages to the sprits of departed relatives. "It's kind of like asking them to put in a good word for them when they meet the big guy," Wolfie explained.

"But your ass is grass ya fuckin pimp!" Wolfie roared as he slapped Mr. Can Do on the back as the dugout rolled from side, to side with the laughter of the snipes.

Mr. Can Do took it in good jest as Wolfie handed him another San Miguel as the dugouts made their way down another canal towards the site of the cobra-mongoose fight promised by Mr. Can Do was to be held. After another ten minutes of cruising, we arrived at a canal side market where they had a cage of glass out back where the action was to be held. Inside the glass, enclosure was a grey cobra of about five feet in length.

As everyone gathered around, there appeared a man carrying a small rattan box containing a Mongoose that he shook to activate the animal. He then opened the top of the glass enclosure and prodded the cobra to get the snake to display the famous hooded defensive position that the whole world knew so well. Once that was achieved, the man threw in the mongoose that quickly pounced on the cobra's head and began chewing the shit out of it. The snake writhed for about fifteen seconds and then was still. That was it. The long anticipated brawl of nature was over in a flash. It was an absolute mismatch, a slaughter of the worst kind, and for this, we had paid thirty-five dollars. The mongoose, whose eyes had flashed red at the onset of the encounter, was now standing on the head of the Cobra staring through the glass with the black beady eyes of the weasel that it was. Cox was livid.

"You shittin me buddy?" he said to the man who had brought the mongoose. "That's it? You doped up a snake and threw in a stretched out rat and collect thirty five bucks?" he asked.

"Mongoose very fast," answered the man.

"Of course he was, the snake was asleep when you woke him up with the stick, and you've been pissing off the rat all morning long," he accused.

"Mongoose very fast," the man replied again as he retrieved the mongoose from the enclosure.

"I think you are the fast one, pal," retorted Cox as he glanced around at the rest of the group who were getting a kick out of the whole exchange. "Probably splitting the take with you, ain't he?" Cox said.

"No, my American friend, I assure you he is not," Mr. Can Do replied. "Mongoose very fast," he agreed.

"How many times do I have to hear that?" Cox asked.

"G.I. Very slow is more like it," Cox muttered as Deadeye pulled him away and pressed another San Miguel into his hand. "If I wanted to get bullshitted, I could have stayed on board and played poker with Boogie and Toungie," Cox complained to Deadeye as they walked away.

"It's another sea story, forget it," Deadeye laughed.

Before everyone climbed back into the dugouts, we all sprung for more beer to take along with some fruit to soak it up with. The sun was high and had burned off the mornings mist as the two Thai boatmen headed back to the market place at a somewhat faster pace now that the big Americans were getting loose drinking beer in the sun. After the fruit had been consumed with Scratch peeling the last banana, he figured now was the time to drop the challenge. "Hey Wolfie, how about getting a little steam up," he asked.

When the Wolfman turned to his right in order to answer him, Scratch hurled the half-eaten banana smack into his bearded face. "Have some chow, fur face!" laughed Scribeci as he reached back and grabbed the throttle handle from the boatman, and gunned the engine sending everyone lurching backwards with the sudden speed.

"Son of a bitch!" roared Wolfie as he did the same, easily commandeering the throttle handle from the diminutive boatman. Mr. Can Do quickly began trying to placate the boatmen as the race was engaged by holding up his hand, and rubbing his thumb, and forefinger together vigorously at them to indicate the promise of more money coming their way because of the Americans impromptu canal race.

It still did not erase their consternation that they wore on their faces as everyone else hung on to the sides of the boat as Wolfie gained on Scratch's boat, and tried to nudge the dugout over, much to the chagrin of the two boatmen.

"S'matter Polack? Can't you steer that thing?" goaded Wolfie as his boat bumped once more and this time much harder on Scratch's craft.

Scribeci countered with a tack to port near the bow of his opponent sending those in Wolfie's boat reeling off balance, and almost capsizing it. The two played chicken for another minute before heading into a flat out race with Scratch's boat winning due to less weight. With the two boatmen finally convincing Scratch and Wolfie to return control of the boats back to them, things finally got back to normal even if the boatmen ran the engines a little faster in order to be rid of the Americans that much sooner back at the market place. Once we had paid off the boatmen along with a generous tip for the canal race, Mr. Can Do suggested dinner back at the hotel, and then later that evening he would take us to see a Thai kick boxing match. Cox was suspect.

"Oh sure, we will probably see Bruce Lee chop up some junkie off the street in one second flat," he complained.

"No No! It's very much more my friend, two men, training same, same," Mr. Can Do replied. "No Mongoose, Mongoose very fast," he added.

"I don't want to hear any more about that fuckin rat pal," Cox said. "As far as I'm concerned we got suckered," he said.

"Thai boxing mo' betta, G.I. see much kick ass, training is same, same," he assured.

"What time?" Wolfie asked.

"Eight P.M. after dinner," replied Mr. Can Do.

"Lighten up, Cox," said Scratch. "I've seen it before, real warriors, no bullshit."

We climbed into the two taxi cabs for the ride back to the hotel with Mr. Can Do still reassuring Cox about the skill level of the contest he was to see that evening. Sensing that if Cox's doubts spread to anyone else he might very well be out some

American money, Mr. Can Do pulled the age-old pimp trick out of his hat when he asked Cox, "You likea pussy?" he grinned.

"Of course I likea pussy," Cox retorted, mimicking him in response.

"OK I can do for you, no charge," he assured.

"No shit?' replied Cox, surprised at the offer.

"You pay for boxing, I pay for pussy, you like?" he asked.

"Now you're talking, Slick," Cox said as the two cabs headed into the Bangkok traffic.

Back at the hotel Mr. Can Do summoned two prostitutes through a runner for Cox to choose from. The wily Machinist mate chose both knowing that there was nothing the pimp was going to do about it because he was worried about Cox influencing anyone else, and therefore losing American money that evening.

"Now G.I. very fast," smiled Cox as he ushered the two girls into his room and shut the door, leaving Mr. Can Do standing there in the hallway.

"Mudda Fucka G.I." muttered Mr. Can Do as he ambled off down the hallway. It was just the price of doing business sometimes. He had encountered streetwise Americans before, and since he was not really paying for Cox to get laid, he was not really losing anything either. Another day, another hustle.

After dinner, everyone piled into another set of cabs, and Mr. Can Do directed the drivers to the club where the contest was to be held. The place had a small ring about three feet off the main floor and was surrounded by tables, and chairs. It had lights overhead while the rest of the club was darkened. The two fighters soon entered, and climbed into the raised ring. Their feet were taped up to the ankles, and small leather gloves fixed to their hands. They appeared to be evenly matched as Cox mimicked to Scribeci, "Training level, same, same."

Scratch threw up his hands, and added matter of factly, "Hey! You screwed both of his whores for nothing; quit bitchin."

Cox was not complaining of course, it was just the day's beer, and the Thai stick in its accumulation. Everyone was in good sprits as the two contestants were introduced to the room and gave slight bows to one another. As the bout commenced, the two warriors judged the distance between them by raising their cocked legs toward each other and giving quick effortless jabs before moving to the other foot, and letting fly with a full flatly placed foot to the midsection of his opponent. They engaged in hand action before one gave a quick round about back kick that drove his heel into the other mans side just above the pelvic area, and just below the ribs where the body has no protection, even if well muscled. The man was clearly hurt but toughed out the rest of the round bravely enough.

"That was his kidney he hit, he's done," Scratch said. As they went into the second round, his opponent wasted no time exploiting the matter. What he did not count on was the spinning back fist that caught him at the base of the skull as he moved in to finish the wounded area with his hands. The speed of the hurt mans maneuver stunned the room with its speed and grace, as the bouts presumed winner headed for the mat, landed face down, and was still.

Cox was on his feet. "Good shot brother! Good fuckin shot! Did you see that?" Cox said to Mr. Can Do, who just grinned as if to say "I told you so."

"I hope you likea all the pussy my American friend," said Mr. Can Do.

"Oh I'm having a great night Slick!" retorted Cox, as the table broke out laughing.

There was one more bout that night that ended up in a draw before Mr. Can Do rounded up some cabs, and we headed back to the hotel around midnight. Once more around the pool in the moonlight, some of Mr. Can Do girls swam with the snipes as Scratch passed around the rest of his Scotch.

"Tell me, boot, do you think the guy that took the kidney shot was supposed to lose, and he bucked fate? Or was he supposed to win anyway, and just happened to catch a stray shot by mistake?"

"I think he pulled one out of his hat when he needed it most to be honest," I replied.

"How do you he didn't fake being hurt in order to lure the guy into going after only one part of his body, therefore setting him up for the spinning back fist," he asked.

"I think he knew his ass was grass if he took another shot on that side, and the back fist was nothing more than a survival move he had practiced five thousand times in training," I said.

"What are you getting at Scratch?" I asked.

"Existentialism-v-Determinism," he said.

"Oh Christ," muttered the Wolfman as he rose and dived into the pool.

Scribeci smiled, and winked at me as he went on with his train of thought. "You know, I'm envious of guys like Wolfie because his whole life has been determined for him, and all he has to do is accept it which as you can see he does wholeheartedly," he said.

"He's been riding the Grey Ghost since the orphanage turned him loose at eighteen. He's got no family, no relatives, no kids, or at least none that he'll own up to," Scratch admitted. "He's all alone in this world, and yet he's surrounded by some of the best friends any man could ask for. Quite a paradox if you ask me. Hell, he's been on five other ships already. He could pipe aboard any ship in the fleet, and it would be like he belonged there."

"Maybe it's because he does," I answered.

"No maybes boot, it's his lot in life, his calling," he replied. "The way I see it is that we have free will, luck, and then we have fate." He continued, "Wolfie's Navy career was fate, pure and simple."

There was silence as Scratch finished his story, sipped his Scotch, and just sat there with that look on his face that conveyed that he still was trying to piece the puzzles together about the incomprehensibility of life.

"The only thing I can make out of all of it is that the meaning of life is to give life meaning, because it's all we have to work with," he finished. "Hey you two, Cox and I can't screw em all," Wolfie bellowed, holding two of Mr. Can Do's girls on each shoulder in the shallow part of the pool. "This part is free will boot, let's get some," he said as we jumped into the pool and picked the girls off Wolfie's shoulders.

Scribeci was a hard one to figure. The rest of the time in Bangkok was spent around the pool drinking beer and smoking Thai stick when the lifers were doing something else. Mr. Can Do's girls were available for a price, and we all partook in the offers. Soon it was time again to set the sea and anchor detail and steam for the open sea. Bangkok had been a great liberty port, and a memorable one at that. The *Juneau* was bound for Subic Bay for a weeks upkeep period, and a few of us were invited to visit the town of San Felipe, about twenty miles north of Olongapo to spend a couple of days with the Cruz family, and experience some real Filipino hospitality, and see how real Filipinos lived, unlike the hustlers, and whores of Magsaysay street.

In the meantime, however, it was time to punch tubes in the boilers so the forward boiler was secured as soon as sea detail was over. We would be four days at sea running on one boiler until the forward boiler had been punched out. The snipes had been given the choice of performing the task underway, or when we reached Subic Bay for the upkeep period, and quickly chose the former so as to have that much more liberty while in port. Two days out Captain Petrowski received news that every commanding officer dreads.

One of the communications officers delivered the message just after noon chow, and the young L.T.J.G. warned the Captain that it was bad, very bad. Captain Petrowski put down the cup of coffee he had been drinking with the Chief Engineer and read the message for a second before exhaling heavily.

"Good God!" he exclaimed as he shook his head from side to side. "What is it Captain?" asked the Engineer. The Captain pushed the message across to the Engineer who read it quickly, and sat there stunned by what it had to say.

"Why do these things have to happen?" he asked to himself as the two men sat there in silence.

"I'll fetch the chaplain sir," he said.

"Thanks Screws," answered Petrowski. "Is he on watch?" he asked.

"Yes sir. He's aft with the Wolfman on the throttledeck." Ensign Benson preferred the free wheeling style of the after engineroom compared with the way Main Control was run up forward. He had apprenticed himself well under Wolfie's steady hand on throttles, and was not far from handling a sea detail on his own. The messenger answered the throttledeck phone, and relayed the message to the Ensign.

"The Captain wants to see you sir, his cabin," he said.

"Thank you, Fireman."

When the Ensign reached the Captain's cabin, he found the door open and the Skipper standing there with the ship's chaplain. At once, he knew something was wrong because of the chaplain's presence, and silently thanked the Captain's presence of mind by not summoning him over the ship's 1mc.

Their faces said it all and Ensign Benson knew it was serious. "How bad is it sir?" he asked the C.O.

"I'm sorry son," said the Captain. "I'm so very sorry."

The skipper turned to the chaplain who was holding the message from the Red Cross. "God bless you, buddy." He left the two men alone and closed the cabin door.

The chaplain then had the gut wrenching job of telling Ensign Benson that his mother, father, and two younger sisters had been killed in an automobile collision with a tractor-trailer in heavy morning fog. Tule fog, as it was known in California's central valley. Fog so thick that it was like trying to drive through a ball of cotton.

Ensign Benson was now an orphan at twenty-three. Captain Petrowski had the Chief Engineer muster all of Bravo, and Mike divisions on the fantail, and without knowing what it was about; we all knew it was serious because the C.O. and the Master at arms, along with the engineering lifers were already there. Once we had assembled, the Captain spoke. "Sailors, we've got a shipmate in trouble, and he's got to get off the ship as soon as possible and back to the world," he began. "I know that you just tore apart # 1 boiler to punch tubes, but it's got to be buttoned back up and lit back off so we can make all speed to Subic Bay," he said. "Your division officer just suffered a family tragedy the likes of which are staggering, and he's going to need some extra cash to take care of business back home. I know you guys won't let him down," he said. "Anything you can spare will be a big help, but for the time being we've got to get that boiler back together and lit back off."

"Deadeye," he said.

"Yes Sir," answered Deadeye. "Your invention is going to get another workout, it's going to be another power run all the way," he said.

"I'll get right on it Sir," Deadeye assured.

"Petty officer Pruitt."

"Yes Sir, Captain," replied the oil king.

"Same as before if you will please."

"Yes Sir," Pruitt said.

"OK Snipes, everyone up forward, and let's get that boiler back on line," he said.

Most of the boiler tubes had already been punched along with the steam drum, de-super heater coil, and dry boxes wire brushed free of boiler scale. The economizer was being completed as well, so that left only the 2,200 tubes of the water drum left to be "short punched" as it was known. It would be a shame not to be able to finish this one last task, but those were the brakes. We would have to drain, and reopen the boiler water drum at Subic and do it then. When Scratch informed the Captain of this, he asked Scribeci how long it would take two men to complete the task if they worked strait through with no breaks.

"To properly short punch 2,200 tubes? Four hours sir," Scratch replied. "That's just punchin, and cussin sir."

"OK. If we are this close then let's go," Petrowski said.

"Scribeci, I'll need a pair of coveralls, and a volunteer." Scratch turned to me and said, "Boot, round up another pair for the Old Man, and start punchin."

After finding a pair that fit the Captain, I grabbed two pneumatic brushes to take into the water drum that the Captain was now crawling into just beneath the deck plates. The Captain's leadership in this respect quickly infected the snipes because punching the water drum tubes was one of the hottest, grubbiest, jobs on ship.

"Well guys, they don't call him Wild Bill for nothing," said the Chief Engineer. Two air hoses were passed into the two of us along with an elephant trunk for fresh air circulation as we attached the brush motors to the hoses, and began setting our face masks on properly to begin short punching all those tubes that loomed over us in the half light. Wild Bill was at the far end of the water drum because he was the first in, and we lay on our backs, and punched up at the rows of tubes. The rest of the snipes crawled all over the boiler to reassemble it. The Master at arms took up station in the fire alley in case of any emergencies concerning the Captain were to arise, and to ensure overall security measures were enforced because the Commanding officer of a ship is always escorted when he moved about the vessel. Tube after tube, hour after hour, and the whine of the pneumatic brushes continued to emanate from the water drum as we narrowed them down to 1,000, 700, 500, and on until 2200 hrs.

When we finished all 2,200 tubes of the water drum: "OK Fireman lets get some coffee," said the Captain.

"Yes Sir," I replied.

The C.O. crawled out just after I did and he was just as filthy as I was which meant we were only a hair more filthy than the rest of the snipes that had just finished buttoning up the boiler, and were ready now to fill it with water and pressurize it to check for leaks. Deadeye's steam assist device had already been hooked up back aft, and the other one was standing by next to the emergency feed pump.

"Are we ready to Hydro yet?" he asked.

"We'll begin filling the boiler shortly Captain," said Scratch, as some of the snipes installed the flex gasket around the opening of the water drum manhole we had just crawled out of, and began to tighten down on the bolts to secure it.

"Fine, but first I'd like to say a few words," he said. The Captain had me call the rest of the sweaty, dirt-caked snipes up to the throttledeck where those standing forward throttles could also hear what he had to say. Someone handed him a cup of coffee as everyone crowded around and grew silent. "Is this everyone, fireman?"

"Yes sir."

"I don't know what scuttlebutt you may have heard in relation to Mr. Benson, so I might as well set the record straight," he began. "An auto accident in California just killed his entire family, his parents, and both sisters."

There was an audible escape of sorrow from every man's throat at this revelation. The Captain took another sip of coffee before he continued. "So you can imagine how hard it is to be cooped up on this ship right now after getting that kind of message. As soon as we bring this boiler on line it'll be a power run all the way to Subic Bay, and that's 900 miles from here," he added. "I know that a lot of you are short on funds because of all the R/R in Bangkok, but I want to ask you to give what you can because it costs a few bucks to bury four people, and Mr. Benson's family were people of modest means. I don't know if we'll ever see him again because these type of things tend to change a man in all kinds of ways. But even if we don't, he's still our Shipmate, and right now we are all he's got," he said.

"OK Snipes, let us pray," he said as he bowed his head. And there we were 23 dirty=faced men led in the Lord's prayer by our dirty-faced Captain, as each man thought his own thoughts, and thanked God that they had been spared what Ensign Benson had not been. After he finished, Wild Bill and the few of us that had been raised Catholic crossed ourselves, and raised our heads. "Scribeci, how soon can you have her on line?" he asked.

"Well Sir, we had to put some fresh refractory mud by the screen wall header, so it hasn't been hot yet," he replied.

"Textbook says six hours for a cold boiler, but then she's only been down two days. I can bring her on line in three hours at the soonest, that's the safest, and soonest I can do Sir," Scratch told him.

"That'll be fine Scribeci, Thank you. Before I go I'd like to donate my cover to the collection effort," he said as he took his Captain's hat from the messenger's booth on the throttledeck where he had placed it when donning the coveralls and handed it to Chief Craddick. It had the officer's gold band across the back of the visor, along with the "scrambled eggs" motif on the bill itself as his symbol of authority. On the inside band of the hat was his name. "Wm. Petrowski, Captain. U.S.N." Not that anyone would contemplate lifting a few dollars from it, but it did get a message across as to whom you would be dealing with if you were caught in the attempt.

"I would be much obliged if you handled this chief," he said.

"Yes Sir, by all means," he replied.

"Thanks Chief. I'll have Boogie heat up some chow for all you men that missed out this evening, so until it's ready I suggest that you all get cleaned up before Pruitt dumps all the fresh water," he warned.

As the hot, tired, dirty-faced meeting broke up, Chief Craddick told Scratch that he wanted him and his watch on light off as soon as the Hydro test was completed on the boiler.

"Hit the showers, grab some chow, and I'll see you back here in one hour," Craddick said. By the time we had showered, ate, and returned to the firealley, Chief Craddick had already filled the boiler with water and was building up pressure with the emergency feed pump from steam cross- connected from the after boiler in order to check for any leaks. Fred and myself checked the de-super heater hand hole plugs, and found them to be tight as well as the flex gasket seals on the steam drum, and water drum. Deadeye had me ferry the other burner barrels down to the firealley where he began to assemble everything for the power run.

We would not be using them right away; instead, we would light off with the size #64 plates in order to heat the new refractory slowly for the first hour. We would then switch to the size#32 plates until we were ready to come on line, in which case we then would come on line with the customized barrels and go to Flank speed. Pruitt was busy dumping all the excess fresh water, which meant that with all the Marines aboard, the crew would be put on water hours again for the duration of the power run. Landon meanwhile, was transferring fuel oil in order to maintain an even keel. Three hours later Scratch rang up main control to inform them that the main steam gage was about to close on 600psi.

"Ready when you are, Smitty," he said.

"We are cross-connecting main feed now. Tell Deadeye it's a go in two minutes," Smitty replied.

Once both boilers main feed had been cross-connected, Deadeye began changing one burner at a time, and replacing them with the drilled out sprayer plates of the customized barrels until all five had been replaced. Cox opened the throttles all the way, and both boilers were at their maximum out put as the *Juneau* began to pick up speed through the South China Sea midnight. It would be a 900-mile power run to Subic Bay. After getting relieved by the midwatch, I headed up to the 04 level to get some fresh air, and cool down. The night was star strewn as always when it was clear, and it was balmy as usual in this part of the South China Sea. I had only been topside a short time allowing my night vision to adapt when further down the rail I noticed another figure strolling towards me. When he came closer, I could see that it was Ensign Benson, and I came to attention.

"As you were Riley," he said.

"Good evening Sir," I said.

"Good morning is more like it," he smiled weakly, and I could see the tired look on his face as he placed his hands on the railing that the Bosun's mates kept painted so white, and I got the feeling that he wanted to talk so I placed my hands back on the railing, and looked down at the Brine being pushed away from the ship, and saw the green light of the phosphorescence.

"We're making good speed I see," he said softly.

"Yes Sir, twenty-six knots again Sir," I replied.

"Twenty six knots and all on account of me. Under the circumstances this is the best present I've ever had," he continued. "I know you guys knocked yourselves out getting that boiler on line, and I'm damn grateful for what you're doing on my behalf."

"Forget about it Sir. You're a Shipmate," I told him.

"Yeah, a Shipmate," he said. "That word has new meaning for me now; I now know the strength of that word… Shipmate." He repeated.

"Is your paperwork all squared away Sir?" I asked him.

"Yes it is, I'll take a Slick from Cubi Point to Clark Field. From there a M.A.C. flight to Guam, and then Pearl, after that on to L.A.," he said. Mr. Benson was silent after that, and I knew that he needed to be alone for the moment, so I bid him goodnight, and wished him the best if I did not see him again which would most likely be the case. He made for a lonely figure there on the 04 level now that I knew what had happened to his family. On any other occasion, he would simply have been enjoying the balmy evening pondering the next day's plans, or taking a well deserved breather from the throttledeck, but not this night. This night would be spent asking God why he had to have all of them. One would have been bad enough to be sure, but all of them? Why all? We continued the power run all the day long, arriving at Subic Bay in the early evening and setting sea detail as the sun was setting. Once we were moored, Ensign Benson left the ship with his sea bag, and garment bag draped over his shoulder to catch a jeep ride to Cubi Point, Clark Field, and the long sad journey home.

"Gonna miss ol' skinny, had the makings of a damn fine officer," Wild Bill said to the Chief Engineer as they watched the Ensign depart in the jeep. "Aye Sir," replied the Engineer.

THE FEAST AT SAN FELIPE

When sea detail had been secured and shore power hooked up, both boilers were secured and bottom blown. The normal workday continued for most of the crew, but the snipes were all granted liberty to either catch up on their sleep, or hit the beach. Scratch, Wolfie, and Smitty decided to head to the Naval Brig to see how Hensen was doing, not having seen him since he went over the hill the last time we were in Subic Bay. Landon, Stewart, and I were busy packing gym bags for the trip to Cruz's place in San Felipe, and while we were excited about the upcoming party, and the legendary Filipino hospitality that was sure to accompany it, we also felt for Ensign Benson and what he must be going through at a time like this.

Cruz told us that there were few Americans that ever visited his hometown and to be on our best behavior, kidding us about the incident in Singapore. Pruitt would be arriving late the next day with one of the other Filipino's from the personnel office now that there was a way to skirt Ensign Benson's edict about Port, and Starboard duty sections for the two Oil Kings. Pruitt had the Wolfman covering the oil lab in case of any problems. When the four of us were ready, Cruz led the way down the Brow and we made our way across the naval base to the Marine gate where we showed our Military I.D. cards, and proceeded across Shit River into Magsaysay Street towards he Seaman's club for a cold San Miguel.

Afterwards, we bought twenty more for the ride to San Felipe, storing them in two large paper bags to try to keep them cool. If they warmed somewhat in the tropical heat, we could handle it. We passed into Subic City, and raised our beers to Marilyn's Club as the Jeepney driver stopped to let off some American sailors from one of the guided missile Destroyers at the base so they could partake in that establishment's famously sordid business, and embarked some more passengers. Soon after we were out of Subic, and into Zambales province as we picked up, or dropped off people here or there. The area became more rural, and the people fewer the farther north we went.

After two hours of stop and go, we arrived in San Felipe's small dirt town square in front of a small white building with a sign that read "The White House." We squared up with the driver, and went inside. It was a bar and grill of sorts frequented by the locals who all knew Efren Cruz, as we sat at one of the picnic tables, that outside of the bar, was the only furniture in the place. "MABUHUY!" Said the Filipino bartender as he saw Cruz and the three of us at the table. They exchanged greetings in Tagalog with a few of the others doing the same. Cruz introduced us to some of the other Filipino's at the other table who nodded hello as Cruz asked the bartender to set them up with another round on him.

Soon after, several small children appeared at the large screen less windows to get a look at the three Americans that had suddenly appeared in town. We got the distinct impression that we were the center of attention, so Cruz spoke to them with us picking out the name Cruz, as they ran off with the greatest of haste when Cruz held up a silver Peso. The other Filipino's laughed as the kids ran shrieking an announcement that a native son of San Felipe was home for a visit.

"I told them that the first one to tell my family we are in the White House would get this Peso," Cruz said. "I'll give them each one, but they don't know that."

By the time we finished our first beer, a lone Filipino, about thirty years old appeared crossing the dusty red square with the children in front of him trying to convince him that they were the first to reach him.

"Ver," Cruz said. "My cousin."

Ver entered the bar and greeted his cousin warmly with the same smile that all Filipinos seem to be born with as Cruz shook his hand and ordered up some more San Miguel. The children quickly confronted Cruz, insisting that each had been the one to get to Ver first. Cruz allowed them to joust for a few seconds before giving each of them a silver Peso. When that round was finished, Ver suggested that we head for Cruz's place close by.

As we left the White House, another Filipino around the same age as us appeared heading our way. "Romy, my cousin," said Cruz. Romy greeted his cousin and was introduced to the three of us as we kept walking towards his parents house with the three Filipino's speaking in Tagalog, and Cruz catching up on the local news.

We arrived soon enough at a wooden structure with a corrugated metal roof set off the ground about five feet on sturdy wooden posts that themselves were on circular concrete pads for support. There was a large banyan tree in the front yard that provided shade that had a small tree fort between two limbs. Cruz led the way up the stairs into the house where we were met with a gleaming Mahogany floor, no doubt hewn from the local jungle. The furniture was the Rattan kind that Americans are always sending home as a novelty. "MABUHUY! Smiled Cruz, "Welcome to my home."

Since the place did not have electricity, Cruz gave Romy some paper peso's and instructed him to round up the outside wheelbarrow, go to the White House, and come back with more San Miguel, along with as much ice the thing could carry. When Romy returned fifteen minutes later, we were well into the newest batch of San Miguel when we heard a bikie sputter up out front. It was one of the usual conveyances so common to the Philippines with attached sidecar, but the driver remained seated as if awaiting a fare. Ver got up, looked out the doorway, and said something to Cruz in Tagalog.

"Sonny," said Cruz. "My cousin." Cruz rose and went outside and shook hands with yet another cousin, and was soon enveloped in an animated discussion in hushed tones with the bikie driver. Ver and Romy spoke to us in passable English for a full ten minutes the two cousins talked out in the street. A few minutes later Sonny headed down the street, and Cruz came back inside and spoke to the two other cousins in Tagalog. They gave off body language that suggested they had no control over what was certainly a conversation about Sonny. Something suddenly did not seem right even with all the beer we had consumed that afternoon, and Cruz sensed our uneasiness.

"No problems guys, just San Felipe politics. MABUHUY!" he said.

"MABUHUY!" Echoed Ver and Romy as they raised their bottles of beer in unison to us. Along the rest of the afternoon, several other people came by, and Cruz introduced them as members of his extended family. Uncles and aunts, great uncles and great aunts, children of all ages, and many young adults of our own ages.

Most of them were paying courtesy calls on San Felipe's newly returned son, and it made an impression on the three of us how fast word had spread that we were in town considering I had yet to observe a single telephone. Two of the uncles quickly partook of the stock of San Miguel, and I noticed that they removed the bottle top by holding the bottle firmly in their left hand, and crooking their right finger under the corrugated cap, then levering that finger against their thumb to remove the cap with a "pop" in one smooth motion. They just grinned at us when they noticed our surprise at what seemed to be a beer drinker's Martial arts move. "MABUHUY!"

They said to us in the Philippine greeting of welcome. Soon after, a military jeep pulled up out front with four armed policemen toting M16 rifles, at least three of them were. The driver of the jeep was older than the other three who looked to be in their twenties. The older man, about fifty, got out of the jeep to reveal a .45 automatic on a pistol belt, grabbed a small knapsack, and bid goodbye to the other three and walked toward the small group of children out in the yard as the jeep pulled away. "Papa" Cruz said. "My Father."

Papa Cruz wore the uniform of the Philippine constabulary along with the surplus military belt that held two canvas magazine pouches for the .45 as the children ran to welcome him home from work, and the start of his annual two-week vacation. We all stood as Cruz's father came up the steps and entered his home. He nodded hellos to Romy and Ver, then hugged his son welcome home. Cruz introduced us one at a time and Papa Cruz answered "Mabuhuy!" to the three of us once learning our names. He removed his sidearm and placed the belt on the mantle piece, removing the magazine, and sliding the pistols slide rearward to ensure it was now unloaded before replacing it in the worn leather holster. One of the uncles handed him a San Miguel, and he removed the bottle cap in the same smooth fashion they had used before.

Papa Cruz spoke good English as he asked us where we were from back in the States, and how we liked the Navy and such when he came around to me, and asked where I was from. When I told him I was from New York, he said, "New York, New York, so big they name it twice!"

"Yes Sir," I responded as the room laughed at Papa Cruz's icebreaker.

When he finished his beer, Papa Cruz excused himself and changed into civilian clothes, as we got ready to return to the White House and resume the party so the women could prepare the evening meal. Before we left, he removed the old .45 from its holster, inserted a magazine, and put one more in his back pocket. He placed the pistol in his waistband, and left his shirt hanging over it. Even on vacation he was required to carry his side arm at all times as a member of the security forces.

Back down the dusty road, we went about twelve strong, with Papa Cruz, and the uncles in the lead. We crossed the small town square and entered the White House that was now mostly deserted. Landon, and Stewart, headed right for the bar, and ordered up San Miguel for everyone because we had more money between the three of us than these people saw all year. The three of us set up round, after round, of San Miguel until it grew late and Papa Cruz suggested that we head back because of the curfew he was sworn to uphold was approaching. When we arrived, the tables were all laid out with Philippine dishes that were all lit up by candle light because the vast majority of the countryside had yet to receive electricity.

"Tomorrow is the Babui," said Cruz in reference to the 40-pound pig that would be roasted for the party. "And you must try some Balut," he kidded, knowing that he had yet to see an American eat one of the Philippine delicacies that they considered slimy.

A "balut" was a fully formed chicken inside the egg that was incubated in the ground for a twenty-day period or thereabouts, and then the shell was peeled like a hard-boiled egg to reveal the chick fetus. The whole thing had turned black, and was the consistency of a gel. The average Filipino thought nothing of popping one into their mouth a half dozen at a time, and most Americans, myself included, could not understand how they did it. All the men ate, and drank, and talked in both English, and Tagalog, with the uncles relating stories from the war, and how one of the uncles had been on Corrigedor when the island fell to the Japanese. He had been one of the lucky ones to escape the Battan death march along the way, and became a Philippine Scout jungle fighter for the duration of the war.

"Japanese very bad to Filipinos, but much bad to G.I.," he added, meaning Americans. "I think Americans know Japanese, they no surrender to them, maybe G.I. fight like all gone," he added as he made a gesture as if he were holding a rifle with a bayonet, and using it to run someone thru.

"Very bad time for G.I. 'Japanese kill many G.I., kill many Filipino's for three years," he said. "General Macarthur come back and bring many G.I.," he said as he opened his arms wide, and flashed a beaming smile, while the others laughed at this understatement of the massive re-invasion of American troops in '44and '45.

"Yes," said Papa Cruz. "Many die, no reason, very bad time for Filipino's." The elders had vivid memories of the war that had ended thirty years before, but like all people who undergo horrific experiences it would always be with them.

"G.I. Very good to Filipinos for long time," added the uncles. "Japanese bye bye."

"Sayonara, son of bitch," cheered the other uncles as we drank on and talked of many things with Cruz translating to those whose English, and Tagalog, were minimal until everyone grew sleepy and reclined on the individual mats that the women had spread out for us. Before dozing off, Cruz warned us not to go anywhere by ourselves the next morning until he could detail someone to escort us. The N.P.A. was active in these parts and the last thing Cruz needed was for us to push our luck by wandering around by ourselves, and tempting fate. It was sound advice, as we were to learn the next morning.

The thing about drinking San Miguel or any other beverage containing alcohol is that it tends to dehydrate the body, and dehydrate it that much faster in the tropical heat. I awoke the next morning with a swollen tongue, and a headache, along with an overpowering thirst for something cold to find Stewart returning from the outside latrine in pretty much the same condition. Everyone else was sound asleep on the floor, the uncles, and the cousins Romy, and Ver.

"I gotta get something cold, boot," he said.

"Let's wake someone up to walk us down to the bar and get some soda pop," I said.

"I ain't no kid boot, we ain't gonna get lost," he replied.

"But Cruz said," I began.

"Hey c'mon, these guys are sound asleep, we're gonna look like a couple of pussies asking someone to hold our hand just down the street," he said. "You want to look like a pussy? Besides, I have insurance," he said with a forefinger to his lips to signal secrecy. He quietly opened his gym bag and fumbled through the skivvies to retrieve the .45 he had gotten from that C-Ration Marine the day before we steamed for the Equator back in February.

It was as Landon had described it back in Singapore, completely refinished, with black plastic grips. Stewart then reached into his back pocket and removed a loaded magazine that he slipped into the magazine well of the pistol that made a soft click, as it seated. "You had that clip on you the whole time?" I whispered.

"Of course, first rule of firearm safety says never store guns, and ammo together," he said. "Or didn't you know that?"

"Of course I did," I replied. "I'm just thinking how it would have looked if it had fallen out last night is all," I said.

"Yeah well it didn't happen, so forget about it. Let's go boot, I got cottonmouth big time." Stewart and I quietly left the sleeping men snoring away, and walked out into the early morning mist headed for the White House.

"Cruz isn't going to like us slipping away like this," I warned.

"We'll be back before anyone knows it, besides, we're gonna bring back enough for everyone, and they'll be in the same shape we are, Hell, they'll thank us for it," he said.

When we arrived at the town square, I noticed a man about our age sitting on the sidecar of his motor bike smoking a cigarette, and talking to another man around the same age. The two men stared at us as we crossed the square, and entered the bar. Soon after the bike sputtered to life as the driver took the mans fare, and drove him up the street we had just walked down. We received two orange sodas from the bartender and chugged them down right away. Stewart then ordered two tumblers of the local Philippine Rum as well.

"Little hair o' the dog is the best thing for that hangover I say," he said.

We dropped the rum down our freshly chilled throats, and told the bartender to sell us a case of orange soda to bring back to the others. "But for now I gotta see a man about a horse," Stewart said.

Stewart ambled outside to the latrine and I paid the bartender for the orange sodas and waited as two Filipinos entered the bar and sat across the room and spoke softly to each other. They each appeared to be intoxicated, and did not look like either man had slept last night. I got the distinct impression that they were eyeballing me the way they just stared my way without speaking. I cracked open my third soda and whished that Stewart would hurry up and return when two more Filipinos entered and sat at the same table as the other two. They all looked like they had all attended the same party, and none of them seemed to be in the friendliest mood. One of them said something to me in Tagalog that I did not understand, and so just shrugged my shoulders in reply. He then said the same thing again, only this time he motioned as if he were drinking from an imaginary bottle.

I assumed that he was referring to the orange soda I was drinking from, so I rose and walked to the bar, and took four sodas from the case that the bartender had placed on the counter and set them on their table. "Here you are fellas," I said. There was silence as I backed away, and it became clear to me that it was alcohol they expected me to buy for them instead. The one that had spoken before stood up, and took the soda bottle by the neck in club fashion as the bartender began to speak rapidly to the man, and I instantly sensed danger. At that moment, Stewart returned and sensed the same tension.

"What's the problem, boot?" he asked.

"They want me to buy a round of drinks," I replied.

"Haven't you already?" he asked, seeing the four of them holding the orange sodas.

"They want booze, they're drunk," I said. It was obvious that they intended to shake us down for a round of hard stuff, and it did not sit well with Stewart.

"Fuck em', they ain't getting nothin," Stewart said under his breath.

"Hey look," I said, remembering his .45. "Let's just buy them a round and get the hell outta here. This is what Cruz warned us about, remember?"

"Cruz ain't here," he said.

"Doesn't matter, let's just buy them a round and split," I pleaded to him. I motioned to the bartender to set them up, but he refused to serve them because they were already shit faced, and causing trouble with the two of us.

This only tended to exacerbate the already tense situation. Something must be done before they made a move, and Stewart pulled the .45, and then we would be in a world of shit. They knew we had money, and were bound to part with it sometime and they just could not see why we should not do it now. Suddenly we heard the sound of a motor bikie arrive out front and quickly leave. Efren Cruz, and Papa Cruz, then entered the room much to our surprise and relief as the four men quickly assumed a somewhat more relaxed stance, and began to open the sodas I had given them, and sat back down. Papa Cruz eyeballed the four and they got the hint that things could get worse for them if we decided to squeal about their attempting to shake us down so they bid the bartender goodbye and left.

Stewart passed out more sodas and quipped to Cruz, "Didn't we drink with those guys last night?"

"No, I would not associate with them if I were you," he said.

"Hell, I can't remember, I figured they were more cousins again," he said. Stewart was trying to cover up as best he could because he did not need Cruz proving himself right on his warning not to stroll about unescorted. Cruz had been un-unnervingly correct.

I grabbed the case that held the sodas after the bartender replenished the missing four bottles, and we left the bar only to find Pruitt, and one of the Filipinos from the ship's personnel office arriving on a Jeepney from Olongapo city. Pruitt came armed with four bottles of Scotch as presents to Papa Cruz, and the uncles that he carried in a gym bag. After introductions, we began the walk back to Cruz's house with him and Stewart at the rear of the group so Cruz could speak with him alone about what he had just done.

"Sonny told us where you were," he began. "Those four men will rob you if they get the chance, I did not give that warning lightly, my friend. Please show respect for my father's position. He has earned his time off. Please do not ignore my warnings again, Stewart, There could be trouble. I know why you did it of course, but please, I am responsible for your safety here."

"Sorry buddy, it won't happen again," Stewart replied sheepishly.

"OK" Cruz smiled. "It is past."

Cruz's cousin Sonny was the one in the square when we entered, and knew that we were guests of his cousin. He had alerted Cruz and the uncles after dropping off his fare up the same road. Sonny had then sped away as if on another fare after dropping them off at the bar so as not to appear as if he were in any way connected to them. There was a reason for the mysterious behavior of Sonny that we would soon learn. We did not know it then, but Sonny was walking a razor thin line between treason and treason, as it were.

The other uncles were awake and smoking by the time we returned, and very grateful for the cold soft drinks, not to mention the four bottles of Scotch Pruitt had thought to bring.

"MABUHUY!" offered the oil king.

"Thanks a bunch," Pruitt replied. "Y'all can call me Calvin."

As the uncles downed the sodas Cruz informed us as to the sequence of events he had planned for the day. First, up was a trip to see the cockfights a mile or so down the road, while the pig was dressed, and prepared for the evening feast. Afterward, Cruz would take us foot fishing in the rice paddy to add to the meal, but for now, we were given some cooked rice and papayas for breakfast by the women. We arrived at the arena about an hour later, and observed around a hundred Filipinos, all men, gathered under a large corrugated metal roof so common to the Philippines with wooden bleachers.

In the center of the dirt floor were two men each holding a colorful cock rooster. Each bird had a two-inch razor attached to their legs that was used to slash the opposing bird once the combat began as many of the men started placing bets with one another. None of us had ever been to such an event so Cruz explained to us, "The birds are very fast."

Stewart started to grin, remembering Mr. Can Do's explanation back in Bangkok.

"They jump in the air and slash with those razors on their legs until one of them pierces the heart of the other," he said. "After that, it's a payday for the winner." We were noticeable in the crowd as the only Americans present so Cruz warned us against placing any bets that were going on all around us. No sense flashing around any of our slush fund money in front of any N.P.A. sympathizers, if there were any. The two rooster men threw their birds at each other and they flashed their razors into feathers, and flesh, with one bird dropping to the dirt floor almost instantly. Money changed hands amongst the crowd as two more birds were taken from the rattan cages and fitted with the razor spurs. Bets were agreed to and the scene repeated again, and again. There were no wounded birds. It was life or death in every dance.

Cruz's cousins Romy and Ver won money on all of their bets coming in handy, as both were unemployed, a common affliction in the rural Philippines. After twenty or so matches, we left the arena, and grabbed a Jeepney back towards Cruz's place. It was time to engage in some San Felipe style foot fishing in the rice paddy. We had the Jeepney stop about a thousand feet from the house along one of the paddies, paid him off, and started removing our shoes, and rolling up our pant legs. We were after Mud Fish that the locals grew in the rice paddies as a bumper crop along with the ever present three times a day meal of rice. The object was to find the fish with your feet, pin it, and then retrieve it with the hands. Some of the young Filipinas of the clan appeared with a basket and giggles at the sight of the three Americans up to their knees among the rice stalks, as the girls waded in and began finding fish right away.

"They're showin you boys up," drawled Pruitt, as he pinned and retrieved his first fish. He held it up for inspection with a smile before throwing it in the basket. "Bout the size of Sunnies I'd say," he added, as he found another fish and bought it up.

"Hey Riley, what's that fishin y'all do up north anyway?"

"Ice fishing," I said.

"I tried that once, but by the time I chopped a hole big enough to put the boat in, it got dark," he said.

"Up your ass Pruitt!" I said good-naturedly.

"Speakin of my ass, I got plans to commission a portrait on it when we hit Hong Kong," he said. "Gonna have ol' Pinky Lo, create a masterpiece on my backside for all time," he added in reference to Pinky Lo, the famous Hong Kong tattooist known to Sailors, and Marines the world over. "Whup, Got another one," he said as he bent down to grasp another mudfish from under his bare foot. So it went, foot fishing in a Philippine rice paddy, and talking about the tattoo's we were going to get when the *Juneau* made Hong Kong in a week or so.

The young Filipinas quickly filled the basket as Stewart, Landon, and I began to pick up one here and there until we had about twenty of the small rice paddy fish. "Ol' Hot Dawg could use a cold one buddy," he said to Cruz as he walked to the bank and stepped out of the paddy.

"OK. We'll go back to the White House where they have them on ice," Cruz replied. The eight-year-old Filipinas grabbed the rattan basket by the handles on each side and said something to Cruz in Tagalog, then bid us adieu as they walked towards the house in their flip- flops while we dried our feet with our socks, and donned our shoes for the walk to the bar.

"They are young," smiled Cruz, as we watched them turn at every few feet and flash that trademark Philippine smile our way and giggle to one another. It was a new experience for them at eight years old.

"You are the first Americans they have ever met, they are surprised that you all have different colored eyes," he said. "They did not know that there was such a thing as green eyes except on a cat," he said to Stewart. "They want to know if you can see better in the dark."

"No shit?" Stewart replied.

"They have never been out of San Felipe in their lives," Cruz said. "They don't know anyone except their family, and their classmates," he shrugged.

Romy and Ver were seated at one of the tables as we entered the White House enjoying some of their winnings from the Cockfights, having declined the fishing part of the afternoon. They were not spending it all, just enjoying a little treat for their good luck. Pruitt informed them that their money was now no good, and he would pick it up while we were here. They thanked him in English, and raised their San Miguel bottles in tandem.

"Y'all welcome just the same. Just wait till *Field and Stream* gets hold of this here fishin story," he grinned. We drank for about an hour before the two Filipinas returned to inform Cruz that everything was ready, and that most of the extended family had arrived for the festivities.

"It is time for the "Babui" Cruz announced as we drained the last of the San Miguel, then ordered four more cases to bring with us. There were about 40 people there when we arrived with the young kids all dressed up in their Sunday best. The women were busy with all the different dishes of food as one of the uncles sat by the pit turning the forty-pound pig that by now was a golden brown color, and the skin beginning to crack. He offered me one of the cracked skin pieces the size of a small wafer, and I found it to be good.

Romy in the meantime had grabbed the wheelbarrow and returned to the White House in order to fill it with ice for all the San Miguel we had bought in. The feast was now in full swing as we were introduced to Efren Cruz's extended family here and there as the afternoon slid into dusk with the children pointing out Stewarts green eyes in amazement. Stewart could do nothing but laugh at his new celebrity status, and crack another San Miguel. We were accorded the same trademark smile from everyone we met except Sonny.

He was not rude, but he was not friendly either, and seemed to keep a cool distance from us, this worried Papa Cruz and the uncles because they knew that he harbored sympathies for the New Peoples Army, and very well may be an active member. He had been warned by Papa Cruz several times not to associate with the group. They had frequent shootouts with the Philippine army, and were known as good jungle fighters like their fathers before them in the war. Sonny was under pressure from one cell operating around San Felipe to set us up for robbery, but refused to do it because we were guests of his cousin's family. He was in a difficult spot because he also could not tell his policeman uncle about any plans to move on us, if there were any.

We had planned to leave in the morning, but Papa Cruz felt it was safer if we left that evening, and insisted on coming with us as far as Subic City, packing his .45 under his shirt while Stewart, clandestinely did the same. He thanked us for the visit, and we thanked him for the famous Filipino hospitality and a chance to see the real Philippines for a change as opposed to the Magsaysay strip. It had been a treat for us Americans, and soon would be another sea story to tell.

We made Magsaysay around 1900hrs. And crossed over Shit River, dropping silver Peso's into the reed Peso catchers of the lovely Cherry Girls as we went back to the ship. Sea detail the next morning was the usual heart in the throat sequence it always was for the burnermen, but I was now up to speed enough to be confident on the burnerfront. Smitty put in an order to Pruitt for some "hot bearing" vodka for the lifers' only Shaft Alley card party, and King Neptune himself was rumored to be interested this time around. It was a two day float to Hong Kong, and a somewhat rough sea detail as Scratch had promised due to all the Merchant shipping between Hong Kong island, and Kowloon where the *Juneau* dropped the hook about three hundred yards from Fenwick pier.

HONG KONG

"Gotta a surprise for them boys at the China Fleet Club this time around," drawled Pruitt as we sat talking in the oil lab after sea detail was over.

"Who's that?" I asked.

"The Brits that hang out there," he replied. "Ya see, Hong Kong's their port, and their always drinkin, and talkin shit about Britannia."

"They think they own the place, any time you get more than five of em' together they start all that singing and stuff. Last time I was here we had some Marines from the *Midway's* security force, and they had to wear their Charlies on the beach," he explained. "Anyway, a bunch of Brit sailors started singing the Marine Corps Hymn with not so nice words attached if you know what I mean. Them boys don't cotton to anybody trashin the Corps like that, and that's a fact. Got ugly real quick like, couple guys from the other group got smacked around because of it," he said.

"The cops got there but there wasn't enough of them to do anything because the Marines were all in uniform, and wouldn't let their guys be taken away. Anyway, it caused a royal headache all around, but then they should have known better than to mess with uniformed Marines."

"So what's the plan?" I asked him.

"Gonna have to out sing em," he answered.

"You're kidding, right? What are we supposed to sing anyway, Pruitt?" I asked.

"I'm workin on it right now at the lithography shop," he said. "Havin a bunch of copies made up of a certain song should set the record straight. You'll see Riley," he assured.

There was no telling what Pruitt had up his sleeve, and I was not sure I cared to know as he sat there grinning like he just screwed the Queen. Hong Kong was the port everyone waited for in order to get any tattoo's they had in mind, such as Pruitt, and the others. Liberty call was commenced just as soon as the water taxies, or Walla Walla's as they were known came alongside the Jacobs ladder the Bosun's mates had lowered to the floating platform Fenwick pier supplied for visiting Navy ships that had to anchor out. There was a British Destroyer of the Type 42 class moored to the pier where *Juneau* sailors were let off to head over to the China Fleet Club just across the street. I had duty that night in the after engineroom under Deadeye as Topwatch, and Case as pumpman, much to the latter's delight because I was confined to the burnerfront, and therefore could not avoid him. Deadeye could not stand Case personally, but knew he was a top-notch pumpman in a pinch.

"He's an asshole," Deadeye would say when Case left the fire alley. "I hope you whip his ass boot, I really do."

"I know he's been on your case since you came aboard back in October. Thing is, though, he shipped over last week," he said.

"You mean he re-enlisted?" I asked. "Yeah. He's getting out on arrival when we get back to San Diego."

"You got about two months to go, hope you did your homework," he said. There was a pause before Deadeye asked further, "Scratch still giving you pointers?"

"Yes, How'd you know?" I asked.

"We talk," he said with a shrug.

"Case's difficult, that's for sure," I sighed.

"Yeah well he's in for a big surprise when we hit 32nd street," Deadeye added.

"How's That?"

"I can't talk about it, it's just Wolfie, and myself right now, you'll see when we hit San Diego." He nodded. "Gonna put a stop to that squeaking wheel."

Case returned with a cup of coffee and took up his roost between the feed pumps under a ventilation duct.

"You been here before, Deadeye?" I asked as I tapped the fuel oil ball valve once to raise the needle of the main steam drum gauge back to 650psi, as we were now in a condition known as – hotel steaming- that is lights, and hot water.

"Lots of times, what do you want to know?" he asked.

"What's this I hear about the China Fleet Club?"

"Not a bad place," he began. "The older guys like it because it's clean, no hookers, good food, that sort of thing. Kind of boring if you ask me, why?" he asked.

"Pruitt says he has a plan to out sing a bunch of Brit sailors," I said.

"Oh yeah, that bunch," he replied. "You oughta hear them after a few. They start singing all that nationalistic shit about how the sun never sets on the empire, and how their Navy rules the waves. It's annoying as hell considering how they're the third best in terms of sea power. Been playing catch up ever since Lend-Lease, when F.D.R. sent them all those four pipers back in the war."

"So what's Pruitt got planned anyway?" he asked.

"He wouldn't tell me, but he's got that look on his face again," I replied.

"Yeah he's a stinker ain't he?" He chuckled. There was a pause as the fireroom noise droned on and I tapped the fuel oil ball valve once more to keep the needle of the main steam gauge at 650psi while Deadeye talked to Case about an ever so slight variance in the pitch of one of the fuel oil service pumps located against the bulkhead at the end of the fire alley. He and Case were so accustomed to the signature noise made by every piece of equipment in the after engineroom that the slightest variance caught their ear right away.

Deadeye answered my unasked question after Case returned to the feed pump station. "Duplex strainer needs to be cleaned, If the basket strainer gets plugged it makes that sucking sound you now hear," he explained. "We'll switch baskets at the end of the watch."

"You going to make it a career, Deadeye?" I asked after awhile wanting to know if he was going to be a Lifer.

"Fuckin Right," he assured with a thumbs up. "The Navy's the best thing that ever happened to me, I love this shit! All the places we go, all these women. OK, so you gotta pay em', so what! At least you don't gotta support em. You oughta see some of the tailor shops in this town. They know how to treat a sailor right," he continued.

"Here's the catch, these tailor shops are a dime a dozen right? So therefore, the prices are good because of all the competition. I'm telling you there are dozens of them and they all have refrigerators stocked with beer. Thing is though, they'll only give you one or two, because they know that people like us will take advantage of the situation while we pretend to look through the catalog like were gonna buy something," he explained. "It's the low cost of the business side of the trade, There's nothing that says we have to buy anything so by the time you hit five, or six tailor shops, you've had eight, or nine San Magoos… All free!" he said as he spread his arms in a ta-hah motion.

"They can measure you up for a great set of Crackerjacks and you can dump that milkman suit they issued you in basic," he added.

"I know what you mean," I responded, remembering the disappointment that day in boot camp when we were issued our dress blues, and everyone was wondering what was going on. They were not the "crackerjack" style so long associated with the Navy that the recruiting poster had advertised.

"Why did they do that anyway?" I asked.

"It's psychology on the Navy's part that backfired, after they stopped the draft everybody started smoking pot and goofing off," he began. "The Navy couldn't keep up on manpower with an all volunteer force so figured they needed a new catch to attract more people that Congress wouldn't let them draft. They figured if they dressed up boots to look like Chiefs, they could get more Indians so to speak. Anyway, it pissed off the Chiefs because they spent ten years earning a hat," Deadeye continued, meaning the Chief's hat with anchor on it that we were issued before we even left basic training.

"Chicks hate it too," he said as he tapped out another Camel from the crumpled pack. "They're suckers for a swabbie who looks like a swabbie, know what I mean? What do you have?" he asked me accusingly. "You have no Crow because you have no rank, You have no Hash marks because you ain't been in long enough to ship over, and the only medal you have is that feel good Gedunk medal they awarded you for getting through boot camp," he said.

"It's like this, even if all you had was that Gedunk medal on a set of Crackerjacks, at least you're still looking sharp, you know? It's that Swabbie uniform they dig. Bank on it!" he said with thumbs up. "May as well spring for a set of blues as well," he advised.

"They can provide the real thing?" I asked.

"Oh yeah, it's all Mil-Spec material, pass any inspection in the Fleet," he replied as he walked back over to the fuel oil service pump, and started checking lube oil temperatures to see if there were any different readings from the few minutes that had passed since he and Case had conferred.

It was at that moment that the torrent of water hit me from above. You see, the burnerman stands under a forced air draft vent when he tends the burnerfront. He has to stay there in order to not only keep from heat exhaustion in the moist heat of the engineroom, but also to monitor, and closely at that, the Main steam gauge pressure. What Case had done was fill a mop bucket with cold water from the D.A. tank, and from the upper level pour it all at once through a gap from about eight feet above allowing the air pressure to blast the cold water all over, and down my back, shoulders, and skull. It was the aquatic equivalent of "BOO" in a darkened room that you are not prepared for. Deadeye spun around and instantly looked up where Case was standing by the gauge glass and the ventilation duct on the upper level.

"Son of a bitch," I yelled at him as I stood there soaking wet while Deadeye searched for the eight inch crows foot he was known to twirl pistol fashion all watch long to throw at him. Case took off towards the evaporator before Deadeye found his trusty Crow's foot, so I decided to go after him myself, or so I thought before Deadeye grabbed me by the web belt and pulled me back to the fire alley and spun me around.

"You ain't been relieved yet, boot," he said. "Save it for the boat deck or you'll find your ass talking to the Man," he advised. "He's looking for the first chance to write you up. Get it? All he was doing was cleaning the boiler front, accidentally knocked over the wash pail, and the next thing he knows he's got some maniac attacking him. He's setting you up." It's serious stuff, boot, the old man will give you 45 and 45 at least, maybe a fine to go with it," he said.

"Let's see, 45 days restriction to the ship only counts when she's in port, so there goes Hong Kong, Okinawa for the two weeks we'll be there, and then Pearl as well."

"Dammit!" I spit, thinking what would have happened had Deadeye not stopped me from clawing my enraged way up the fire alley ladder, and doing exactly what the bastard wanted me to do. He was playing me like a fish, just waiting to set the hook, and then reel me all the way up to Captain Petrowski's cabin. A place I did not want to go again because of the still fresh incident in Singapore.

Everyone had had a good laugh about how Pruitt had bullshitted us out of a jam, but it was now clear that Case was going to use that along with being an agent provocateur to see me in

Wild Bills sights once more, and once more not to his liking.

"Boot, under any other circumstances I'd like to see you go after Case and fire him up, but not on my watch," Deadeye confessed. "The X.O. will set up another smoker when we hit White Beach; he does it every Wes-Pac for this very reason." He was referring to my present problem with Case. "You go thirty days at sea, and C.T. starts to notice a shiner here, a fat lip there, at chowtime, so he relays that information to the X.O."

Deadeye fingered another Camel from the pack, and stepped away from the still moisture spraying ventilation duct, in order not to blow out the flame that popped up from the Zippo he cupped in his hands. "It keeps things real, no bullshit, all the piss gets out in a safe way," he said. "We get relieved in an hour so then its liberty call, don't blow it now. Besides, you ain't made out of sugar boot, you won't melt none."

It was still humiliating standing there soaking wet knowing that some of the Machinist mates on the upper level were laughing at the situation. Third class petty officers like Case did not do any of the general cleaning in the engineroom because that is what boots like me were for. When they saw Case bleeding off the ice-cold water from the D.A. tank into the pail, they knew that the boot from the forward fireroom was going to get a bath. The after fireroom under Wolfie, and Deadeye, was different from the forward fireroom under Smitty, and Scratch. Nobody would dare soak Scribeci's burnerman on his watch. It was a precursor of what I could expect from Case if ever I were to find myself transferred back aft and had the misfortune to find myself under him when he made Topwatch soon enough.

Scratch had been right, so had Fred, and now Deadeye, in their assumption that I must square with the hairy, gloating, Case eventually. It would be very soon. It would be on the port boat deck at White Beach. It would be him and me, along with other guys that had beefs with one another from other divisions, and there would be other challengers as well that just liked to brawl, But it was the grudge matches that everyone wanted to see because those guys fought with more intensity compared to the rest and everyone knew it.

I looked over at the feed pump station where the hairy one smirked from under the ventilation vent.

"You're done hassling me, pal," I muttered under my breath. Case saw my mouth moving in his direction and knew I was bad mouthing him, so he came over to where I was standing to ask if I had a problem. I remembered Deadeye's advice not to sass him, or make any furtive movements on my part knowing that he was just itching to cheat me out of Hong Kong liberty.

"Yeah, I got a problem," I replied.

"And what might your problem be, Mr. Boot?" he asked.

"I can't seem to find the boat deck these days, I was just wondering out loud if you could show me sometime when we hit White Beach," I responded.

Case eyed me coolly for a second before asking me with a smirk, "You calling me out, boot?"

This was it, I thought. I had finally done it; there could be no waffling now that I had just dropped a challenge.

"Yes," I replied, looking into his beady eyes.

"Sure you're up to it?"

"If it wasn't for Captain's Mast I'd just as soon we go to the well deck right now," I said.

"Temper, temper, Boot," He teased. "I'm all for it except on second thought I think I'd like to invite the deck department to see the one responsible for their headaches get his ass whipped. They'd love to do it themselves except it would start a war with Engineering, and they don't want that, the next best thing would be to have someone they know do it," he explained.

"I'll be there, Case," I answered firmly.

"I know you will, boot, you don't have a choice now."

Case walked away to the feed pump station with his last words ringing in my ears as I thought about what I had just done.

"We'll be pulling for you, boot," Deadeye assured. "Stay away from him till we hit White Beach."

Our reliefs arrived soon after, and Deadeye walked with me up to the flight deck to look at the lights of Hong Kong, and Kowloon. The harbor was all lit up as we gazed at the high rises of Hong Kong crowded up against Victoria Peak.

"There's the China Fleet Club," Deadeye pointed out as I looked at the large San Miguel bottle, and glass all neon lit that marked its location. It was right across the street from Fenwick pier where there was a water taxi unloading *Juneau* sailors going on liberty.

"Aberdeen's down that way," he said as he pointed farther down the shore. "Wanchi district's over this way, but it's off limits because of all the Brown Rock Heroin you can get there," he explained. "The Navy loses three guys a year because of it, potent stuff. And straight ahead is all the free beer you can drink." Deadeye pointed past the China Fleet Club into the heart of the city, referring of course, to all the tailor shops. "Bring some money with you and we'll get you a decent uniform, till then hit the rack."

The next morning after quarters, everyone was discussing the tattoos they were going to get over at the world famous Pinky Lo's tattoo shop as soon as liberty call was sounded. The place was known for the way they tattooed sailors anywhere on their anatomy they pointed to... anywhere. When liberty call was announced, the water taxi's lined up on the port side Jacobs's ladder as *Juneau* sailors piled in for the three hundred ride to Fenwick pier.

"First stop is the China Fleet Club, We'll eat lunch there when it's time," Deadeye said. The place was a large affair with restaurant, barroom, and gift shop downstairs, with rooms to rent upstairs.

"Like I say, it's a clean joint, but it's mostly merchant seamen that come here, them and the Brits of course. This is where we'll night cap it before catching a water taxi back to the ship."

We left the China Fleet Club and headed up the street with Deadeye pointing out the various tailor shops, and listing the order in which we would hit them with the last one being the closest to the China Fleet Club. We entered the first one and sat down on the couch that had a coffee table covered with catalogues of different styles of dress.

The tailor asked us if we wanted something to drink, and we asked him if he had any beer on hand. He nodded and fetched up two cold San Miguel's. We looked through the magazines for a while before asking him the price of a pair of dress blue crackerjacks. He quoted a price, and Deadeye pretended to waver a bit once the initial bargaining had begun. The tailor brought two more beers as Deadeye gave a quick wink to me as the man turned away. "He's no dummy, we won't get another one until we ask to get measured up, actually he quoted a fair price so go ahead and order here, and they'll be ready tomorrow."

After informing the shop owner that I needed a set of blues, and whites as well, he measured me length, and width, and I gave him the down payment he asked for. They would be ready for pick up tomorrow afternoon he informed me as he bought two more San Miguels from the shop refrigerator. "Well, there's one six pack," Deadeye gloated as we drained the bottles and stood up. "Let's go mine some more San Miguel Gold. Later Slick." Deadeye waved as we left the shop.

We walked down the street and entered another, then another, and yet another until we had consumed the better part of a case of San Miguel between the two of us. By that time, it was around noon and he suggested that we head back to the China Fleet Club, and get something in our guts to soak up the morning's beer. "Or we'll be wiped by three if we don't,'" he advised.

Once inside the club we ran into Pruitt, Scratch, and Lutz, and joined them at their table. They said they were off to Pinky Lo's for tattoos, or at least he and Lutz were. Scratch was not interested in tattoos because he said you should not disrespect your body that way. "But then to each their own." He shrugged.

Scribeci was the only lifer in Engineering that did not have a single tattoo on his body. Some guys like Smitty, and Wolfie, and the ship's Master Chief had –Sailors grave- tattoos on their upper arms, while still others had their Crow, and Chevrons on their upper left arms, and several red hash marks tattooed on their left forearms with each one denoting four years of service in the fleet. Whenever they went up in rank, they would tattoo another Chevron under the old one. Third, class, second class, first class, and so on. When they shipped over for another four years, they had another red hash mark tattooed below the last one.

Hard core, real hard-core. Even out of uniform at the beach, you had only to look at their naked left arm to tell their whole life story. They did not care; they reveled in this life of booze, and broads, different ports, and different ships and the eternal sea. Tattoos went with the territory. This being a Saturday, some of the British sailors from the type 42 destroyer were at what could rightfully be called their table, and were casting glances our way as Pruitt drawled out the description of the ass master piece he was going to get at Pinky's tattoo shop.

"I don't believe it," Scratch said.

"I do," snorted Lutz.

"No fuckin way," added Deadeye.

"There's another one," pointed Pruitt.

After we had some lunch, the old Rockola jukebox started up with Elton John's "Saturday Night's All Right For Fighting" as one of the Brit sailors went through the selections.

"If it ain't one of em' then it's another," Pruitt drawled, referring to the English rocker.

"OK Gentlemen, it's time to get Pinky Lo Van Gogh started on another masterpiece, y'all welcome to watch," Pruitt said to Deadeye.

"This I just have to see," Deadeye replied.

The five of us walked back up the street and two blocks over to Pinky Lo's tattoo shop. The inside of the shop had a few Brit sailors drinking beer from the shop refrigerator while one of their shipmates had a large Union Jack put on his arm. The walls were covered all around with designs of every tattoo one could imagine, along with pictures of tattooed men as Pinky Lo finished the Union Jack.

He placed a sterile gauze bandage on the mans arm, and took a drink of water as we filled our eyes with all the pictures on the walls. Every conceivable tattoo a man could want was on those walls. Pinky Lo was an artist whose canvas was Human skin, and he was known worldwide for his mastery of the craft.

"Sailor man want beer?" he asked Scratch, pointing to where the ice cold San Miguel was stored. Scratch opened the door of the fridge to reveal nothing but San Miguel as far as beer went, and a couple six packs of soda pop in the lower shelf.

"Only San Miguel?" Scratch asked.

"Sailor man only drink San Miguel," Pinky Lo answered. "Numba one."

"Ain't it the truth brother," Scratch replied as he palmed two bottles then inserted the tops into the opener screwed into the side of the fridge, and popped them off, and handed them to Deadeye, and Lutz. He repeated the sequence for Pruitt, and myself, and grabbed one as well. We drank the beer, and looked at all the tattoos pictured on the walls for a while before slowly drifting off to a different part of the shop before Scratch nudged me, and cocked his head towards Pruitt.

"Check it out," he smiled. I looked over at Pinky Lo listening to Pruitt pantomime to him about the kind of tattoo he wanted him to do. Pruitt would point to a tattoo of a red devil with a pitchfork, which he said he wanted him to change to a shovel. He then placed his left hand on his left buttock. He then walked down the wall a few feet and pointed to a hot rod that had flames sweeping out of the hood, and placed his right hand on his right buttock. It was funny as hell to see Pruitt standing there grabbing his ass as Pinky Lo broke out laughing as if it were some kind of joke.

"I'm serious, Chief," Pruitt protested in earnest as the famous tattooist chuckled in return.

"You chasing dragon in Wanchai today?" he asked Pruitt, meaning had he been to the infamous rooftop district where all the brown rock Heroin was to be had.

"Your hands please," Pinky asked.

"What for?" asked Pruitt.

"Your hands please," he repeated.

Pruitt held out his hands as Pinky sniffed them carefully knowing that if Pruitt had handled any opium, or heroin, it could be detected hours afterward. The tattooist had learned from years of experience that drunks were one thing, but when someone was on heroin or opium, and asked for one tattoo or another, they might not like what they saw when the drug wore off. The last thing he needed was some sailor coming back in an unpleasant mood.

"OK if you like," Pinky replied, once he was convinced that Pruitt was on the level. Pruitt climbed up on the table used for such purposes, and removed his pants to his knees revealing the skivvies underneath that were marked B-DIV, to connote Bravo Division, so as to be able to get them back from the ship's laundry while at sea. He then peeled them down as well and rolled onto his stomach as Pinky changed the needle and arranged his inkstand nearer the table. "Any doubters left?" he asked Deadeye.

"Not any more you wild bastard," Deadeye answered. "Hey Scratch, Grab ol' Hot Dawg another beer if you would please, Gonna be here a spell I'd say."

There was another tattooist present, and Pinky introduced him to us as Rickey, his apprentice, who would someday take over the business when the master retired. Rickey was setting up to tattoo a "Flying Asshole" on Lutz's forearm as the pen like tattoo gun started up with an angry bee like noise and began tracing the outline of the horned devil on Pruitt's left ass cheek. "Gonna get one, boot?" Deadeye asked.

"Yeah, Screaming Eagle with a rising sun," I replied.

"Sure you want it?" he asked.

"I guess."

"Don't guess boot, once it's on, it's on for life," Deadeye responded.

"Hey, If Pruitt can live with that on his Ass then I can live with an Eagle on my shoulder blade," I said.

Half an hour later Lutz was done and Pinky Lo had finished the red devil portion on Pruitt's Ass, and was tracing out the sweeping flames portion on the other half. I removed my shirt and straddled the chair in reverse as Rickey traced out the Eagle, and rising Sun on my shoulder blade. He changed the needle, and inserted another color cartridge, and the angry bee noise began anew.

A few minutes later, the skin began to grow numb around the area of the needle as I drank from the bottle of San Miguel. Ten minutes later Rickey announced that it was finished, and applied a bandage to my new lifetime partner. Pruitt's tattoo took a half hour longer which suited him just fine considering all the free beer he was getting in return. When it was finished Pinky Lo placed bandages on both butt cheeks, and Pruitt rose off the table and pulled his pants up over the bandages.

"Feels like I'm back in diapers," he grinned.

"You crazy fuck!" Deadeye laughed, as he gave Pruitt the high five.

It was getting dark now as the five of us headed back to Fenwick pier to catch the water taxi back to the ship. The next day at liberty call, I returned to the tailor shop and paid off the tailor for the two new sets of Crackerjacks I had ordered hardly believing the quality product I received for the shamefully low price he asked in return. Deadeye had been right on target; Hong Kong was a tailor shop bargain indeed. I had duty on the third day with Scratch's mid watch, and at 0400, he sent me up to the berthing compartment to wake our reliefs.

I went to my rack to get my flashlight, and as I opened the lock, I heard someone sobbing softly near the hatch that led to the Airdale's berthing compartment. I flicked on the flashlight, and made my way towards the red lens night light to find a man sitting on the scuttle wheel of the hatch where the Storekeeper's supply compartment was located, with his knees drawn up, and holding his head in his hands. All around him were white bandages that he had stripped off and scattered on the deck. At first I thought that he'd been beat up until my light caught the sight of all the tattoos, thirteen to be exact!

"Look what I done to myself," he sobbed to me.

"Oh my God!" I gasped in the glow of the red lens lamp. This poor kid from Deck division had hit the beach with a pocket full of money, half of which he used to get shitfaced, and the other half to get tattooed to the point that he looked like a comic book.

As the beam of my flashlight went from one tattoo to another I saw Yosemite Sam with raised pistols, and above that the words "Back Off." There was Wiley Coyote strangling the Road runner with, "Beep, Beep, Yer Ass," Elmer Fudd shooting his shotgun, and yelling, "Silly Wabbit." Olive Oil was giving Popeye a blowjob, and on his back, a tattoo of a hunter bent over a log with his pants down being covered by a buck deer with a full rack, and a scowl, humping him from behind and announcing, "Here's your deer meat Pal."

When he cradled his head in his hands once more looking for all the world like one of its more miserable inhabitants, the beam of my flashlight caught one more tattoo on his right hand. It was on the karate chop part of the palm extending along the pinky finger, and it read, "Fuck the Navy." That was what any officer would see when this poor bastard gave a salute… Not good!

"Why didn't y'all stop me," he sighed.

"I wasn't with you," I replied.

"Well then who was?" he sobbed.

"How do I know, I'm a hole snipe, Your from deck right?" I asked.

"What are you doing here then?" he asked. "I live here, this is Bravo division Buddy, and you're in the wrong compartment." I said.

"Bravo division?" he asked suddenly, and with a flicker of clarity as opposed to his misery now that the relief watches had been awakened from our conversation, and were starting to gather around him trying to figure out the situation.

"What's the problem?" asked Deadeye as he came over tucking in his dungaree shirt tails.   "Drunk Deck Ape," I replied. "Look what he did to himself," I said as I passed the flashlight beam over his naked torso from one tattoo, to another, as the other three men of the relief watch came over: Danshaw, Fred, and Moe.

"What's he doing here," Deadeye asked still not fully awake.

"He's drunk and confused," I said.

"Y'all not gonna grease me are you," he pleaded.

The four broke out laughing at the fear on the part of the Bosun mate who found himself in hole snipe country, and at a numerical disadvantage at that.

"Naw kid, you greased yourself well enough for one night I'd say," said Deadeye.

"Wait till he gives a salute, then he's really in a world of shit," I said.

"How's that?" Deadeye asked, still not quite awake. The young deck ape by this time had risen and donned his civilian button up shirt, and was going through the sequence as I shined the beam on his right hand while it climbed the button ladder.

Deadeye looked closer in order to understand why one tattoo could possibly be any worse than what he had seen thus far.

Then he saw it: "Fuck you," "Fuck the Navy" as it was, but Deadeye saw the former because that is how lifers like him saw it. The sleepiness drained from Deadeye's face as fast as the disbelief, and then jaw-tightening anger replaced it.

"Fuck Me? Is that it, you little fuck?" Deadeye took a quick step forward, grabbed the kid by the lapels of his shirt, and slapped him across the side of the head twice before Danshaw, and Fred grabbed him from behind, and Moe, and me jerked the hatch open to the Airdale's berthing compartment, and pulled the hapless kid away from the scene.

"Lemme loose Fred, Dammit," Deadeye demanded as Danshaw pinned both him and Fred against the ladder with his bigger frame until Deadeye calmed down enough so that even Fred could handle him gently. Danshaw then stood in front of the hatchway and told Deadeye, "Ain't goin dis way," thereby giving Moe and myself time enough to lead the kid up to the Foc'sle compartment where he bunked.

"Lemme loose Fred, I'm cool," Deadeye said as Fred let loose. "Yeah well, I got in a couple shots anyway," he shrugged. "Fuck him! Little Bastard!" He tucked his shirt back in. "Gonna talk to Neptune after watch, gonna have to correct that bullshit, bet on it!" Deadeye assured the others, and then headed down to the fireroom.

When Deadeye's watch had been relieved, he headed up to the Chiefs mess and told Neptune, who among being the ship's oldest Shellback, was also a Bosun mate, about last night's incident. Neptune put down his coffee mug in disbelief. "Fuck my Navy"? he asked. "You're kidding, He's got that shit tattooed on his saluting hand?" he asked.

"Saw it with my own eyes just before I smacked him around a bit," Deadeye replied.

"Good for you Snipe!" Neptune said. "First, or second division?" he asked.

"They dropped him off in first division berthing, but he could be second for all we know," Deadeye replied.

"I'll find out soon enough," Neptune said as he rose from his chair and got on the phone to the Quarterdeck. A moment later came the announcement over the 1mc. "1ST and 2nd divisions muster on the Foc'sle."

Neptune told Deadeye to follow him as he started out of the Chiefs mess, and forward to the starboard main deck passageway towards the Foc'sle. The two men stood in front of the paint locker as the deck division assembled wondering why they had been summoned to Quarters a half hour early.

"That's him," said Deadeye as a very hung over, and dejected looking deck ape made his way to one of the Capstans and sat down.

"O.K. Snipe, I'll take it from here," he said.

"Thanks Neptune," Deadeye said, and left the Foc'sle.

Neptune walked up to the man and told him to go below now that the berthing compartment was empty. Once they were alone, the Master Chief asked him to turn over his Bosun knife. "What for?" he asked.

"Because I'm telling you to, no telling what else you're gonna stick yourself with next," replied the Master Chief.

"You're not to handle any Marlinspikes either, not even a paint chipper," he said. The kid just stood there with a blank look on his face as Neptune stuck the clasp knife that all deck division sailors carry into his pocket.

"Got any money left?" he asked the kid.

"I'm broke," he replied.

"OK Then you're gonna owe me the cost of a tattoo this morning," he said.

"Put your civvies back on, and meet me on the Quarterdeck in five minutes," he ordered. "Where we goin?" he asked. "Pinky Lo's" answered Neptune. "I have an idea how to fix that bullshit on your hand before you end up saluting Wild Bill some morning before he's had his coffee yet" "Yes, Chief," said the sullen youth.

Neptune stopped, and turned around, his face crimson, as he braced the young man, "MASTER CHIEF!" Neptune yelled into his face. "It's MASTER CHIEF…SEAMAN, UNDERSTAND!"

"Aye, Aye, Master Chief," answered the corrected youth.

"Five minutes sailor, be there in four, and bring your dress blues with you because you'll be wearing them when we return," he said.

"Aye, Aye, Master Chief," he responded as Neptune left the compartment to change into civilian clothes.

The kid met Neptune on the Quarterdeck promptly and the two descended the Jacobs ladder to the small platform where the water taxi bounced in the chop as Quarters was called for the rest of the crew.

The Master Chief was silent until the water taxi pulled alongside Fenwick pier. "Where you from sailor?" he asked.

"Mobile, Alabama Master Chief," he replied.

"Any other problems?" he scowled at him before climbing onto the pier with the young man in tow. As they walked towards Pinky Lo's tattoo shop, Neptune asked the kid where he had all his tattoos put on.

"I don't remember Master Chief," he said.

"What do you remember anyway?" Neptune pressed.

"Well, it was downstairs, and the guy ran his needle off a car battery," he said. "Oh Christ!"   "A real pro that one," Neptune muttered. "Do you remember whether or not he changed the needle?"

"No, Why?" he asked. Neptune stopped in his tracks and stared hard at his newest charge.

"Why? Hepatitis, that's why! Do you know what it does to your liver? Do you know you carry it for the rest of your life?" He pressed.

"I don't even know what it is," pleaded the youth.

"You get it from infected people who get tattoos from fly by night operators like the one who painted you up," he replied. "It's a blood disease, and it ain't nice. Look kid, was there anybody getting tattoos before you that looked like they were from Bumfuck, Egypt. Or someplace like that?" Neptune asked.

"I can't remember Master Chief," the kid answered as he hung his head down and stared at the sidewalk as people filed past them with only furtive glances.

"OK Blood work will tell, let's go," Neptune said.

They arrived at Pinky's place and Neptune grabbed a cold San Miguel from the fridge as the kid stood there with his garment bag containing his dress blue uniform waiting for whatever the Master Chief had in mind.

"You don't get one," Neptune said, and then took a long slug of the bottle, draining half of it.

"Yes gentlemen," said Pinky Lo as he came over to them.

"Got a request for you Pinky," Neptune said, as he took a pen from his shirt pocket, along with one of Pinky's cards on the door of the fridge, and began to scrawl on it the following words,- ROCK THE NAVY- and then handed it to the world famous tattooist with a slight bow. By closing off the side of the letter F and then adding a leg to it, and then closing off the letter U, to make it an O, Pinky turned the word FUCK, into the word ROCK, so now when the kid saluted the Quarterdeck O.O.D. he would present,- ROCK THE NAVY- and not the other phrase.

"Whadda say kid?" asked Neptune after Pinky Lo had changed the lettering on the kids hand, "Beats having ol' boats take your finger off , Aye?"

"Anything's better than that Master Chief," he mumbled in response.

"You owe me a saw buck payday, don't be ducking me," Neptune said as he paid Pinky off. "You owe any slushers in deck?"

"No" he replied. "Engineering?" Neptune asked.

"No"

"Good, now put your blues on, we're headed back to the

ship," he said.

The kid changed into his dress blues, and followed Neptune back to Fenwick pier where they boarded one of the water taxi's for the ship. They climbed the ladder to the Quarterdeck, where the kid turned aft to face the American flag popping in the breeze at the fantail, and saluted the colors. He then showed both his I.D. card, along with his *Juneau* card, and requested permission to come aboard as is the custom regardless of how long you had been aboard ship, giving the Quarterdeck O.O.D. a salute bearing the new tattoo, "ROCK THE NAVY," because Neptune had the kid remove the bandage in the water taxi.

"Permission granted," replied the O.O.D. The Master Chief did the same and the O.O.D. replied in turn, as they walked past the Gunners Mate armed with the shotgun that was now always present on the Quarterdeck after the Singapore incident.

In Neptune's eye that was the only way to settle the matter all around before he would recommend that the kid be discharged back in the states. The kid had lackluster performance reviews as it was, but then so did many guys on their first hitch. A growing process could be corrected in time, even the stupid tattoos one through twelve, could be overlooked, but not that thirteenth tattoo on his hand. That tattoo went to the very core of everything lifers like him stood for. He lived and breathed United States Navy. It was in fact the only life he had ever known; it was as if the kid had insulted his own Mother.

In almost thirty years in the fleet, he thought he had seen it all, but the audacity of some punk kid to spit in his face was too much to take. It was about the only thing that could make a salt like him blush, and what would make him blush would make a dog drop a bone. He wanted a drink.

The two San Miguels at Pinky's helped him calm down enough to keep from giving the kid a harangue that would have been wasted anyway, but now he wanted something stronger, and he knew just who to see about getting it. Pruitt was in the oil lab testing Phosphate in boiler water for the forward boiler when Neptune knocked on the door.

"If it ain't a rebel to the cause, ain't no cause to be here," drawled Pruitt, which was fast becoming his usual response to anyone interrupting him when he was busy.

"Neptune Sweetheart," said Neptune, remembering the oil king from the beauty contest when they crossed the Equator back in February. The oil king opened the door, and the Master Chief stepped in, and got right to the point of his visit.

"Doctor Pruitt, I seem to have a bit of a cold lately, and I was just wondering if you had any Russian Penicillin on hand," he said, in reference as to whether Pruitt had any Vodka left in stock. "

"Y'all got a prescription?" Pruitt asked.

"Yeah, Doctor Jackson signed it," Neptune answered as he tossed a twenty-dollar bill on the stainless steel counter top.

"Looks legit to me," replied Pruitt as he pocketed the twenty. "Y'all go on up to the Chiefs lounge and relax a bit, as soon as I get done here, I'll run you up a pint," he said.

"Thanks Pruitt," Neptune nodded.

"No sweat, If that condition persists though, I want y'all back for another consultation, ya hear?" he grinned.

"Will do," he responded as he closed the oil lab door behind him. Pruitt needed the time for two reasons, the first was to finish testing the boiler feed water for hardness on the forward boiler. The second of course was to open a fresh can of Orange HI-C that the vodka was stored in, and transfer three or so pints of the vodka into plastic bottles with screw on caps that were stored under the stainless steel counter. He did not need anyone else knowing the trick of how we got the stuff aboard. After testing the feed water, he found that while the boiler water was not hard, he still needed to add Sulfite, so therefore the boiler had to come first.

Pruitt called up to the Chief's quarters and told Neptune that he had to make a house call on a sick boiler, so it would be about a half an hour before he could reach him with the much awaited Russian Penicillin. "I'll tough it out," Neptune said, and hung up the phone.

When Pruitt had finished circulating chemicals through the boiler, he ran the booze up to the Chief's lounge and had a chat with Neptune about Deadeye smacking the kid around in Bravo division berthing the previous night. He did not mind it under the circumstances of course, with Deadeyes heart, being in the right place as far as Neptune was concerned, but the kid had complained to his division Petty Officer, who in turn had just left the Chiefs Lounge prior to Pruitt's arrival.

"They've already got it out for Riley because he almost scalded them twice," he said to Pruitt. "But Deadeyes a second class Petty Officer, he shouldn't have done that, he knows better. They want some kind of payback, and soon."

"What do y'all have in mind for a solution?" Pruitt asked.

"Boat deck for starters, some of the guys in second division want a crack at him," he said.

"Something else we oughta do as well since we'll be at White Beach for two weeks," he added.

"How's that, Master Chief?" Pruitt asked.

"Something good for everyone, I'm thinking along the lines of a football game between Deck, and Engineering," he said. "Give everyone a chance to get the piss out before we start back across the pond."

"Oh were good for that," Pruitt responded with his trademark grin.

"Yeah well, I figured you guys were," Neptune replied. "Scuttlebutt in the Wardroom says that the CLEVELAND will relieve us on May 6th, so how about we plan for the 3rd?"

"I'll pass the word to the snipes," Pruitt said.

"Thanks Pruitt." Once again Neptune had figured out a way to avoid a bigger hassle for what was really a Captains Mast offense against Deadeye for striking the kid in the first place. Whether his heart was in the right place or not, was irrelevant as far as the Uniform Code of Military Justice was concerned. Assault was assault, and the Master Chief of the *Juneau* could not bear to see a go- getter like Deadeye, a fellow member of – his Navy-, be hauled in front of Wild Bill for what Neptune himself felt like doing when he heard the news that morning.

The boat deck and football game with all involved would be a cleaning of animosity. It would also be good for morale, and a hell of a lot of fun to boot. It would also spare Deadeye a blemish on his service record. It was all in a day's work for the Master Chief Petty officer of the Command, *U.S.S. Juneau* [LPD-10] He lived for this stuff. The last day in port, most of the crew was content to hang around the bar of the China Fleet Club, and swap stories about the last eight months of Wes-Pac now that it was nearing the end of the deployment. Hong Kong was to be the last real liberty port of the cruise before heading back to White Beach for a two-week upkeep period, and to await the arrival of the CLEVELAND to relieve us. The crew would be working half days, and swimming, sunning, drinking, and just relaxing before our transit across the Pacific. Everyone had by now been screwed, blued, and tattooed, as the fleet axiom went. We had shed our Pollywog status, and been ordained with the "Trusty Shellback" title in its place. We had shed sweat, tears, some blood here and there, and a hell of a lot of Virginity in the process, along with any lingering adolescence. It had only been eight months, but seemed like an eternity to most of the younger guys, and the married guys as well. To other sailors like Wolfie, Deadeye, and the rest it was over all too quickly. The *Juneau* could remain in the Orient forever as far as they were concerned, and so went the various conversations at the tables in the barroom of the China Fleet Club.

The late afternoon sun disappeared into a light drizzle as twenty or so *Juneau* sailors partied on oblivious to the thickening crowd of English sailors from the type 42 destroyer, now that their liberty call had been announced. After an hour or so the Brits, now feeling their beer began singing in unison one nationalistic song after another, and generally hogging the air space, along with becoming quite annoying in general.

"Been waiting for this all week," Pruitt drawled.

The Oil King reached into his pocket and produced a handful of neatly printed cards fresh from the lithography shop. He handed some to Wolfie's table, and then to other *Juneau* sailors from deck, and air division as well. By this time the Brits were caterwauling, their way through their second rendition of "Oh Britannia" when Pruitt approached the juke box and slugged in a quarter. Then standing there like a portly composer he began to conduct his carefully chosen revenge.

"Y'all sing along with Sweet Daddy," he grinned. The jukebox selected the preplanned song from Country singer Johnny Horton, "Battle of New Orleans."

BATTLE OF NEW ORLEANS, BY JOHNNY HORTON

"Well in 1814 I took a little trip, and I went with Colonel Jackson down the mighty Missip. We took a little bacon, and we took a little beans, and we went to meet the British, down in New Orleans. Chorus!" yelled Pruitt at the other tables with *Juneau* sailors.

"We fired our guns, and the British kep'a comin, there wasn't quite a many as there was a while ago, we fired once more and they began a runnin, down the Mississippi to the Gulf of Mexico! Well they ran through the briars, and they ran through the bushes, and they ran through places where a rabbit couldn't go, they ran so fast that the hounds couldn't catch em' down the Mississippi to the Gulf of Mexico!"

The stanzas repeated themselves again as the *Juneau* crowd

got it together louder than before as the Brits now found themselves drowned out by the jukebox as well. "They ran so fast that the hounds couldn't catch em' down the Mississippi to the Gulf of Mexico!" Pruitt looked funny as hell, standing there with both hands conducting Johnny Horton's masterpiece, and yelling, "Chorus!" as the *Juneau* crowd's voices rose in unison. No one really saw the culprit that threw the beer glass towards Pruitt as he conducted his long-awaited concert, it did not really matter as Wolfie's table of Scratch, Deadeye, Lutz, and Smitty erupted towards the Brit table, and they in turn rose with a spilling of beer glasses to repel the snipes.

"*Juneau* sailors in!" yelled Pruitt as pandemonium befell the room followed by a rebel yell from the Oil King.

Broken glasses and foul language were the order of the evening as the close quarter combat began to turn the tide in favor of the snipes. Man for man, the Brits comported themselves very well, but that signature rebel yell from Pruitt simply galvanized the *Juneau* sailors into the steamroller they could not defeat.

One Chinese bartender was on the phone to the Hong Kong Police, while the other one had charged a CO_2 fire extinguisher, and was spraying the brawling men with cold CO_2 foam. As soon as the other man had hung up the phone, he grabbed a second fire extinguisher, and began to do the same as those still in their push, and shove routine continued to scrap. One Brit sailor was out cold on the floor, a recipient of an overhand right from Scratch, who himself had a nicely split lip.

Deadeye was rubbing the back of his head full of CO_2 foam while Lutz was dragging Pruitt across the floor away from danger after being decked by a British knuckle just before Scratch laid the man out. There were no real winners, or losers as it were, just some who gave some, and those who took some.

"Cops on the way, people!" yelled Wolfie, "Lets pull out!" he ordered, and with that, the *Juneau* sailors massed out the front doors of the China Fleet Club.

"Spread out!" ordered Smitty, knowing that the police would put two, and two together rather quickly with everyone headed towards Fenwick pier together.

"How's Pruitt?" he asked Lutz.

"He's alright, just had his bell rung a little," replied the Burnerman. Pruitt was growing a knot smack in the center of his forehead from the Brit knuckle just before Scratch gave the man one of his own.

"Serves him right," said Deadeye still rubbing the back of his head, and noticing a bump of his own. "This guy gets into more jams than anyone I ever met. How are we gonna get back to the ship now that Fenwick pier is gonna be crawling with cops?" he asked to no one in particular.

"We're gonna swim back," Scratch said.

"Be my guest Scribeci," Pruitt replied.

"You're going too," Scratch said.

"Ah cain't swim Scratch," Pruitt pleaded.

"Tough shit, you're going with us," Scratch insisted. "Just roll on your back and we'll pull over," he replied.

"You can't be serious?" Smitty implored.

"Look, we have to light-off the boiler at 0400, Pruitt has feed water to test, we can't do it sitting in the Hoosegow," Scratch said.

"It's only about three hundred yards or so, and it's slack tide, we're fine," he said.

"He's got a point Smitty," Wolfie said. "We have to get back, and we can't go by way of Fenwick pier. I was in the Hong Kong Jail three Wes-Pacs ago and it ain't nice. They wrote me up U.A. on top of it, and I even missed ships movement because of it, and it'll be the same thing now. That's why I'm not a Chief now; the whole thing set me back three years. Besides, it's just another sea story, Scratch is right. We have to swim for it."

"Ah still cain't swim Scratch," Pruitt repeated.

"Stow it Pruitt, you'll be fine."

"Ah still cain't swim Scratch," he pleaded even louder.

"You're the ship's Oil King Sweet Daddy, Landon can't do it alone."

"You're going, so forget about it and relax. Stash your wallets down your skivvie shorts guys, put your sneakers in your back pockets," urged Scratch as everyone began to comply.

Scribeci and Lutz jumped down the three-foot sea wall into the water, and as soon as they came up Deadeye pushed Pruitt in, and they all jumped in to help with Pruitt.

"Just relax, and scissor your legs when we do," Scribeci repeated as they began to pull for the ship as Pruitt began to pray.

"Ah cain't believe I let y'all talk me into this maneuver," Pruitt said. "That Rascal done hit me too hard, Ah ain't thinkin right."

With the other five swimming, and talking and laughing, about the absurdity of the evening's events, Pruitt calmed down somewhat and concentrated on timing his scissor kicks to coincide with the men pulling him.

"Ain't this a trip?" laughed Smitty as they stroked towards the ship.

"Save your breath," retorted Wolfie. "You're gonna need it to blow up your date."

The men laughed, talked, and swam while the Oil King prayed and kicked, and prayed and kicked some more.

After five minutes Lutz and Wolfie relieved Scratch and Deadeye. It was a little more than 300 yards but everyone was in good enough shape so as not to compromise safety. A few minutes later, they reached the port side Jacobs's ladder, and clambered up to the Quarterdeck where Wolfie informed the O.O.D. that some guys from deck might need the Motor Whale Boat to go get them before the Hong Kong police took them in for questioning.

"Had to do it Sir," Scratch insisted to the L.T.J.G. standing quarterdeck watch. "We have a boiler to light-off at 0400, and Pruitt's got feed water to test, we can't take a chance on missing ship's movement," he explained.

"OK, it's like this guys, I'm going to let the Captain deal with this because the C.O. of the Brit destroyer called over to inquire as to the fight at the club. Says that he wants a report or something of that nature from us. You guys wait over here in the helo hangar until the Captain gets here," he instructed the group.

The six soaking wet men waited for the Captain to arrive at the hangar bay, and when he did the O.O.D. called Attention on deck, and they snapped to. When Captain Petrowski arrived and saw them standing there all wet, he did not quite know what to think. Since Wolfie was senior man present, Petrowski centered on him first.

"Petty officer Wolfe, You're the senior ranking Sea Daddy here, what happened?" he asked Wolfie.

"Well Sir, it's like this," he began. "Everybody was having a good time since we were coming to the end of another Wes-Pac, and all of a sudden the place started filling up with Brit sailors from that inport Destroyer. Anyway Sir, they started all that singing that they are known for, and it got kind of boring because it's all yesterday's bullshit Sir."

"Anyway Sir," Deadeye added, "Pruitt had a plan to out sing em' with some cards he had printed up just for this occasion."

"What! Pruitt again!" the C.O. said as he looked over at the wet Oil King. "And just what was on those cards Petty Officer Wolfe?" he asked.

"A Johnny Horton song Sir," Wolfie replied. "Which song?" he asked, almost cringing at what the reply would be.

"Well Sir, Pruitt chose "The Battle of New Orleans," Sir." Wolfie said.

"Yeah well that's enough to get it started anywhere in the world with that bunch," Petrowski agreed.

"We were about to wrap it up when one of them threw a

glass at Pruitt, and it all fell apart Sir. It was knuckles away after that Sir," Wolfie finished.

Captain Petrowski centered his attention on Smitty. "And?"

"It's like Wolfie says Sir. It's that "glassing" thing the Brits have when they disagree about something or another, it's dangerous shit Sir, and it called for a response because I mean, what are we supposed to do? Let Pruitt take a hit over a song Sir?" he asked the C.O.

"You know Sir, the Aussies may turn a glass over here and there, but I've never seen an Aussie sailor throw a glass," Smitty said. "They consider it to be unsportsmanlike, a cheap shot, and so do I Sir. I like punchin em' Sir," Smitty smiled.

"And so you all swam back?"

"Yes Sir," Smitty replied.

"Who's idea was that?" Petrowski asked.

"Mine Sir," Scratch volunteered. "We had to swim for it Sir, because we have a boiler to light-off at 0400, and Pruitt's got feed water to test. Look who's in front of you Sir," Scratch advised. "Four Topwatches, an Oil King, and a burnerman Sir. I was thinking about the readiness of the *Juneau* when we get underway tomorrow Sir. "If Wolfie misses ship's movement again he'll never make Chief in this lifetime Sir."

Captain Petrowski asked Lutz his side of the events, and he explained that he was busy protecting Pruitt after one of the Brit sailors nailed him in the forehead.

"Besides Sir, I had to help with Pruitt on the way back to the ship," he said. The C.O. then came to Pruitt finally.

"First Singapore, now Hong Kong, so tell me Pruitt, what do you have planned for your next trick?"

"Wasn't planning on any tricks Sir, Just shuttin em' up with some historical singin Sir," Pruitt answered. "It ain't our fault they don't like being on the losing side of history Sir," "They started it Sir," Pruitt said matter-of-factly.

"Yes, I know," Petrowski said. "They always do. Fellas,

here's the thing, their Captain wants me to submit a report to him, and I just finished telling him that I do not report to him, or anyone else in the British Navy. I told him that he could come to the *Juneau*, and we would discuss the matter, but he's hesitant to do so because he doesn't want it to appear that he's reporting to me," Petrowski explained. "It's that false sense of superiority they have, hubris is more like it. So therefore we have a bit of a standoff because of his sense of national pride about to be pricked. So unless the Hong Kong Police have any problems... Pruitt! Then I don't have a problem with how you guys handled yourselves tonight," he said. "Besides, I'm proud of the resource-fulness on the decision to swim back. However, I want to get the point across that I'm not all warm and fuzzy about getting calls from other Navies concerning possible legal situations like this," he explained.

"Therefore you men will stay on the Quarterdeck soaking wet until the midwatch is relieved," he said. "You can run in place to get warm, or you can roll the Quarterdeck dice to your hearts content, but you will remain uncovered until then, any man poops out will be placed on report for disobeying a direct order. Any problems with that directive?" he asked the group.

"No Sir," they replied in unison.

Captain Petrowski nodded to the O.O.D. as to his instructions to hold them there in their soaking wet, and soon to be shivering condition to make them think about any future mistakes. The six would have to spend the next four hours of the midwatch under the drizzly night sky in their wet, clammy, civvies.

In the meantime, the ship's Motor Whale boat was going back and forth picking up the rest of the crew that couldn't allow themselves to be stopped at Fenwick pier because of all the po-lice now there attempting to sort out the Americans, and Brits that may have been involved. When 0400 rolled around, Scratch and the rest were released from the Quarterdeck to assume the light-off watch, and after both boilers had been brought on line at 0700, the *Juneau* set sea detail, and hauled up the hook to get underway for White Beach, arriving two days later. The weather was that unique form of latitude called sub tropical. Lots of warm, sunny days, and only slightly cooler nights.

WHITE BEACH STANDOWN

The *Fort Fisher* was moored across the pier to the west to await its relief from one of the ships of its own class [LSD] having been on Wes-Pac with *Juneau* the last eight months. Both ships were having division parties on the beach along with Horseshoes, softball, and football, while other sailors were enjoying the colorful reef off shore with fins, and mask. There was a stand own of sorts now that another Wes-Pac was coming to pass.

"Here's to number nine," said Wolfie with a toast of his beer can. "Number ten on the way," he added.

While Neptune had more years in the Navy overall, the Wolfman had made more Wes-Pacs than anyone else aboard *Juneau* at present. It was strange because he only had sixteen years in service. Usually when someone shipped over, there was a two-year stint of shore duty attached. BT1 Wolfe had purposely avoided shore duty by requesting a swap with someone of equal rank on a ship just starting a Wes-Pac. That then put him on what was known as an "operational hold" status by mere fact that his new command was deployed. There was always someone who wasn't wild about leaving the wife and kids back in San Diego, and were looking for guys like Wolfie and Smitty, who lived for this stuff, to make a swap with, thereby remaining in San Diego for another seven months.

Sea duty was tough on young families, and tougher on teenagers in school. There were times when dad simply had to be there in a kid's life, and sea duty simply could not permit it.

Those were the brakes for many a military child, regardless of branch, and that is where Wolfie, and the rest came in.

It was not long before Neptune and Chief Craddick arranged the football game between Deck, and Engineering for May 3rd, but first would be the smoker on the boat deck, and Case. It had been on my mind since we left Hong Kong a week ago. I had been training with Scratch in a clandestine fashion down in lower vehicle storage, and doing my sit-ups at an increasingly faster pace now that it seemed to mean so much more, like cramming for a final exam you were not sure you were going to pass. Not having any formal training for this sort of thing, I was about as ready as I was going to be.

Everything else was mental, and that was the hard part. Scratch was telling me that Case was going to throw T.V. punches like those that they did on Gunsmoke, Hail Mary haymakers with no follow up shots.

"He'll throw ten or twelve and wind himself," he said. "You just cover up, and stay in close, wait for the duck then upper cut him like I showed you. I'm telling you he won't have any wind for round two."

That was the game plan Scratch said I should use considering that I was still a pussy. The smoker would start after knock off ship's work at 1630, and Scratch advised me not to eat anything at breakfast except two oranges. He said that Boxers, and Bullfighters, fasted before going into the ring because if they took a hard one in the gut, the doctors could not operate if the stomach was digesting food. I had noticed Case with a full tray at noon chow, and felt like I had won a mental victory.

"Just working against himself," Scratch opined.

Since I was standing the mid-watch on the operational boiler, and the 1200-1600 during the day, I had to wait to be relived before I could go to the boat deck where some of the off watch guys had already rolled out the mats, and various buckets of water for the mouthpieces. There had already been four or five engagements as I made my way up the fireroom ladder, and met up with Pruitt in the well deck where he told me that Case was on the boat deck along with Scratch, and everyone else except those guys that could not wait to down some beer at the enlisted club. There were about thirty guys there when Pruitt and I arrived, and watched a match between a guy from Navigation, and the Black guy from deck who made the hissing sound when he threw a punch. He was the same guy I had witnessed at my first smoker off Mindoro. He drew even with the guy from Navigation. I saw Case off to my left looking at me as he unbuttoned his dungaree shirt, and I began doing the same. It was showtime!

I saw Scratch looking at me with a grin as Danshaw laced up my gloves and stuck a mouthpiece in me.

"You de' the man, boot," he said, as he moved out of the way to expose Case in the same readiness. I had had nothing to eat since morning chow other than two oranges, so I was as light as I could be. Case and I touched gloves and backed up a second to measure one another up for an opening shot. As the case would have it, I threw a couple of punches at Case's gloves not quite knowing how to get an advantage when Scratch weighed in on the matter. "Punch him in the Fuckin head!"

Case began to do just what Scratch said he would do when he launched into a haymaker mode as I moved head into my gloves toward him, shot out my left to touch his right bicep, and thus robbed him of his first attempt. He countered with another and grazed the top of my head in such a way as to make me think if that was the speed he had fresh, along with a surprising lack of power, then Scratch was right on that call as well. I slipped one all or nothing shot after another, while robbing him of his attempts by touching his bicep until he dropped his gloves, and I launched one of my own. It caught him square on the side of the head, and he stepped back and covered up.

"About time, boot," Scratch yelled. I quickly moved in and

launched another shot that caught him in the same fashion because he peek-a-booed me half way through my arc. The boat deck erupted upon both contacts as it did with other contestants when a good shot landed as Case hauled back to Haymaker position, and I stepped into him with a short right hook to the Jaw. He then bought his gloves to his face and covered up as I landed another shot on the side of his head. Case then did what Scratch said he would do when faced by too many shots.

He started to duck down towards me and it was at that moment that everything began to move in slow motion. After eight months of Case's harassment, and bullying of me in the fireroom, his turning the deck division against me because of the safeties lifting, and his pointing me out to them on the messdecks that day, his soaking me on watch in Hong Kong in an attempt to get me charged at Captains Mast, but mostly because he was so miserable to put up with, all ran before me as my feet quickly changed position in order to use my right that was now coming straight up between Case's gloves, parting them perfectly, and connecting again with his face.   BOOM! he dropped like a sack of rocks, just like Scratch said he would, and exactly the way he had demonstrated it to me in the well deck on the way to Subic Bay.

The boat deck erupted in a roar at the shortness of the bout that the effect of making me look like a bad ass, but only because of Scratch's training of me to-lead- Case into his own defeat. That was it. Case was done for as he looked for someone to untie his gloves, and I did the same. What a difference a little training can make.

"Good work, boot," Scratch said as Danshaw slapped me on the back

"You de' man, boot." He grinned to me.

"Thanks guys," I replied.

Case's gloves were untied as he stood there with the most quizzical look on his face not quite believing it was over that fast, but having no desire to go another round. Pruitt announced that drinks were on him over at the enlisted club for all members of Bravo division that cared to go over.

"You going over Riley?" he asked.

"Maybe later, I think I'll go for a swim before it gets dark," I answered.

I put my shirt back on and left the boat deck for the berthing compartment to retrieve swim trunks, fins, and mask. Then headed for the small rock islands that were still pockmarked with WW2 shell holes acquired during the battle for Okinawa thirty years before. During low tide, you could walk out to the outer island just off the beach from the club. I was still pumped from the boat deck, and needed to burn off all the adrenalin, and a good long swim was just the thing to do it as I entered the water and snorkeled out on the reef. The elation soon began to wear off and was replaced by a sense of confidence that was beginning to feel familiar after the last eight adventure filled months of sea duty. Yet one more dash of salt had been added to my naval career, and I was becoming less, and less, a "boot" every day. With the sunlight beginning to fade, I returned to the island to use the rest of it to dry off, change back into dungarees, and then head to the enlisted club where I met up with Pruitt, and the rest of Bravo, and Mike divisions. They were in fine form, with Deadeye sporting a small shiner from one of the guys in deck that he received on the boat deck later that day.

"Gonna get even tomorrow when we play football," he said. "Gonna check em' good the first chance I get."

There were about two hundred sailors from the *Juneau* and *Fort Fisher*, and the Schlitz malt liquor never tasted better that night as I reflected on the events of the day. The snipes were planning for the game tomorrow against deck, and it was agreed that Chief Craddick would be quarterbacking due to Neptune assuming that role for deck. Danshaw, Swensen, and some of the bigger Machinist Mates would hold the line, while others such as me would go long or short, as the situation called for until the club secured at 2300.

The next day Neptune, and Craddick, turned their divisions loose at knock off for noon chow, and everyone headed for the field at the end of the pier for the showdown. The snipes stripped off their shirts before deck did so we got to be –skins- In order to tell the two teams apart. Craddick and Neptune went odds, or evens with deck receiving. It was fast and rough for the first three plays until everyone sized everyone else up for a weak link near the fifteen-yard line when deck massed left, and Neptune scrambled for a touchdown. The snipes then fought their way up the field to no avail when the guy that had given Deadeye the shiner, intercepted a pass and ran damn near the full length of the field until Scratch took him down. Once again, Neptune scrambled for a second touchdown.

"What do you say about some half time Neptune?" Deadeye asked.

It was not a hard decision to make on Neptune's part since there was already an exodus towards the beer-filled garbage cans brought by both teams. Game as it was, there was still stand down time to be had, and the mood was infecting all. Two cans of beer later, Deadeye suggested that Craddick drill the interceptor deliberately so he and Danshaw could pincer move to cut him in half, with Deadeye getting the upper half in order to even the score from the boat deck. It also served to lump up one of decks stronger players. After the interceptor's bell had been rung enough to keep him out of the snipes business for a while, Danshaw managed to bull his way to a first down. A snipe fumble, and deck recovery, put Neptune in charge once more.

The beer was taking its toll under the Okinawa sun, and things were becoming disorganized because of it. After the hike, Neptune scrambled again only to be floored by Stewart, and Cox, who were now wise to his moves. He got up slowly, feeling the effect of the hit, and decided that it was enough glory days for one day, and headed for the beer and a seat. "Getting to old for this stuff I guess," he said to no one in particular.

"Why is it so bright out all of a sudden?" he asked again to no one as he headed off the field, and opened a can of beer, leaned back against the picnic table, and took a long pull from the can. "Two down" chuckled Deadeye. "Now maybe we can get somewhere," he said as Neptune removed his shirt, lathered up with Coppertone, and reclined on top of the table.

"I scored twice, apes," he said. "Kick some ass."

The game resumed for another ten minutes without him, with Engineering managing to score a touchdown, at which time another exodus ensued for the beer, and ice station near where Neptune was sunning himself.

"Better put a shirt on Master Chief, Y'all gonna burn in this sun," Pruitt advised.

"Wouldn't know it to look at him though, Hell, he looks like he's turning blue," added another as he nudged Neptune, and saw his jaw relax.

"Neptune!" he yelled as it quickly became clear that something was wrong with the Master Chief.

"Something's wrong with him," the man announced now that everyone's attention had turned to the table. Neptune's sunglasses were removed to reveal the blank, lifeless eyes of a dead man.

"He's having a heart attack, get him to the ship," he said.

There were no vehicles handy, and the only thing motorized was a front end loader being used by one of the Seabees stationed at White Beach to build one of the fuel farm berms about two hundred yards away. One of the deck crew ran towards the loader gesticulating wildly, and explaining the situation while pointing at the group of men that were waving him over. The Seabee dropped the bucket of soil, and headed towards the group that was running to the street carrying Neptune's body with them.

They laid him in the bucket of the loader, and clambered all over it as the driver roared off down the White Beach pier as fast as it could go covered with *Juneau* sailors as the rest ran after it. L.T.J.G. Shott was the O.O.D as the loader pulled up to the Brow, and as soon as Mr. Schott was informed as to the situation, he grabbed the 1mc. and passed the word for the duty Corpsman to lay the pier on the double. With that terse announcement, everyone not on watch headed for the flight deck to see what the emergency was.

"Get him outta there," the corpsman ordered as another man ran down the brow with his medical bag. Neptune was lifted out of the bucket and placed on the pier where the Corpsman checked for a pulse, and began Heart massage to no avail as Captain Petrowski, and the Chief Engineer looked on. After a few moments, the Corpsman used his stethoscope for a heartbeat that would not be there ever again.

"He's gone, Sir," the Corpsman said to Petrowski.

"Oh for Christ's sake!" the Captain hissed under his breath. "Can you believe this Screws?" he asked.

"No Sir, I can't," answered the engineer as they both looked down at Neptune's blue face.

"Get a stretcher down here," Petrowski ordered. "Mr. Schott, I need an ambulance please,"

"It's already on the way from Kadena Sir," Schott replied.

"Mr. Schott, I need the Master at arms to secure the hangar bay, and post a guard that reports directly to you," he said. "Aye Aye, Captain," replied the O.O.D. An immediate pall came over those present as Neptune's body was lifted onto a Stokes stretcher, and carried up the Brow to the Quarterdeck, and into the hangar bay, where he was covered with a blanket and set on the deck.

"What happened, Craddick?" he asked the Chief.

"I don't know Sir," Craddick began. "I mean he was fine, he was quarterbacking almost a half hour, scrambled for two touchdowns, and then took a hit and called it quits," he said. "Last we saw he was drinking beer, and sunning himself on the picnic table… just kicking back," he added. "It's the strangest thing Captain," Craddick said softly. "He just laid down and went away Sir."

"Well was he in pain or what?" Petrowski asked.

"He didn't mention anything Sir," Craddick replied. "We assumed that he was winded, and wanted a beer, and a breather, oh yeah, now as I recall, he wanted to know why it was so bright out all of a sudden," Craddick added.

"He what?" Petrowski asked.

"Yes Sir, after he got hit he wanted to know why it was so bright out all of a sudden Sir."

"Who hit him, Chief?"

"Stewart, and Cox, Sir," he replied.

"OK. I'll need to speak to them in my cabin as soon as possible."

"Yes Sir, we'll be up right away," Craddick replied, and then told Scratch to round up Stewart and Cox.

The blue Air Force ambulance arrived twenty minutes later from Kadena Air Force Base, and they loaded Neptune's body into the back, and took him to the base dispensary for an Autopsy. The next morning at Quarters, Captain Petrowski addressed the crew on the flight deck as to the sudden death of the Master Chief, so that every one got the official story, and ordered the rest of the day off as a sign of mourning, and the following day the official Autopsy results came in that Neptune possessed an enlarged heart that suffered an infarction, and led to a massive coronary as he lay on the picnic table.

"Quicker than dead," Petrowski thought to himself as he read the report, and remembered what Craddick had told him on the pier that day.

"Lucky Bastard," he thought as he shook his premature grey head from side, to side, and wondered where he was going to

find another Master Chief Petty Officer of the Command anywhere like him.

It had been a tough start to his newest command since arriving aboard *Juneau*. First was the almost international incident in
Singapore, then the Ensign's family tragedy, after that it was the
China Fleet Club brawl, and his tense conversation with the Brit
destroyer Captain, and now the strange, surreal, loss of an otherwise healthy, hearty, forty-nine-year-old Master Chief.... What
next?

That question was answered the following day when he received word from the Chief Engineer that Smitty, Wolfie, and
some of the other lifers Neptune shared quarters with had put
in a request to speak with him on Neptune's behalf. The Chief
Engineer let the men into the Wardroom after morning chow,
and they seated themselves around Petrowski. Each man had
his personnel folder in front of him as Wolfie spoke first.

"Any word from Red Cross Sir?"

"Nothing they can find," Petrowski answered.

"It's the same with us as well Sir," Wolfie continued, as he
opened his personnel folder to the entry where normally there
was a "next of kin" space that read "Present command," and
handed it to the Captain.

The C.O. read the space aloud, and looked at the Wolfman.

"No Shit?" he asked. "Them too, Sir," Wolfie replied, as the
other three lifers pushed their folders towards the Captain.

He glanced briefly at the space that all had "Present Command" entered where the "next of kin" space was before Wolfie
spoke again.

"At this point in my life, I don't have anyone back in the
world that would miss my carcass Sir," he began. "Where I'm
at, is where I'm at, if anything should happen to me Sir, right
now I belong to the *Juneau*, and that's where I would want to be
sent."

"Sea burial Sir, Sailors Grave," he said.

"Been awhile since I've seen one of those," Petrowski mused as his memory flashed back to 66' when he was X.O. on the *John Thomaston*, and they sent a second-class storekeeper over the side on Yankee Station.

The fleet wasn't full of them because nearly everyone had someone back in the states that could claim the body, but every now and then this kind of situation arose, and the Navy was called on to bury one of their own in the time honored tradition, "Sailor's Grave."

"I understand your concern, fellas," Petrowski began. "Problem is, Neptune's had that in his records for years, and may have forgotten all about it. Time goes on and people change, things change. He may have forgotten to update it as he grew older, and I just want to make sure that there's no other claim to the body. I'll explain the situation to the C.O. at Kadena, and have him prepare Neptune for sea burial," he said. "We'll be two weeks from here to Pearl, so that should be enough time to satisfy any other claims. If there's no word by 180 meridian, I'll order a burial at sea with full Honors," he promised the quartet.

"Thank you Sir," they murmured, as none of them would want anything less at this point in their lives.

"You're true Shipmates, Neptune has been honored."

"Aye, Aye, Sir" they said as they stood at attention, and were dismissed.

TRANSIT TO PEARL HARBOR

The U.S.S. *Cleveland* [LPD-7] stood into Buckner Bay at 0830 to the sheer joy of many, and the –all good things must pass-shrug of others who lived for this stuff. The ship had been refueled, and food stocks taken on, with the last of any mail, when the blue Air Force ambulance arrived shortly after and the *Juneau* guard pulled the aluminum shipping casket from the rear, and carried it up the brow where the Quarterdeck watch saluted smartly as they carried the Master Chief around to the hangar bay, and placed it on the makeshift bier the Hull Techs had constructed the day before.

The watch secured the area and remained on station. After Wild Bill, and the Master at arms, had returned from briefing/de-briefing the C.O. of the *Cleveland*, sea detail was called, and the *Juneau* shifted colors, cast off her mooring lines, and stood out of Buckner Bay bound for Pearl Harbor. The normal at sea routine commenced, and the days went by sunny, and warm revolving around watch standing, and chowtime until after a week, Captain Petrowski let it be known that there was no-one to be found that had legal claim to Neptune.

"He's ours," he said to the Engineer.

"We're approaching the international dateline," Petrowski said. "It's fitting that we leave him on this side of the world, Eternal Wes-Pac. He'd want it that way."

"Aye Sir," Screws replied. "I'm sure he would."

With that said, all department heads were made aware at quarters that burial would be at noon, and that the uniform of the day would be full dress blues, with ribbons. Full Ships Company present.

"Anyone in Sick Bay?" he asked the Medical officer.

"No Sir" he replied.

"Anyone in the Brig?" he asked C.T.

"No Sir." C.T. replied.

Towards 1100, the crew began changing into dress blues, with ribbons, and headed to the flight deck where the honor guard stood with a stretcher upon which Neptune's shipping casket lay on the starboard catwalk railing. The crew assembled by division the full length of the flight deck, and there were in excess of 300 of us with those on watch the only ones excused. The engine rooms received bells to come down to one third, and the ship given time to coast to that speed before Captain

Petrowski stepped to the microphone that had been set up and spoke into it, "United States Ship *Juneau*. Attention on Deck!" he ordered.

The sound of three hundred men coming to attention in unison was riveting because most of the crew had never been in such a large formation before. It was a smart move when performed by 54 recruits in boot camp, but 300 salts was something all together different. There was professionalism, all mixed with a sense of urgency that had been drilled into our heads back in basic training, and now I understood why.

Captain Petrowski began with how we had just lost a shipmate in the strangest of ways, and how life is such a fragile, unpredictable thing, and a total mystery, before moving on to how important Neptune was as *Juneau's* command Master Chief, and admitting not knowing him but only a few months, felt as close to him as any shipmate he'd ever known. The C.O. then read Neptune's service record spanning 29 years, and containing almost every service ribbon the Navy had to offer. The Master Chief had served on Submarines, and Battleships, Cruisers, and Carriers. He had been from Inchon, to Wonsan, during Korea.

He was at Beirut, in 58' to land the Marines, blockaded Cuba in 62' during the missile crisis, and was back in the Gator Navy three years later when President Johnson ordered the Marines into Santo Domingo, Dominican Republic, in 65'. He did his time on Yankee Station, off Viet Nam before two tours at R.T.C. San Diego, before being assigned to the Gator Navy one more time with *Juneau*. "Shipped a lot of green in his day," added the C.O.

After a brief silence, the ship's Chaplain stepped to the microphone to deliver the Benediction, and he finished with the Navy Submarine Prayer.

LORD GOD, OUR POWER EVERMORE
WHOSE ARM DOTH REACH THE OCEAN FLOOR
DIVE WITH OUR MEN BENEATH THE SEA

TRAVERSE THE DEPTHS PROTECTIVLY
O, HEAR US WHEN WE PRAY, AND KEEP
THEM SAFE FROM PERIL IN THE DEEP

The chaplain figured that of the three versions of the Navy
Prayer, the one he delivered fit the occasion best since Neptune
once served as a "bubblehead," that is, a submariner, and was
now returning to the deep.

It was also necessary because the chaplain had to give a non
denominational service due to the fact that in Neptune's service
record where the box marked "religion" was, Neptune had the
personnel office of long ago type the words "just enough" in that
space. He was a pistol.

The crew then rendered a hand salute, while the seven-man
squad opened up with three volleys of their M14 rifles for a
twenty-one gun salute, and the ship's Pennant, and American
flag were dropped to half mast. With a nod from the chaplain,
the honor guard then raised the rear of the stokes stretcher, and
Neptune's weighted shipping casket entered the vast Pacific
Ocean at 23 degrees West Latitude/ 178 degrees north longi-
tude,… Sailors Grave!

"God I love this stuff," murmured the Wolfman. "Just like
it's supposed to be."

The *Juneau's* flag, and pennant were then run back up to
proper position, and the engine rooms given bells for ahead full,
to cross the 180th Meridian at 1600, putting us back in the world
as the saying went when returning from a Wes-Pac deployment.
Crossing the International Date Line also meant that for the first
time in eight months Scratch, and the rest of the older guys now
called me by my name instead of –boot– now that I had completed an official Wes-Pac. We made Pearl two days later, and
Wild Bill had the off watch crew change into Tropical White long
as the summer uniform was known in order to Man the rail
upon entering Pearl Harbor in order to render honors while

passing the U.S.S. *Arizona* memorial on our port side.

After that, the ship came to an all stop as the tugs roped on, and pushed her against the mooring donut. After shore power was engaged, both boilers were secured and allowed to settle out before being bottom blown, and the duty section took over working parties for Mail, and foodstuffs consumed during the two-week steam from Okinawa. There was a refueling party forming up on the starboard flight deck while the rest of Bravo division manned fuel oil tank sounding tubes, and donned headphones. The rest of the snipes headed to the port shaft alley to Skate out of working party as usual. Some of the off-watch guys had planned to rent cars and tour the circumference of the island, and Pruitt suggested we do the same so we ponied up the cost of the rental and gas at 50 cents a gallon.

When liberty was called at noon chow, Pruitt Landon, Fred, and myself, headed down the brow with swim gear, and suntan lotion because the islands were only 20 degrees above the Equator. We were headed to Waikiki beach to check out all the White women that had been missing the last eight months since the Miss Americas had put on a show to remember at the enlisted club. After picking up the rental car, Pruitt got behind the wheel and we headed to the beach parking lot, and then right into the surf, at least we did. Pruitt said that he had enough of water at Hong Kong.

"Scratch ain't here, I ain't goin," he said. "Y'all no longer the top of the food chain in there," he advised.

There were some other snipes down the beach that soon came over with Stewart among them. They were grinning like fools, and their eyes were bloodshot from a combination of seawater, and something Stewart called "Maui Wowie" that he had scored from one of the local boys. He produced a banana size bud from his towel and held it up for inspection.

"It's a whole ounce for a hundred bucks," he said. He broke off a small end of it, stuffed it into the cellophane from his cigarette pack, and crammed in some rolling papers with it. "Don't drive with this stuff Pruitt," he warned.

"Don't worry ol' stick, that's for the Doobie brothers here," he said as he pointed towards Landon, and me.

"It ain't for me, but thanks just the same."

Stewart and his group were headed around to the North shore to see if any rollers were coming in, and what the surfing action was like. With Pruitt abstaining, the three of us rolled up our own joints, and put the match to them and soon found out why it was called what it was.

"WOW! Sure glad you're driving Pruitt," said Fred as he stubbed out his joint after only one hit. "One of these could last me a week."

"Half a week." I countered.

"Two days," added Landon, as we all broke out grinning the same way we had just saw Stewarts group doing.

"Think y'all better swim some of that stuff off before we get started around the island, or y'all not gonna make a lick of sense." Pruitt drawled. We swam for another hour before it was time to get out of the sun, and head for chow somewhere. Burgers and fries, American style.

It had been eight months since I'd had those, and a properly made chocolate shake. They went down great before we again got on the road, stopping to check out the Blowhole, before proceeding on to the North shore to watch the locals surf, and check out the Babes watching as well.

After a few hours, the sun began to set as Pruitt suggested we complete our circumnavigation of Oahu, and return the rental car. With the four of us feeling the effects of too much sun, mixed with the Maui Wowie Stewart had given us, Pruitt pulled into the road and we headed back to Pearl, returned the rental, and hailed a cab back to the base. We were only in port for two days, and had duty on the second day, so Pearl made for a short visit.

THE LAST LEG

Both boilers had been lit off at 0300, and so were already on line when Scratch up forward, and Deadeyes watch aft, reported they were manned and ready when the sea detail was called. It was an easy sea detail compared to many, and when we cleared the channel Scratch said to me, "One more Riley, and were home. You're taking her in when we hit Dago."

He was referring to the way many sailors called San Diego. After sea detail was secured, I went topside for great views of Oahu, and Molokai along with what must be some of the Pacific Oceans bluest water. I had never seen any part as blue as I could see now, and it stood out in brilliant contrast to the white foamy wake churning behind the ship.

We would be four days at sea at eighteen knots, and as the days passed, the excitement among the crew was evident knowing that eight months was now behind us. The Navigation department set up a mooring pool, and passed the cube-checkered sheet amongst the other divisions. Meanwhile Deadeye, and Wolfie, were making plans of their own, even if those plans were somewhat more sinister. They were discreetly consulting people from other divisions like A-Gang, and Repair division, until they had eight volunteers for the plan that was to take place once the ship was secured from sea detail at 32nd street.

There was another plan the snipes had in store, and once again, it involved Pruitt, who would be standing Smokewatch on the way in, and when the *Juneau* passed under the Coronado Bridge. The last night at sea, there was not anyone that could sleep knowing that the World was waiting for us in about ten hours. The human energy level could be felt through out the ship as everyone talked about what they were going to do on the ship's thirty-day stand own granted to every ship completing a Wes-Pac.

HOME!

"NOW SET THE SPECIAL SEA AND ANCHOR DETAIL!"
I noticed how that announcement that I'd heard the last eight
months seemed to carry a sense of urgency to it, and it received
a cheer from the bridge, to the messdecks, to the Engine rooms,
as everyone went about their duty in the best of moods. The
mooring lines were played out on the foc'sle in the early morning haze so common to the California coast as the ship's 1mc.
was heard again: "ALL HANDS NOT ON WATCH, MAN THE
RAIL!"
Tropical White long was the uniform of the day for all hands
topside, and they began forming up at arms length until the entire perimeter of the ship was manned. Pruitt plugged into the
sound powered circuit on the 04 level where the Smokewatch
stood, and reported to the two engine rooms that he was
Manned, and Ready. After picking up the harbor pilot, we resumed one third ahead until out of the coastal haze, Pruitt could
just make out the sandstone end of Point Loma on the ship's port
side.
"Point Loma visible y'all," he said as the engine rooms let out
a cheer on their respective Throttle decks knowing that the
World was now in sight.
Five minutes later Pruitt called down to say we were passing
the submarine base, and five minutes later said, " passing boot
camp" With that announcement my mind flashed back to the day
I started basic training, and it seemed like another world ago
compared to now. "Passing Broadway pier," he said as the *Juneau*
headed to the Coronado Bridge and began to pass under it.
"I'd prepare for an all stop if I were y'all," Pruitt said, thereby
giving both firerooms the code word to bring a blower down to
around 500 rpms, and cause thick black smoke to pour from both

stacks, and "smoke the Bridge" as we passed under it thereby officially ending another Wes-Pac deployment.

Pruitt, of course, had to call down and report heavy smoke as the pumpmen forward, and aft brought the blowers back up to three thousand rpms. It had been a Wes-Pac custom for the last six years since the bridge had been built to smoke the bridge only after completing a deployment. A few minutes later both firerooms went down to one burner apiece as the tugs roped on, and began to push the ship against the mooring donut with that all too familiar bump followed by the word everyone shipside, and pierside longed to hear after so much time at sea:

"MOORED!"

Came the announcement as another fist pumping cheer was heard throughout the ship, and down on the pier from all the civilians gathered there. The Bosun's mates began attaching the pier side brow as people on the pier began surging to board the ship, and Mr. Schott began directing civilians around to the hangar bay where Boogies crew had set up messdecks tables covered with cupcakes, and Lemonade, along with little triangle sandwiches with, and you might have guessed it, "Juneau steak," as roast beef had been named by the crew a year ago.

The messdecks were filling up with civilians, and children, and a very festive air filled the ship when Pruitt called down again. "Y'all ain't gonna believe who's talkin to Mr. Schott on the quarterdeck right now," he said. "Who's that Pruitt?" Scratch asked through headphones. "Ensign Benson, That's who!" Pruitt replied. "No shit?" he asked, "that's affirmative snipes, in the flesh," Ensign Benson had made the long journey home and buried his entire family, after which he swung his backpack, and headed for the safety of the woods where everything made sense. After two weeks alone and contemplating the chaos of civilian life, he had decided to return to the only family he had left.

"Welcome back Benson!" Schott said as he pumped the Ensigns hand.

"Welcome back Skinny!" Schott repeated from a beaming face.

Mr. Benson smiled and stated matter-of-factly, "There's no where else to go now. The Navy's all I've got."

NOW SECURE THE SPECIAL SEA AND ANCHOR DETAIL!

With that announcement, along with shore power presently hooked up, both firerooms pulled fires, and secured. The pump drains on the machinery were opened to drain condensate, and I used the last of the steam to blow down the burner barrels.

Meanwhile back aft, Deadeye held up a can of ball, and roller bearing grease, and said to the Wolfman, "Anytime now."

Mixed into that can of #5 ball, and roller bearing grease was coffee grounds, Three dozen busted egg shells from the messdecks that morning, and last , but not least was an entire tube of Prussian Bluing compound, the likes of which had graced both my fingers, and Ensign Bensons ear, just before the power run with *Fort Fisher*. The Wolfman rang up the Quarterdeck and asked Mr. Schott to pass the word.

Bravo division working party lay the after engineroom. Mr. Schott had no idea what was about to happen on the upper level next to the Evaporator some three or four minutes later because that was hole snipe business. It sounded normal enough as the Wolfman had requested a summons for this fireman, or that fireman to "lay" all deployment long as was needed, and he always needed to conduct legitimate business.

The fact that Bravo division always Skated out of working parties left many of them puzzled at the request. All but eight of them. They mustered fast, very fast! Case was cooling it under a vent with a cup of cold water from the D.A. tank next to the evaporator when all of a sudden it seemed that the rest of the watch had disappeared. He had prepared the boiler for a bottom blow, and was now just waiting for the sediment to settle for an hour or so in the water drum. This was his last sea detail on *Juneau*, and the miserable Bastard was re-enlisting for two years shore duty much to everyone's delight.

He looked around, and wondered where everyone was, and then saw the first of eight masked conspirators that promptly threw him to the deck plates, cut his web belt, and began hauling down his dungaree trousers, and skivvie shorts. Then using latex gloves provided by a certain Oil King, began to smear grease and all its contents from Case's chest to his knees!

He yelled, and yelled, much to the working parties delight as they rolled him over, and worked him over, with the five pound can of bearing grease until it was empty.

"You'll go to Mast for this!" he swore at Deadeye. "And you'll go to shore duty, asshole," retorted Deadeye. Wasn't that the truth. Part of that reenlistment consisted of a physical that he would now have to attend with his entire torso stained Prussian Blue. The eight men then left the grease smeared man on the deck plates, and made good their escape as Case began to collect himself. The forward fire alley phone rang with that turkey gobble sound that it did, and Scratch answered it as I was finishing up with the burner barrels. He returned the phone to its holder and called me over.

"Chief needs to see you in D.C. Central," he said. Upon entering the air-conditioned compartment, I saw Craddick, and Pruitt going over refueling operations now that Pruitt had secured from smokewatch.

"What's up, Chief?" I asked.

Craddick pointed behind me at a new man standing there in that same stupid looking salt-and-pepper boot camp issue uniform I had reported aboard in at White Beach.

"New Boot, take him below and get him a rack, and a locker. Square him away, after that, have him put on his dungarees and take him down to the forward hole, and turn him over to Scratch, show him how to bottom blow the boiler," he said.

In looking at him, he seemed to be a Boy Scout that had been given the wrong uniform, and address, as the last eight months seemed to flood my mind with how much this kid had just missed one hell of a Wes-Pac. I cocked my head towards the hatchway and said, "Follow me, Boot!"

THE END

BALLAD OF THE HOLE SNIPE

The folks in San Diego, have gazed upon the sea, and watched the warships standing out to keep this country free, and most of them have read a book, or heard a salty tale, about the men who steam these ships through Lighting, wind, and Hail. But there's one place they don't know, that even sailors fear to go.

So little is known about this place sailors call the Hole. It's down below the waterline, and it takes a Human toll. It houses Engines run by steam that makes the shafts go round, a place of fire, noise, and heat, that beats a body down.

Where boilers with a hellish heart, and blood of angry steam, that any minute could escape, and burn the entire team. Where Turbines scream like tortured souls alone and lost in hell, as ordered from the bridge above, we answer every bell. The snipes that keep the fires lit, and make the engines run, are strangers to the world of light, and seldom see the sun. Their hardness pays no living thing the tribute of a tear, for deep within this nether world, there's no tolerance of fear. There's not much that men can do, that these men have not done, beneath the decks deep in the hole, to make the engines run. So every day's a war down here where gages all read red, six hundred pounds of surly steam can kill you very dead. But I can talk about this place, and try to help you see, the dangerous life of men down here because one of them was me. I've seen these exhausted men toil in superheated air, to keep their ship alive, and lit, the glory is all theirs. Thus, they'll toil for ages on, until warships steam no more, amid the boilers brutal heat, and the turbines mighty roar. So when you see a ship pull out to meet another foe, Remember kindly if you will, THE HOLE SNIPES DOWN BELOW!

The author wholeheartedly supports the effort to add the names of the 74 crewmen who lost their lives at sea while aboard the U.S.S.FRANK E. EVANS [DD-754] on June 3, 1969, to the Viet Nam Memorial Wall.

Their recognition is earned, and deserved.

Lest we forget.

About The Author

Joey Fogarty served in the US Navy from 1975-1979 in the Western Pacific aboard the *U.S.S. Juneau* LPD-10. He currently splits his time between California and Maine.

ABOOKS

ALIVE Book Publishing and ALIVE Publishing Group
are imprints of Advanced Publishing LLC,
3200 A Danville Blvd., Suite 204, Alamo, California 94507

Telephone: 925.837.7303
alivebookpublishing.com

CPSIA information can be obtained
at www.ICGtesting.com
Printed in the USA
BVHW081207091221
623626BV00006B/116